Traynham

QUISLING
The Career and Political Ideas of Vidkun Quisling
1887-1945

(By courtesy of *Aftenposten*, Oslo

Vidkun Quisling 1887–1945

QUISLING

The Career and Political Ideas of Vidkun Quisling
1887 - 1945

Paul M. Hayes

 Indiana University Press
Bloomington & London

Published 1972 by Indiana University Press
Copyright 1971 © by Paul M. Hayes

Published in Canada by Fitzhenry & Whiteside Limited,
Don Mills, Ontario
Library of Congress catalog card number: 78-184523
ISBN: 0-253-34760-2
Manufactured in Great Britain

2-5-73

IN MEMORY OF J. M. HANDFORD
(1 May 1947–2 June 1968)

CONTENTS

PREFACE

THE OBJECT of this study is to examine in detail the life of Vidkun Quisling. In so doing it is hoped that light will be thrown on Quisling's actions in April 1940, and the reasons for them. As a result of the events of 9 April 1940, he gained world-wide notoriety. The conventional picture of 'Quisling the traitor' was formed during the brief interval between the invasions of Scandinavia and the Low Countries in the spring of 1940. In the political and military conditions of the time a rapid judgement of his character was made: it has lasted ever since.

There have recently, however, been several attempts by former followers or other admirers of Quisling to refurbish his tarnished image. A picture of him as a misunderstood and much maligned man has emerged from these writings. So seriously have these admirers of Quisling been regarded in Norway that several actions for libel have been brought. There has even been published a serious work by three Norwegian academics, giving a factual account of the events which led to the German invasion of Norway, in an attempt to rebut hostile allegations.

When the present study was begun, this recent revival of interest in Quisling and his actions was still in the future. The attraction of Quisling lay not in his topicality but in his enigmatic character. Opinions about his ability and his intelligence differed widely. Feeling among Norwegians had not greatly diminished since 1945; he was still hated by most as much as he had been hated during the war. Yet there were still those who swore that he had been unjustly executed, the victim of personal rancour and political revenge.

It soon became clear that for an adequate study of Quisling's behaviour in April 1940 there was needed, above all, a knowledge of his life and actions before that date. This suggested a complete biography, in which Quisling's political ideas could be set in the context of his life. This study represents an attempt to fulfil that idea.

Already a number of attempts have been made by historians, psychiatrists and journalists to examine Quisling's political ideas in relation to his actions. None has produced a satisfactory analysis; all have been confronted with the same inconsistencies which broke the logical pattern of Quisling's ideas. Yet the belief persists that if only a missing link in his

9

character could be discovered, then all his actions would fall into place and all his ideas appear consistent. For my part, I believe that this is an inadequate basis for explaining the complexity of character which led a man who was passionately devoted to his country to commit high treason. Instead of attempting to impose a preconceived formula, it has seemed better to allow Quisling's actions and words to speak for themselves, in the belief that when this is done problems of interpretation will be reduced to a minimum.

Most of the events here dealt with have already been surveyed; many of the citations indicate a debt to secondary works. Any claims to originality must rest in the first place on the extensive use of unpublished material made available by the Norwegian government; and, secondly, on the approach to the problem, outlined above. The works of others have been drawn on heavily and, I hope, not uncritically, but in every case the use of original material has been preferred.

Chapter 1 EARLY YEARS

TELEMARK IN southern Norway, where Quisling was born, is an area for individualists. The terrain is rocky, full of trees, high mountains, deep valleys and cold lakes. It is beautiful country, country for those who like peace and solitude. Its people, known as the *teler*, have played a notable part in Norwegian history. A lifelong student of Norway has written:

> the 'teler' have shown themselves all through history to have been individualists who resented rule or discipline of any kind. They appear to have taken a prominent part in any and every anti-monarchical movement and to have defied governmental decrees from their remote valleys. The last notorious 'teler' rebel was none other than Vidkun Quisling.[1]

Vidkun Abraham Lauritz Jonssøn Quisling was born at Fyresdal, a small scattered village, on 18 July 1887.[2] Although his mother's family had originally come from Denmark the family into which he was born was well-known locally. For several generations his ancestors had provided the local pastor, as well as a series of yeomen farmers and soldiers. The strong connexion with Fyresdal was never forgotten later in Quisling's life, and he always hoped to return to Telemark in order to pursue the simple life of a farmer.

Jon Lauritz Quisling, his father, was village priest at Fyresdal and rural dean of the Lutheran pastors. He was eccentric even by the standards of country parsons with curious hobbies. Intellectually able, he wrote several religious, historical and political tracts as well as his autobiography.[3] He was an avid reader, showing keen interest in national history and great enthusiasm for the Norwegian independence movement. Like his son, Vidkun, he was fascinated by genealogical trees. He traced the name Quisling back to Susanne Magdalene Quislin, his great-grandfather's mother. She was a great-granddaughter of the royal priest Lauritz Ibsen Quisling, and daughter of a priest from Tinn.[4] Through this side of the family Quisling was distantly related to the dramatist Henrik Ibsen.

Quisling's mother, born Anna Caroline Bang, belonged to a junior branch of the Hvide family.[5] Her father, a shipowner from Grimstad, was third cousin to the author Bjørnstjerne Bjørnson, and to Rikard Nordraak, the musician and composer. Vidkun was not an only child; he had two brothers and a sister, all younger than himself. His eldest brother was Jørgen, two years his junior. Then came his sister Esther, and finally Arne. All were of exceptional intelligence. Arne became an engineer and later emigrated, while Jørgen became a chemist and a doctor. Esther died at the age of nineteen of an injury to her brain, attributed to too much work at school.

Quisling was very proud of his ancestry, especially of the fact that his family had for centuries been living in Telemark. That his roots lay deep in Norwegian soil made him feel that he was a true Norwegian. Something of this passionate belief was revealed at his trial:

> I was brought up among viking graves, amidst scriptural history and the sagas. I belonged to an ancient house and I was inculcated with a belief in family pride, family history and our responsibility to our people. Bjørnson and Ibsen were of the same stock, so dishwater did not run in my veins. The name Quisling is no foreign name, but an ancient Nordic name, meaning a cadet branch of a royal house. Q is not an outlandish Latin letter but an ancient protective rune.[6]

Loyalty to his home and to his family were thus impressed upon Quisling from a very early age. These were sentiments which he never forgot. His delusions of grandeur – for his derivation from royal ancestry was highly suspect – and his visions of destiny were created in childhood and remained all his life.

Thus, the family background was somewhat unusual. Quisling's parents were much more intellectual than those of most of his own age. His mother had little in common with other mothers in Fyresdal, for her youth had been spent in an artistic and literary circle. Consequently she brought up her children to believe that they were different, thus contributing a great deal towards their sense of isolation.[7] Quisling's parents had strong, individualistic views which had considerable influence on their children's characters. Quisling derived his love of abstruse argument from his father and his driving ambition from his mother. Their two characters found common ground in enthusiasm for education, so that Quisling was encouraged to read and to study from a very early age.

Despite the different personalities of father and mother Quisling's home was happy. His mother was a capable housewife and an understanding parent, who seems to have hoped that her children would fulfil their early promise in a way their father had not fulfilled his. Perhaps her ambitions were realised by all three of her sons entering professions rather than becoming priests or farmers. Quisling himself recognised that the passionate love of learning acquired in his childhood had set him apart from others. At his trial he recalled:

> I was brought up in an erudite home. My father was a priest, but he was more philosopher than pastor. He was a historian and a linguist. I was introduced to history at a young age. I read all I could find about the sagas,

Norwegian and world history. All my savings were spent on books. I was perhaps a lonely boy, but this was because I never found in another what I was willing to give in friendship, namely everything.[8]

Opinions have differed as to the influence of his family on Quisling's character. According to a schoolfellow, Vilhelm Ullmann, Quisling lived in 'a charming home, a good harmonious household, one where I loved the whole family'.[9] Some accounts, however, have suggested that Quisling's mother was not only ambitious for her children but also condescending to their contemporaries. As she dominated her eldest son he had perhaps acquired his feeling of superiority from her conduct. This opinion also is controversial. A recent biographer of Quisling considers that 'Vidkun worshipped her to his dying day and she was probably the strongest influence in his life. She had no chance of fulfilling her ambitions through her husband, to whom she was sometimes intolerant, and so she planted them in her children.'[10] If this were true it would certainly lead one to suppose that Quisling inherited from her his intellectual arrogance, which was to militate so greatly against him when he entered Norwegian politics. On the other hand his official biographer has praised the warm and sympathetic character of Quisling's mother and has suggested that 'it seems to be from his father that Quisling obtained both his characteristic talents and his reserved and brooding nature'.[11]

Quisling's rural childhood meant that he spoke the local dialect, which was difficult for other Norwegians to understand. In 1893 Jon Quisling moved to the small living of Strømsø, near Drammen on the Oslofjord. When young Quisling first went to school, at the age of seven, in 1894, he spoke only the dialect of Fyresdal. His curious accent amused his schoolfellows and was a cause of loneliness. This was a difficult burden for a child to bear, and Quisling became miserable and discontented. Recalling these days, he recounted at his trial: 'When I was seven years old I was sent to the town to go to school, but I soon became very homesick.' His natural aloofness hindered him from establishing an easy relationship with his schoolfellows. The years at Drammen seem to have intensified his feelings and his determination to impress his fellow pupils. When he first entered school he was 'bottom of the class', but he 'took hold of himself, and in not many months was at the top'.[12] It was a position which he was to hold for the rest of his schooldays. According to a wartime apologist this superiority 'cost him but little effort'.[13] A less enthusiastic commentator of the same era, however, has written:

the boy was very gifted, and he received a good education, such as Norway provides for all. People who knew him during his school years say that he was a 'shining light' and that he was ambitious far beyond the ordinary. He was regularly the highest in his class, and if he did not manage to maintain that position by honourable means he did not hesitate to employ others. He *insisted* upon being first – in the classroom and among his comrades. And if he thought he had been wronged, he never forgot it.[14]

13

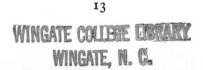

At the age of twelve, Quisling changed schools. In May 1900 his father was transferred from Drammen to Gjerpen, a small village near Skien, in Telemark. Vidkun Quisling was accordingly sent to Skien high school. The move accentuated his loneliness and reserve. Without many friends he was obliged to find other interests. He was fond of nature and often went for long solitary walks in the fields and forests. The effect of this period of Quisling's life was crucial in the formation of his character. 'I grew up', he wrote of his beloved Telemark, 'in a narrow mountain valley which was then still wild in prospect and where lawless people may still have lived.'[15]

If Quisling gained much from exercising his imagination he also lost a great deal in never acquiring the art of making casual friends. Relationships with Quisling either went much deeper or did not exist at all. He felt very strongly about those of his own age. At his trial he declared: 'I had a good friend who betrayed me, and I nearly killed him for that. He betrayed me and I thrashed him because of his betrayal of our friendship.'[16] On the other hand his friends were lasting. Ullmann, who first knew him in 1902, remained a friend even in 1945. At Quisling's trial Ullmann reported that he had spoken with some of Quisling's former fellow pupils about their early days together, concluding his remarks by stating: 'I am sure that I speak on behalf of all the form, when I recall him as a very true, courteous and good friend.'

Quisling's career at Skien high school was brilliant. He became the star pupil and easily surpassed the record of Ibsen, a former pupil. The secret of his success, according to Ullmann, lay in his exceptionally receptive and retentive mind, coupled with an unusually wide range of interests. He was respected for his intellect by his colleagues who 'put him on a pedestal'.[17] Quisling, however, never felt entirely at ease; 'what I was looking for lay outside the school system, and I drank with an unquenchable thirst for knowledge'. He agreed that his interests ranged widely, but his chief pleasure lay in mathematics and history, which had been the interests his father sought to encourage. In Ullmann's opinion, Quisling ought to have become a scientist, since a scientific career would have provided an outlet for his exceptional mathematical ability. There is strong evidence to support Ullmann. Quisling himself stated that 'as a young boy I took up higher mathematics by myself, out of school hours. I read Abel's collected works while still at the high school.'[18] While he was still a pupil at Skien, Quisling discovered a new method of solving an Abelian problem. His solution later became a standard reference in a number of Norwegian mathematical textbooks.[19] He devoted much of his spare time to logical analysis of complex equations. At his trial he recalled that his 'mathematics teacher was grieved when I chose to become an officer'.[20] His explanation for this decision was that, although mathematics fascinated him, his interest shifted from subject to subject at school, and he was not sure that he would always retain his devotion to mathematics.

Quisling left Skien school in 1905 with an excellent academic record. Among his many triumphs the one which probably gave him most satisfaction, particularly after his poor start at school, was his achievement in obtaining the 'Artium' with the highest marks in the school.[21] To the surprise of most people who knew him well he decided to enrol as a cadet at the Military Academy. The reasons for this decision were closely related to affairs in Norway in 1905, when independence from Sweden was finally attained. 'I chose to become an officer on account of my historical reading and the dissolution of the union with Sweden', he wrote. 'I was filled with affection for my country and people, and was willing to offer my life for them.'[22]

Patriotism was a very strong force in Norway at the end of the nineteenth century and it was not long before love for his country developed in Quisling a desire to serve it in some striking way, as Nansen had. In this way the bases of his future attitudes were laid down. His decision to pursue a career of service to Norway eventually grew into a passion which was to dominate his life. Some indication of the depths of Quisling's patriotism has been given by Fru Mollø Christensen, who lived in the rectory at Gjerpen during the winter of 1913-14.

The brothers Vidkun and Jørgen, though not Arne, who became an engineer in the U.S.A., were outstandingly active. Diligent one might more properly call them. They could never stop. It was a mania. I had asked Vidkun what he wanted for Christmas, and he asked me to sew a silk flag with a gold cross on a red field, which was the ancient Norwegian flag, St Olav's flag. Thus very early was Quisling attached to the sagas.[23]

For Quisling the legends and sagas of former Norwegian greatness were very important. His interest in Nordic destiny had been fostered assiduously by his father during childhood and further promoted by the agitation for Norwegian independence, which reached a climax during his high school days. He felt that he had a personal part to play in Norway's new destiny. The fact that he had been born on 18 July he believed to be of great significance. It was the anniversary of the battle of Havsfjord, c AD 872, as a result of which Norway had become one kingdom. Quisling believed that the date of his birth was no mere coincidence but a sure indication of destiny. Thus, from the beginning patriotism and personal ambition were closely related.

Quisling's decision to enter the army met with full approval from his family and schoolfellows, with the sole exception of Ullmann, with whom he had struck up a firm friendship and frequently discussed his future. According to Ullmann the young Quisling at one time or another considered being either a scientist or a priest.[24] Eventually, however, his patriotism drove him towards a military career. It was this enthusiasm for Norwegian independence, coupled with his brilliant academic achievements, which gave Quisling considerable popularity at school. He was never again to be as well liked as he was at school. If he made very few close friends during his schooldays, he seems to have made few, if any, enemies. There was still an attractive warmth about his personality which later he lost. For the rest of his career his natural reserve was constantly mistaken for hauteur or arrogance, an impression only reinforced by his high ambitions.

In 1905 Quisling became a cadet at the Norwegian Military Academy, where his career was even more distinguished than at school and his examination results were unsurpassed. He was a hard worker, 'applying himself to his studies with great energy and interest, and was always first'.[25] He was not particularly interested in the prescribed military and physical exercises, preferring to focus his attention on more academic subjects. He was enthusiastic about studying the art of war, strategy and military history, absorbing all the books on these subjects available in the General Staff library.[26] He was respected by his colleagues both for his ability and his industry, and for all three years of the course he held first place in the class. In his first two years he was clearly the best candidate, and in the third year tangible proof of his excellence was shown by his becoming sergeant-major of the cadets.[27] He also exceeded all expectations in physical endurance. One legendary episode was, according to Captain Odd Melsom, cited years later as an example of his keenness.[28] In 1907 Quisling travelled forty miles across country, alone, at night, during the winter and in mountainous country, in the course of a routine reconnaissance.

In 1908 Quisling was rewarded for his intellectual and physical exertions. He graduated at the head of his class and was gazetted as a lieutenant. He did not, however, join the General Staff immediately, as had been predicted. Instead he returned to his old school at Skien, to teach for a year, until the summer of 1909. He enjoyed this year, but he decided to resume his military career in the autumn of 1909, when he joined the Military High School. Once again this decision surprised most of his colleagues, who had been sure, in view of his outstanding record, that he would immediately join the General Staff. The reason for the decision was Quisling's wish to extend his technical knowledge. During his period as a cadet he had acquired a special interest in artillery and engineering and he now felt that he should devote more attention to these subjects. Henceforth his particular field of interest lay in these subjects.[29]

Quisling left the Military High School in 1911. He had achieved a unique standard of all-round brilliance. At his trial Quisling's pride in that achievement was still evident – 'I obtained the best results anyone had ever obtained throughout the century of the Military High School's existence.' The achievement earned instant recognition. For the first time in the school's history the honour of presentation to the King in an interview was conferred, a distinction which has never been repeated, though the school has now been in existence for over one hundred and fifty years. Quisling's bearing at his interview with King Haakon confirmed the high reputation he had earned.

16

A career full of honour seemed to await Quisling whenever he decided to join the General Staff. He finally enrolled as a probationary officer on the General Staff in the autumn of 1911, becoming personal assistant and adjutant to General Holtfodt.[30] Although he was enthusiastic about his new tasks he still retained an exceptionally wide range of interests, which occupied most of his free time. His intensive concentration on military studies since 1905 had not restricted either his reading or his appetite for knowledge. By this time he spoke several languages fluently, including English and German, and had become an eager student of philosophy and political science. Among the writers in whom he showed particular interest were Nietzsche and the German geopolitical school. The breadth of his reading was of considerable assistance to him in his military studies; for example, his interest in geopolitics enlarged his knowledge of strategy and the theory of war. Although still an aspirant, his general knowledge of military science was at least as good as that of his superior officers. It seemed obvious to all who came into contact with him that he would acquit himself with distinction once he became a full officer on the General Staff.

A requirement made of those who aspired to join the General Staff was the intensive examination of a particular country. Quisling chose Russia.[31] He learned the language and read a great deal of Russian literature. He also made a close study of the Russian economy, especially the rates of production and export/import statistics, which he felt were relevant to any accurate estimate of Russian war potential. During the winter of 1912–13 he wrote a technical study on the country for the General Staff, and this remained the standard work on the military potential of Russia for some years[32] until the firm establishment of the Communist regime altered the facts upon which he had made his judgements.

During the years 1911–15 Quisling was not just a desk soldier. Despite a vast amount of paper work he found time to carry out the normal duties of a regular officer. According to his own testimony the life he led was singularly energetic.

> I lived like an ascetic. When I was out marching I had a bag of nuts in my pack, and I drank the milk which was issued to soldiers. That was what I lived upon. I refused to lie in front of the stove in the winter so that I might harden myself. That is how I lived as a young man. I rose at five in the morning the better to prepare myself for my occupation as an officer and my service, as an officer, to my country.[33]

This account was not retrospective self-glorification; it was supported at his trial by Lieutenant-General Otto Ruge, a man in no way sympathetic towards Quisling, who stated that 'he was an intelligent man, outstandingly industrious and ascetic in his personal behaviour'.[34]

Quisling believed that this period of service to Norway clarified his ideas: 'I began to understand what it was to guide a nation, to control the destiny of a nation. It began to seem clear to me what a nation was.'

Certainly he felt that he was doing service to his country and at his trial remembered these years with pride and pleasure. He was happy in the army and later recalled: 'As a young battery lieutenant stationed in North Norway I commanded the best soldiers I ever had.' Quisling must have been happy for he had at least one chance to take up a very profitable post elsewhere.

> I was asked to go to China. I don't know what this really involved. I was invited to be an instructor in the then Imperial Chinese Army, and offered a high rank considering my age. Also I taught myself Chinese. I threw away, as one might say, a great deal of time teaching myself the language. Meanwhile the Chinese revolution took place and put an end to it all.[35]

In 1915 this period as a probationary officer on the General Staff ended successfully, and Quisling transferred to the Artillery at his own request, taking up in 1916 the position of adjutant to the Inspector-General of Field Artillery.[36] During 1916 and 1917 he specialised in the study of ballistics and was awarded the Royal Norwegian Gold Medal for Ballistics.[37] In 1917 he returned to the General Staff; he was promoted to the rank of captain, and remained attached to the General Staff until 1923. During 1917 he continued his study of Russia, which had acquired additional interest owing to the change of government. This study contrasted strongly with his normal work, which mainly involved tedious paper work; Quisling gradually lost interest and began to long for a life of action. He asked that his specialised knowledge of Russia and its language be made use of and that he be transferred to a more active post as military attaché in Russia.[38] This decision was perhaps the most momentous in Quisling's career, marking an abrupt change in his hitherto well-ordered progress. With his attainments and abilities he would almost certainly have reached the top ranks of the General Staff. General Ruge, a few years older than Quisling, was the key officer in the army in 1940, a man of lesser ability, though infinitely greater balance.

In 1918 Quisling had excellent prospects which he was prepared to put at risk. His decision to go to Russia completely changed the pattern of his life. After 1918 he became increasingly erratic in the use of his gifts, and more obsessive in the pursuit of his interests. The years he spent in Russia were crucial in the making of the man, and more than any others yield information about the change in attitude which led to the Quisling of 1918 becoming the Quisling of 1940.

The application which he made was successful,[39] and on 5 April 1918 he was ordered to proceed to Petrograd, at that time still the diplomatic capital of Russia. Before he departed Quisling was presented to the King. He wrote to his parents, 'On Saturday I had an audience with the King. I talked to him for about half an hour. He was very amiable and I found what he said reasonable.'[40]

Quisling encountered some difficulty before he could reach his new post. According to his own account, 'some time passed before I could arrive, owing to the civil war and revolution in Finland, but eventually I obtained permission to travel via the eastern front through Germany'. He arrived at the closing stage of the Russian revolution, when the Bolsheviks were consolidating their supremacy. Quisling noted that the general opinion among the Russians was that the revolution was purely a passing phase and would soon be over. He, however, saw it as another phase of the world crisis which had begun with the defeat of Russia by Japan in 1904–5. That defeat had thrown Russia back into European affairs, thus precipitating the world war, which would in turn, he believed, lead to serious internal and external convulsions. The extent to which this opinion was based on hindsight is hard to judge. Certainly trained observers did not find it easy to assess the Russian situation in 1918. For all his background knowledge, it is hard to accept that Quisling was at that time a better judge of the situation.

Quisling did not remain in Petrograd. He made several journeys, and added considerably to his store of knowledge. He visited the war front, where the Red and White armies were engaged in a bitter struggle, and where, he states, an offer was made to him which would have led to his leaving the Norwegian Army.

> I was at the front, attached to Trotsky. At one of the decisive battles on the eastern front Trotsky asked me for my opinion on the situation at Kazan, where the Northern Army Group and the Eastern Army Group of the Whites were in the process of joining together in order to crush the Bolsheviks. He asked me what I thought he should do in this situation. I discussed this with Trotsky, and made such a strong impression on him that he wanted me to become his chief of staff and remain with him on the eastern front.[41]

Quisling, however, rejected the offer.[42]

Russia continued to fascinate the military attaché. He believed the Russians had strong connexions with the Nordic peoples. 'Russia', he said, 'is a Nordic land. The original Russians were Germanic.' He even traced a connexion between the names of places on the lower Dnieper and his own Telemark, and came to the conclusion that 'the greater part of the Russian aristocracy were of Norwegian and Scandinavian blood'.[43] Later in his life he came to feel strongly about the decay of Teutonic influence in Russia and bemoaned the fall of the Russian nobility; which he considered could have been prevented had the thirty-two German divisions on the Russian front in 1917 been used to put an end to Bolshevism rather than expended on a fruitless offensive in the West. In 1918 his opinions were very different.

Quisling used to discuss these and allied matters with an acquaintance called Frederik Prytz, a timber merchant and entrepreneur, who was at that time chargé d'affaires at Petrograd and with whom he struck up what was to be a long enduring friendship. As men on the spot, they appreciated how tenuous was Bolshevik control in 1918–19. Quisling realised that the Red Army was very weak, and recalled at his trial how, on his way from Petrograd to Moscow and on to the eastern front, he had come across only a single patrol of the Red Army.[44] The land awaited the return of firm and effective government.

Quisling's letters to his parents and his brother Jørgen reveal the chaotic state of affairs in Russia.

> There is famine here. The bread ration is no more than a small roll a day, and that mixed with straw. Sugar costs nearly 100 roubles a kilo, flour 40, portion of soup in a good restaurant 25. There are epidemics here in the city, famine, erysipelas, scurvy, dysentery. By the roadside are lying numbers of cripples and beggars.[45]

He saw that the old order had been totally overthrown, and that the aristocracy were in no better position than the peasants. 'Some had patrimonies which were greater than a Norwegian county. Now all that is over, and they live on twenty-five grams of black bread and five salt herrings a day; sometimes perhaps they cannot even obtain the bread.'[46] The confusion and distress brought about by the revolution greatly worried Quisling,[47] and these experiences undoubtedly influenced his subsequent decision to return to Russia to work with Nansen in his mission of relief.

Despite his wanderings in the battle zone Quisling tried to live the life of an ordinary diplomat. Although the Bolshevik seizure of power had changed many things in Russia it had not destroyed the habit of entertainment. In a letter to Jørgen, Quisling related how he and nearly all the legation staff were invited to a reception at the house of the Danish Ambassador, Herr Scavenius. Present at this reception were 'many of the old Russian nobility, whose names read like a chapter from one of Tolstoy's novels'.[48] Despite all his military and social engagements – or perhaps even arising out of them – Quisling found time to visit Trotsky at his home in Moscow. Certainly his stay in Russia was full of activity, and he had little time for relaxation. Nevertheless, although he was devoted to his work, it was not long before events conspired to return him to Norway, and perhaps in many ways he was not sorry to have the chance of getting away and recovering from his exhausting experiences.

As the year 1918 drew to a close the situation in Russia became more dangerous, and eventually the Foreign Minister, Ihlen, decided to close the Norwegian legation in Petrograd. Most of the staff left Russia in December 1918; Quisling followed early in 1919.

> We broke off relations with the Soviet Union. We were among the last to leave Russia. We had represented a number of other countries and in the course of this contact I noticed many things. . . . I had observed that the English and the French had concocted a conspiracy to topple the Bolshevik government, though I was not personally involved in it.[49]

Quisling returned straight to Norway, intending to rejoin the General Staff. First, however, he visited Ullmann for a short stay. According to

Ullmann, Quisling had, on professional grounds, been most reluctant to leave Petrograd, particularly in view of the opening of the war of intervention. Apparently he did not blame solely the Bolsheviks for this crisis, and gave a judicious and balanced survey of the situation.[50]

For a short period Quisling rejoined the General Staff,[51] and during the winter of 1919–20 he gave some lectures on Russia to the influential Oslo Military Society. His lectures came as a shock to many of the officers, who were surprised to find him defending the Communist system.[52] Apart from his well-known nationalism he had shown no previous sign of political leanings. He did not stay long in Norway, however. Almost immediately after returning to normal duties with the General Staff he was sent to Helsingfors, whither the legation staff from Russia had retreated. Finland, after initial post-war convulsions, had acquired a stable government in April 1919 when a democratic election brought the Liberal Party to power. The Finnish capital was thus a relatively peaceful vantage point from which to observe developments in Russia.

It was believed that Quisling's knowledge of Russian affairs and his excellent command of the language would be invaluable to the Norwegian Minister in Finland, Andreas Tostrup Urbye. On 8 October 1920, therefore, Quisling was ordered to Helsingfors to take up the post of joint military attaché and legation secretary. The latter was a posting of some importance, justifying Quisling's transfer from the General Staff. Quisling at his trial recalled: 'At the same time I was deputy for Urbye when he was away, and I had also charge of Russian affairs in so far as we could cope with them in Helsingfors.'[53] His loss to the General Staff was soon felt; shortly after his transfer, his former chief, General Holtfodt, met Urbye, and congratulated him 'on having obtained such a man as an assistant in the legation'.[54] Within a short time Urbye also thought highly of Quisling's abilities, and in an interview given on 3 December 1938, after his retirement, he declared: 'When I worked with Quisling I felt an idiot, so sharp was his brain, so nimble were his wits, so great was his logical power.'[55] Nor was this only an assessment in retrospect, for it was Urbye who recommended Quisling to Nansen, as a result of the excellent work he had done.[56] Not only was it the minister who was impressed with Quisling's work but also the rest of the embassy staff, who appreciated the scope of his interests and the trouble he took to do his work thoroughly.[57] His short stay in Finland confirmed both his ability and his industry in the eyes of his superiors.

On 27 May 1921 Quisling's period of duty in Finland ended and he was ordered back to Norway.[58] Here he expected to re-establish himself on the General Staff and resume his regular duties. But once again his return to his military career was postponed. While at Helsingfors, he had aided Nansen in his repatriation work. After the First World War there were more than two million prisoners of war in Russia, and Nansen had been appointed High Commissioner by the League of Nations, with the task of solving this problem.[59] Many other difficulties faced Russia after 1918, and Nansen required able assistants. In 1920 he began to recruit men for his next task, which was to be the relief of the starving Russian peasantry. He knew that Quisling spoke Russian fluently, and that he knew the country and many of its leaders. Accordingly Nansen asked Urbye for his candid opinion of Quisling. Urbye recommended him very warmly. Even after an interval of a quarter of a century, at Quisling's trial in 1945, Urbye refused to change his original assessment. 'He was a very conscientious man, a man of his word, who had wide interests and was well informed.'[60] Not surprisingly, therefore, Quisling received a request from Nansen asking him to assist in the work of relief. He had no difficulty in obtaining leave of absence from the General Staff, for officials in Norway, unlike those in many other lands, were eager to assist Nansen. By the end of 1921 Quisling was ready to return to Russia.

In January 1922, then, Quisling set out for Russia, with no illusions as to the difficulty of the tasks ahead. As he was about to depart he encountered a Norwegian called Koepcke, a former consul who had only just returned from Russia. Koepcke told him that if he went he would be lucky to survive. Even this dismal prophecy did not shake Quisling's determination; he arrived in Russia late in January, and travelled by way of Petrograd and Moscow to the district to which he had been assigned – the Ukraine. The winter was a hard one; both Petrograd and Moscow were abnormally snowbound. Quisling had to go out into the countryside and work on his own, for the roads, such as they were, were more easily passable by one person than by a company. The conditions were abominable, and the task was made even more difficult by the Bolshevik government's ignorance or neglect of the true state of affairs.[61]

In the years immediately after the Bolshevik revolution conditions in Russia had been aggravated by political strife. Acute xenophobia was widespread, originating perhaps in defeat at the hands of Imperial Germany and intensified by the excesses of the Poles and the foreign-assisted Whites.[62] The government of the Soviet Union, apprehensive of the presence of aliens on Russian soil, placed unnecessary obstacles in the way of all offers of assistance until 1921. The Bolsheviks were particularly suspicious of all foreign-based organisations, and wanted to channel assistance to devastated areas, if they could, through their own administrative machine. In these early days, however, the Bolshevik administration was no more efficient than that of the Tsars, and eventually the Soviet government was obliged to admit the fact by allowing foreign organisations to work in those large areas where its writ did not run.

Even the International Russian Relief Executive [63] encountered grave difficulties in getting permission to operate. The Soviet government feared lest this mission of mercy might be used for political purposes. When the scheme was first suggested in 1919, G. V. Chicherin, the Commissar for Foreign Affairs, had sent a telegram to Nansen stating that his government was 'ready to lend every assistance to your scheme so far as it bears the character you have ascribed to it in your letter, [but] we at the same time do not wish to be the object of foul play'.[64] It was thus not until 1921 that any action became possible, and even then only because

the Governments and the business world also found their attitude towards Russia much affected and complicated by the famine, of unparalleled severity, which devastated Russia after the harvest of 1921 had failed in the most fertile regions, especially in the Volga districts and in Southern Ukraine.[65]

Soon after the existence of famine had become evident Nansen was requested by the International Conference of Red Cross and Philanthropic Associations, which had met at Geneva on 15 August 1921, to put himself at the head of the relief work for Russia. This was the basis of the International Russian Relief Executive (henceforward called the Commission).

By the time the Commission was ready to start operations war conditions had existed in parts of Russia for over seven years, and a speedy return to peacetime existence had become impossible. Thus on his arrival in the Ukraine Quisling faced a formidable task. His official designation was that of Secretary to the Commission in the Ukraine, with headquarters at Kharkov. There his presence was to prove invaluable, for he had not only contacts with the Bolshevik government but a fluent command of Russian; which was sorely needed, since Nansen was unable to speak the language. At the office in Moscow where the Commission dealt directly with the central administration, a knowledge of German did almost as well, but in the provinces Russian was essential, and Quisling was able to remedy immediately the Commission's lack of a competent linguist. Travel in Russia was, if anything, slower than under the Tsars and Quisling did not arrive in the Ukraine until 12 February 1922.[66] On his arrival Nansen gave him full powers to grapple with local problems while he himself left to use his name and diplomatic skill in order to secure international co-operation in this humanitarian work.

The most immediate problem was that of food. Nansen himself remembered with horror

the Russian famine in 1921 and 1922 when the Volga region and the most fertile parts of Russia were ravaged by a terrible drought, when something like thirty million people or more were starving and dying – dying by the thousand.[67]

Little could be done to relieve so many. Nevertheless a start was made in the Ukraine, despite dreadful difficulties. Civilisation had almost completely collapsed and the fertile Ukraine, once the corn belt of Russia, remained uncultivated. Gangs of hungry peasants roamed the countryside, looting what little property still existed, and terrorising those who still tried to farm the land. The conditions resembled those in Ireland in the 1840s. There were outbreaks of cannibalism; the only food otherwise available was rotten fish – and of this there was too much. The resources of the Bolshevik government were totally inadequate, and were further strained by the inevitable outbreaks of fevers and other diseases which swept the country and killed millions of people weakened by insufficient food. Quisling thus had grave problems even without the political complications arising from working in Soviet Russia.

The Ukraine had been one of the principal battlefields in the recent civil war. Not only was disorganisation widespread but the central government was doubtful of the political reliability of the area. The most serious initial problem was that of food transport to the starving millions. In this Quisling was greatly assisted by previous actions of the Soviet government. Originally the Bolsheviks had, for military reasons, placed the control of the railway system under Trotsky, who had greatly improved its efficiency. Then a unified Commissariat of Traffic, headed by the ruthless Feliks Dzerzhinsky, had been created, which incorporated not only the state railways but also canals and river transport. Although the total amount of inland traffic was only about a quarter of what it had been before the war,[68] the mobilisation of existing resources under a responsible minister who was prepared to allocate priorities eased Quisling's task. Nansen himself wrote:

> under Trotsky's dictatorship an immense effort was made to restore a little order and to repair the ruined railways. . . . It brought about a considerable improvement in the working of the whole system of transport, an improvement of which I have been able to convince myself by the numerous reports from our delegates who have had to superintend the transport of the food-stuffs despatched to the starving populations of the Volga and the Ukraine.[69]

Despite these improvements the transport system still suffered from its long neglect since the outbreak of war in 1914, and in particular the lack of new track, sleepers and rolling stock effectively hindered the swift transmission of relief supplies.

Quisling did his best to cope with this situation, and his fluent knowledge of Russian was of considerable help. His diplomacy seems to have lulled many suspicions about the role of the new Commission. He was even able to persuade large numbers of Russian students to work for the Commission, and to prevent the local commissars from interfering. His authority was considerable, though its exact extent is now difficult to determine. He appears to have been directly responsible to Nansen, and not, as one biographer has suggested, to an Englishman named John Gorvin.[70] No less improbable, on the other hand, is the suggestion of another biographer:

> he controlled 60 per cent of the creaking Russian railways, which were nominally requisitioned by the Soviets for the military purposes of Trotsky and the Red army. Hence subsequent denials by Moscow that they ever gave foreigners administrative authority over the railways. That is a quibble.

24

Only Quisling's capacity for self-deception can have inspired his own statement that his power was like that of 'Caesar Augustus'.[71]

In fact the evidence suggests that the Commission was in a very privileged position in Russia, and that this position derived not so much from the efforts of Quisling as from the co-operative attitude of the Soviet government. Nansen recorded that although

> the Russian transport system still works rather slowly and rather badly, I have not received any personal impression of this, as the Russian Government, with the most perfect Russian hospitality, placed the finest saloon-cars at my disposal on my journeys in 1921, 1922 and 1923. I cannot even say that our delegates in the famine relief work have suffered overmuch under the transport difficulties, except in the spring of 1922 when, *inter alia*, they went from Samara to Moscow by a train which was three weeks late. They have, moreover, enjoyed facilities and diplomatic privileges secured by the agreement that I concluded with Tchitcherin before the relief work began. Similarly our goods transports have always enjoyed special privileges: gratis carriage, priority, protection of the sealed wagons by soldiers of the Red army, etc.[72]

Quisling's role appears, therefore, to have been more limited than he later remembered. If Nansen is to be believed, the Bolshevik government was very much more active than Quisling suggested. The inevitable conclusion is that Quisling never exercised those wide discretionary powers which in retrospect he claimed to have possessed. Where he actually did exercise power was in his dealings with local officials. Even if considerable authority had been delegated to him by the Soviet government – and there is no evidence for this – that government was so remote from the Ukraine that it would have found great difficulty in enforcing obedience to Quisling's orders. The Commission in the Ukraine operated on a basis of agreement rather than of compulsion. The advancement of famine relief depended more on local relationships than on directives from Moscow. It seems likely that the privileges which the Commission obtained at this level stemmed largely from Quisling's linguistic skill and his persuasiveness. Hence his value to Nansen.

Although his task demanded his presence in the Ukraine, Quisling still maintained contact with the outside world. There were offices of the Commission in Berlin, Moscow and Geneva, and through these offices came news of the political repercussions of the work he was doing. The months spent in Kharkov made Quisling bitter against political intrigues in Russia and the West, for he felt that these hindered the progress of his work. It is not surprising that he became more sympathetic towards the Bolshevik government. He was later to state that 'in the beginning the Bolsheviks were well-intentioned and desired the welfare of the people. It was not they who started the terror.'[73] This sympathy, however, seems to have arisen more out of pity for the dreadful condition of the Russian people and the misery inflicted on them by Denikin and Kolchak, the White commanders, than from ideological sympathy with Communism.

The charge, alleged to have been made by the Polish government that Quisling deliberately aided the Bolsheviks in the Ukraine appears to have little substance. Indeed, one of his notable feats probably hindered the Red Army, for he stole some of Budënny's horses, to be slaughtered for food.[74] The Red Army commander is reported to have greeted the news of this disaster with the comment that Quisling was merely doing his duty in the way to be expected of a soldier.[75]

Relations with the outside world seem to have been complicated not only by political events but also by the curious structure of the Commission. There is some controversy over the exact working of this body,[76] though its founder, Nansen, had little doubt about the way in which it was intended to function. Nansen's daughter wrote that

> it was further arranged that the Nansen Mission was to be administered from a central office in Geneva, . . . and to have a sub-office in Berlin, which would be in direct communication with the Nansen office in Moscow, ...
> As well as the office in Moscow for Great Russia and the Volga valley, there was to be a branch office in Kharkov for Ukraine and Crimea.[77]

Quisling was in charge of the office in Kharkov, but the odd procedure by which aid had to be channelled through Moscow, and often through Berlin as well, made his job unnecessarily complicated.

Although administration absorbed a large amount of Quisling's time it was not his sole function. He was expected to travel in the Ukraine and assist in the practical distribution of relief. His first task was to set up centres for the starving and the diseased to attend. This work was quickly completed, and the centres were soon operating to full capacity. Known as 'Nansen kitchens', they swiftly reduced the rate of mortality. The kitchens fed huge numbers of people, particularly children, and, by supplying decent food, began also to reduce the incidence of diseases connected with malnutrition. The only matter for regret was, as Nansen himself admitted, that it was impossible to supply food to all who required it. Thus, while thousands were saved, thousands were also left to die, though the Commission did its best.

Nansen himself pointed out that it was better that half should survive the whole winter than that all should survive half the winter and then once more be exposed to starvation.[78] Nansen was particularly affected by the plight of the young.

> I believe that the thousands of kitchens opened by foreign relief organisations, where the children came for a meal every day, saved millions of little starving creatures from a cruel death. . . . According to a report which I have just received from my representative in Ukraine, Captain Quisling, the conditions among homeless children seem to be very bad there, even though they may be less bad than those described above. Out of Ukraine's 11 million children more than a million are orphans or semi-orphans. . . . The mortality is therefore very high, being up to 80 per cent for new-born infants. . . . In 1922, 12,204 criminals under fourteen years of age were registered.[79]

As if these problems were not sufficient to keep the Commission busy, there was also that of the students, who required a different type of treatment. Student relief in the area centred on Simferopol and Kharkov, and the aid to the students was in time repaid by the assistance they gave the Commission in its routine work.[80]

Problems were not solved merely by the provision of meals. Both Quisling and Nansen realised that little would be accomplished without a long-term plan.[81] It was evident in 1922 that there would be an even more serious problem in 1923. The very saving of life created fresh problems. Between twelve and fifteen million people were fed in 1922, and many of them depended for their continued survival on the meals supplied by the Commission. The only satisfactory solution was to persuade the peasants to return to tilling the land, thus increasing food production. Many buildings and much machinery, however, had been destroyed, or allowed to decay since 1914; still more of the remaining buildings had been requisitioned for use by the Commission as centres, so that these too were not available for agricultural purposes. Much of the seed corn had been consumed in order to stave off impending starvation. To remedy this situation Quisling tried to obtain fresh supplies of seed corn and new machinery. By the time he left the Ukraine, for the last time, in autumn 1923, conditions had much improved, and agriculture was flourishing once more.

Quisling was profoundly moved by the suffering he had witnessed. At his trial he recalled some of his emotions; he felt 'that there was no one in government circles in Moscow who knew what was going on in the famine-affected areas'. This lack of knowledge proved a handicap for those involved in the work of relief, and it was perhaps at this time that Quisling began to question once again the merits of the Soviet system. He was, after all, well-placed to observe the clumsy working of the government as he travelled through the Ukraine. 'For three months I travelled in the stricken areas among the starving people, and I lived like a dog, plagued by vermin, hunger and disease, cholera, smallpox and fever.' He regularly sent reports to Nansen about the location and prevalence of these diseases, thus acting as a public health inspector in addition to all his other jobs. Not unreasonably he was proud of his work and later claimed to have 'saved more people than he could remember, though it must have been some hundreds of thousands'.[82] He added that he had remained at his post without regard for his own interests. And indeed it seems unlikely that the Quisling of the early 1920s was much concerned with his own well-being: his activities in the Ukraine rather suggest that he was a humane man, with a conscience and a real sense of duty.[83] By 1945 irrevocable changes had been wrought in his character.

During the spring and summer of 1922 Quisling acquired a working knowledge of several more Russian dialects, and made good use of his linguistic ability to investigate the social, economic and political background of the Ukraine. It is said that at some point during these months he married a girl called Alexandra.[84] According to this story she was only about eighteen years old, but was a political refugee, and the only way Quisling could help her escape from Russia was by marrying her. Once they were safely outside Russia a divorce by consent followed. The whole story is shrouded in mystery. Although certain details about Alexandra were current, she was never given a surname, nor is there any record of either marriage or divorce. Quisling himself offered no information on this matter at his trial, and his former supporters seem to be divided in their opinions of the truth of the story. Even assuming that, owing to the disturbed conditions then in Russia, the relevant papers have all been lost, it is still not easy to believe that in 1922 Quisling was so far alienated from the Bolshevik regime as to act in this way. It would have been even more unlike him not to discuss the affair once he had left Kharkov in the autumn of 1922. Having returned to Norway for the winter, it seems inconceivable that he should not have disclosed this romantic adventure to any of his friends or relations. Finally, and perhaps most important of all, his wife, whom he married in 1923, has denied that there was ever any truth in the matter. The mystery remains unsolved.

After his return to Norway Quisling did his best to arouse interest in the valuable work being done under Nansen's command, and to raise more money for the Commission. His stay was short, and early in 1923 he returned to the Ukraine, where he remained until September. The work of the Commission in the Ukraine then ended, not because there was no more to be done, but because there were other and more urgent tasks. During these few months Quisling met and married his wife. She was appreciably younger than he, having been born at Kiev on 12 October 1900. Her maiden name was Maria Vasilievna Pasek, and she was a member of an old aristocratic Russian family, though not one of the first rank, being well known in the Ukraine rather than nationally.[85] Apparently she was both very beautiful and intelligent, and, given the poverty of Ukrainian social life at this time, it is easy to perceive the attraction that they must have held for each other. They were married on 10 September 1923,[86] and soon after left the Ukraine for ever. By early October Quisling was once again resident in Norway.

Quisling's leave of absence from the General Staff had in fact expired in the summer of 1923, but he had stayed on in order to complete his mission. Once the affairs of the Commission had been wound up, he left Kharkov in mid-September. On his departure from the Ukraine he received a letter from the local Red Cross in which it was recorded: 'We consider that a large part of the success of the work of the mission may be attributed to your personal qualities, your tact and your noble and sincere friendship for our country and people.'[87] Nansen, in his account of the work of the Commission, also expressed his appreciation of the task Quisling had performed.

Quisling left the Ukraine with a strong emotional attachment to Russia. In part, perhaps, this attachment arose from his belief that

28

Russia was a Nordic land. So passionately was he wedded to this idea that he always insisted that his wife was of Nordic descent. In 1930, at the time of the jubilee of his class of 1905, he described her in his biographical notes as 'a Russian of Dinaric-Nordic extraction'.[88] That this was a genuine belief seems consistent with his character, though some critics have suggested that Quisling put forward this theory because in Norway his dark-haired wife was frequently thought to be a Jewess.

Quisling's return to Norway created a minor stir, for in an article published soon afterwards in one of Norway's leading newspapers, *Tidens Tegn*, he advocated recognition of the Soviet government.[89] The article was given considerable prominence and dealt not only with the vexed question of recognition but with a much wider range of Russian topics. Despite the attention brought him by this and other similar articles and letters to the press, Quisling settled down in Oslo, apparently with the intention of resuming his much interrupted military career. He and his wife eventually bought a house in a pleasant residential district,[90] and lived there until they moved to 'Gimle', his official residence, late in 1941.

As events turned out, Quisling did not rejoin the General Staff. His failure to resume his military career is one of the most curious developments in a life full of conundrums. The reason seems to have lain in Quisling's personal feelings. Obviously there would have been difficulties in his way, but none of them was insuperable. The most serious obstacle was that, as a result of his service in Russia first as attaché and then as assistant to Nansen, he had never taken the necessary examinations. A second difficulty was that, by now, because of his earlier brilliance in army examinations, his meritorious service and his unrivalled knowledge of Russian affairs and the Russian language, he had come to deem himself indispensable. The effort to settle down as a regular member of the General Staff would have been intellectually small but morally taxing. He would have had little difficulty in passing the army examinations, but after virtually ruling large areas of the Ukraine he would have found it almost impossible to defer to those in higher positions who had enjoyed less practical exercise of authority. Perhaps, too, he was correct in his belief that a career in the General Staff held no future for him since already he knew far more than most of his fellow officers, and this superior knowledge would be resented.

Yet when Quisling had taken up his post as military attaché in Petrograd, he had believed that step would aid rather than hinder his future military career. Again, when he sought permission to assist Nansen, he felt that he was performing a service for Norway, and he seems to have expected, quite reasonably, that the years from 1918 to 1923 would have counted towards his service on the General Staff. It was particularly galling to discover that men of lesser ability and experience had, through their devotion to one career, overtaken him in the race for preferment. In his calculations he had failed to allow for the inflexibility of the rules of the officer corps, the army and the War Department. Instead of proving an asset, the years spent away from Norway were to be a disadvantage. It is hardly surprising that Quisling felt bitter about such stupidity, and although the viewpoint of the Norwegian authorities may be defended, it must not be forgotten that as a result of this decision the Norwegian army lost one who, to judge from examination results, was the ablest soldier, without exception, that it had ever recruited.

It seems improbable, however, that these were the only reasons for Quisling's failure to rejoin the General Staff. One factor which may have weighed heavily against him was the impression he had given many of his fellow officers that he was sympathetic to Communism. The suspicions aroused by the views he had expressed in the winter of 1919–20 were further strengthened by the articles he published in October 1923, which were distinctly favourable towards Russia. Another important factor was the length of time he had spent away from the army on non-military affairs. On at least one occasion he had overstayed his leave. It is hardly surprising that in these circumstances many officers had serious reservations about his return to active duty. So, in late 1923, the General Staff and Quisling parted company. He remained attached to the army, with the rank of captain, and was placed in the reserve, on half pay. But he was not assigned any formal duty.[91]

Quisling's own view of the matter was that he had been very badly treated by the army, though at his trial he declared: 'I refused to take the matter up again, and I can honestly swear that the affair caused no bitterness on my part.'[92] Whatever his feelings in 1945, in 1923 and the months that followed he seems to have been both disappointed and disillusioned. In 1927 he still felt sufficiently strongly to write to King Haakon about the matter. In his letter of 1 November, written from Moscow, he recalled that early in 1922 Nansen had asked him to travel to Russia as representative in the Ukraine for the international relief commission which Nansen headed and to which Norway was officially committed. Upon Nansen's suggestion the chief of the War Department had given Quisling permission to join the mission. On the basis of this fact alone he felt that his service should count towards seniority, since the work which he did redounded to the credit of Norway. By 1927, of course, it was much too late for this letter to have any effect, and the King took no action.

During 1922–3 Quisling had continued to work for the General Staff for short periods between his other activities in the Ukraine. It had been at the personal request of Nansen that he had been released for special duty in the autumn of 1922. Quisling was fully aware of the circumstances, for he later recalled that 'the conditions imposed on me by the military authorities were the same as before, though it was now pointed out that this would be the last occasion'.[93] Quisling knew that this leave had been granted only for a very limited period but later complained:

On 1 July 1923 my leave ran out. I had had permission from the General Staff, I personally had paid my replacement in the General Staff . . . but the liquidation of my work in Russia would require at least two more months . . . and for this I was denied permission.[94]

When he decided to stay in Russia in defiance of orders, the consequences must have been clear to him.

It would have been improper for me to leave my post at that time, but on the other hand I had been denied permission to continue, and if I wished to complete my work in Russia, then, much against my will, I had to give up my position on the General Staff and in the army and go on the reserve list.[95]

Quisling chose to count upon his reputation to save him from the consequences of his act, but in this he was mistaken. 'Nansen wanted to take up the case,' stated Quisling in 1945, 'but I said no, for it would have caused too much trouble.' It remains a mystery why he failed to take advantage of Nansen's generous offer, for Nansen alone had the power to save his career. The most plausible explanation is that a man with Quisling's outlook on life wanted to be taken back on his own terms or not at all.

The terms which Quisling demanded were much too high. He was shocked and enraged to discover that, even if allowed to rejoin the General Staff, he would not rank in seniority according to the years he had spent in the army, but according to the time he had spent on military affairs. He concluded that the army had no proper order of priorities, and complained that, although he had not been granted two extra months, 'a Norwegian officer, who was looking for a position in a bank, received leave of absence'. At the same time he claimed that all he would have been doing on the General Staff was 'sitting and writing some orders of the day, or some such stuff, for the two months, or perhaps would even have been on holiday for that period'.[96] All Quisling's efforts were in vain, and by mid-October 1923 it was clear to him that he would not be allowed to resume his career as if the events of the previous five years had not taken place. Despite this he disclaimed any bitterness, stating at his trial that he had 'never felt any animosity either against the Norwegian military service or against General Bauck,[97] who handled the case. Everything was lost, but it was a fact which had to be faced.'[98] Once his initial irritation had passed, this was probably true.

Thus in late 1923 Quisling, although nominally attached to the army, had no fixed occupation. From being the arbiter of the fate of thousands of Russians, he had declined to a position in which his prospects were very poor. It is scarcely to be wondered at that he felt ill-used. What seems to have hurt him most of all was the failure of the General Staff to recognise the value of the work he had done. Not only was it work for Norway, but Quisling also felt that 'my work was for all practical purposes General Staff work',[99] and that his knowledge could have been invaluable to the army.

One thing at least is clear from the whole episode – the General Staff's reservations about Quisling's suitability on disciplinary grounds were amply justified. Quisling evidently felt that he was dealing with men of inferior minds, and the General Staff knew this and resented it. One biographer has, not unjustly, characterised Quisling's attitude at this time thus: 'What was the importance of these trifling jobs back in Norway? Was a formal, provincial standard to be imposed upon his work? As a captain he had supplied and administered a greater number of people than in the fully mobilized Norwegian army.'[100] It is clear why the General Staff would not take Quisling back.

While Quisling was still struggling with the army authorities he was fortunate enough to receive a letter from Nansen which offered him some prospect of employment. In late 1923 Nansen was enjoying a well-deserved rest at his home in Lysaker, while preparing plans for further work for the League of Nations. Nansen's letter, dated 17 October, invited his former assistant to help in the solution of certain problems which had arisen in Bulgaria, in connexion with refugees, work with which Quisling was familiar. The letter was, indirectly, a testimonial to the value of the work which Quisling had previously done: 'I am wholly in agreement,' Nansen wrote, 'with Major Johnson, Frick and Gorvin, that we could not find a better man, if it were possible that you could take on the job.' The letter contained advice on the measures Quisling would be obliged to take if he were to accept Nansen's offer and concluded by regretting that Nansen could not see Quisling personally, since 'there was so much I would have liked to discuss . . . and I would be glad to thank you personally for your first class work in Russia'.[101] Nansen's declaration of confidence encouraged Quisling, and he accepted the offer.

Late in 1923, Quisling departed for Bulgaria in order to assist in the repatriation of Russian refugees. A start had been made early in 1923, but so far the problem appeared almost as difficult as ever, particularly since there was no common frontier between Russia and Bulgaria. Before Quisling's arrival the Commission had been using ss *Varna*, an old and unreliable cargo ship, to transport the refugees. This proved to be a slow method, and by the end of 1923 only a few hundred had been returned to their native land. The work was further complicated by the suspicions of the Soviet government, which feared the infiltration of spies hired by the West or by the *émigré* regime. At one point the whole scheme had been put into question by such doubts, but luckily,

> in response to the appeal from many thousands of refugees in Bulgaria who expressed the desire to return to Russia, the High Commission opened negotiations with the Soviet Government in order to ascertain on what conditions the Soviet Government would allow such refugees to re-enter Russia.[102]

Happily an agreement was reached between the Commission and Russia,[103]

Quisling spent about eighteen months in the Balkans and went on to act as a roving agent for Nansen and the Commission, once his first task in Bulgaria had been completed. His principal contribution to the solution of the Bulgarian problem was to arrange transport by rail through Bulgaria, Romania and Russia for large parties of refugees. Once this delicate piece of diplomacy had been completed, the problem was largely freed from the possibility of international repercussions; there still remained, however, the problems of food and accommodation. As a result of the Balkan Wars, the Great War and then the civil war in Russia, there was terrible dislocation in most of the Balkan states; not only had whole populations been uprooted by the redrawing of frontiers, but there had also been vast physical damage to civil amenities. The problems of organising shelter, water and food supplies were almost insuperable. Eastern Europe had fallen into chaos, 'there were 30,000 refugees in Finland; Latvia and Esthonia were flooded with them; there were at least 25,000 in Czechoslovakia, 50,000 in Yugoslavia, 35,000 in Bulgaria, over 70,000 in the East'.[104] In view of the size of the problem, and the economic difficulties of the Allies, it was not easy for the Commission to obtain adequate finance. Recourse to a regular lottery had been made at an early stage in the activities of the Commission, and Quisling was put in charge of the lottery run in Bulgaria. After the deduction of all expenses the scheme yielded a net profit of 520,000 leva.[105] The money was devoted exclusively to the relief of Russian refugees in Bulgaria, and was not put at the disposal of the Soviet government, as some enemies of the Commission alleged.

Apart from a few brief visits to Norway Quisling passed the months from the autumn of 1923 to the early summer of 1925 working in the Balkan states. He was responsible to the central office of the Commission in Geneva, but was allowed considerable discretionary power. After Bulgaria he turned his attention, like Nansen, to Greece, which was still in a state of turmoil after the unsuccessful war with Turkey. In addition to all the refugees from Asia Minor and Turkey-in-Europe, which amounted to a total of about one-and-a-half million, there were also large contingents of Bulgars, Albanians and pro-Tsarist Russians. 'The worst place was Constantinople. . . . Now, there were 170,000 Russians registered there, of whom 125,000 were men from Wrangel's beaten army with their families.'[106] Thus both in Greece and in Turkey, Quisling had an additional problem to solve, for many of the refugees would not consider repatriation. Old communities were transformed in appearance, new villages were constructed. Quisling had the task of supervising much of the resettlement, and this occupied him fully until the summer of 1925. Even after that date, because of his great experience, he was sometimes consulted about Balkan problems. In 1926, 10,000 Bulgars were unceremoniously ejected from Macedonia by the Greek government, and Quisling was asked by the Commission to draw up a plan for their resettlement. His work and that of Nansen, Frick and Gorvin, received the well-merited personal thanks of King Boris of Bulgaria.

In the summer of 1925, as the work of the Commission was drawing to a close, a new and urgent task was presented to Nansen – the problem of the Armenian refugees from Turkey. After severe repression during the course of the war, the surviving members of that unhappy race had left Turkey during the wave of xenophobia which swept that country after her defeat in 1918. The Council of the League of Nations had repeatedly discussed whether something could be done for these refugees, 'who were living in great destitution in various countries'.[107] Eventually Nansen was persuaded to conduct investigations into the problem and started to recruit suitable men.

The Armenians had submitted to the League of Nations a project for transferring 50,000 refugees to the Sardarabad area in the newly created Republic of Armenia. This area, although at that time a near-desert, was judged to be capable of supporting a large population, once it had been irrigated and cultivated. The Armenian representatives therefore asked the League to try to raise the capital, estimated at £1m, which would be needed to build a dam. The scope of such a scheme, and the size of the sum required, made it necessary for the details to be studied at first hand by the League's own experts. There was strong pressure on the League to look upon the scheme favourably; by so doing, the ideal of a national home for the Armenians, to which the Allies were committed, might become a practical possibility. The Commission which was deputed to look into Armenian conditions, including its head, Nansen, numbered five. The other members were described by Nansen as

> Mr. C. E. Dupuis, an English engineer, formerly adviser to the Egyptian Ministry of Labour, and a first-rate hydraulic expert; Monsieur G. Carle, who was recommended by the French Ministry for Agriculture, and had had much experience, particularly of subtropical agriculture; and the Italian engineer, Signor Pio Lo Savio, an expert in hydraulic constructional work, who was recommended by the Italian Commissioner for Emigration. Captain V. Quisling, a Norwegian, was the secretary of the commission.

The five members found it easy to work together and Nansen added that he wished to avail himself 'of this opportunity to express my heartfelt thanks to my kind and indefatigable colleagues for their efficient and self-sacrificing work throughout our journey, and for their invaluable collaboration'.[108] Although Quisling was a very junior member of the Commission, his was a key appointment, for, as frequently in Russia, he alone had a working knowledge of any language which was likely to be of use to the Commission. Throughout Nansen's account tribute is paid to Quisling for his linguistic and organisational ability.

The Soviet government, however, again regarded the Commission with suspicion. Finally, Nansen prevailed over the caution of Chicherin and obtained permission to journey to Erivan, the capital of the new Armenian Republic. Even this concession was obtained only at the price of abandoning the official status of the Commission as a representative body of the League, an organisation which at this time remained un-recognised by the Soviet government. A further condition was attached: the Commission was required to co-operate with a committee to be appointed by the Armenian Republic. These tiresome provisions were accepted by Nansen rather than see the complete frustration of the mission, and fortunately it proved to be easy to work with the official Armenian committee.

The members of the Commission assembled at Geneva in the summer of 1925 and travelled to Trieste, where they arrived on the afternoon of 4 June, to take a passage on board the Italian steamer *Semiramis*. After a leisurely journey through the Adriatic and Aegean the party reached Constantinople on 8 June, in time to meet representatives of the Armenian refugees there, who numbered some 5,000. The next day, while Nansen was waiting for a boat to take his party to Batum, the Commission had time to interview some Russian refugees who had arrived in Turkey as a result of a dispute between the Soviet and Bulgarian authorities. The refugees had sailed from Varna to Odessa and thence to Constantinople in a frail vessel named the *Triton*. Their travelling conditions had been abominable, but they had high hopes for the future. 'With Mr. Quisling as interpreter I talked with some of them', wrote Nansen. 'Their one wish was to get to some place where they could work and support them-selves, for their present life was intolerable.'[109] As a result of the efforts of the Commission the Soviet government was persuaded to take back the refugees.

In the afternoon of Wednesday 10 June the Commission left on a French steamer bound for Batum, where the party arrived the following Sunday. A large deputation representing the various governments con-cerned (those of Acharistan, Georgia, the Transcaucasian Federated Republic and the USSR) arrived to welcome the Commission. The party was escorted to a special railway carriage, in which the Commission was to travel to Tiflis later in the day, and speeches of welcome were made.

> I said a few words in reply in English [Nansen recalls] which was trans-lated into Russian by Captain Quisling, assuring them that we had come with excellent intentions to do our best for the Armenian refugees and the Armenians generally, but that we anticipated great difficulties and did not as yet know what could be done.[110]

Nansen's speech was well received, thus beginning the work of the Commission well. They reached Tiflis on Monday 15 June, and the next day drove out to near-by Mtskhetha, a town on the River Kura, where a new power station and dam were being built. The scheme was carefully inspected by the technical experts while Nansen and Quisling slipped away to look at a local church, which was a monument of some historical interest. Both Norwegians were eager to acquaint themselves with the history and culture of Armenia as well as with the routine facts about economic and social development. They were continually finding simi-

larities between the Armenian and Scandinavian races and languages.
Later on 16 June, the Commission, its investigation in Mtskhetha completed, left by train for Aleksandropol, to be met on arrival the following
day by Ersingian, the Commissar for Armenian agriculture.

The Commission now began a programme of visits and surveys of the
resources of the new Armenian Republic. On 18 June the irrigation
works in the Sardarabad desert were inspected, and on 20 June those at
Alagöz. On Sunday 21 June the Commission returned to Aleksandropol
as it was 'the great day of the opening of the new Shiraksky Canal,
whereby about 20,000 acres of new, dry land was to be irrigated and
rendered fertile'.[111] As a result of much hard work the Armenian government had successfully completed a difficult engineering feat and Nansen
was full of praise for the work.

> As we had come to Armenia specially to study the prospects of artificial
> irrigation and the cultivation of new land, we were particularly lucky to
> have been present at the opening of a new canal, and to have seen how a
> great undertaking of that kind could be carried out.[112]

The Commission also fulfilled the second part of its duties, the
examination of measures being taken by the organisation for relief in the
Near East. The day after the opening of the canal the supervised community of Kazachi was visited, and on 23 June the 'Polygon' settlement.
Later in the week the Commission investigated the school of agriculture
at Stepanova and paid a short visit to some villages in the Kirr region,
completing their tour at Echmiadzin on 28 June. Long talks with
Ersingian followed on the 29th, when the Commission declared, in a
report written by Quisling, that 'the impression we got from all that we
saw was that the plans were sound, and that they could be carried out
without much difficulty and at a very reasonable cost'.[113] The Commission was, however, unable to recommend the Sardarabad desert project
since it was estimated that it would cost up to twenty million gold roubles
and would take three years to complete. To raise such a loan was felt to
be impossible. Eventually the secretaries of the negotiating bodies agreed
that a loan from the League to the Armenian Republic, guaranteed by the
Soviet government, would be the best way of financing the other schemes
which the Commission was prepared to recommend. After a final tour of
inspection to the new electric power station in the Zanga valley near
Erivan on 30 June, the Commission completed its work and departed for
Tiflis on 2 July.

At this point the Commission officially disbanded, though Quisling and
Nansen decided to travel back to Norway together. They stayed at Tiflis
for a few days, making excursions into the neighbourhood and continuing
their investigations into possible common elements of culture between
this area and Scandinavia. On the whole they felt that their visit to
Armenia had been a success. Nansen later recorded that 'we had spent some
crowded weeks together, and believed we had done some good work'.[114]

The travellers left Tiflis by car on 6 July for Vladikavkaz where they caught a train to Petrovsk, arriving the next day. At the station they were met by Samursky, the President of Daghestan, and the Soviet Commissar, Korkmazov. The President was an old friend of Nansen and had taken advantage of his visit to Armenia to persuade him to break his long journey back to Norway at Petrovsk. Quisling was willing to accompany Nansen, for he wished to have an opportunity to compare conditions in the Caucasus with those in Armenia and the Ukraine. From Nansen's point of view he not only had Quisling's company but his invaluable assistance as interpreter. On 8 July the travellers continued their explorations by visiting the Derbent lowlands, though they were unable to visit Derbent itself, where there was a settlement in which they were interested, owing to a feverish attack which temporarily immobilised Nansen.[115] By 11 July Nansen had recovered sufficiently to attend a meeting of the Daghestan Commissariat, at which he and Quisling reported upon the use made of mineral resources in the republic. Having reached a satisfactory conclusion on this matter, Nansen found that the official tasks assigned to him had been completed. After a farewell party the two Norwegians left on 12 July by steamer across the Caspian to Astrakhan.

Nansen and Quisling arrived at Astrakhan on 13 July, leaving the same evening by boat up the Volga, bound for Saratov, which they reached on 16 July. Thence they travelled by train to Moscow and on to Oslo, arriving home after an expedition lasting just six weeks. Quisling had been of invaluable assistance to Nansen, who recorded his indebtedness by giving 'hearty thanks to Captain Vidkun Quisling for his untiring kindness as a travelling companion, and for the valuable help he has given the author through his knowledge of Russian and his many-sided attainments'.[116]

The two Norwegians stayed in Oslo for a few weeks, after which Nansen returned to make his report to the sixth assembly of the League of Nations at Geneva. Quisling drafted this document, which advised the adoption of a scheme to drain and irrigate some 36,000 hectares of land at a cost of £900,000. However, there were still many doubters in the assembly, which

> decided . . . to send a further technical commission to examine the possibility of the plan. This commission sent out two officers to Armenia; one was Captain Quisling and the other, W. McIntosh, an engineering expert. The latter worked in the country for six months.[117]

Quisling thus returned to Armenia for a short time, arriving back in Norway at the end of 1925, in time to spend Christmas with his wife.

Once again Quisling's work with Nansen had ended, and there was no prospect of immediate employment. In this emergency he remembered his old friend Prytz. During the years since Quisling had last seen Prytz, the timber merchant had prospered greatly. He had started his own company at Archangel in 1913, but had been obliged to abandon his interests there owing to the outbreak of war.[118] After the Great War he had returned to the business world, founding a new company in 1923, which he called The Russo–Norwegian Onega Wood Co Ltd. This company operated mainly in the remote area near Lake Onega, but proved to be highly profitable, and Prytz had become a very wealthy man. Fortunately for Quisling, he had corresponded regularly with Prytz during the years he spent away from Russia, so it was natural for him to turn to Prytz for help early in 1926.

By a lucky chance Prytz was able to offer Quisling an ideal opening for his talents. In February 1926 he opened a new office in Moscow, which was placed under Quisling's management. The chief function of this office, it has been alleged, was to 'change currency outside official channels'.[119] Obviously, if this was true, Quisling must have had some idea of the purpose of the office, although his apologist has claimed that 'Quisling was not implicated in Prytz's shady business'.[120] The standard procedure was for businessmen who earned Russian currency to give their roubles to the office, which then arranged a credit note for them in London, thus evading the exchange rates imposed by the Soviet government. Quisling, however, was not on a commission basis but drew a regular salary. This enabled him to escape the wrath of the government when, in 1927, its agents exposed the swindle. Prytz was obliged to leave the Soviet Union in some haste, having amassed a considerable fortune.[121] Quisling was left to explain that Prytz had assured him that nothing illegal was being done, and that all the transactions were a legitimate part of company business.[122] Luckily for him his statement seems to have been accepted by the Soviet government.

Quisling, although grateful to Prytz, was glad to be able to leave his employment soon after the exposure of the frauds. In May 1927 diplomatic relations between Britain and the Soviet Union were broken off in consequence of the Arcos affair, and Norway took over the task of protecting British interests. As Quisling had considerable diplomatic experience, spoke English well and had the advantage of being resident in Moscow, he was an obvious candidate for this task. At the end of May 1927, therefore, he found himself invited by the Norwegian Foreign Ministry to take up the post of secretary to the Norwegian Legation in Moscow, 'until diplomatic relations between the two countries were resumed'.[123] As it turned out, they were not resumed until October 1929, so that Quisling held the post for about two-and-a-half years.

During these years Quisling learned a great deal about the conduct of international relations and came into contact with many important political figures. These years were also important for the development of his attitude towards social and political issues. When he went back to the Soviet Union in 1926 he was, at the very least, sympathetically inclined towards Communism. By the time of his return to Norway at the end of 1929 he had travelled almost the whole width of the political spectrum. This change seems to have been gradual. His conversion owed something to his surroundings, for by the end of the decade the Communist system had clearly departed from the idealistic path envisaged in 1917; but it probably owed more to the views of his companions and to his official contacts.

Most of the work which Quisling performed on behalf of Britain was purely routine – the duties which a vice-consul would normally be able to perform. Consequently he had some free time at his disposal, and this he used in a number of ways. Until he finally severed his connexion with the Norwegian army in 1930 he managed to keep abreast of military affairs,[124] but after 1928 he concentrated increasingly on political questions. At the same time he and his wife led an active social life and regularly came into contact with leading Communists, travelling quite widely within the Soviet Union, which, considering the restrictions on foreigners at this time, was remarkable. Nor was this a normal feature of Quisling's life, for in Norway he and his wife led a very quiet social life, while in Russia social activity was forced upon them by Quisling's position in the legation. The contacts he made enabled him to perform his duties very competently, and so conscientious was he that at one point he lived in the former British Embassy, so that he might have closer access to the files and archives.[125] His work was so highly valued that after the conclusion of his mission he was awarded the CBE, then a highly valued decoration. This award was to cause the British much embarrassment in 1940.

Beside all his other activities Quisling found time to continue with some administrative work in aid of Nansen's Armenian projects, though he was too busy to devote as much time as he would have liked to this cause. He frequently saw many of the prominent members of the Communist party, though the only one he knew well was Trotsky, who, by the end of the decade, was in disgrace. None the less Quisling's contacts played a material part in changing his views. The idealism to which he had paid tribute in his articles and letters in the early 1920s had been replaced by Stalin's repressive reaction. Changes in the higher ranks of government had swept away most of Quisling's acquaintances. He himself was under observation by the OGPU, not merely because of his connexion with Prytz's currency frauds, but also because he was known to have been a friend of Trotsky.[126]

Political developments in the Soviet Union were thus quickly revealed to Quisling, and it is plain from his later writings that on the whole they did not meet with his approval. In 1926 he was still thought to be in sympathy with Communism, but by 1929 few, if any, of his acquaintances held such an impression. Almost certainly the strongest influence in turning Quisling away from the regime was the economic and agricultural policy pursued by Stalin. The importance of this factor has been stressed by one biographer.

It should be kept in mind that Quisling was in favor of the Russian revolution up to about 1926, especially after the adoption of the New Economic

Policy in 1921. The masses generally owned, occupied, and worked their own areas of land. But, when the Stalin faction in 1928 moved against the peasants and nationalized the land into large factory farms, then Quisling, the man of the soil, reacted violently against all of it. In that mood he returned to Norway. And the programs of the left-of-center parties in Norway indicated the same fate for the people of Norway; to Quisling that meant a catastrophe.[127]

Quisling certainly was deeply impressed by the distress of the agrarian population, and in his book on Russia outlined dramatically the desperate condition of Soviet agriculture at the end of the 1920s. 'Perhaps the most damning verdict on this policy', he wrote, 'lies in what a Siberian farmer told me—"our work has become our enemy." '[128]

Quisling came to believe that in many ways the Tsarist regime of 1906–17 had been better, and there was a considerable amount of evidence to support this conclusion.

In 1929 [he wrote later] corn production was estimated to be 78m. tons, as against 82m. tons before the war. But of that, 68m. tons and 61m. tons respectively were absorbed by the rural districts. For eventual export or for the towns, therefore, there were thus only 10m. tons as against 21m. tons prior to the war. As the population in the towns had increased by more than 20 per cent the shortage of bread can easily be understood. The export of corn, which before the war had been as much as 14m. tons a year, was greatly reduced.[129]

Quisling thus felt that the lot of the peasant farmer and the urban worker had been made harder rather than eased during the decade since the Bolshevik seizure of power.

If the repressive measures of Stalin's agricultural policy began Quisling's political conversion, the political mismanagement coupled with the policy of purge and terror turned him into a convinced opponent of the Soviet system. The erstwhile friend became the eloquent critic who denounced Stalinist Russia, where 'the state has come to dominate not only all political activity but all aspects of life, social, economic and cultural. The state is everything. The individual is nothing.'[130] The political position occupied by Quisling in 1929 was thus very different from that he had held before 1926.

Although Quisling was supposed to be representing British interests rather than examining Stalinist policies, he had a very good reason for wishing to keep in close touch with happenings in Russia. His interest was derived mainly from the fear that the Soviet Union threatened Norwegian security. The activities of the left-wing politicians from Norway who visited the Soviet Union seem to have caused him particular concern. Quisling was alarmed about the actions of 'members of the Comintern and other international commissions, with funds to spend for international political purposes'.[131] According to another biographer Quisling was able to use his position as British representative to investigate these activities: 'in this twin diplomatic role he completed his dossier of Norwegian Socialists' intrigues with the Third International – ammunition which he was to fire off at home when he went into politics shortly afterwards'.[132] The manner in which Quisling used his position to promote the completion of his supposed dossier is, however, not quite clear. In view of his known suspicion of the Stalinist regime, it seems unlikely that the Soviet authorities would have allowed him to amass much information about relations between the Comintern or their own agents and the Norwegian left-wing politicians. Since this issue was to play a dramatic part in his political career in the early 1930s it is unfortunate that there exists no definite evidence.

Quisling still managed to maintain some of his other interests. In 1929, according to the evidence given in 1945, he was once again heavily involved with Armenian problems.[133] He corresponded frequently with Nansen, although both of them were far from the scene of the events in which they shared an interest. In reply to a letter and a telegram sent by Quisling on 1 June 1929, for example, Nansen bemoaned the bureaucratic delays and inefficiencies of the Armenian government, which had failed to carry out most of Quisling's recommendations until too late. In the same letter Nansen expressed thanks to Quisling for 'your distinguished work on this matter, and regret that your exertions have been so poorly rewarded – particularly after there had seemed to be good reason for believing they would be successful'.[134] There is thus clear evidence to show that Quisling maintained his interest in Nansen's humanitarian work almost until the moment of his departure from Russia.

Quisling's duties in Russia came to a sudden end in 1929, when diplomatic relations between Britain and the Soviet Union were resumed. On 3 October a protocol was signed by Henderson and Dovgalevsky, and negotiations then began for the exchange of accredited representatives.[135] By early December, through the good offices of Urbye, the Norwegian ambassador in Moscow, the formal business was completed. By 13 December Sir Esmond Ovey, the new British ambassador, was ready to take up his post.[136] On 22 December he presented his credentials.[137] In late December 1929, after close contact with Russia for more than a decade Quisling severed his extensive links with that country for good. Thereafter his visits to other countries were brief, in connexion with political or business activities.

Though it is clear that Quisling's views at the time he left Russia in 1929 were different from those he had held in 1926, the reasons for this political conversion remain somewhat unclear. They may to a certain extent be seen in his political experiences during his time as British representative. On the other hand there is reason to think that his conversion began rather earlier, though the direct evidence for such a belief dates only from the early 1930s. The point is more important than may first appear, because Quisling became involved in political controversy in the 1930s, during which one of the principal matters in dispute was the degree to which he had identified himself with the Communist cause.

For Quisling the importance of the issue lay in the left-wing challenge to his political integrity. When he became a minister in the Kolstad government in 1931 a curious episode was revealed to the Storting (the Norwegian Parliament) by some of his political enemies, who alleged that some years earlier he had made overtures in turn to the Labour Party and the Communist Party by offering each his services. The affair made a considerable political impact, for it occurred at the very beginning of Quisling's parliamentary career, and gave him a bad start. The wider importance of the matter, the timing of Quisling's conversion from admiration to detestation of the Soviet Union, was not fully considered at the time, though some light is thrown upon this issue in retrospect by the debate of 1931.

The overtures made by Quisling were supposed to have taken place in the winter of 1924–5. Although at this time he was ostensibly working in the Balkans he made periodical visits to Norway, one of which occurred shortly before Christmas 1924. A brief holiday eventually lengthened into a stay of about two months. It was alleged by Quisling's opponents that during the course of this visit he came to see them, without any encouragement on their part, and offered to assist them in recruiting a paramilitary organisation for the protection of the left-wing parties. This offer of assistance was rejected by both left-wing parties, and Quisling passed out of the lives of these politicians until 1931, when he reappeared as a minister in a hostile government. Not surprisingly the Labour Party tried to use the story of these overtures to discredit him, end his political career and encompass the defeat of the government. The allegations led to a stormy debate in the Storting in 1931, which proved a victory for Quisling, albeit a Pyrrhic victory. The incident was again the subject of debate at his trial in 1945, when the decision of 1931 was, in effect, reversed. The sole result of these two emotional encounters has been to obscure the truth, so that it seems improbable that the full story will ever be revealed.

The first approach was made to the Labour Party through the person of Alfred Madsen, a prominent member of the Storting. Quisling went to see Madsen, who stated in 1931: 'I understood him thus – he was very enthusiastic about the Soviet Union and wished to place his services at the disposal of the Labour Party.'[138] Madsen then suggested that Quisling should see Martin Tranmæl, the editor of *Arbeiderbladet*, the leading left-wing newspaper, who testified at Quisling's trial:

> He sought me out without encouragement or an appointment; . . . when he came to the office he stated that the Labour Party ought to realise when it came to power it would need to have some forces at its disposal – in other words 'red guards'. He offered himself as leader of such a body. He felt that as he was an officer and had served in Russia he was well qualified for the task. I rejected his offer and he left the office. Since then I have heard nothing from him.

Quisling denied that his visit had had any such purpose, and in 1945 pointed out that the Labour Party had its own 'bully-boys' already. Yet under cross-examination he was unable to find any convincing explanation for his visit, merely stating that it was just 'to greet Tranmæl and have a chat'.[139] When pressed to enlarge upon the topic of their conversation he became very muddled and made a poor impression.

After rejection by the Labour Party, Quisling addressed himself to the Communists. He made contact with Jakob Friis, at that time one of the editors of *Norges Kommunistblad*, a Communist news sheet, and arranged an appointment at Friis's home[140] in order to meet both Friis and Olav Scheflo, then the chief editor. According to Friis this meeting took place in January or February 1925: 'Quisling offered to re-enter the General Staff and serve our interests there. We declared that it would be of great importance to us to have a man like Quisling on the General Staff.'[141] Scheflo, the other participant, though less precise about the date, was much more detailed in his description of the meeting. In 1932 he wrote:

> Quisling told us that the General Staff systematically spied upon both the Communist and Labour parties and had full information about all the activities of both parties. . . . Later in the conversation Quisling told us that he thought he could re-enter the General Staff if he so wished and asked if we, as Communists, would be interested if he were to join the General Staff and provide us with information. I answered that, as Communists, we were naturally very eager to be informed about all questions, but that Quisling could not reckon upon any reward for his work. After that we did not discuss the matter further.[142]

Quisling's account of this incident was rather different. The story told by Friis and Scheflo, he maintained, was a total fabrication.[143] By the time of his trial Scheflo had died, so Quisling was spared the difficulty of trying to rebut the stories of two witnesses, and in fact was able to advance a story of some plausibility. According to this, the purpose of his visit was to discuss an article on Russia which he hoped was going to appear in *Norges Kommunistblad*. Since an article actually appeared in the issue of 21 February 1925, this explanation cannot be rejected out of hand. Quisling's apologist, however, has advanced a novel explanation for the visit: Quisling 'had merely contacted the Left in 1924–6 to warn them with first-hand evidence of the drift which Stalin was starting away from Lenin's hopeful New Economic Policy'.[144]

Finally, later in 1925, Quisling met Peder Furubotn, at that time leader of the Communist Party, together with another Communist, Christian Hilt, at his own home. They discussed the possibility of a revolution in Norway and examined the means of its promotion. Nothing came of this conversation. If the meeting took place it must have been at the end of 1925, after Quisling's return from Armenia; though this particular point did not come up either in 1931 or in 1945.[145]

It is difficult to know what to believe and what to discount in these conflicting stories. Certainly Quisling had been sympathetic towards communism earlier in his career, though it is less clear that he was still so by 1924. On the other hand, the article which appeared in *Norges Kommunistblad* early in 1925 was couched in terms favourable to the Soviet Union. Even if the Communist leaders were not willing to entrust Quisling with the task of raising a paramilitary organisation they were obviously happy to use his reputation for the purpose of propaganda. This is plainly apparent from Scheflo's testimony, for he wrote: 'We were agreed that Quisling should support the party by means of an interview on the language policy of the Soviet Union.' There is thus a strong probability that Quisling was still pro-Communist in 1925, though this conclusion is no proof of the truth of the first part of the allegations made against him.

The rival accounts contain many inconsistencies. Quisling's feeble explanations at his trial were not convincing, even allowing for an imperfect recollection of events which were by then twenty years old. It does not, for example, seem probable that he went out of his way to pay a social call upon Tranmæl in late 1924. To begin with, Tranmæl and Quisling had never met previously, and secondly, this version leaves unexplained the object of Quisling's visit to Madsen. Quisling's account of his visit to Friis, likewise a social call, is more plausible, for he had met Friis during his stay at Helsingfors, had been of assistance to him there, and knew of his interest in Russia. Quisling recalled that he had 'met Friis many times, and frequently visited his home, both in Neuberggaten and Munkedamsveien'.[146] He insisted that his purpose in visiting Friis was to have a friendly discussion on matters of common interest.

In 1924 Quisling was aware that there was no possibility of his return to the General Staff, for he knew of General Bauck's decision. Either, therefore, the story of his willingness to act as a spy on the General Staff was a fabrication by left-wing politicians, based upon ignorance of the true position, or they were misled by Quisling. The only purpose Quisling might have had in misleading them was presumably to increase his chances of being employed by them to raise a 'red guard', an occupation clearly incompatible with employment in the army. If the whole story was concocted by left-wing politicians, as Quisling maintained, it seems strange that, since the breakdown of the alliance between the Labour and Communist parties in Norway, no indication of a conspiracy has been discovered. It is unlikely that the necessary collusion could have escaped undetected or that politicians, however ignorant of military affairs, could have believed that Quisling would be entrusted with confidential work on the General Staff while openly supporting a revolutionary organisation. It is difficult, therefore, to see any point in Quisling's alleged political *démarche*. The evidence suggests rather that he could not gain from his overtures, if he made them, since the people he approached were not likely to be deceived.

There is a further problem. If, despite the balance of probabilities, the Communists actually believed that Quisling could return to the General Staff, why were they so eager to reject his services? Even had they been sure that the scheme was a fantasy it could hardly have harmed their interests to encourage him to go on with his scheme, since if it were to succeed it would pay them enormously. If Quisling were to be of any permanent use to the party, it would necessarily be through his special military knowledge and contacts, and, according to their own testimony, his services were believed to be worth commanding. If he were to fail in his mission then he would be the one to suffer, and the Communists would have acquired the additional information that the security arm of the army was better informed than they had thought, which might in turn help them to tighten security precautions within the party ranks. Thus the aim of the Communists ought to have been to place Quisling on the General Staff, unless they believed that he was a double agent who would pass them nothing of value while gleaning information for the General Staff about their activities.

Through this tangle of truth, half-truth and lies it is hard, at this distance, to judge the case. There seem to be many reasons for rejecting the allegations out of hand. Quisling knew he could not return to the General Staff, and therefore had no good reason to offer his services in this way. Secondly, in 1924–5 the left-wing parties had no proof of his insincerity, and therefore it seems strange that his offer was not accepted – or at least carefully considered rather than immediately rejected. Further, the background to Quisling's rise to ministerial rank in the Kolstad government provided an excellent motive for members of the left-wing parties who wished to destroy his political career. Finally, if Quisling's commitment to Communism were accepted sufficiently fully to be used for propaganda purposes, why should his sincerity have been doubted in other connected matters?

Against these powerful reasons must be balanced other facts. Quisling's denials were feeble. He was unable to produce a reasoned defence, nor was he able to deny that he had visited several left-wing politicians, and clearly with those he had visited he had discussed political matters. Finally, his article in the Communist newspaper lends authority to the view at that time he was at least inclined towards Communism.

By combining the rival versions it is possible to arrive at a reasonable reconstruction of events. Quisling did visit all the politicians named and did offer them his services. Almost certainly he overestimated his importance to them and discovered that his offer to write articles on their behalf was not received with the rapturous enthusiasm he had expected. At this point he may have spoken of his potential use. He may have suggested, for instance, that as an army officer he could be of assistance to them if they were thinking of raising a paramilitary force. He may even have suggested that, as a member of the General Staff, he possessed information of possible value to them.

Quisling was the kind of man who would have used arguments of this sort to convince a sceptical audience of his value. Either, therefore, the left-wing politicians took his measure and discounted the possibility of using him, or they feared that he was an *agent provocateur* sent by the General Staff to provoke the Left into an act of folly. Then, when Quisling became a minister, their suspicions were confirmed, and a desire to punish him for his impudence led to the left-wing attack. In these circumstances any casual remarks made by Quisling could have been taken out of context or even deliberately misconstrued. This would partly explain the difference in the emphasis placed upon the conversations by Quisling and by his opponents. It would also account for his difficulty in explaining away his alleged remarks. It was obviously hard to admit to the conversation and yet to deny that all parts of it were true. Yet Quisling followed this course, when it would have been simpler to deny that the conversations took place at all. It seems probable, therefore, that he was telling the truth and that any remarks made about red guards or the General Staff were casual and unprepared. Whether the left wing deliberately misinterpreted these remarks for political purposes, as Quisling contended, or were genuinely unable to distinguish between the serious and the vainglorious elements in Quisling's conversation does not affect the plausibility of such a reconstruction. It would seem probable that all the parties concerned in this curious episode told the truth as they saw it.

The incidents of 1924–5 thus provide valuable information about Quisling. His enthusiasm for Communism probably received a severe setback in 1925, when his overtures were rejected. This blow to his hopes, combined with his observation of conditions in Russia between 1926 and 1929, caused him to lose confidence in the whole Communist movement, thus reshaping his political philosophy. Nor was this the sole consequence of the episode, for it had far-reaching effects upon Quisling's relationship with the Left at the moment of his entry into Norwegian politics. In 1931 he was still remembered for the views he had expressed in *Norges Kommunistblad* six years before. The continuous process of disillusionment with the Communist system which had developed in the intervening years came as a sudden shock to the Labour and Communist leaders. They saw Quisling as a political turncoat, failing to realise that they had not known him very well, even in 1925. Feelings ran high because opinions about him were inevitably based upon disconnected items of information, which in aggregate were frequently misleading. The years spent in Russia were therefore important not only for the development of Quisling's personality and ideas, but also for the formation of attitudes towards him of those involved in politics.

Chapter 2 QUISLING AS POLITICIAN

QUISLING ARRIVED back in Oslo either late in 1929[1] or very early in 1930. His position was by no means enviable. Neither in Norway nor in Russia was there any obvious career for him to adopt. In his homeland he had long since abandoned the army career for which he had been trained, and his standing in Russia had been severely shaken by the currency affair.[2] He had prestige and some important contacts, like Nansen, but little else. He was not wealthy, nor had he made himself indispensable in any walk of life. He had been careless of his own interests in the 1920s, and had been continually both surprised and aggrieved when others had failed to look after interests which he himself had neglected. Though he had not been a dilettante, his habit of flitting from one employment to another in the years after 1918, and his willingness to take risks, had deprived him of that security which his intelligence and industry should have been able to guarantee. Thus, at the age of forty-two, Quisling had the problem of trying to decide his future career.

In these circumstances he turned to Nansen for advice. Nansen had been the main influence upon him in the early 1920s, and in the spring of 1930 he was to play one last significant part in Quisling's life. At the time of his return from Russia, Quisling had some political aspirations, based principally upon his experiences under the Soviet system. Nansen too had political ambitions, though by 1930 he seems to have recognised that they were impossible of fulfilment. Nevertheless he encouraged Quisling to embark upon a political career. Quisling's writings reveal the extent to which he was indebted to Nansen's political ideas.[3] There was much common ground between them. Originally both had been sympathetic towards the revolutionary government in Russia; then, after the consolidation of the Stalinist regime, this friendly interest had turned into a deep-seated suspicion of the aims of the leadership. Both men were disillusioned idealists, who recognised that the Soviet Union now posed a serious threat to the stability of the democratic systems of Western Europe. Both were eager to serve their country by saving Norway from this danger. Only Quisling, however, could play an active part in Norwegian politics, since Nansen was already an old man of sixty-eight. It is not known if Nansen regarded Quisling as the inheritor of his mantle, but

47

that Quisling felt himself to be Nansen's natural spiritual successor is indisputable.

Convinced that he had a political mission to perform, Quisling saw his task as that of warning the Norwegian people of the dangerous nature of the policies being pursued by the Soviet Union, and, if possible, of preventing supporters of those policies from coming to power in Norway. 'I travelled back to Norway, filled with one desire, namely, to do what I could for my fatherland and try to prevent it from being swallowed up in that maelstrom which I knew existed there.'[4] In this task Quisling hoped to have the active support of Nansen, and firmly believed that together they would become an irresistible force in Norwegian politics, sweeping aside their opponents.

The exact part played by Nansen in fostering Quisling's political ambitions and formulating his programme is a matter of some controversy. Much of this stems from a later period, when admirers of Nansen were eager to avoid recognition of any link connecting their hero and the villainous Quisling. So far did this propaganda extend that the official biographer of Quisling claims that Quisling and Nansen hardly knew each other, and were certainly not on intimate terms.[5] Chief among the perpetrators of this myth were, perhaps not surprisingly, Odd Nansen and Liv Nansen Høyer. Both facts and probability, however, tell against these very one-sided witnesses.

In view of the political situation in Norway at the end of the 1920s the connexion between Nansen and Quisling is obvious. The similarity of their ideas was close, and to a large degree may be attributed to the confused nature of Norwegian politics in the preceding decade, impelling both men in the same direction. As in Britain, the post-war boom had come to an end in 1920, and thenceforth economic conditions had been poor. Inevitably there arose social and political unrest, which, coupled with the growth of a multi-party system, led to chronic governmental instability. Political extremism, both of left and right, began to flourish, and the quiet, comfortable, pre-war political world, peopled by relatively moderate Conservatives and Liberals, disappeared. Even the precarious fabric of Norwegian democracy, founded upon the events of 1905, seemed about to crumble. In 1921 and again in 1923–4 a whole series of strikes, fomented by ardent revolutionaries, threatened the security of the state.[6] In the election of 1927 the Labour Party became the largest political group, with 59 seats in the Storting. In 1928, there was a brief Labour government, led by Christopher Hornsrud, whose wish 'to bring about a Socialist order of society in Norway'[7] brought about the fall of his minority government at the hands of the alarmed bourgeois parties.

In 1929, therefore, Quisling found a situation of political confusion. A class struggle was already under way, and the middle classes were in search of a national leader who could provide stability. In default of such a leader, and in reply to the bellicose workers' organisations already in existence, they had started to form paramilitary organisations. The most prominent of these was the right-wing Samfundsvernet, or Community Defence Organisation. At the same time a political body with roughly similar aims, and with considerable duplication of membership, was set up, under the name of 'Fedrelandslaget' ('the Fatherland League'). Its future leader, Viktor Mogens, recorded:

A strong anti-marxist wave of feeling swept the land. The Fatherland League had been founded and had obtained tremendous backing . . . including men like Fridtjof Nansen, Michelsen, Thommesen, Gulbranson, Lund. Young people flocked to join. It showed Quisling the way, showed how the land lay, gave him ideas. He too joined the Fatherland League.[8]

A biographer of Quisling has written:

The two most famous and revered personalities in the country, Christian Michelsen and Fridtjof Nansen, felt disheartened, just like Quisling, at the social-economic-political developments. . . . In the late 1920s the two men organized a group of patriots into the Fatherland League, whose purpose was to combat the prevailing class struggle and multi-party politics and to try to save the traditional culture, according to 'sound political principles'.[9]

From the start, the Fatherland League had some prospect of gaining power. It had been founded as a result of the political confusion of 1925, and of the strong initiative taken by the newspaper *Tidens Tegn*, which during the winter of 1926–7 ran a campaign in favour of raising Nansen to the post of premier. It was thus well before Quisling's entry into Norwegian politics that the possibility of a non-partisan body, bent on national unification, was first seriously advocated. Further, although Nansen would not lend himself to open violation of customary democratic procedures, his adherence to the Fatherland League indicated considerable support for that body's criticisms of the working of Norwegian democracy. By 1926, therefore, Nansen had lost much of his old sympathy for political radicalism and had taken refuge in the conservative camp.

The appeal of the Fatherland League, however, was very limited, and not even the prestige of Nansen's name was able to save the movement from early political obscurity. The Fatherland League's chief influence on Quisling was not that it provided him with all his ideas and future supporters, but that it gave him an example. The suggestion that Quisling and Nansen had little or nothing in common as far as political views and aims were concerned is as demonstrably false as the allegation that the two men had little personal contact. At Quisling's trial the defence rebutted allegations that Nansen had not valued his services and had never known him intimately. An original draft message from Nansen 'which he had sent to Quisling on New Year's Eve 1929, with his wishes that 1930 should be a fortunate year for Quisling',[10] might reasonably be interpreted as an expression of sympathy for Quisling's political aspirations.[11]

In 1930 a series of events conspired to make Quisling think that the moment for his entry into politics had arrived. It was evident that the Labour Party had lost much of its appeal of 1927, and that the political tide was running strongly in favour of the non-socialist parties. In the elections which followed, the Labour Party was reduced to 47 seats. In addition the propaganda of the Fatherland League was more successful early in 1930 than at any other time in its existence. In a New Year message *Tidens Tegn* declared that this body 'represents an effective and unifying element'[12] which would be vital in the impending elections. A letter, signed by a number of prominent Norwegian figures, was sent to *Tidens Tegn*, in celebration of the anniversary day of the organisation, in which it was claimed that 'the Fatherland League has in the course of these five years grown up to become one of our country's strongest organisations'.[13] Among the signatories were Nansen, Erling Sandberg, a bank director and financier, and Joakim Lehmkuhl, an engineering consultant, all well known in Norway for non-political reasons. Thus the party to which Quisling attached himself early in 1930 had high hopes, and it did not seem inconceivable that the Fatherland League should gain some measure of power. Certainly the Labour Party was far from happy about the progress of the movement, and particularly about the support it was drawing from among the middle classes, especially in the army. In fact, the party even claimed that membership of the armed forces was incompatible with membership of the Community Defence Organisation. This view was strongly opposed by many members of the Fatherland League, including Quisling, and eventually by the Storting itself, which rejected a Labour Party motion to this effect by 82 votes to 55.[14]

This was the situation to which Quisling had returned. The opinions of his friends and his experiences in the Soviet Union combined to push him towards a political career. Men whose opinions he valued waxed poetic in their warnings about the dangers of socialism. Major Ragnar Hvoslef, later a colleague of Quisling, albeit unwillingly, and famous in the 1930s for his right-wing views, eloquently denounced, in a letter appearing in *Tidens Tegn* on 2 April, the attitude of the Labour Party towards the Fatherland League and the Community Defence Organisation. Quisling was eager not to be left in the rear of the battle. His sole problem was how to make his way in, and this was solved by Nansen's death on 13 May 1930. This not only removed the one famous international figure from Norwegian life but also released a great flood of emotion amongst the Norwegian people, who were anxious to learn as much as possible about the life of the dead hero. Quisling was not the only acquaintance of Nansen who tried to cash in on his former friendship, but whereas others sought only money or reflected glory, he sought political power. *Tidens Tegn*, the faithful supporter of the Fatherland League, provided Quisling with a vehicle for his publicity campaign. Almost immediately after Nansen's death Quisling was billed as the author of a series of articles entitled 'Political Thoughts upon the Occasion of Fridtjof Nansen's Death'. As the colleague of Nansen in Russia, and as one in sympathy with many of Nansen's political aims, Quisling had apparently found the opportunity for which he had been waiting.

A week before Quisling's first article was due to appear, an article written by Ronald Fangen, on Nansen as a Norwegian national symbol, appeared in *Tidens Tegn*. It provided welcome publicity for Quisling's forthcoming political testament by drawing attention to some of the incidents prominent in Nansen's life. On 24 May Quisling's first article appeared as a major feature in the newspaper, occupying the whole of the front page. Its theme and form were remarkable; the article attributed to Nansen ideas and intentions which in all probability he never held or even thought of. Even if Quisling's assessment of Nansen's views accurately reflected certain of Nansen's statements, these views were never part of a consistent philosophy, as Quisling claimed. In his article Quisling reported that

> the political task which Nansen saw for himself in Norway was, as is well known, to free the fatherland from class warfare and party politics, and to carry through national revival and unification upon a basis of sound political and economic principles.[15]

He went even further by claiming that Norway now needed a new leader to replace the dead Nansen, implying that, from his own long connexion with Nansen and his intimate knowledge of his beliefs, he himself was the most suitable successor.

Quisling's initiative met with a very mixed reception. From the Labour Party there was hostility; that he had expected. What he did not enjoy was a number of attacks from unexpected quarters. One in particular, by Lehmkuhl, seems to have enraged him and created in him an abiding dislike for its author. Lehmkuhl's attack, published in *Tidens Tegn* on 29 May, roundly assailed Quisling's manipulation of Nansen's name to support his own *démarche*. On the other hand, Quisling also received strong support for his interpretation, as in another letter appearing in the paper on 31 May from Hans Bauge, a country priest, who felt that Quisling had rendered valuable service to the Norwegian nation by drawing attention to Nansen's beliefs. Quisling's aim, if only to focus interest upon himself and his activities, had certainly succeeded.

Attention was reinforced by the second of Quisling's articles, which was published on 4 June. It was entitled 'Nasjonal Samling' ('National Unity'), the name which Quisling later gave to his own movement. The article contained a slashing attack upon Lehmkuhl, whom Quisling accused of believing in violent social conflict – 'Lehmkuhl wants to hit the workers on the head and then to talk to them from a bourgeois standpoint.' He claimed that social unity was the basis for his new ideology; he wanted to set up politically neutral unification committees at a local level, 'which can then grow together and build up an organisation'.[16] Yet

Quisling remained uncertain in his intentions. He was not sure whether he should cut his connexion with the Fatherland League and found his own party, or continue in an attempt to mould the Fatherland League to his own liking. Meanwhile *Tidens Tegn* had persuaded him to write more articles – this time on the subject of Russia and her place in the world.

During the summer of 1930 Quisling busied himself with the task of writing these articles, and eventually produced a series entitled 'Russia and Ourselves'. The first instalment appeared on 15 September and the last, the thirteenth, on 3 December. Once again articles from his pen received a considerable amount and range of attention. As the series contained a great deal of criticism of the Communist system in Russia, Quisling's views met with a stormy reception from the Left, in particular from members of the Labour and Communist parties. The organ of the Labour Party, *Arbeiderbladet*, was especially hostile, thus demonstrating that the Labour Party still retained a naïve belief in the virtues of the Soviet system. The natural identification of Quisling with the anti-Communist lobby consequent upon these articles was to have important effects upon his subsequent political career.

Although Quisling had thus attracted considerable attention by the overt expression of his beliefs, he remained unsure as to how best to turn this to advantage. Nor was his indecision cured by the advice of his friends. Certain of Quisling's biographers have seen Prytz as his *éminence grise*, and have suggested that at this vital moment in his career it was Prtyz's advice that prevailed. Vogt has asserted that it was Prytz who inspired Quisling to write about Nansen's death, implying that it was Prytz who really mapped out Quisling's course.[17] Hartmann also has laid great weight upon Prytz's influence. But it seems more likely that the decision was Quisling's own. The delay and confusion in the making of the decision perhaps provides an early example of those characteristics which were to mark out Quisling later in the decade. Prytz probably did enjoy a very extensive influence over Quisling in the early 1930s, just as Hagelin was close to him after the outbreak of war, but Quisling seems to have possessed a very self-centred nature which ultimately made any decision his own.

Political circumstances probably contributed much to Quisling's decision to attach himself to the bourgeois cause in the elections of 1930. It was clear from the beginning of the campaign that the Labour Party would lose a number of seats, and Quisling threw himself enthusiastically into the fray – not on behalf of any particular party, but as an anti-Socialist. He denounced the social revolution for which the Labour Party was fighting, since he felt that it would destroy Norway's Nordic civilisation. Quisling's campaign met with some support. Major Hvoslef, in an article in *Tidens Tegn*, declared that 'Captain Quisling will have the thanks of all patriotic Norwegians for his sober and edifying articles on the situation in Russia'.[18] Quisling was also ready to take an active political part, and on 5 October addressed a meeting of the Agrarian Party.

His speech, which was very well received, contained a serious appeal for the unity of the bourgeois parties so that they might be better equipped to combat the Labour Party.

After the election Quisling continued to make political speeches, and even to engage in public debate, as on 7 November, when he and a barrister named Hansteen discussed various political issues. During the autumn of 1930, therefore, he was able to recruit a considerable amount of support for his notions among the bourgeoisie. He created for himself the image of the respectable friend of Nansen, eager to use his experience of life in Russia to warn the middle classes in Norway of the dangers which threatened them. He also set about reviving his connexion with the military. The views which he held in 1930 were rather more palatable to members of the armed forces than those which he had advocated almost a decade earlier, after his first experience in Russia. On 17 November he gave a talk on Russia to members of the Military Society. Among those present were the King and the Crown Prince. The talk was well liked, and Quisling made a good impression. By the time that the last of his articles was published he had re-entered Norwegian society, and had in fact established himself in a strong position.

On 17 December 1930 the articles which he had written for *Tidens Tegn* were published in book form, under the same title, *Russland og vi* ('Russia and Ourselves'). The book was political in every sense, and expressed in definite terms the direction in which his ideology was leading. In this way the publication of Quisling's ideas in late 1930 was much more important than the articles which he wrote only a few days after the death of Nansen. In late 1930, for the first time, Quisling seriously considered making these theories the ideological basis of a political party. He wished, in effect, to introduce a corporate state system into Norway.[19] In his eagerness to devote as much time as possible to the development of a new party, Quisling decided to try to reduce his other commitments, slight though they were. In late 1930 his tenuous link with the army was severed, though he was promoted to major on his retirement.[20] It was at this time too that the first contact between Quisling and the Nazi Party was made. Whether this connexion was purely fortuitous, as seems most likely, or was part of a definite commitment to Nazism, as Hartmann seems to believe, will probably never be known.

The actual contact between Quisling and the Nazi Party at this stage was certainly both brief and slight. On 7 December Quisling visited at the Oslo Missionshotel the veteran Nazi, Max Pferdekämper, a close colleague of Hitler from the Munich Beer Hall days. After a discussion, they went on to attend the opening of the new Norwegian-German Association headquarters. The following day Pferdekämper sent a report of the meeting to Himmler. The significance of this meeting is much disputed. Hartmann claims: 'One thing is definite – for Quisling this meeting must have been a strong stimulus. Here he had a chance to come into contact with Hitler, leader of Germany's second largest party.'[21] On the other hand Hewins casually dismisses the significance of the whole episode, declaring: 'That Quisling sought a meeting with Hitler and tried to secure Nazi funds is mere speculation.'[22] Neither assertion can be proved, but if Quisling did try to get in touch with the Nazi Party then it seems strange that for a long time after 1930 his contacts with Germany remained superficial.

Quisling thus had a cause, anti-Communism, but no means of fulfilling his aims. He had made many enemies on the left, but had not won for himself equal support on the right, though he had gained considerable goodwill. He therefore began to sound his contacts for support in creating his new classless party. By early 1931 he had made some progress. The principal difficulty was that 'his simultaneous attack on socialism and capitalism was too comprehensive for the tiny Norwegian nation. In discarding *both* wings of potential support, he left a rump too small to provide adequate backing for true and effective national unification.'[23] Nevertheless, early in 1931, some of the more obvious obstacles had been overcome and Quisling was ready to launch his new party. Apart from himself, the moving spirits behind the party were Prytz, Hermann Harris Aall, a philosopher and lawyer, who, though Norwegian by birth, spent most of his time in Sweden or Germany, and J. Throne-Holst, an industrial magnate, director of the Freia chocolate firm and a noted anti-Communist, who had first met Quisling at a private meeting at which he had been impressed by his eloquence. As Throne-Holst was very wealthy his support provided just that financial stimulus necessary to start the movement. After short preliminary negotiations a meeting was held on 17 March at the Oslo headquarters of the Handicrafts and Industrial Union to celebrate the foundation of the new movement, which was named 'Nordisk Folkereisning' ('Nordic Folk Awakening').

The movement's first meeting was held under the chairmanship of Prytz, who announced that the purpose was to found a movement devoted to the preservation of the Nordic heritage. There were about thirty men present believed to be potential supporters of the movement, and, after Prytz had made his introductory speech, Quisling took charge in an attempt to convert sympathy into active support. His speech reflected Nazi ideology in many ways. He condemned the bloody social revolution which, he claimed, lay behind the policies of the left-wing parties. He insisted that the social unity of Norway was in great danger, and that the cure lay in his 'politico-religious party'. Moreover, co-operation with other Germanic races was necessary – 'the future of our people hangs upon the preservation of the Nordic race.'[24] The obvious parallel between Quisling's ideas and those of Hitler possibly cooled the enthusiasm of many of those invited to the meeting, or perhaps many of them had never fully appreciated its purpose. Whatever the cause, Quisling's movement did not start as well as he had hoped. Reactions to the new organisation were almost uniformly hostile from the outset, especially on the left, and the label of 'Nazi' was immediately attached to the party.

Before the end of the meeting on 17 March, however, some of the enthusiasts had made provision for the future administration of the movement. A proposal from the chair was accepted that a Central Committee of thirteen members should be set up. Quisling and Prytz had prepared a list of likely candidates in advance, and these names were accepted by acclamation. Nor were these supporters disheartened by the hostile reaction in the press to the formation of the party; for they went ahead with their plans for promoting its popularity. On 25 March the Central Committee held its first meeting, at which the financial problems confronting the new movement were the main topic of discussion. A second meeting was held on 8 April in order to resolve certain constitutional problems. A constitutional committee was appointed, consisting of Aall, Halvor Hansson, an officer on the General Staff, and Halvor Egeberg, a wealthy financier and speculator. Among the problems with which this committee had to deal was the public launching of the party and its official recognition as a public body rather than a private organisation. Ironically, the internal problems of organisation were solved largely by copying the system then existing in the Soviet Union. Hartmann has even suggested that Quisling 'wished to build up a Communist system, supported by opponents of that system in Norway'.[25] It was never intended, however, that the ends of such a system should be Communist.

It is difficult in retrospect to see what Quisling and Prytz hoped to achieve through their movement. Right from the start, support was so limited that even the most sanguine adherent must have had serious reservations about its future part in the political life of Norway. It would seem almost as if the movement really did represent, in Quisling's mind at least, an attempt to rise above party. Quisling had no great faith in any of the old parties, and it is characteristic that in the 1930 elections the party he had supported was the newest of the major parties – the Agrarians. He certainly believed that it was possible, in some instances, for men to rise above personalities and parties in politics; one biographer has written that 'he had little desire to form his own political party – he wished rather to stand above in order to unite, and formation of a new party would only lead to further splits'.[26] 'Nordic Folk Awakening', then, represented, if anything, an attempt by Quisling to put his theories to the test. Fortunately for his self-confidence the progress of political events early in 1931 rendered this particular attempt redundant before its inevitable failure became plain to see. After Quisling's virtual withdrawal from the movement, its source of energy ceased to exist. On 13 May Quisling gave up his post as leader of the movement and later that day the Central Committee met and elected Prytz in his stead. Thereafter 'Nordic Folk Awakening' gradually faded away, despite brave statements that the programme would be continued and a new campaign mounted. Without Quisling's open adherence the movement was moribund.

It was at this moment in Quisling's career that he became directly involved in Norwegian politics at the highest level. After the elections of

1930 the Liberal government of J. L. Mowinckel had continued in office, though dependent as before upon support from the Conservative and Agrarian parties. The accumulated follies of the Liberal Party, however, eventually led to a parliamentary crisis and to the defeat of the Mowinckel government on 7 May 1931 by 57 votes to 54.[27] A new government had therefore to be found, and while it would perhaps have been best to hand the task to the Conservatives as the largest of the non-Socialist parties, their leader was anxious that the new government should enjoy the support of the Liberals, if possible. Thus it was the leader of the Agrarian Party, Peder Kolstad, who was entrusted with the task of trying to resolve this difficult political situation. The Conservatives promised him their full support, as did the small ultra right-wing Free Liberal Party. Most of the posts in the prospective Agrarian Party government gave Kolstad little trouble, but in two cases he had some difficulty – the portfolios of Justice and Defence. Eventually he chose Asbjørn Lindboe, who had been a member of the party for some years, as Minister of Justice, and Vidkun Quisling as Minister of Defence. The fact that neither of them had had any previous political career was felt to be no disadvantage. In fact, in view of the way the Norwegian political system worked, Kolstad probably felt that the introduction of specialists would strengthen rather than weaken his government.

The appointment of Quisling was at once controversial. Political commentators of all parties seem to have been surprised at Kolstad's choice. It was on 9 May that Quisling's probable appointment was first reported; and as late as the previous afternoon responsible newspapers had been suggesting that the choice lay between two or three obvious candidates, of whom Quisling was not one. The moderately Conservative *Aftenposten*, for example, had suggested that there were 'two candidates, namely Carl Mork and Otto Ruge',[28] both of whom were majors in the army. Other candidates were mentioned, but on the whole the consensus of opinion seems to have favoured Ruge for the post. It was certainly very far from true that 'as the former paragon of the General Staff and an international expert, Quisling was obviously the man for the job'.[29] Why, then, was Quisling preferred to the other candidates?

Most probably the reason was that Kolstad was under pressure from various factions within his own party. It had been by no means certain that he would be selected as the Agrarian Party's candidate for the post of premier; many members of the Storting would have preferred Jens Hundseid, a prominent member of the party since 1924, and later to be premier. Further, Kolstad had had difficulty in persuading Jon Sundby to take the portfolio of Agriculture; and the post of Foreign Minister had been offered to two other candidates before it was finally accepted by Braadland. Kolstad therefore was anxious to avoid further controversy within the party. At this point a 'Quisling for Defence Minister' lobby began to make itself felt. Prytz had visited Thorvald Aadahl, editor of *Nationen*, the mouthpiece of the Agrarian Party, and urged him to press for Quisling as Minister of Defence. Aadahl certainly passed the message on to Kolstad, and probably, though not certainly, supported the proposal.[30] In any event, Kolstad wanted a strong Defence Minister, able to cope with the very serious problems relating to Norwegian security. From the point of view of Kolstad the choice of Quisling did not seem unreasonable. There were many within the Agrarian Party who believed that Quisling was of ministerial calibre – he had clear and firm views on defence problems, and had supported the party in the 1930 elections. As recently as 28 February Quisling had made a good, non-partisan speech at Bergen upon these very issues of security.[31] The political movement which he had since launched claimed to be above party, rather than competing for power, so that this provided small reason for rejecting him. Finally, Kolstad may well have been more than a little exasperated with those counsellors who disliked the choice of Quisling but were quite unable to agree upon any other and better candidate.

It was thus probably a mixture of motives which led Kolstad to put forward the name of Quisling at a top-level party meeting on 10 May. Already rumours had begun to spread that Quisling would be chosen. *Arbeiderbladet*, on 9 May, claimed that 'definite information . . . from reliable sources . . . indicated the choice of Quisling as Defence Minister'.[32] At the party meeting nothing was heard of the candidature of Ruge, nor did Kolstad give any reasons for his unexpected choice. The premier did not even indicate who had suggested Quisling's name to him. He obviously felt that Quisling would be able to perform his duties at least as well as any of the other candidates, and possibly, in view of his distinguished army career and knowledge of foreign affairs, rather better. The disunity of Quisling's opponents almost certainly irritated Kolstad, a very practical man who disliked abandoning one possibility before it was clear that there was a better alternative. Finally there were undoubtedly strong influences at work on behalf of Quisling. It is plain, both from their previous and their subsequent support of Quisling in their newspapers, that Aadahl in his *Nationen* and Rolf Thommesen of *Tidens Tegn* regularly used their editorial influence on Quisling's behalf. It would seem not at all unlikely, therefore, that they did so on this occasion. Kolstad, given all his other difficulties, would have been unwilling to challenge these influential men on this issue.

Certainly both Aadahl and Thommesen were suspected by their contemporaries of being at least partly responsible for the choice of Quisling. Dr Arnold Ræstad, formerly Foreign Minister, who had worked closely with Kolstad at the League of Nations and knew him well, expressed the opinion that it was 'editor Aadahl who had given Kolstad the advice to employ Quisling'.[33] Later evidence suggests strongly that Thommesen also was eager to install Quisling at the Ministry of Defence. He had represented the right-wing Free Liberal Party in the Storting from 1927 to 1930, and during these three years had largely concerned himself with defence questions. It was he who had permitted the use of *Tidens Tegn* as a vehicle for Quisling's ideas, as he held similar views. Through Thommesen's social standing Quisling met many of the people, such as Throne-Holst,[34] whom he hoped to persuade to sponsor his new political movement. Hans Holten, who was executive secretary of the Agrarian Party in 1931, was 'inclined to believe that Thommesen was father to the idea of Quisling becoming Defence Minister'.[35] This view has been supported by others with some knowledge of the government crisis of 1931.

Thus it was that Quisling was chosen. His apologist has suggested somewhat different reasons:

> Kolstad may even have hoped to profit from Quisling's high standing in influential business, military and intellectual circles, for the Farmers' party was only ten years old, part Liberal and part Conservative, and this was the beginning of its first and only term of office.

This view is based upon totally false premises. Had Quisling really possessed sufficient influence in these circles to be useful to Kolstad, then his own movement, 'Nordic Folk Awakening', would have attracted more support. Quisling never held a position of such high standing; the nearest he ever came to achieving it was after he had been appointed minister, and before he became involved in a number of controversial incidents.

On 12 May the Kolstad government was formally announced in the Storting. At once it was Quisling's appointment which attracted most attention. *Nationen* and *Tidens Tegn* welcomed it warmly. *Aftenposten*, which had previously reserved judgement, was much more cautious. *Arbeiderbladet* and *Dagbladet* were very hostile; so indeed was *Arbeideren*, the mouthpiece of the Communist Party. Thus, the suggestion that 'Quisling's government appointment was well received in the Press except by *Arbeiderbladet*'[36] is quite inaccurate. The attacks on Quisling from the left were mainly in response to his known anti-socialism. Further, his connexion with the 'Nordic Folk Awakening' movement made him a much easier target. The movement was described in the left-wing press as Fascist and reactionary, and Quisling was branded as a Nazi. Predictably, the right-wing press reacted almost as strongly in his favour, the army journal *Vår Hær*[37] welcoming his appointment with some enthusiasm. It was not long, however, before the principal scene of controversy shifted from the press and public debate to the Storting itself.

The first meeting of the new government took place on 11 May, the day before formal presentation to the Storting. Kolstad introduced the various members of his cabinet who were unacquainted with one another, and briefly reviewed the political situation. In particular he examined the country's financial problems, which were so serious that at one time he had considered giving up the attempt to form a government.[38] He also emphasised that it was absolutely essential for the Agrarian Party to work harmoniously with the other bourgeois parties.[39] Then the cabinet settled down to produce a draft programme which could be presented to the

Storting. Once this had been prepared and Kolstad had been convinced that he would be able to lead a government, the names of his ministers were officially released.[40] The same day the outgoing Liberal government formally proffered its resignation to the King.

Immediately the official announcement had been made on 11 May, Quisling went to his new office to have a preliminary look at some papers, assuming that the government would in due course obtain a vote of confidence from the Storting. But no sooner had Quisling's appointment been confirmed on 12 May than a storm broke about the unfortunate Kolstad's head. On 13 May *Arbeiderbladet* launched a vitriolic attack upon Quisling, describing his appointment as amazing, and introducing openly for the first time the allegations about the incidents of 1924–5. At the same time Quisling was accused of being in the pay of England. The article suggested that the government ought not to be confirmed if Quisling were to be included as a minister and ended by insisting that 'it was nothing less than a scandal that a man who had behaved publicly as he had done should be summoned to the King's council'.[41] A few days later the Communist journal joined in the chorus of condemnation; Jakob Friis made a most abusive attack upon Quisling, accusing him of being 'a British spy and *agent provocateur*, under orders from London to spy out the possibilities of military revolution . . . and an eventual British intervention in the Soviet Union'.[42] These attacks from the left, coupled with sharp criticism from the orthodox conservative *Morgenbladet* of the appointment of Lindboe as Minister of Justice,[43] must have dispirited the weary Kolstad, who had been struggling to solve the government crisis for almost a week. However, his faith in both Quisling and Lindboe remained unshaken.

Quisling and his fellow ministers meanwhile settled down to their various tasks as best they could. All of them must have realised that their political futures would be decided by the debate on the vote of confidence due to begin on 19 May. In the meantime *Arbeiderbladet* continued its daily criticism of Quisling's appointment. On 19 May Alfred Madsen took up the attack in the Storting, repeating the whole range of accusations against Quisling, including the allegations about his former overtures to the left. Madsen's speech, indeed, almost ceased to be a denunciation of the Kolstad government, against which he was supposed to be moving a motion of no confidence, and became a violent and highly personal attack upon Quisling. He did, however, break off his invective long enough to describe the Kolstad government as 'a mouth with no teeth'. After his speech a period of relative calm ensued while Hambro, President of the Storting and a Conservative, reviewed the merits of the government rather than the personalities in it, and ended by offering Kolstad as much support as possible. When Kolstad rose to reply to Madsen he was in a very difficult position. As Vogt has written, Kolstad 'could hardly have known in advance the storm of protest with which the nomination of Quisling would be received by the left-wing parties'.[44] His concern was to preserve his government, not to go into details of what might have happened in 1924 or 1925; he was therefore bound to defend Quisling – though, of course, he was unable to do so save in general terms. He knew no more about the matter than most members of the Storting, and he contented himself with a brief survey of Quisling's excellent humanitarian work, adding that he thought it was foolish to 'judge a man as superficially as the Labour press had done'.[45]

After this attempt to turn the debate into more normal and regular channels, Mowinckel introduced the personal element once again by attacking Hundseid, between whom and himself there was much animosity.[46] It was thus in an acrimonious atmosphere that Quisling rose to defend himself, and, by implication, the judgement of Kolstad. Quisling dismissed Madsen's account as a fabrication: 'That I should have offered to obtain weapons and ammunition is a complete fantasy.'[47] He denied that he had ever made any overtures in the way alleged, but he was not able to produce any satisfactory explanation for his visit and it is doubtful whether he carried conviction to most of his hearers. Lindboe recorded in his diary: 'To my mind Quisling's defence was not very successful',[48] and this seems to have been the general reaction. After Quisling had spoken, Nygaardsvold, the future leader of the Labour Party, returned to the attack; remarking that Quisling's speech had been an admission of guilt, he added: 'It would have been better if Quisling had taken the consequences, picked up his hat, and said good-bye. That would have served the Agrarian Party best.' Quisling was then defended by Mjøen, who remarked that he could understand how Quisling had once been a revolutionary – many people throughout the world were glad that the Tsarist regime had been destroyed. This did not mean that such people were inconsistent in subsequently denouncing revolution.

At this juncture Madsen returned to the rostrum and resumed his onslaught, introducing all manner of new charges. Chief among these was an attack upon Quisling's financial dealings while in Russia, accusing him of 'exchange transactions, which the Russians reported were in conflict with Russian law. The Russians themselves believed that they had lost about two million roubles through these dealings.' Thus to his other grave allegations Madsen added the charge that Quisling was a swindler. This stung Quisling into a much stronger denial. He went over the 'Red Guards' case, stating that on the only occasion he ever visited Madsen it had nothing to do with the affair as Madsen had described it. On the matter of the financial swindle Quisling grew indignant, pointing out that he had 'never heard anything about it from the Russian authorities, quite the opposite'. In this, at least, he was supported by the former Conservative premier, Lykke, who confirmed that when Norway took over the protection of British interests in Russia there was no complaint about the employment of Quisling. Nygaardsvold, however, had the last word in the debate by remarking that he 'would content himself with wishing the Agrarian Party joy of Quisling'.[49]

The whole affair was a grave embarrassment to Kolstad, who had hoped that his government would manage to avoid such difficulties, which had contributed so largely to the fall of the Mowinckel government. Attacks on the new Defence Minister did not end even when the government was obviously bound to obtain its vote of confidence. On 22 May *Arbeideren* made further allegations about Quisling's role in Russia, and a few days later *Arbeiderbladet* launched a massive attack upon the aims of 'Nordic Folk Awakening', ignoring the fact that Quisling was no longer officially associated with the movement. The newspaper accused Quisling of wishing to set up 'a new organisation with Fascist tendencies',[50] and made much of the insignia used by the movement, which, it stated, were Nazi in inspiration. As the symbol referred to was the gold cross of Saint Olav on a red background, this seems an unnecessary distortion of the truth. More damaging allegations, better founded on fact, could have been made. On 6 June *Arbeiderbladet* made a much more wounding attack, contemptuously dismissing the movement as a 'compound of Fascism, nonsense, childishness and balderdash'. The newspaper did not hesitate to point out the lack of support for Quisling on this issue – 'of the important newspapers it is only the government organ, *Nationen*, which defends this upstart movement. But then, Aadahl himself is a member.'[51] Perhaps it was fortunate for Quisling that Kolstad did not take much notice of this press campaign, once his immediate parliamentary problems had been overcome. According to evidence given by Sundby to Hartmann, the reason was that Kolstad regarded the whole affair as a tactical manoeuvre by the Labour Party to split his government. Thus, at least to the outside world, he maintained his faith in Quisling.

Kolstad was probably wise. Norway could not have faced another drawn-out governmental crisis; it was desirable for the Agrarians to weather the storm outside the Storting rather than try to change course. In addition, Kolstad was a shrewd and perceptive man, who may have felt that the Labour Party was exaggerating Quisling's Fascist leanings. If he did, he showed greater judgement than his contemporaries, for although the attacks of *Arbeiderbladet* proved correct in 1933, matters were rather different in 1931. By 1933 Quisling did believe in a kind of Fascism; in 1931 such an allegation was less plausible. In 1931 *Arbeiderbladet* identified Quisling as a Fascist because of his connexion with 'Nordic Folk Awakening', but it is doubtful if the movement was modelled on Fascism either in theory or in practice. Quisling was at the time no special friend either of Germany or of the Nazi Party. Throughout his life he never learnt to speak German really well, whereas he spoke excellent English. Nor did he admire the German system; like Nansen, he had an abiding respect for that of Britain. Further, it was Britain, not Germany, which in the 1920s had led the crusade against the Soviet Union. Quisling, therefore, as a deeply committed anti-Communist, thought chiefly in terms of a British-sponsored anti-Bolshevik front, of which 'Nordic Folk Awakening' was to be the Norwegian wing. In this he was supported by Prytz, whose connexions also were British rather than German, and it was not until later in his career, when he became deeply involved with Aall and Hagelin, that Quisling turned towards Germany. Nor, for all their anti-Communism, were men like Throne-Holst and Thommesen either Fascists or Nazis, and it seems doubtful if Quisling would ever have gained their support had his movement been inclined towards Fascism. It is worth noting that when he did found a Fascist party in 1933 he almost immediately lost support from this section of the community.

The mistake made by *Arbeiderbladet* was to confuse the sound of Quisling's perorations with their substance. Quisling was eager to root out Communism in Norway, and at the inaugural meeting of his movement he had declared that it was necessary 'to shape a new society, based upon a new political system'.[52] Not unreasonably, supporters of the Labour Party believed that this would mean the establishment of a system in Norway not unlike that in Italy. In fact, this was far from true. Quisling wished to establish a bi-cameral system in Norway with a 'Riksting' ('Council of the Kingdom') as well as a Storting. Like many of his critics, Quisling confused hard facts with theory, and believed that what he defined as a moral society could be achieved by tinkering with a few institutions. So much in Quisling's ideas about the ideal state was vague and paternalistic that in retrospect it is difficult to believe he was a thorough-going Fascist in 1931. His beliefs at this time may best be defined in his own words. He felt his goal 'was a national revival of the Nordic spirit; ... not only anti-Bolshevism, but principally a positive policy based upon realities, with a powerful and noble end in view, in fact something to live and die for'.[53] Such a policy, however unrealistic, was not Fascist, and Quisling seems to have been mystified by many of the attacks made on him. He and his opponents did not live in the same world and could not communicate with each other. Few of his contemporaries seem to have ever realised this fact; perhaps Kolstad, with his greater insight, was one of the few.[54]

Not all Kolstad's colleagues seem to have been as pleased with the outcome of the debate of 19 May. Lindboe needed reassuring by his senior civil servant, Carl Platou, in a conversation on 20 May, that although 'Quisling's answer could not be described as wholly satisfactory, the government had on the whole performed well'.[55] The political and economic situation in Norway in the summer of 1931, as in Britain, was so serious that the members of the government wished to avoid, almost at any cost, any threat to governmental stability. Unfortunately for them, a crisis suddenly arose in the form of a particularly intractable labour dispute.

The dispute started at Menstad, in Telemark, in an area which was, by Norwegian standards, heavily industrialised. The workers involved in the labour dispute came from the area near Porsgrunn and worked at the Norsk Hydro plant near Menstad, at that time the largest single industrial unit in Norway. According to Hewins, the timing and the place can hardly have been coincidental. Obviously it was aimed at placing the new Defence Minister in a predicament, which would accomplish his fall, and possibly at sparking off nation-wide disturbances, which would be the prelude to revolution on the Russian model.[56]

While it is possible that some hotheads may have hoped that a large industrial dispute would lead to a political and social revolution, there seems to be no evidence for believing that the strikes were deliberately engineered to get rid of Quisling as Defence Minister. The factory had had a long series of disputes between labour and management, including a serious conflict as recently as 1924, and it would seem more likely that this particular incident was, as another biographer of Quisling has written, 'just an incident in the class struggle'.[57] The seriousness of the outbreak at Menstad in 1931 was due to two factors – the extensive use of violence, and the general economic problems of Norway which exacerbated social relations throughout the whole country; in Britain, at the same time, the vexed question of unemployment benefits was creating major difficulties.

On 30 May and 2 June there were large demonstrations as the result of a dispute over the exact terms of a contract entered into in 1924 which led to a strike and a lockout. For various reasons the situation deteriorated during the next few days – the company wished to hold the workers to the contract, and the workers wanted some relief of their position. Both sides allowed themselves to be guided by extremists. After a week of tension the long awaited battle began on 8 June. The actual amount of violence used seems to have come as a surprise to most people. Lindboe, as Minister of Justice, had a particular interest in the affair; he appreciated the serious nature of the dispute, and had taken the precaution of increasing the number of police available, but he seems still to have placed his faith in negotiations, though by 4 June he had discussed with Platou the possibility of arming the police effectively.[58]

On 8 June two large processions of workers, about a thousand strong, led by fifty or sixty 'Workers' Guards', marched on Menstad. They were armed with hose-piping and bludgeons.[59] On their arrival at the entrance to the plant the demonstrators found their way blocked by a mixed force of police and company employees. A general mêlée ensued in which a number were injured on both sides, and several policemen were taken to hospital. The police were routed, and the victorious workers were left in possession of the field. In the meantime the government had taken far-reaching measures to prevent a recurrence of such disturbances. It was this that involved Quisling in yet another head-on collision with the Labour Party.

During the disturbances, a fierce debate had been waged in the Storting. Anton Jenssen, a leading figure in the Labour Party, had accused the government of trickery and provocation in 'sending police directed against the working class'. Despite a series of emotional, but irrational, speeches from the Labour Party, the government won the

63

argument, and the support of the other parties, merely by presenting a more moderate case. It was a double victory; since earlier in the day the Kolstad cabinet had at last obtained its vote of confidence, by 89 votes to 45.[60] While the Storting was still in session a message was delivered to Lindboe, informing him of the events at Menstad. He contacted Kolstad, who agreed to hold a cabinet meeting to discuss the affair. When the cabinet met Lindboe reviewed the facts of the situation and urged that 'troops be sent to Porsgrunn, for law and order could not be maintained without such assistance'. The situation was serious and it was felt that the militants among the workers might get out of hand. No one spoke against Lindboe's suggestion, and Trædal, the Minister of Church Affairs, supported him very strongly. Curiously, Quisling was silent throughout the discussion. In the end 'it was unanimously agreed that military support should be sent'. After some discussion it was decided that one company of troops would be enough, and 'Quisling went out in order to telephone the Commander-in-Chief, so that he could give the appropriate orders'.[61] The cabinet meeting then came to an end, and ministers departed to resume their normal duties.

Thus Quisling clearly had little or nothing to do with the cabinet decision to send troops to Menstad. His sole part in the affair was to act as the minister charged with carrying out that decision. In the circumstances, however, it was almost inevitable that he should be held responsible. His supporters naturally, though incorrectly, saw him as the strong man of the cabinet. His enemies believed that his known views on social unrest must have made him the driving power behind the decision to put down the riots by force. This assumption was equally fallacious, but had far-reaching consequences. Despite the evidence available, the temptation to assign to Quisling a major role in the affair is still strong. Hewins, for example, has written:

> Quisling feared that the rebels would seize the arms in a neighbouring armoury. He sent in a company of local infantry militiamen and a few other troops.... Society had shown that it could defend itself and Quisling became the hero of the hour – supported by the Cabinet to a man – and hailed as the one person who knew how to stand up to the Reds.[62]

Such an interpretation of the incident directly conflicts with the facts – but then the whole of Quisling's life as a politician was marked by emotional attitudes on the part of supporters or opponents which make it particularly hard to discover the facts of any issue.

The government decision had a very mixed reception in the next day's press. *Arbeiderbladet* attacked it strongly, and imputed much of the blame to Quisling. On the other hand, most of the press approved the government's action. *Aftenposten* called the Menstad affair a 'Communist-inspired riot'[63] and took the view that the cabinet could have come to no other decision. On 9 June the cabinet held another meeting to decide whether further measures would be needed. The police authorities had asked Lindboe for larger reinforcements, and it was agreed to send 'two torpedo boats and two minelayers'.[64] Beyond these measures matters were left to Quisling, who ordered a limited degree of mobilisation in Telemark. This was entirely justifiable in view of the weakness of the police in the area, and of the proximity of an army arsenal to the scene of the riots. According to Hewins, Quisling also persuaded the Community Guard to lend a hand,[65] but Harald Franklin Knudsen, later Quisling's secretary, in his account of the affair, reports that the Community Defence Guard 'was scattered to the four winds of heaven'.[66] As the troops were never actually required to take action it would seem very unlikely that Quisling called upon this unofficial body to assist him.

When the news was released that the government had sent four ships to Porsgrunn, *Arbeiderbladet* was highly indignant. The Labour Party organ declared that it was 'Defence Minister Quisling who had pushed this matter through the government and stood behind this comprehensive mobilisation' and launched a tremendous personal attack upon Quisling, claiming that 'in order to crown his work the half crazy Minister of Defence has gone over to general mobilisation in Telemark. . . . We have had a further confirmation of the way in which the Norwegian armed forces will be employed.'[67] Quisling made no attempt to deny the truth of these accusations and they therefore stuck. As Hartmann has pointed out, 'It was understandable that the public thought that it was Quisling who had pushed through the decision to send troops to Menstad. He was the recipient of both the honour and the reproaches; and he never made any denial.'[68] Quisling was perhaps not unwilling to assume the role of strong man in the government. Certainly, later in the month, when the situation was much less serious, he created this impression when he told a reporter from *Aftenposten* that the 'torpedo boats would be withdrawn when their presence was no longer necessary'.[69]

Even after the Menstad affair had been settled the troubles of the new government were by no means over. The Lilleborg concession, which had led to the fall of the Mowinckel government, was the subject of long disputes within the cabinet during June and July. Quisling did not play a central part in the dispute but as the cabinet was evenly divided, every vote was important. Eventually, in the critical cabinet votes of 9–10 July, Quisling voted with the majority, which decided to grant the concession.[70] As this matter came so soon after the Menstad affair it did considerable harm, for it emphasised the differences of opinion within a cabinet which itself depended upon a party holding only 25 out of the 150 seats in the Storting.

At the same time another serious issue arose out of the aftermath of the Menstad affair. On 15 June a message from the Oslo Telegraph Office was sent to Lindboe, enclosing a transcript of an intercepted telegram from Peder Furubotn to an agent in Oslo. Furubotn, a prominent member of the Norwegian Communist Party, was at that time in Moscow working for the Comintern.[71] The telegram, sent from Moscow on 13

June, ordered a resumption of agitation in Norway by the working class, and suggested various means of increasing unrest; particularly prominent among these were strikes, demands for higher wages, the organisation of a workers' militia, and attempts to foment disloyalty among the police and the armed forces. Clearly, Furubotn and his followers hoped to make use of the Menstad affair to produce a social revolution. The cabinet, after discussion, left the matter to Lindboe and Quisling, who, in consultation with Welhaven, the chief of police, were able to deal with the matter. They forwarded the telegram to its destination, but alerted the appropriate authorities so that any necessary counter-measures might be taken. The incident was important in that it convinced Quisling that the current disorders were all part of a complex plot to overthrow the state. Henceforth he became even more suspicious of the Communist and Labour politicians, with results which were to have a profound effect upon his political career in 1932.

During the summer of 1931 Quisling and Lindboe were working together closely. They were both concerned with the social and political problems which stemmed from the severe depression that had hit Norway – Quisling because of the threat to security, and Lindboe as a result of the legal problems involved. Ever since March 1931 there had been a series of strikes, boycotts and lockouts, of which the Menstad affair had been the most serious. Attempts had been made to reduce wages in order to bring down prices, but such efforts were no more successful in Norway than elsewhere in Europe. Incidents were perpetually occurring between angry workers and the police. Feeling ran so high that even in the Storting wild statements were made, and Johan Nygaardsvold, later to be premier, declared that 'a policeman who entered the service of capitalism ought not to be awarded any compensation'.[72] Intemperate statements of this kind did not ease the government's task, and after certain incidents at Skien at the beginning of July, Quisling asked his colleagues to be allowed to use the military if a situation arose similar to that at Menstad. Lindboe and the other members of the cabinet overruled this dangerous proposal.

At a cabinet meeting on 29 August it was finally resolved that in emergency a small directory, consisting of the premier and the Ministers of Justice and Defence, should have the authority to deal with the vexed question of the employment of troops. The cabinet also approved a plan for the defence of Oslo, drawn up by the Commander-in-Chief, and presented by Quisling. Quisling and Lindboe were very much concerned about threats to security, despite the energetic efforts made by an industrial peacemaker to settle the situation. In particular they were alarmed by continuing disturbances in Skien, where most of those who had been arrested at Menstad were held in custody. They met Kolstad on 30 August to discuss this problem, and the caucus decided not to call in soldiers but to leave the police to deal with any trouble. The prisoners, however, were to be removed to Arendal, which was believed to be rather

more secure. The day before there had been disturbances at Graten-
moen, and on 31 August troops had to be sent, thus causing another
political outcry. Lindboe at first thought that this action had been
authorised by both Kolstad and Quisling, but it transpired that the
decision had been taken solely by the Minister of Defence.

After the agreement of 29 August this action looked like a direct breach
of faith. Although the left-wing press had no knowledge of the cabinet
resolution it was quick to attack Quisling on entirely different grounds.
The civil and the police authorities in Skien denied having asked for
help, and the affair seemed to be an arbitrary act of dictatorship on his
part. Lindboe recorded that Quisling was fortunately able to convince his
colleagues that his action had been correct, since it had been based upon
a telegram from the military authorities in the area.

> Quisling told the press that it was not the local civil authorities which had
> asked for help, but the local military command, which had responsibility
> for the security of the military depots, fearing lest the depots be stormed
> and weapons be given to the demonstrators.[73]

Even this statement did not ward off all attacks. The premier was furious
about the incident, and ordered a full investigation by Lindboe's department. Investigation showed that both Quisling and the local commander
had acted in perfectly good faith, believing that there was serious risk of
an outbreak of violence, as they had been informed that there was to be an
attempt to release the Menstad detainees. The cause of the trouble was
the local chief of police, who had inspired the alarmist telegram, having
treated seriously certain wild statements in a local paper.[74] It is hard to
see how else Quisling could have acted, and this his colleagues recognised; even Kolstad must, by this time, have been a little weary of the
way in which Quisling managed to attract unfavourable publicity for the
government.

While Quisling was involved in a series of disputes through his concern
for internal security, he was also preoccupied with a number of difficult
tasks concerning external defence. The real problem was the lack of any
inter-party agreement on defence. The Labour Party, like its British
counterpart, had a naïve belief in the possibility of disarmament, and a
very influential pacifist wing. It also contained a number of fellow-
travellers, who were not averse from trying to take advantage of the beliefs of their more idealistic brethren. Thus the attitude of the Labour
Party became one of hostility to all expenditure on armaments. The post
of Defence Minister had been the grave of political reputations greater
than Quisling's, and in 1931 the tasks were more onerous than usual. As a
minister Quisling had to try to reduce government expenditure, but he
also realised that the needs of his own department demanded a large increase in its share of the budget. This was an impossible position from
the very first, and Quisling would have been well advised to have abandoned the task as soon as he was aware of its unrewarding nature. At

Quisling's trial Halvor Hansson outlined the magnitude of the problem which faced Quisling, pointing out: 'The period from 1930 onwards was one of decline for our defence . . . the problem for the friends of defence was not how to build up but how to hinder any further decline. I am absolutely certain that Quisling did everything possible.'[75]

There had been a great decline in Norwegian strength since the end of the First World War. Jon Skeie, in his account of Norwegian defence policy, wrote: 'When the First World War came to an end we had a very good defence system. In 1940, when the Germans attacked us we were very poorly equipped. Our authorities had neglected our defence.'[76] Quisling was obliged to bow to the realities of the political situation and could do very little to arrest the decline. The Agrarian Party government was dependent upon the support of the Liberal Party in the Storting, and it was under the Liberals that the real drop in necessary expenditure had taken place. The government could not afford to depart too far from the line taken by the Mowinckel government lest it lose the support of the Liberals. Defence had been one of the major problems standing in the way of a bourgeois coalition in 1928, and throughout the next ten years it continued to divide the Liberals from the Conservatives and Agrarians.

Quisling's best hope was to try to reorganise the defence system so that increased efficiency might compensate for lack of money. In this, at least, he was moderately successful. He also managed to obtain a small increase in the amount of money allocated to his department. When Quisling entered the government the budget had already been prepared by the outgoing party, which had expected that expenditure would be in the region of 32m kroner. By dint of some hard bargaining Quisling was able to obtain an increase of 3m kroner.[77] One of the main obstacles in his way was the Storting committee for Defence, which consisted of equal numbers of those for and those against increased expenditure, but had as chairman Alf Mjøen, who was against spending more money. Mjøen's casting vote seems to have been frequently decisive.[78] Even those who objected to increased expenditure did not try to prevent Quisling's other activities in the Ministry of Defence. The result of his work was a useful revision of the structure of the army, which subsequently had a first line of two divisions, and a second line of six divisions. Military service was increased to ninety days and garrison duty to six months.[79] These changes were welcomed by regular officers.

Later in his career Quisling always laid great weight upon his period of office as Defence Minister, claiming that he had always done his best for Norway. It was the line of defence he chose at his trial, and it was, in general, supported by the testimony of Halvor Hansson. Lieutenant-General Ruge, who worked with Quisling during 1931–3, was rather more critical of his efforts.[80] The criticisms made by Lindboe, however, are much more serious, since he was in a position to know all the facts. Lindboe and Trædal were the two ministers most enthusiastic about the rebuilding of Norway's defence,[81] and Lindboe was most critical of

Quisling's defence policy. He alleged that Quisling let himself be influenced too much by those on the committee who wished to economise on expenditure – 'Had Quisling taken a standpoint more in accordance with his party colleagues on the committee, then the majority might have been very different. This was the opinion also of most of the representatives of the Agrarian Party on the committee.'[82] Quisling was also unduly influenced, Lindboe felt, by the opinions of Laake, the Commander-in-Chief,[83] and other supporters of the Liberal point of view. This was clearly demonstrated when the Conservative and Agrarian parties put forward a proposal for the remodelling of the Ministry of Defence in the summer of 1931.[84] Quisling, had he been a real 'friend of defence', should have given the motion his support, but in fact he opposed it, and it was rejected by 76 votes to 66.[85] This forced the Agrarians and Conservatives to support the proposals of the Liberals, since they were at least more acceptable than those proposed by the Labour Party. As Lindboe pointed out, 'The voting thus gave Mowinckel's defence policy a completely different parliamentary basis from that which it really enjoyed; at the moment when Quisling could have thrown his weight behind Norway's defence, he betrayed it instead.'[86] Lindboe has also supported his view by reference to Quisling's second budget proposals, which reduced expenditure to 30·6m kroner, a sum 4·5m kroner lower than the amount Quisling had declared to be the essential minimum in the previous year. Quisling's role as a 'friend of defence' was thus no more free from controversy than any of his other activities at the time.

The summer of 1931 was untypical, in that political activity was unusually great. In addition to the affairs previously mentioned, the government found itself involved in a wrangle with Denmark over part of East Greenland, commonly known as Erik the Red's Land. During the last days of the Mowinckel government a rare outbreak of irredentist feeling had infected the Norwegian public, and it had been suggested that moves should be made to occupy part of the disputed territory, thus involving the government in a dispute with Denmark, whose claims to the area had hitherto been almost unchallenged. Kolstad's government was unfortunate enough to inherit this legacy, and the possibility of military action, though soon abandoned, initially made Quisling's opinions important. It was generally believed by the more aggressive newspapers, such as *Nationen* and *Tidens Tegn*, that Quisling was leader of the party within the cabinet which was in favour of firm action. This assumption was almost certainly incorrect, for Quisling seems to have played little part in the determination of policy in 1931, though in 1932 matters were to be quite different. The matter was, however, extensively discussed in cabinet meetings, especially between 29 June and 10 July, when 'in those 12 days we had 27 government meetings, both on Sundays and weekdays, and of these 23 were either wholly or principally concerned with the Greenland dispute'.[87] At one of these meetings, on 8 July, Quisling did suggest openly the possibility of military occupation, but repented later in the day of this bold line and indicated that 'his proposal was only intended as a basis for discussion'.[88] In the event, the cabinet did not pursue the chauvinistic policy of the Mowinckel government, and agreed to submit the case to an impartial tribunal at The Hague. If, as Hewins has suggested, 'this remote incident [the occupation of East Greenland by some fishermen and traders] touched off the ingrained "Nordic imperialism" in Norway and particularly stirred Quisling', though he did not 'get the support which he expected from his own government',[89] Quisling gave little indication of this belief. As in the Menstad affair, he seems to have seen his role, retrospectively, as rather larger than strict historical accuracy would warrant.

The rest of the year was relatively peaceful. Quisling, although a regular target in the left-wing press, refrained from any further controversial action. Kolstad was even able to go away for a short holiday, leaving Trædal in charge – an eventuality which had seemed most improbable a few weeks earlier. During the autumn of 1931 Quisling was principally occupied with ministerial business. Preparation of the estimates of his department for the coming year left him very little time for other activities. As a relaxation from work he occupied himself with medieval Norwegian history, and interested himself particularly in the reconstruction of a medieval castle. This and similar innocent interests kept him out of the public eye. The period of peace, however, proved to be merely the calm before the storm.

On 12 January 1932 the King opened the new session of the Storting. By the end of the month Quisling was involved in another controversy, this time quite unwillingly. On 20 January a German Nazi, Captain Horst von Pflugk-Harttung, arrived in Norway from Sweden. His arrival was greeted with howls of protest from the left-wing press; two days later *Arbeiderbladet* ran an article under the headline 'The Murderer of Karl Liebknecht is now in the City'. It was claimed that Pflugk-Harttung had come to Norway in order to contact certain Fascist interests, and not, as he claimed, to seek refuge from vengeful Communists. The left-wing press demanded that the Ministry of Justice refuse to allow him to stay. On 27 January *Arbeiderbladet* insisted that 'Karl Liebknecht's murderer must leave the country'. Opinion in other newspapers was rather more moderate. *Aftenposten* pointed out that Pflugk-Harttung had entered the country perfectly legally and that, provided he attended only to his new profession of journalism and did not intervene in politics, there was no reason to refuse him permission to stay.[90]

The controversy did not abate, and on 29 January a protest meeting was held under the auspices of the Labour Party; inflammatory speeches were made and a poem on Liebknecht recited. As nothing could be proved against Pflugk-Harttung, the Ministry of Justice was reluctant to take action; the left-wing press therefore cast about to find someone to blame for this reluctance, and Quisling was the obvious choice. *Arbeiderbladet*, without a shred of evidence, accused him of 'having a finger in the pie'.[91] Hartmann, thirty years later, even suggested that Quisling had direct communication with Pflugk-Harttung,[92] thus implying that already, early in 1932, Quisling was turning towards Nazism. The left-wing press claimed that Quisling had put pressure on his colleagues to permit the German to remain in Norway. This allegation has been decisively rebutted by Lindboe, who states that 'when the Pflugk-Harttung question was most urgent, there was no application by Quisling on his behalf'. The Minister of Justice further states that he could not remember Quisling raising the matter; none of his colleagues could ever believe that 'the Minister of Defence had secret contacts with Nazi circles'. On the contrary, pressure was put on the government from another source: this was 'the Fatherland League, through Advocate Christopher Borchgrevink, together with the President of the Storting, C. J. Hambro, and former premier Johan Mowinckel'. The two party leaders called Platou and Lindboe to Hambro's office, where they 'strongly pressed for asylum to be given to Pflugk-Harttung in Norway'.[93] The accusations against Quisling must therefore be discounted. His interest in the matter, if any, can only have been passive, and in no way deserving of the allegations made so freely by his political opponents. The whole affair was, in any event, swiftly forgotten in the interest aroused by another incident involving Quisling in February 1932. On 19 March Pflugk-Harttung, on the basis of information received from Sweden, was ordered to leave Norway, an action which was heartily approved on the next day by *Arbeiderbladet*. As Lindboe wryly observed, it was not every day that he received bouquets from that quarter.[94]

The most curious incident of Quisling's ministerial career occurred, according to his own evidence, on 2 February. That afternoon he had lunch with a friend at some time between three and four o'clock. At about a quarter to five he left for the Ministry of Defence, intending to collect some papers and then to go to the Storting. He collected the keys to his room from the janitor, but on reaching his office discovered that the door was open. This was quite out of order; even worse, the door to the conference room also stood open. The room was dark, and Quisling thought that he saw a black Gladstone-bag. As he stepped inside to have a closer look he was suddenly assailed by a small but agile stranger,[95] who attacked him with a knife. Quisling seized his assailant by the coat, but he then had pepper thrown in his eyes, received a blow on the head and collapsed unconscious.[96] When he regained consciousness he was lying on the carpet and his assailant had disappeared. He lay down on a sofa for some time, but did not raise the alarm. Eventually he left the building at about half past six, giving the keys back to the janitor, but without mentioning that anything unusual had taken place. He walked a short distance and then went home by taxi.

As he climbed the stairs at his home his wife noticed that 'his steps were heavy and dragging'.[97] When he saw Maria the first thing he told her was that he had been attacked. He then lay down on the sofa in the dark, because the light hurt his eyes. He was supposed to be going out that evening to an entertainment organised by Prytz, and when he did not arrive Prytz came round to see him. The whole story was soon told, though Quisling was still very weak – almost fainting when he tried to rise to greet his friend.[98] The police were then informed of the incident and an investigation was set in train after Quisling had received medical treatment. The next day he returned to work, and on 4 February made a statement to his cabinet colleagues about the affair. The following day a statement was released through the press, offering a reward of 5,000 kroner for information leading to an arrest.[99] The police statement, like most of the press, accepted Quisling's version of the incident. Inevitably, the attitude of *Arbeiderbladet* was far from friendly. Whereas *Aftenposten* observed that there had been 'an attempt at espionage in the department of Defence',[100] which was a not unreasonable interpretation of the events, the Labour Party journal entitled its account 'A Criminal Film in the Ministry of Defence'[101] and made numerous allegations, some of which were entirely fabricated, such as the suggestion that Quisling drove himself home after the incident. The result of this attack was a flood of speculation and rumour. Before long it was being openly suggested that the whole affair had taken place only in the mind of the Defence Minister.

The evidence is quite unclear. Initially there were two schools of thought – those who believed Quisling's story and those who called it a fabrication. To these must be added a third – those who thought that Quisling imagined the whole incident as a result of some mental or physical disability. All three theories have some plausibility.

Those who suggest that from start to finish Quisling told the truth have probably the strongest case. Police investigations discovered pepper on the floor of the office and found that Quisling's clothes had indeed been ripped with a knife or some such weapon. The medical evidence provided by two very respectable doctors showed that Quisling was suffering from a form of amnesia consistent with concussion. In addition he had contusions and lesions hardly consistent with self-infliction. Further, no trace of the weapon was discovered. Finally, Quisling's inability to be positive that there had been only one man involved was hardly consistent with a well-planned fake attack.

On the other hand, those who suspected a simulated attack also had reasons. The fact that Quisling failed at any point to raise the alarm until he returned home, seems difficult to explain if the attack were genuine. So too does the failure of the janitor to remember the entry or exit of anyone answering to Quisling's description of his assailant. Nor did the janitor see Quisling's face as he came out of the office, as he apparently turned away deliberately.[102]

Those who have attempted a synthesis of these conflicting points by ascribing the affair to a delusion on Quisling's part have, perhaps, had the most unrewarding task of all. The poet Nordahl Grieg and Dr Scharffenberg, a famous Norwegian medical scientist, suggested that

Quisling had suffered from a malarial attack and had imagined the incident. In favour of this hypothesis were the facts of Quisling's suffering from malaria in Russia in 1923, and of his sudden recovery about three or four days after the incident – this would have been consistent with a common type of malaria.[103] This theory would also explain his failure to summon aid and his inability to remember details clearly.

Various solutions are therefore possible. Hartmann has attempted a reconstruction of events involving a complex network of double agents and an international spy-ring, dragging in Pflugk-Harttung and a German Communist named Wollweber.[104] It seems unlikely that any reconstruction can be totally satisfactory, but Hartmann's theory, based as it is on a series of ill-connected suppositions, seems more improbable than the plot in even the crudest type of spy thriller. Perhaps Quisling's own story is the most probable. Both of the other explanations founder on a series of unexplained facts. Quisling's story has only one basic flaw – his peculiar behaviour after the attack. The clue may be his concussion. A man who has been concussed may well act abnormally, and it is worth noting that the doctors who examined Quisling made this point in their report. Quisling, then, may quite well have performed a series of normal every-day acts while on his way home, and only then have begun to recover. Anything abnormal, such as summoning the police, would not have occurred to him while he was in this trance-like state. Such a theory seems to leave fewer occurrences unexplained than any other. None the less it is not entirely satisfactory, and it would not be wise to draw any firm conclusions from it.

Whatever the truth of the matter, it was certainly no help to Quisling. Nor to the government, then struggling with the inevitable budgetary problems. The only factors favouring the government were Kolstad's determination, and the reluctance of any other party to take office in a period of economic disaster. Unfortunately for the government Kolstad fell ill, became much worse on 28 February, and died on 5 March. The Agrarian Party never made good his loss; no one else seemed to have his clear vision or his ability to heal dissension. His death, at a critical time, was a loss that the Norwegians could ill afford. The year of his premiership had been uneasy, but it would almost certainly have been a good deal worse without his guiding hand.[105] His successor was Jens Hundseid, a man of great talent but without that evenness of temper and spiritual balance which so distinguished Kolstad. From Quisling's point of view the substitution of Hundseid for Kolstad held only one conceivable advantage – he was less well able to control his ministers. According to Hartmann, Hundseid wished to get rid of Quisling immediately, but was prevented by the threat of the resignation of Trædal and Sundby. 'It is not possible to dismiss the government's only gentleman',[106] Trædal is reported to have said to Hundseid. The truth of this story is difficult to establish, but one thing is indisputable – between Quisling and Hundseid there was not the most amiable of relationships.

The new government, with some reorganisation of portfolios, proceeded with the same policies, unpalatable though they were. Most unpopular of the proposals was the compulsory reduction of departmental budgets by 20 per cent. This probably affected Quisling worst, as it made any chance of a revival of Norwegian defence totally impossible. The economic situation was desperate; for much of 1932 about 200,000 trade unionists were unemployed. In addition, the financial position of many small farmers and shopkeepers was parlous. The political atmosphere was electric, and feeling between the parties ran very high. It was with some trepidation, therefore, that the new government and its leader faced their first major test in the 'Speech from the Throne' debate, which began on 5 April.

As if the debate were not controversial enough, a personal attack upon Quisling by Nygaardsvold introduced what proved to be a direct confrontation between Quisling and his opponents. Nygaardsvold suggested openly in the chamber that Quisling's story of what had happened on 2 February was untrue. He also launched a violent attack upon Quisling's previous conduct as a minister, including his handling of the Menstad affair. The next day Quisling was ably defended by Jon Sundby, who criticised strongly the personal abuse in Nygaardsvold's speech.[107] In the meantime, Quisling was preparing his defence, in accordance with instructions from Hundseid.[108] He was, however, rather nervous about the use to which he intended to put certain documents, and consulted Lindboe, telling him that the documents were for his own personal defence, and making no suggestion that they would be used 'in the direction of treason or anything that would in any way be compromising for the Labour Party'. Accepting Quisling's assurances, Lindboe naturally exhorted him to defend himself. On the morning of the third day of the debate Lindboe had a curious discussion with Hundseid, during which the premier told Lindboe that he had a speech in each pocket: one supported Quisling, the other dissociated himself from his Minister of Defence. Hundseid offered to read them to Lindboe in order to have his advice. The Minister of Justice refused this Greek gift, remarking that 'either he must lay the question before the whole government or he must take the decision himself as head of the government'.[109] Lindboe had no intention of giving advice behind the backs of his colleagues. Thus, for Hundseid, Quisling's fate clearly depended upon the impression he made in the Storting. A bad speech would mean his demission from office, for he would have forfeited the premier's confidence.

Quisling did not make a bad speech. On the contrary, he made one of the very few good speeches of his career. Far from contenting himself with a defence of the policies of the government and of his personal actions, Quisling launched into a violent denunciation of the Labour and Communist parties. Such an assault was completely unexpected. In his previous speeches Quisling had shown no debating ability whatsoever. His sudden access of confidence seems to have come as a very unpleasant surprise to his opponents. Even more displeasing and disconcerting was the matter of the speech. Quisling began by warning Nygaardsvold that 'he ought to remember there is a nemesis in life for those who act illegally, even if it is against that which he believes to be unjust'. Quisling also recalled that 'right from my first entrance into our political life I have been the target for a systematic and shameful attack from the revolutionaries in our country'. He then went on to dismiss with contempt the assertion that he had ever supported either the Labour or the Communist parties.

If Quisling had stopped at this point in his speech his political career might have been happier. Among the bourgeois parties there were many who realised the justice of much that he had said. There were probably, if the truth be known, many decent men in the Labour Party who felt some sympathy for the unhappy Minister of Defence. However, Quisling proceeded to lay about him verbally, returning with interest the many blows the Labour Party had showered upon him. It was a performance which Hundseid, his eyes naturally fixed upon a smooth parliamentary passage for his government, found very disturbing. Quisling asserted that he had nothing to be ashamed of in his political career; the suggestion that he and his ministerial colleagues were lackeys of foreign capital was absurd. In reality it was not any of the bourgeois parties but the Labour Party which was in the service of foreign interests. Quisling proclaimed triumphantly that he had a large body of evidence against both Labour and Communist parties. He had documents to show that the Communist Party 'was financed from abroad, and had in 1928–9 received 500,000 kroner from this foreign power'. He also revealed that the Communist Party had been guilty of a great deal of subversive activity, especially in the armed forces.

Quisling next turned his attention to the Labour Party. He pointed out that it was a revolutionary party and cited its members' adherence to Trotsky – 'a man who is too red even for Russia'. Unlike his opponents, he did not 'intend to indulge in personalities', but would keep to the facts. Looking through the files of his ministry, he had come across papers which were 'in the highest degree compromising for certain of the leaders of the Labour Party'. He warned them of the dangers of attempting social revolution, reminding them that it was neither the Girondins in France nor the Social Democrats in Russia who were finally victorious. Quisling also criticised sharply the workers' organisations for defence, which he claimed did not exist simply to prevent a Fascist *coup*, but were militant and aggressive bodies. Once again he asserted that it was the government's duty to uphold law and order; a government was entitled to use those organisations which helped in such a task, and to curb those which opposed the preservation of internal security. Quisling concluded by declaring that 'the organised forces of capital and labour must be replaced by organisations for co-operation'.[110]

This powerful speech produced strong reactions. Some of the more extreme right-wing figures of the Storting were delighted. Ameln even made a speech defending Quisling's attack on the left. Nygaardsvold and other members of the Labour Party counter-attacked vigorously. Nygaardsvold recalled that Quisling had still given no proper explanation of the attack on 2 February, and he further demanded to know whether he had severed his links with such bodies as the Fatherland League and 'Nordic Folk Awakening'. Finally, he insisted that Quisling should lay the allegedly compromising documents before the Storting. Mowinckel then rose to put the view of the Liberal Party, but exposed its embarrassment by failing to take any clear line in the dispute. He was succeeded by Hambro, who promptly moved that all papers concerned with the 'Pepper Affair', the Menstad incident and Quisling's assertions be put before a special investigatory committee, to be appointed by the Storting. The debate concluded with a further demand to see the papers, this time from Hundseid, and an assertion on behalf of the Labour Party by Olsen-Hagen that the group of which he was a member had nothing to fear from such an investigation. The proposal for a special committee was accepted without a vote.

After the debate, whatever the result of the committee of investigation, it was impossible that peace could ever be achieved between Quisling and the Labour Party. Moreover, the debate led to a further decline in personal relations between Jens Hundseid and Quisling. The premier's speech had been unclear; like Mowinckel, he had taken no firm position. Unlike the Liberal leader, Hundseid had no tactical justification for vacillating. Asbjørn Lindboe believed that 'the evident hostility and the subsequent open struggle between Quisling and the premier really originated with the Prime Minister's speech in the Storting that day'.[111] It was clear that Quisling had raised issues with important bearing on the government's future. Lindboe disapproved of Quisling's attack on the Labour Party, arguing that it showed little loyalty to his fellow ministers, and he formed the opinion that 'the premier had good grounds for asking Quisling for his resignation'.[112] He seems to have forgotten that Quisling could hardly be sure of his colleagues' loyal backing, and therefore probably believed he would obtain maximum support if he routed the enemy. Certain curious features surrounding Quisling's speech cast some doubt on this charge of disloyalty. As Lindboe himself indicated, the fact that Hundseid had two speeches prepared suggests that he had a closer knowledge of the contents of the documents than Lindboe supposed. If the premier knew what the documents contained, then he could guess how Quisling would use them, and it was he rather than Quisling who failed to keep his colleagues adequately informed. Further, if Quisling thought that what he intended to do was known to Hundseid, this would explain not only his own failure, so strongly criticised by Lindboe, to inform his colleagues of his proposed *démarche*, but also his subsequent anger at Hundseid's attitude.

The speech created a sensation in the press, and during the following week Quisling's ministerial future was widely discussed. *Arbeiderbladet* was eager to see him discomfited, and agitated repeatedly for the Storting to proceed with the investigation.[113] Prodded by his colleagues, Nygaards-vold continued his demand to know where the papers were; a week was ample time in which to produce them. Hundseid informed the Storting that the papers were being sorted and classified, while Gabriel Moseid, the leader of the parliamentary Agrarian Party, remarked: 'No one could have a greater interest in the speedy presentation of the papers than Minister Quisling, the government and our party.'[114] Meanwhile inter-party talks about the formation of the committee were being held, and on 26 April a committee of eight was elected, including representatives of all four major parties: the Liberals supplied Myklebust (chairman) and Peersen; the Agrarian Party provided Moseid (vice-chairman) and Østby-Deglum; the Labour Party was allotted the post of secretary, filled by Anton Jenssen, and also provided Monsen; finally the Conserva-tives had two representatives, Fjalstad and Lykke.[115] It was generally agreed that these men would form a fair and impartial body of investiga-tion.

The committee had some initial difficulties in assembling evidence, especially for the 'Pepper Affair', into which the police were still conduct-ing investigations.[116] This problem was overcome, and so was the prob-lem of the secret nature of the documents to be examined; the latter, by holding a number of meetings of the committee *in camera*.[117] Towards the end of June it became clear that the work of the committee was drawing to a close, and that a report could be expected soon. Although the report was made known on 23 June,[118] the debate was not opened until the 29th, as the Storting had a great deal of other business to handle. Matters were somewhat confused, as the committee had been unable to agree on a joint report. There was a majority report, signed by the six members of the committee drawn from the bourgeois parties, and a minority report from the two members of the Labour Party; thus, from the moment the report was produced, it was evident that there would be a serious par-liamentary debate on its contents.

The minority report was very brief, being confined to three points. It suggested that 'Minister Quisling, by his unsupported statements, had committed a grave error of judgement in view of his position as a minister'. The minority also recommended that 'the Intelligence Agency of the General Staff should cease to concern itself with domestic affairs'.[119] Finally, the report demanded that a much more thorough investigation of the affair of 2 February should be instituted. In short, it was a thoroughly recalcitrant and partisan document bearing little relation to the evidence before the tribunal. In addition, the two Labour Party members belatedly began to complain of the procedure and composition of the special committee. Whatever their personal opinions about the majority report, the conduct of the Labour Party, and in particular that of Monsen, over this matter was one of the worst examples of partisan politics in the inter-war years. It must be remembered that the majority of the committee were not stooges of Quisling; they had judged the evidence on its merits. That they came to a different conclusion from the Labour Party members, who seem to have made no attempt to apply this basic criterion, is not surprising.

On most of the issues raised the majority of the committee upheld Quisling, who had provided approximately 200 documents. Upon these papers the majority based their report. This supported Quisling's statements about revolutionary activity and the Communist Party, noting that there were 'ample reasons for the statement made by the minister'. The role of the Labour Party as a revolutionary party was also examined, and here the majority declared that 'they were in agreement with what the minister had said'. As a matter of historical accuracy, so long as the Labour Party was bound by its programme of 1930, any investigation could hardly have come to any other conclusion. The Menstad incident was also reviewed, and again the majority upheld Quisling, saying that he had 'reasonable grounds for his statements in the Storting on the Menstad affair'.[120] The majority clearly found the task of discussing the parts played by individual members of the Labour Party somewhat invidious. It was made particularly awkward owing to the denials of involvement by Støstad and other members of the Labour Party; the committee therefore, quite properly, found that the matter did not warrant further investigation. The question of the 'Red Guards' affair of 1924-5 was also left undecided. As in each case the committee was called upon to judge between two rival oral statements, there was little else it could do. These two points apart, the majority of the committee had upheld the truth of Quisling's assertions – a bitter draught for the Labour Party to swallow.

The debate, on 29-30 June 1932, revealed the depth of anti-Quisling feeling in the Labour Party. After Monsen's ill-conceived criticisms of the committee, Fjalstad, designated as spokesman for the majority, defended both the report and the working of the committee. It was a moderate and sensible speech designed to reconcile the Labour Party to the realities of the political situation. Fjalstad was followed by Østby-Deglum, who attacked the press campaign against Quisling, justly singling out *Dagbladet* for special criticism. Østby-Deglum attacked the Labour Party also, describing it as a 'revolutionary party which has not cut all its connexions with Moscow'. Peersen criticised Jenssen and Monsen particularly for their bigoted attitude. Jenssen, in reply the next day, created a very poor impression with an inaccurate and tedious defence of the Labour Party. Quisling in an unusually brief and well-received speech thanked the committee for all its work, and declared that he was not in the least surprised by the Labour Party's attitude. Some heated exchanges followed between Ameln and Nygaardsvold. Mowinckel recalled the debate to its purpose by deploring the attitude of the Labour leaders and he concluded that the result of the investigations was, 'and this we must be glad about, that there was a basis for Quisling's speech'. He was sorry that Quisling had attacked the Labour Party so strongly, and added that he thought 'Quisling was an idealist . . . but that he was not sure that it was entirely desirable that a Norwegian government should at this time be guided by idealism'.[121] The debate then continued on conventional lines, except for a tribute to Quisling from Moseid, who declared that, although he had not known Quisling before he had become Minister of Defence, he had acquired great respect for his character and talents. After this eulogy the debate dragged to an end, and in the vote which followed the Labour Party was able to muster only 42 votes out of 150 for its minority report.[122] With this vote the matter was officially closed – but not forgotten.

If Quisling had hoped that the bourgeois parties would take strong action against the Labour Party he was disappointed. They had to live with the Labour movement and saw little reason to alienate its supporters still further. Their inactivity was made the more easy by the end of the session of the Storting, which automatically postponed any major parliamentary action for several months. Ironically, it was probably the Labour Party which benefited most from its defeat in the 'Quisling case'. Defeat and humiliation had brought it home to the Labour Party that it would never be trusted by the other parties while it continued to advocate extreme policies. The fate of the Labour Party in Great Britain in the previous year stood as an awful warning. Change began to permeate the ranks of the party, and it gradually lost its revolutionary image.

In Quisling's eyes, however, the Labour Party never changed. For him the Labour Party of 1939 was the same as it had been in 1929, or even in 1919. He believed that he had been betrayed by the bourgeois parties, and during the following year his actions altered accordingly. His apologist has seen the failure of the bourgeois parties to proceed against the Labour Party as 'the decisive moment in Norwegian history between 1905 and 1940'. He has also suggested that

> if the Right had followed the logic of its vote for Quisling and had continued to stand together, the conspirators and pacifists of the Left could have been brought to book or contained. . . . But logic and reason, cohesion and perseverance, are not Norwegian specialities. They like their parish pump and to do things the hard way. . . . So the Norwegian people were left to their fate. This was the treason of the Right, as well as the Left – of the blind, opinionated and selfish individuals and groups whom Quisling castigated.[123]

To propound such a thesis is to fail to understand the logic of the voting on the 'Quisling case'. Quisling was supported because he had been proven correct by the documentary evidence. His views on action against the Labour Party were not supported, because they involved destroying all hope of the Labour Party becoming like the other political parties. Intelligent leaders of non-Socialist parties elsewhere in Europe, such as Baldwin in Britain, favoured similar conciliatory policies. If the summer of 1932 represented a decisive moment in Norwegian politics it was not the betrayal of Quisling which was significant, but the gradual realisation that Norwegian interests would not be served by a sterile and unproductive class war.

Although most of the publicity attached to Quisling during this period was naturally associated with the various incidents with which his name was connected, he devoted most of his attention to the affairs of his ministry. As regards defence, he had an increasingly difficult task in 1932. The only solutions to defence problems were either increased expenditure or disarmament, as advocated by the Labour Party. Quisling had to cope with a third line of policy – reduction in expenditure. The improvements in efficiency which he suggested could not compensate for this policy beyond a certain point. He spent a great deal of time in the Storting actively defending his policy, which seemed to enjoy neither Right nor Left approval. In early May there was a particularly important debate in the Storting, lasting some three days. Quisling's policy came under sharp attack from Nygaardsvold, who alleged that the armed forces existed only to protect the interests of the capitalist classes rather than those of the whole people. He also insisted that 'the Labour Party is against militarism in principle . . . as a party we have always stood for complete demilitarisation'.[124] Støstad, an extremist of the Labour Party, declared that one of the worst features of the armed forces was their use for the suppression of Labour. It was hardly surprising that Quisling could make little headway against such views, although his policy was approved by a vote of 79 to 36. In the political situation of 1932 his views on defence were completely out of place, and he would perhaps have been better advised to resign than to try to struggle on with policies which he cannot have supported wholeheartedly. As Halvor Hansson pointed out in 1945, 'his performance must then be judged in accordance with the background'.[125] By this standard, Quisling's period of office was not a disaster for Norwegian defence, but a personal disaster for himself. Many officers who had welcomed the advent of a 'friend of defence' as minister in 1931 failed to appreciate the pressures to which he was subjected, and had lost much of their faith in him by 1932. Thus, Quisling's retention of office while pursuing a policy of which he subsequently claimed to have disapproved exposed him to the charge of loving office, and the power which it brought, so much that he could not steel himself to resign.[126]. It exposed him also, by a twist of history, to the charge of being partly responsible for the weakness of Norwegian defence in 1940. To Quisling this must have been the bitterest blow of all – a belated nemesis for his fatal inconsistency in 1931–2.

Although the summer months were normally the season of political inactivity in Norway, the Hundseid government did not have a peaceful passage in 1932. The main cause of anxiety was a revival of the East Greenland affair. Advocate Smedal, who had been one of the moving spirits behind Norwegian activity in East Greenland, had in 1931 put pressure upon members of the government, demanding some action from them to protect Norwegian claims. Lindboe, whom Smedal first approached, passed him on to Quisling: 'I advised him to ask for a discussion with acting Foreign Minister Quisling, and was instrumental in bringing about such a conference.'[127] After their discussion Smedal produced a memorandum which had formed the basis of the claims of the Norwegian government in the summer of 1931 and had led to the decision to submit its claims to the International Court. In the summer of 1932 Smedal resumed his activity, particularly as it now seemed unlikely that Norway would win its case. As a result the government held a meeting on 5 July to discuss the possibility of a renewed attempt at occupation, but owing to the strong opposition of Hundseid and the Foreign Minister, Braadland, the suggestion was temporarily left in abeyance until further discussions could be held. Fruitless meetings were held on 6, 7 and 8 July. On 10 July the decision to occupy part of Greenland was taken, though not without some heated discussion, and on 12 July a formal resolution was passed, incorporating part of East Greenland into the Kingdom of Norway. This action led to astonishing complications during the next few months, and involved Hundseid in some rather curious negotiations behind the backs of the rest of the cabinet. The reservations felt by both Quisling and Lindboe in the summer proved amply justified by the autumn of 1932, though both were inevitably accused of being the moving spirits behind the renewal of an active Greenland policy. Both were judged by their past actions and statements rather than by the facts of the situation.

The closing months of 1932 were disastrous for the unity of the Agrarian Party government. Open strife between its members revolved around three main issues – the quarrel between Quisling and Hundseid, the East Greenland dispute, and finally the case of Captain Kullmann. The quarrel between the premier and the Minister of Defence was greatly exacerbated by the other issues, and finally led to a cabinet crisis. Chronologically the Kullmann case came first in the unhappy sequence of events. At the end of August 1932[128] an anti-war congress was held at Amsterdam. Present among the delegates, and prominent among the speakers, was Captain Olaf Kullmann, a naval officer on active service. By the beginning of September, reports of his activities had started to filter back to Norway, and on 5 September *Dagbladet* revealed the whole story. Kullmann had made a sensational speech in which he informed his audience that 'the war has already begun', and, after referring to the campaign in Norway against the policy of peace pursued by the Soviet Union, concluded by urging that 'so long as the overtures of the Soviet Union on behalf of disarmanent are not accepted by imperialism it is the duty of officers to be alert against these war-mongering governments. Should these criminals try to wage war the officers must strike.'[129] Such sentiments were extreme in ordinary circumstances, but when expressed by a serving officer they created a sensation.

Kullmann was sent for by his commanding officer on 6 September, after the report in *Dagbladet* had become common knowledge. He was quite unabashed and refused to recant. In the meantime the Ministry of Defence, under orders from Quisling, had taken the matter up with the Commanding Admiral, who, on account of sensational press reports, was ordered to investigate. Kullmann gave him no more satisfaction than he had his commanding officer at Oscarsborg, and blandly informed him that he had said many other things also.[130] On 24 September Kullmann addressed a meeting of the Student Union, at which he advised officers and men to refuse to do their military service.[131] The admiral was left with no choice but to suspend him from his duties from 30 September. On that day the Labour Party organised a meeting at party headquarters in support of Kullmann. The next day *Arbeiderbladet* ran an article under the title of 'An Army Ready to Fight against War'. The newspaper also observed sarcastically that here there existed plenty more material for Quisling's archives, and that he would do well to remember that behind Kullmann stood thousands of Oslo workers. The newspaper thus resumed its direct attacks upon Quisling; before long he replied in kind.

Quisling was furious about Kullmann's behaviour and the use made of it by *Arbeiderbladet*. Encouraged by articles in the non-Socialist press which suggested that Kullmann was guilty of treason, Quisling began to prepare a case against him. His determination was reinforced by the opening of a campaign in *Arbeiderbladet* on 12 October aimed at the dismemberment of the existing defence system. Quisling opened his campain against Kullmann on 14 October with a letter from the Ministry of Defence to the Ministry of Justice. It had, according to Lindboe, 'a markedly political character'.[132] It bore the stamp rather of a political testament than of the opening of a formal prosecution against Kullmann, and this was perhaps the reason why it was not laid before the cabinet for consideration. Quisling demanded the prosecution for treason of both Kullmann and those political supporters who had given him encouragement, in particular Tranmæl, the editor of *Arbeiderbladet*. He wanted, moreover, the investigation of possible revolutionary cells formed in the armed forces with the object of obstructing national defence. Finally, Quisling referred to the article in *Arbeiderbladet* on 12 October, which showed, he claimed, that 'the leaders of the Labour Party, in collusion with the trade union leaders, had gone over to the organisation of treason'.[133]

The document alarmed Lindboe, who rightly saw that even if the case proved to be politically sound, it could not be described as legally watertight. In his diary for 15 October he notes that he has 'telephoned the premier, and we agreed to deal with the case at a cabinet meeting the next Tuesday'.[134] It was obvious that both Lindboe and Hundseid wished to keep the matter as quiet as possible. However, by the Monday any such hopes had been completely destroyed, as on Sunday 16 October, Quisling had announced to the Norwegian Telegraph Agency his intention of proceeding with a case against Kullmann, and had given some indication of the lines the prosecution would follow. He had also added the ominous comment that a case 'would be brought against some of those outside the armed forces who were implicated'.[135] Thus a cabinet conference on the matter had become superfluous, and the need for a meeting to discuss Quisling's gaffe was imperative. The matter had become very urgent, since *Arbeiderbladet* had assumed, correctly, that Quisling had issued his statement without Hundseid's prior knowledge, and had featured prominently an article entitled 'Quisling on the War Path Again'.[136] The newspaper confessed itself puzzled by Quisling's cryptic utterances and demanded to know if it was his intention to prosecute the whole of the Labour Party leadership. The stage was set for yet another duel between Quisling and the Labour Party.

Hundseid must have been enraged by Quisling's kite. Certainly the rest of the cabinet seems to have been alarmed. Lindboe was at a loss to know who had been responsible for the legal advice given to Quisling, and why he 'had not consulted with the Attorney-General'.[137] Fortunately for the cabinet, Quisling had at no time stated how soon a prosecution would be taken up. The government was therefore in no way bound to take quick action. In fact, the cabinet gave instructions to the Attorney-General to look into the matter, which was tantamount to postponing any prosecution. The press, however, did not forget the incident, and Hundseid was under constant pressure to make the attitude of the government clear. Opinion in the press was by no means totally hostile; support for the government was forthcoming from *Aftenposten* and other moderate newspapers, which on 19–20 October attacked the foolish campaign being waged in the name of freedom by the left-wing press. Despite this qualified support, Quisling found that his position within the cabinet had become very awkward. He owed these difficulties not to his political views but to his maladroitness in releasing to the press a statement of major consequence without having consulted his colleagues. This important issue, however, was soon submerged in a flood of recrimination, accusation and counter-charge within the cabinet, culminating in a serious government crisis.

The crisis had its origins not only in the Kullmann affair but also in the East Greenland dispute. In addition to the deep rifts in the cabinet over the correct policy to be pursued, Hundseid had carried out negotiations with the Danish government without either the consent or even the knowledge of his colleagues. This fact came to light at a meeting called by Smedal at the Bristol Hotel on 11 October. As Lindboe recalled, 'the situation was a little uncomfortable, as the premier himself was present'; more than a little uncomfortable, indeed, since, although Hundseid had previously denied that he had been negotiating in secret, Smedal revealed at the meeting that he had been negotiating with the Danish government through Wedel Jarlsberg, a diplomat. On 12 October the cabinet held a meeting to discuss this issue, and the premier came under sharp fire from several ministers, particularly Trædal, Lindboe and Kirkeby-Garstad.[138]

Quisling, on the other hand, seems to have been oddly uninterested and contributed almost nothing to the discussion. He was presumably pre-occupied with the Kullmann case and was wondering what effect Hundseid's error of judgement might have on his own position. It was probably no coincidence that his sensational press release was made only a few days after this cabinet meeting; the premier struggling with his fellow ministers over his own lapse could hardly take strong action against Quisling. If the Minister of Defence reasoned thus, his judgement was correct; Hundseid could do nothing. The premier did not, however, forget this piece of political opportunism on Quisling's part.

During these critical October days Quisling seems to have made up his mind to try to oust Hundseid from the premiership and, if possible, take his place. However fanciful this project may seem in retrospect, it must be remembered that the situation looked very different to Quisling. He discounted all the adverse publicity in the left-wing press as a matter of course, and overestimated the support given him by the conservative newspapers. He also believed, not without reason, that Hundseid had lost the confidence of the rest of the cabinet, and that it was time for a change in the leadership of the Agrarian Party. Once more, Quisling probably judged feeling within political circles fairly accurately. His miscalculation was in believing that his colleagues would want to replace Hundseid by himself. Quisling, in fact, grossly overestimated both his own value to the government and his own popularity with the rest of the cabinet. He also misjudged his standing in right-wing circles, and as the days went by with no official action over the Kullmann case the moderate press began to dissociate itself from something that was beginning to look like another Quisling canard.[139] Meanwhile, Quisling started to organise his campaign.

Although the Minister of Defence had created trouble for himself within the government by his activities, he had assured himself of the support of a large number of very right-wing figures outside normal political life. As Hewins has correctly pointed out, 'for many Norwegians he had become a symbol and a rallying-point – the strong man who could stop dissension and stem the Socialist-Communist wave'.[140] Among people of this political persuasion Quisling had become a statesman of some importance. In Lindboe's opinion, he had strengthened his position outside the government at the expense of his standing within it. Lindboe explained this change as the result of a number of events –

> many thought that Quisling had been the driving force behind the move-ment of troops to Menstad. His attack on the Labour Party in 1932 . . . and the outcome in the Storting added to his authority, which was further strengthened by the Kullmann case. The vicious attacks upon him in the radical press increased his standing, for political assault can be a two-edged sword.[141]

Quisling thus hoped to rally support for himself outside the Storting and so put pressure on his colleagues.

To a certain extent he was successful, for his colleagues paid close attention to his activities. Hundseid, in view of his own position, was able to do little more than fulminate against his Minister of Defence, but Lindboe, through the agency of Platou, who knew many of Quisling's contacts intimately, contrived to uncover a large amount of information. Quisling had made contact with a body named 'Vort Land' ('Our Land'), a largely informal movement with vague political aims. It was nationalist and anti-Socialist, but did not intervene actively in politics. Indeed, its members differed in their beliefs – some belonged to the Free Liberal Party and others to the Agrarian Party. Encouraged by Prytz, Quisling agreed to attend a private meeting of the movement on 25 October. Present, besides Prytz, were Aall, J. B. Hjorth, a clever lawyer, later prominent in Nasjonal Samling, A. F. Munthe, a regular officer interested in defence problems, and Throne-Holst, at whose home the meeting was held. According to the evidence obtained for Lindboe by Platou, the discussion followed very ambitious lines. The old plan for the destruction of the Storting was revived, and the desirability of a dictatorship considered. In order to overcome economic problems 'the krone was to be devalued to 50 øre, and a programme of public spending to cure unemployment adopted'.[142] It is not easy to judge how seriously this meeting should be regarded, but the emphasis on extra-constitutional methods suggests that Quisling was rapidly tiring of his political difficulties and wished to find a way out that would leave him in a powerful position. The initial meeting impressed a number of people, but the important gathering was held the next day, in the form of a general assembly of 'Vort Land'. At the second meeting a much larger number of important people were present, including Jens Bratlie, a former Conservative politician, Østby-Deglum, Aadahl, Aanstad, Chairman of the Free Workers' Association, Seierstad, Chairman of the Emergency Help Organisation, Hvoslef and various others of like convictions. The discussion followed lines similar to those of the previous day, and Quisling seems to have been well received, particularly by Østby-Deglum. Bratlie, as befitted a former premier, was firm in his view that, whatever the provocation, there must be no unconstitutional action by either Quisling or the government.

The meeting achieved little; its importance lay rather in the presence of a large number of supporters of the Agrarian and Conservative parties. Many of them were top-ranking politicians. Thus the knowledge of Quisling's latest form of activity spread rapidly. Hundseid was affronted. On 27 October, the day after the second meeting, he rang up Lindboe and was 'rather choleric about Quisling', claiming that he had shown 'an improper lack of government solidarity'. As Lindboe curtly observes in his diary, there were at least two members of the government apparently open to this allegation – Quisling and Hundseid. It was evident, therefore, by the end of October that Quisling had embarked upon a plan of some political importance. Consequently his enemies began to prepare a counter-attack. Platou, no friend of Quisling, advised Lindboe that influential men in conservative circles felt that the government would be happier without Quisling.[143] The problem was how to be rid of him. Most members of the Conservative Party in the Storting believed that the government ought to jettison him, as this would leave the Agrarian Party room for political manoeuvre. The arguments of this group were supported by the view taken by the Attorney-General that, although Kullmann's statements had been unwise, they were not sufficient to warrant a prosecution for treason. Nor, of course, did the support given to Kullmann by certain members of the Labour Party constitute a treasonable offence.[144] Quisling had thus taken up an untenable position, which provided his enemies within the government with an excellent excuse for demanding his resignation.

In early November the shape of the conflict to come began to emerge from the confusion. Within the Agrarian Party serious divisions of opinion became apparent. There were those who wished to drop Quisling and those who wished to remove Hundseid. Finally, there was a not insignificant group, fortified by support from the Conservative Party, who felt that the Agrarian Party had best be quit of the pair of them. Conservatives said of Quisling, and may equally well have said it of Hundseid, that 'sooner or later he would compromise the Agrarian Party'.[145] Hundseid, however, was determined that it was Quisling's head, not his own, that should be laid upon the block. On 8 November, after a meeting on the budget, leading members of the Agrarian Party held another meeting, at Hundseid's request. Present were Dietrichson, the general secretary of the Farmers' Union, Trædal, Sundby, Braadland, Lindboe and Hundseid. According to Lindboe, the position of Quisling was the subject of discussion:

> The premier was very eager to throw Quisling overboard. So too was Braadland. Trædal wished to have the facts established and was undecided. Sundby was firmly against. I said that nothing must be done before the premier had spoken with Quisling. We went away as undecided as we had come.

On 10 November Lindboe and Dietrichson discussed the Quisling affair, and decided that if Quisling were to go it must be of his own free will, which they admitted was 'unthinkable'.[146] The danger to be feared from removing Quisling against his will was that it might lead to other resignations from the cabinet and a split within the party which could not be concealed from the public. The moderates within the party thus occupied an unenviable position.

Matters were further complicated by the renewal of Labour Party attacks on Quisling. On 11 November Nygaardsvold addressed a meeting at Trondheim and declared that 'Quisling had arranged the Pepper Affair himself'.[147] After the publication of this statement, *Dagbladet* arranged an interview with Quisling in order to discover his views, but Quisling merely remarked that in no case did he take the slightest notice of what Nygaardsvold said. On 16 November *Arbeiderbladet* insisted that Quisling must go, reporting that as a result of his desire to ape the dictator 'he was a dangerous man for the country, and also for the Agrarian Party'.[148] The newspaper returned to the charge the next day with an attack upon Quisling's friends. A very bitter article disclosed that for advice on certain policies Quisling leaned very heavily upon acquaintances outside the government. It also suggested that the basis of Quisling's political views placed him outside the normal political system. These attacks made the task of those within the Agrarian Party who wished to remove Quisling more difficult, for if Quisling were to be thrown overboard at this juncture it would have appeared as if the government were bowing to pressure from the Labour Party, which would have been politically disastrous.

Unknown to his colleagues, Quisling had at this time once more come into contact with the Nazis. On 18 November Max Pferdekämper visited Quisling at his office and had a long talk. In his account of the meeting afterwards sent to Himmler, Pferdekämper reported that the contacts which he had made almost two years before had not been followed up, and that this had been displeasing to Quisling as well as to himself.[149] Even if allowance is made for the usual exaggeration practised by Nazi officials, it seems clear that Quisling was moving towards a position of greater sympathy for the Nazi movement and its ideas. It was fortunate for him that Pferdekämper's visit went unobserved by his enemies. Had it been revealed that Quisling was in direct contact with known Nazis, the resulting political storm would certainly have impelled his colleagues to cast him overboard in an attempt to unburden the ship of state. Despite this visit, and the construction that would inevitably have been placed upon it, there is, as Hewins has pointed out, 'no evidence that Quisling was in league with the Nazis' at this time.[150]

Conscious that his own political position was rapidly becoming precarious, Quisling went over to the attack. On 20 November he composed a memorandum, which was circulated among his colleagues six days later, stating that he 'could no longer accept the present leader of the government'. As if this action were not serious enough, and despite the document being marked 'Strictly Confidential', Quisling sent copies to a number of people not in the government, both within and outside the Agrarian Party. His gravamen against the premier was that 'Hundseid had betrayed the Agrarian Party's national policy, which Quisling believed he represented first and foremost'.[151] The memorandum was some sixteen pages long, and included a lengthy justification of his own actions. Quisling declared that Hundseid had been fully aware of the matters with which he intended to deal in the debate of 7 April 1932, and that his lack of support had been disgraceful. Quisling compared his role in the government with that of Ramsay MacDonald in the British crisis of 1931 – that of a man who had tried to do his duty. The memorandum also contained some suggestions about the future policy of the government. According to Quisling there were five important issues, all of which could be solved, but none of which Hundseid had tackled: these were a rational monetary policy, the problem of unemployment, the agricultural and fishing crisis, industrial unrest and municipal maladministration. Quisling did not suggest exactly how these enormous problems should be solved, but merely urged that they should be attacked in a different way: the government's actions thus far he dismissed as aimless.

As might have been expected, Quisling's attack on Hundseid was not greeted with rapturous applause by his colleagues. Many of them seem to have thought that his burning concern with Norwegian problems was just a front for his personal objections to Hundseid. Lindboe noted, for example: 'I cannot remember that Quisling once put forward his views upon the solution of these questions.' He believed that Quisling had dragged these matters into his memorandum in order 'to give greater breadth to his attack on the premier'.[152] If Quisling's colleagues were justifiably sceptical about the motives behind his *démarche*, Hundseid was rendered almost speechless with rage when the document was presented to him on 26 November. According to Hartmann's account, 'beside himself with fury, Hundseid tore the pro-memoria to shreds'.[153] The most curious facet of the whole affair was that neither Quisling nor the premier laid the memorandum before the cabinet for official consideration. From Quisling's point of view this was unnecessary; circulation of the document was action enough. Hundseid's inaction can only be plausibly explained by fear that he did not enjoy the full confidence of his colleagues. In retrospect, it would appear that in this matter Hundseid misjudged his fellow ministers, for it was Lindboe's view that 'even though Hundseid's authority had been greatly weakened by his handling of the Greenland dispute, there was little doubt but that, had he sought our advice, we would all have dissuaded him from following Quisling's advice'.

Although there were considerable reservations in the minds of many of the members of the cabinet about the value of Hundseid as premier, there were few who would have 'been willing to belong to a Quisling government',[154] if this should prove to be the consequence of the demission of Hundseid. The dispute between the two men, even if not the subject of formal discussion, interfered with the normal work of the cabinet. On Thursday, 24 November, at a conference on the budget, there was a clash between Quisling and Hundseid, though Sundby and Trædal tried to smooth matters over. Hundseid, after the meeting, said openly that Quisling must resign, and became annoyed with Sundby, who persisted in trying to make peace. On 25 November there was another row in the cabinet, as a result of an open letter sent by Quisling to Nesse, the editor of *Aftenposten*, a missive which, in Hundseid's view, showed further disloyalty to the government. The following day the fateful memorandum was presented to Hundseid and the other members of the cabinet. On the same day Quisling sent a short note to Hundseid, referring to the memorandum, the contents of which he had already briefly outlined at a cabinet meeting on 21 November, and requesting Hundseid to resign.[155] Hundseid was very angry, and at first declared that he was tired of all these wrangles and would be glad to have them ended. After his first fury had subsided, however, he began to consider how best he might outmanoeuvre his rival.

First, Hundseid made inquiries about Quisling's activities, in order to discover if he had managed to create a lobby in his favour within the cabinet, but could discover no evidence of this. Of all his colleagues he seems to have suspected Sundby most, not only because of his attempts to mediate between himself and Quisling after Kolstad's death and his preventing Quisling's dismissal but also because of differences on economic matters. On 27 November Leirfall, who was the party secretary, on his way to consult with Trædal, met the premier, who poured out his troubles, declaring that he was determined to get rid not only of Quisling but also of Sundby.[156] Leirfall, agitated at this news, hurried off to tell Trædal of this unexpected development. If Sundby and Quisling left the government at the same time it would certainly fall, largely owing to Sundby's well-deserved popularity among the regular supporters of the Agrarian Party. Trædal decided that under no circumstances could Sundby be allowed to resign, and that the best solution of the Quisling problem would be a party investigation. Trædal himself, as representative of the cabinet, Moseid as representative of the parliamentary party, and Jakob Vik, the Minister for Social Affairs, as personal representative of Hundseid, whose close friend he was, decided to act as a reconciliation committee.

Despite the unpromising situation, this three-man committee had remarkable success. Quisling was very awkward, and, as usual, found it difficult to understand any point of view but his own. In a message sent to Trædal on 5 December, he made it clear not only that he expected Hundseid to resign but also that the government should support his struggle against the revolutionaries. He hoped, too, to lead a united Agrarian Party, but of this, according to Lindboe, there was 'not the remotest possibility'. Nor was Hunseid very co-operative, refusing to consider Quisling's difficulties over the Kullmann affair. Trædal was, fortunately, able to overcome the obstinacy both of the Minister of Defence and of the Prime Minister. During the early days of December he managed to make both the rivals realise that their positions were fundamentally weak, and that their colleagues were determined to put an end to their open enmity. Early in December, therefore, a compromise was reached. It was agreed that the Kullmann affair should be further investigated by Quisling, that any legal action should await the outcome of this research, and that Quisling's provocative memorandum should be quietly forgotten. The premier was appeased by this firm rejection of the

threat to his authority.[157] The agreement had been reached only just in
time, for rumours of a split in the government and its imminent collapse
had begun to appear in the press.

In a sense the reports in the newspapers were correct. The differences
within the government had only been papered over. The personal gulf
between Quisling and Hundseid was as wide as ever. During the short
period of time left to the government each was very much occupied with
his own affairs. Hundseid was fully involved with the East Greenland
problem and the preparation of the budget. Quisling had the affairs of
his ministry to handle and his case against Kullmann to prepare. Consequently they had little to do with each other. In the meantime, however,
they both received a rough handling from the radical press, in particular
Dagbladet, for their mistakes. Despite these attacks this period was the
calmest in the whole of the troubled existence of the Hundseid government.

After the opening of the new session the government was attacked
vigorously in the Storting. Among the most alarming features of these
debates were the lack of Conservative enthusiasm for the government,
and the increasingly hostile attitude of the Liberal Party. At the end of
January 1933 Quisling's authoritarian inclinations came under heavy fire
from the Labour Party benches. He was accused of having armed certain
non-official organisations at the time of the Menstad strike, and of being
plainly sympathetic towards Fascism. Hundseid was obliged to defend
Quisling's policy and in order to maintain governmental solidarity he had
to declare his support for Quisling over the Kullmann case. The premier
also delivered a stinging rebuke to *Dagbladet*, and denied vehemently
that there was any disunity within the government. Quisling defended
himself quite ably, rebutting the charges levelled against him by Nygaardsvold, and standing firmly by the principle that the first duty of the state
was to maintain law and order.[158] Both Quisling and Hundseid conducted
themselves, for once, as if they were members of the same administration.

Quisling also had some difficulty with his defence proposals, and spent
a large amount of time during February explaining the situation to a
hostile Storting. During these debates he had to ward off a number of
personal attacks. On 10 February, for example, he had difficulty in rebutting allegations made by Mjøen about his connexion with Hvoslef
through 'Nordic Folk Awakening'.[159] February was a busy month for
Quisling; by the same date he had prepared another memorandum, this
time relating to the Kullmann case. It was very long, some thirty-one
pages, and full of legalistic quibbles. The unfortunate Attorney-General
had to deal with the matter, after Quisling had refused to be satisfied
with the reply he had received from the Ministry of Justice. During the
rest of February the document travelled from one government department to another, failing to evoke even the most lukewarm enthusiasm.
Throughout the government crisis at the end of the month Quisling
occupied himself with this problem, to the virtual exclusion of more

important matters. Even after the defeat of the government in the Storting, Quisling still pressed on with his case, and on 28 February Lindboe and Hundseid were surprised to read part of the text of Quisling's memorandum of 10 February in *Nationen*. Thus, despite the Attorney-General's rejection of his document, Quisling was evidently determined that Kullmann should be put on trial, even if the case had to be brought by a future government. As late as 2 March he took the field against the premier for his failure to act, a move which must rank as one of the wildest acts of political optimism in a career studded with actions based on hope rather than reason.

In the meantime the government had fallen. The decisive blow was struck in the Finance Debate, held on 24 February. Long before a word had been uttered it was clear that the government was doomed, owing to the hostility of the Liberal Party. As the Labour and Liberal parties between them controlled 80 out of the 150 votes in the Storting, the fall of the Hundseid government became a foregone conclusion, once it was known that the Liberals were prepared to vote against the budget. The Agrarian administration, however, did not surrender tamely; it went down fighting. Prominent among those who criticised the attitude of the Liberals was Quisling. It was, perhaps, the best speech of his career. He predicted accurately that the Liberal Party would come to regret its action; 'he who rides two horses does not ride long.' Quisling also suggested that what was really necessary for the country was 'an end to political nonsense . . . and the creation of a national government, unlimited by party politics, which shall have full powers to carry out a political and economic revival'. He did not hesitate to use the opportunity given him to attack his opponents. Mowinckel, leader of the Liberals, he contemptuously dismissed in a memorable phrase: 'Russia's Mowinckel, Kerensky, had his February, but he also had his October.' Finally, Quisling insisted that he had always been a non-party man, that he had wished only to serve Norway, and that he was convinced there were many of his fellow-countrymen who shared his views. He concluded by stating that people of this persuasion would soon be back in power, and that 'sooner or later, ours will be the victory'.[160]

This speech, like nearly every public utterance of Quisling's, caused a sensation. Nygaardsvold demanded to know if the speech had been made with the full consent of the government. Hundseid did not reply to this question, and Lindboe felt that this was a mistake, for 'it was a completely unexpected chance for him to put the record straight'. Quisling's swan song gave him a great deal of publicity in the press, and before long he attempted to cash in on his good fortune. Despite all the eloquence of the government leaders, their proposals were rejected by a vote of 80 to 67. Hundseid then rose to inform the Storting that the government would offer its resignation to the King the next day. In accordance with established practice, however, the government remained in office until another administration had been found. There was much bitterness among the rank and file of the Agrarian Party, but in Lindboe's view, there was within the cabinet much relief mingled with regret: 'I can say for myself that the fall of the government felt to me almost like a release. The struggle between Hundseid and Quisling made working in the government very painful.'[161]

During the next few days Quisling wound up his affairs at the Ministry of Defence, apart from the Kullmann case, to which he still devoted most of his attention. By the end of February only routine paper work was left for any of the ministers, and on 3 March, once it had become clear that Mowinckel would be able to form a government, all work ceased. Four days later the Liberal ministry received a vote of confidence, and the short and stormy period of Agrarian Party government had ended.[162]

The twenty-two months during which Quisling had been Minister of Defence had wrought tremendous changes in him. He could neither forgive nor forget the attacks launched against him by the Labour Party, and, to a lesser extent, by the Liberals. Nor could he forget that, in his opinion, he had been let down by the Conservative and Agrarian parties, though he never bore these parties the ill-will which he reserved for the left-wing groups. He had acquired during these months a certain toughness and obstinacy, almost inflexibility, which he had never possessed before. Political experience had brought not only disillusionment with party politics but a liking for power. He had also absorbed certain views on social and economic questions which changed very little thereafter. The man who had entered the cabinet as the 'friend of defence' paid so little attention to this cause that by the time of his memorandum of 20 November 1932 the topic of defence did not rate a place in his mind as a problem of great importance.

In many ways, on the other hand, these months made no change in Quisling. He was still the lone wolf. He was never fully trusted by his colleagues (except perhaps by Kolstad) and they had good reasons for their reserved attitude. He never learned to accept the views of others or the fact that others saw his actions in a different light. Finally, and most important of all, working with able colleagues never shook Quisling's belief that he alone could see issues clearly. His self-confidence was boundless, and the faith of those who supported him has in some cases survived to the present day. It was a trust of which he was never worthy, and in time this fact became apparent to an ever-widening circle of his acquaintances.

Chapter 3 NASJONAL SAMLING

ALTHOUGH, LATE in 1932, Quisling suspended open warfare against Jens Hundseid, the differences between the two men had not been eliminated. Towards the end of the period of Agrarian Party government their rivalry began to revive. As the fate of the government became increasingly obvious, the need lessened for concealing its disunity. Quisling became more convinced than ever that the ills of the Agrarian Party could be cured only by the removal of its leader. His view was shared by many party members, particularly by those who had followed Sundby's lead and voted for Kolstad in 1931. What Quisling failed to realise was that the powerful section of the party which wanted to remove Hundseid would never support his own claims to the leadership, since he possessed, in a higher degree, all Hundseid's failings.[1] In the political situation of early 1933, however, he had not yet accepted this unpalatable fact; he believed that in its confusion the Agrarian Party would look to him for rescue.

Several people helped to convince Quisling that the best way of achieving his objective was to challenge Hundseid's leadership. They were mainly his acquaintances, such as Prytz, outside the party, but they included the influential Aadahl, whose *Nationen* poured out continual pro-Quisling propaganda. Soon after the fatal debate of 24 February Quisling began his campaign. On 27 February an article by him was given great prominence in *Nationen*. The burden of his argument was simple; it followed the lines of his final speech in the Storting. Apart from certain new ideas, it was largely devoted to emphasising how clear his policy had been when in office, compared with the pathetic vacillation of the rest of the cabinet. He particularly stressed the importance of supporting agriculture, one of the securest foundations for the economy of any country. Special attention should be paid to the needs of the farmers. By this he did not mean to speak for only one part of the nation; he was 'representative, and always had been, of a national party. . . . My work within the Agrarian Party has always had an appeal transcending the frontiers of party.'[2] But he added the significant rider that so long as this suited the Agrarian Party he would remain an enthusiastic member. Quisling's strictures on his colleagues did not create the sensation which they might

93

have done a few weeks earlier, for it was now known that the government was a caretaker administration. Nevertheless, his agitation did not pass unnoticed, despite *Arbeiderbladet*'s curt dismissal of his claims to national importance. Inside the Agrarian Party there were many who disapproved of the timing of his initiative. They did not wish the party to be dubbed unstable at a period of crisis in its fortunes. The possibility of a leadership crisis caused them considerable disquiet.

Quisling soon broadened his campaign in an attempt to attract support from other right-wing groups. A few days after his article in *Nationen*, *Tidens Tegn* gave his views equal prominence under the title, 'Lines of Direction'. This second article, spread all over the front page, took the form of a message to the Norwegian people. Quisling maintained that he had no wish to descend to the kind of personal attack made by his opponents; he chose rather to appeal to 'the noble and deep feelings of every Norwegian'.[3] So far as his public statements were concerned, there was some truth in the assertion, but considering his private activities and his propaganda against Hundseid it was nothing but rank hypocrisy. Even during the government's last few days Quisling did not cease to harass his opponent. Whenever possible, he tried to embarrass Hundseid, and the premier proved no more capable than before of dealing with his wayward lieutenant. The problem was that 'Quisling understood and despised Hundseid, but Hundseid did not understand Quisling'.[4] Thus, Quisling had a very considerable advantage. Fortunately, however, some influential members of the Agrarian Party judged Quisling's intentions more accurately than Hundseid did, and thus were more successful in resisting his political machinations. The whole affair was terminated by Hundseid's re-election on 9 March 1933.[5]

This was by no means an overwhelming victory for the anti-Quisling lobby. There was some dispute before Hundseid's supporters carried the day. Quisling was unfortunate in that most of his strongest supporters were not members of the Storting, whereas Hundseid's supporters were, and were therefore able to ensure that their views were accepted. Thus it becomes clear that practical reasons as well as issues of principle and personality weighed heavily against Quisling. Hundseid's re-election must not, however, be viewed as a strong vote of confidence. Quite apart from the objections of the pro-Quisling faction there was a much wider feeling of dissatisfaction. Lindboe, for example, records: 'Kirkeby-Garstad, Trædal and I, who were all summoned to the meeting, harboured such doubts that we did not attend.'[6] None of these three had any desire to replace Hundseid with Quisling, and they stood for a very powerful section of opinion within the party. Despite the prevalence of this opinion, Quisling continued to mount intrigues. His final effort, on 24 March, was to circulate a letter to all members of the Agrarian Party parliamentary group. In this letter, some sixteen pages long, he summarised all the arguments he had ever used, and insisted that the party must make a final choice between himself and Hundseid. 'Already a great deal of time has been lost and many opportunities let slip', he wrote.[7] This letter was coolly received by the members of the parliamentary group, who had already made their choice on 9 March. Hundseid himself was not particularly popular, but an attack on veteran leaders of the Agrarian Party was bound to be disliked. In this matter, as in so many others, Quisling showed remarkable insensitivity to other people's feelings. It ought to have been obvious to him that to achieve his ends he had to win the support of a number of influential figures in the party; to subject them to scathing attacks was scarcely the way to enlist their support.

During the next month or so he gradually came to see the truth. By the end of April it was clear that he had no chance of becoming leader of the Agrarian Party. He had prepared to meet this possibility, and had discussed it with his circle of intimates. In early May, *Arbeiderbladet* in a series of attacks upon him accused him of attempting to drag the Agrarian Party into a new national combination of which he hoped to become the leader. To a certain extent he was guilty of these charges: inquiry reveals that during April 1933 he made overtures to a number of nationalist groups and in an article in *Tidens Tegn* on 1 May he proposed the formation of a Free Popular Party. Among other ideas he suggested that the best way to promote the interests of all patriotic Norwegians was to create a new party resembling the almost defunct Free Liberal Party, thus making a strong bid for the backing of a number of prominent Norwegian industrialists and businessmen. The publication of this article provoked an onslaught from the radical press. Quisling was openly accused by *Arbeiderbladet* of sympathy with the Nazi Party, an accusation which had hitherto been only hinted at. 'It is the former minister, Quisling, and Aadahl, the editor of *Nationen*, who are at the head of this venture. Aadahl has worked for the integration of the Agrarian Party into a National Party . . . with Quisling as its leader.'[8] The left-wing press did not hesitate to point out the many similarities between a party of this kind and Hitler's Nazi Party.

There was little possibility, in fact, of such a powerful combination emerging. Quisling was not a sufficiently imposing figure to reconcile the conflicting interests of the various nationalist groups in Norway. Nor did all of them wish to participate in politics. Many were loosely-knit associations of patriotic Norwegians with strongly conservative leanings; politically, they were content to support the Conservative Party. Action of a more dramatic kind would have been abhorrent to them. Further, the bad personal relations between Quisling and some of the leaders of these nationalist groups – for example, Viktor Mogens, leader of the Fatherland League, with whom his rivalry was of long standing – ruled out the possibility of any combination under his leadership. Quisling was therefore obliged to give up the idea of such a combination and to cast about for another solution. The formation of an entirely new party, with himself as leader, became increasingly attractive. This was partly due to the feeling of several of his supporters that a totally new party was more likely to appeal to uncommitted voters than a loose federation of groups already known to the public. Early in May, Quisling, Prytz and Aadahl began to discuss this project seriously. The problems facing them were immense, involving questions not only of policy and fundamental doctrine, but also of organisation. Their hurried attempts to solve these problems led to strain in their personal relationships, and later to serious division of opinion about practical policies. This basic disunity permanently affected the nature of the new party.

Negotiations for the formation of such a party began in May 1933. On 1 May a political newsletter entitled *Fronten* published an open avowal of support for National Socialism. The regular readers of this publication, which had only a very small circulation, had apparently expressed interest in the creation of a Norwegian Fascist Party on the lines of recent movements in Sweden and Finland. The editor, Adolf Egeberg, a member of a rather curious organisation called the National Club, was convinced by Quisling's article of 1 May that his proposals had much in common with Quisling's. He was therefore anxious to get into touch with him. He succeeded in doing so through the agency of a business acquaintance, Walter Fürst. The National Club had been set up in 1932, and during the winter of 1932–3 its members had heard a series of lectures on Fascism, Nationalism and National Socialism. Among the speakers were Lise Lindbæk and Adolf Egeberg himself. After some difficulty Fürst, the founder, had persuaded Quisling also to address the group,[9] thus introducing him formally to intellectual pro-Fascist circles. According to Hewins, 'early in 1932, Fürst had approached Quisling several times in the Defence Ministry, urging him to revive the Fatherland League, but had received no encouragement'.[10] This, however, seems most improbable, for at that time the Fatherland League was by no means in need of revival. Nor would any intervention by Quisling have been welcome to the leader of that association. In any event, Fürst had established relations with Quisling by the end of 1932. He was thus well placed to forward Egeberg's overtures to him. Fürst and Egeberg, like Quisling and many others throughout Europe, were primarily interested in National Socialism as an antidote to Marxism. On this basis Fürst went to see Quisling armed with a copy of Egeberg's newsletter, and hoping to persuade him to found a party bearing a close resemblance to the organisations favoured by the readers of *Fronten*.

Fürst's initial approach was well received. The two had much in common, and Quisling accepted Egeberg's suggestions with some enthusiasm. Fürst had at that time an office vacant, and he suggested to Quisling that he might like to use it as the administrative headquarters of the new party they had agreed on. It was situated in the very centre of Oslo, at Prinsensgate 7, and would therefore provide Quisling with the operational base he had long needed.[11] He accepted Fürst's offer with alacrity. The friendship between them was heartily approved by Prytz, who believed that at last the chance he had waited for had come. Fürst and Prytz, as the two most practical men in Quisling's entourage, settled down to work out details. In the first week of May 1933 preparations for the founding of the new party went forward swiftly. As well as Egeberg there were other useful recruits: E. O. Hauge, who had been active in supporting *Fronten,* and another businessman called Thor Schyberg, of whose adherence Fürst, mistakenly, felt sure. It was hoped that very soon a large number of businessmen would rally round the new movement, supplying the financial support which was badly needed.

Fürst and Prytz proceeded to construct a provisional committee for the party. An inaugural meeting was to be held at the Grand Hotel on 8 May. To this meeting were invited a large number of potential supporters. Meanwhile, Quisling called upon Aadahl to inform him of his intentions and gain his support. He proposed to call the new party 'Nasjonal Samling', literally 'National Unification' (henceforward referred to as 'NS'). Aadahl seems to have been horrified to hear that Quisling was proposing to fight in the elections due to be held later that year. Aadahl reasoned that the new party would have no time to make its ideas known or set its organisation in working order; the election could end only in catastrophe. Quisling, according to Hartmann, 'would not listen to a word'.[12] Thus, from the start, Aadahl was a very doubtful adherent; his lukewarmness was a serious setback, for his newspaper had a large circulation, especially among likely recruits. He objected to the formation of NS, however, less on principle than on practical grounds, and Quisling hoped that a good showing by the new party would lead him to change his mind. But Quisling's own behaviour at the inaugural meeting was a further discouragement. When the founders of the party, about a dozen in number, assembled at the Grand Hotel on 8 May, Quisling failed to arrive. An embarrassed Prytz promised that he would appear the next day. Quisling's absence, however, had made a poor impression on businessmen like Throne-Holst and Schyberg. The next day there were fourteen people present, including Quisling, who by all accounts seems to have been reluctant to address the meeting.[13] Finally prevailed upon to speak, he was uncertain and hesitant. His speech mainly consisted of vague proposals for a moral and political movement 'based upon modern knowledge and technology'. This did not arouse much enthusiasm among the audience, who were plainly very dissatisfied.

The businessmen and journalists present had undoubtedly hoped for a much more specific approach to the problems which Quisling had mentioned only in passing. One of his listeners asked how a new party could be established and who would back Quisling up. Fürst replied that it was necessary to agree that the stupidity of the conduct of all the old parties had left them no choice but to found an entirely new party. Once again, this vague answer met with a poor reception. Prytz, on the other hand, showed that there were people within the new party who were capable of organising its affairs sensibly, announcing that the committee had 'set itself the goal of raising 500,000 kroner, and had thus far received 37,000'.

He also reported that no one was backing Quisling, except the vast number of ordinary people who supported his political ideas. There would be no foreign backing of the type given to the Communist Party. Schyberg insisted: 'We must be sure we shall win the day. I will not join the party unless it has a real chance of success.'[14] Prytz in reply pointed out that the new party would be very different from the old 'Nordic Folk Awakening'; there was much more time to make preparations, and thus less chance of a fiasco. At this stage Quisling felt that he could contribute something to the debate, and he proposed that the best solution for the problems of the government of Norway was the introduction of a bi-cameral system. He was, however, reluctant to specify further practical remedies.

After the meeting Quisling left further arrangements to his colleagues. They met again on 11 May in order to discuss various details of the proposed party programme and the practical problems of launching it. Not surprisingly, very little progress was made in the short time available. On 16 May Quisling amplified his views in an article in *Tidens Tegn*, but, as usual, they were vague and inadequately thought out. The same day another meeting at the Grand Hotel marked the official founding of the party. Quisling, with his sense of history, had wished to launch NS on 17 May, Norway's national day, by making an important speech at Eidsvoll, revered in Norway as the place where the Constitution had its birth. The local council refused permission on the grounds that the speech might lead to disturbances. Quisling, therefore, had to be content with a meeting on the previous day, though he was later to claim that he had founded NS on 17 May, being eager to profit from his nationalist image. After the meeting he went down to the offices in Prinsensgate. There he and his administrative staff decided to appoint Major Hvoslef as executive secretary to the party, and Quisling drafted a plan for the new party's organisation. According to Hartmann, it was modelled upon the system used by the Communist Party in Russia;[15] the aim was, to fight communism with its own weapons.

The foundation of NS was a haphazard affair, confused and incompetent. An analysis of the membership and the intentions of its members clearly demonstrates that from its beginning the party had little unity. Quisling himself at its head had few constructive ideas, relying principally on a variety of vague and inconsistent proposals. Supporting him were several hard-headed businessmen, such as Prytz and Fürst, who seem to have hoped that the new party might serve to protect their interests, much as certain industrialists aided the Nazi Party in Germany. The party also contained a number of intellectual enthusiasts for National Socialism; among them, Adolf Egeberg and Aall. Unlike Quisling, both these men had a firm grasp of political affairs and could distinguish theory from reality. From such men as Throne-Holst NS received tacit support, but very little financial assistance, which should have been their main contribution. Finally, the party was encouraged by Aadahl, through the medium of *Nationen*, and by the editor of *Tidens Tegn*. Thus the new party depended from its earliest days upon goodwill rather than firm and convinced support. It needed money and a clear programme in order to make any political impact, but the circumstances in which it was created ensured that neither of these requirements was met. Even Hewins has criticised the manner in which NS was founded: 'Considering all the anxiety, thought and discussion which had preceded the formation of some such party in Norway for a generation, it was a shaky and haphazard start.'[16]

To a very large extent the responsibility for this poor introduction to the Norwegian electorate was Quisling's: he failed to understand the simple political truth that in order to gain support a party must participate in political affairs. He should have taken the Nazi Party's success in Germany as a model; instead he stood aloof, waiting to be summoned by an eager electorate. As leader of the party he should have been in the forefront of the struggle, speaking and canvassing. It was up to him to convince potential supporters that NS had great opportunities. Only he could have transmitted enthusiasm to all ranks of the party. His failure to rise to the occasion on 9 May was to be the first in a long line of missed opportunities. Considering all these handicaps, it is surprising that NS was capable even of the moderate achievements which it did attain.

The first problem confronting Quisling was the establishment of a party machine to contest the General Election. This task he left largely to the ingenuity of Fürst and Prytz. In certain areas it proved easy to organise party cadres; enthusiastic supporters had come over from the Fatherland League, the Community Defence Organisation and other similar bodies. Characteristic of this section of the party, which was always the most successful, was Harald Franklin Knudsen, who came from Porsgrunn in Telemark. Like many others, Knudsen was seized with enthusiasm when he heard of the foundation of NS: 'His appeal for Nasjonal Samling acted like a clarion call, and on the very next morning May 18, 1933, I brought some good friends into line and started a local organization of Nasjonal Samling in my home county.'[17] Another useful recruit during the early days was J. B. Hjorth, an exceptionally able lawyer, whose influence on the development of the movement was to be immense. The enthusiasm of such recruits did much to compensate for Quisling's inactivity. Unfortunately for NS, the party did not find men of this calibre in every electoral district. The result was that the strength of the movement was concentrated in certain areas, principally Oslo, Opland and Telemark. In other areas, notably Hedmark, Finnmark and Troms, the party was very weak. These real regional differences reinforced the arguments of the sceptics who insisted that NS was not a truly national party, since it leaned far too heavily upon the enthusiasm of individuals holding key posts. Since NS was not fortunate enough to possess a thoroughly competent central executive the party was never able to avoid giving the impression that it lacked cohesion and firm direction. Again, this defect was primarily the fault of Quisling. The party had a leader who rarely gave precise directions, and this proved to be too serious a handicap.

The NS election programme similarly lacked purpose; this was, of course, eagerly seized upon by Quisling's opponents. Its principal proposals were much too general for the electorate to accept. These proposals were mainly based upon Quisling's memorandum of 20 November 1932. The brochures issued by the party proclaimed sound financial management, the provision of work for the unemployed, industrial co-operation and the rebuilding of agriculture as the foremost goals of an NS administration. Similar proposals, however, in variant forms, had appeared in all the major party programmes in the election campaign of 1933. The chief difference lay in the fact that whereas the other parties gave details of the measures they proposed, NS asked for a blank cheque. Thus, it was easy to accuse Quisling of attempting to create a Fascist party, and it was difficult for him to deny the charge when he declined to elaborate his programme. In addition, he had declared his belief in the principle of leadership, as defined by Hitler, thus exposing himself again to the charge that he wanted a dictatorship in Norway. There was sufficient truth behind these allegations for the electorate to believe them and to be frightened off.

In view of the hostility which Quisling had always encountered from the left-wing press it was essential for him to remain on good terms with the editors of the more moderate newspapers. His frenzied attacks on all the other parties, however, soon alienated their supporters, including the newspapers. Consequently, during the campaign of 1933, only *Nationen* and *Tidens Tegn* showed any friendliness towards the new party. This proved to be a very serious setback. Aadahl had hoped that NS might co-operate with some of the bourgeois parties, thus avoiding a serious split in the anti-Socialist vote. But his hopes for a policy of gradual development, based on Mussolini's example of alliance with the right-wing parties, were soon dashed. Quisling wrecked the plan before it had had a chance of success. On 17 May in a speech, later published as an open letter, Quisling declared that his aim was for 'all sections of the community to work together in NS', and promptly proceeded to put this aim beyond reach by dwelling upon the folly and iniquities of the other parties. In the course of a savage attack he declared: 'The old parties have failed us badly – in such troubled times we need a stronger body than they can provide.'[18] Finally, he accused the bourgeois parties of being so anxious to gain their petty victories over one another that they failed to perceive the danger of socialism which was flourishing as a result of their disunity.

It is hardly surprising that Quisling's pronouncements were paid scant attention by the other party leaders. They had no reason to agree to the co-ordination of the anti-Socialist forces under his leadership while he was attacking the very men with whom he would have to co-operate. The press strongly rejected Quisling's overtures, some newspapers pointing out repeatedly that he was himself doing more than any other bourgeois politician to split the anti-Socialist vote. Quisling sought to rebut this particularly damaging charge in an article in *Nationen* in which he stated: 'Today we need national unification, and we must begin at some point; the belief that NS has caused a split arises out of undue regard for the other parties.' Potential allies within the bourgeois parties were turned into opponents by his intransigent attitude. Quisling's former colleagues within the Agrarian Party were especially wounded by his attacks, in particular by his accusation that 'he had worked in the Agrarian Party in the hope that it would prove to be flexible enough for him to adapt its beliefs, but unfortunately such was not the case'.[19] His monumental political conceit and ingratitude thus seriously restricted his party's prospects from the very start.

Nor was NS united when it entered the political fray. Several of its more important members thought it unwise for NS to contest the 1933 elections. Among them were Hjorth and Aadahl, but they were strongly opposed by Fürst and Prytz, who believed that the sooner NS began to fight elections, the sooner it would make some lasting impression on the electorate. They had bitter memories of the failures of the Fatherland League and other similar political bodies which had talked but had not fought. Although, in retrospect, Aadahl's and Hjorth's assessment was clearly correct, the activists could adduce powerful reasons in favour of their policy. Superficially, the political situation favoured NS. The old parties had failed to cope with the problems of the depression and there was much disillusionment. The activists undoubtedly hoped to benefit electorally from the rising tide of unrest, just as Hitler had in Germany. In addition, Prytz and Fürst believed that NS ought to try to take advantage of the publicity Quisling had received as Minister of Defence, while he was still remembered by the electorate. Aadahl and Hjorth argued that these reasons, powerful and weighty as they were, did not compensate for the handicap under which NS would be placing itself; it was foolish to enter an election with no proper election fund or party organisation. Furthermore, the party would have only a very short time in which to make its programme known. These fears were to prove fully justified.

From first to last, the campaign waged by NS was a dismal failure. The party had no financial resources to meet the expenses of a national campaign nor any front-line speakers to attract large audiences. Quisling made a number of speeches, but the press reviewed them badly. His usual theme held little interest for most of the people of Norway; they wanted to hear practical solutions to their problems, not long lectures on the destiny of the Norwegian race. Quisling was the object of a series of sarcastic editorials in the radical press. This was largely his own fault for introducing all manner of fantastic notions into his speeches – demanding, for example, that Marxism should be rooted out, party politics and parliament abolished, strikes and lockouts forbidden, a corporate state introduced and a small council elected in order to give advice to the leader, who should appoint experts to carry out administration. One biographer has rightly commented:

> Obviously such a program could not possibly appeal to any but a few Norwegians of the modern age who were afraid of losing their landed properties and investments in an age of the new culture. It smacked too much of Hitler, who was just then making headway in Germany in a manner that was anathema to Liberals, Socialists and Communists.[20]

Quisling was naturally accused by *Arbeiderbladet* of wishing to introduce a dictatorship of Italian or German type – an allegation to which he never found a convincing reply.

Nevertheless, it is doubtful if Quisling intended to establish a dictatorship along these lines. He was much too nervous about taking decisions to be a successful autocrat; he always leaned heavily upon the advice of men like Prytz. Although he continually emphasised the principle of leadership, he also accepted the condition that he should be advised by a small body of intimates. Had he obtained power in the pre-war years, the form of government would have been an oligarchy rather than an autocracy, and it is by no means clear from the events of 1940–5 that Quisling would have been the dominating force in his administration, though no doubt he would have remained titular head. Throughout his political career after 1933, Quisling's colleagues were constantly asked who stood behind him. The image of Quisling as a strong man seemed so improbable to the general public that it was always believed that more powerful and sinister forces were using him for their own ends. In 1933 such a suspicion contained little truth; by 1940 it was well founded.

The attacks to which Quisling was subjected caused him to reply in kind, usually at NS meetings which often ended in riots. In 1933, at least, these disturbances must be attributed largely to the presence in the audience of numbers of belligerent Communists and Socialists. In Knudsen's view

> the opposition was fierce, and drastic. The Marxist elements saw, from the beginning, that Quisling was more dangerous to them than any of the old party leaders, . . . they immediately commenced a fierce offensive against him. They sent out their 'storm columns' to destroy his meetings.[21]

In later years the fault lay equally between NS and bands of militant workers, but in its first election campaign Quisling's party may largely be acquitted of blame. As the campaign progressed, the disturbances spread. Meetings at Gjøvik, Oslo and Bergen ended in fighting. News of these brawls did not help Quisling to secure votes from the more conservative sections of the electorate, and he grew more desperate in his attacks on the other parties.

By the end of the campaign Quisling had forfeited any chance of attracting a large bourgeois vote by the immoderate tone of his assault on the established parties. Shortly before polling day, at a meeting at Lillehammer, he proclaimed that NS was Norway's only hope of escaping from her political and economic difficulties; the old parties had coped with none of the problems, and the objective of the Labour Party was 'world revolution and Red Moscow dictatorship over the whole world'. Quisling demanded that this plague be stamped out and social unification be achieved through NS: 'The old parties do not understand that a new era has dawned.' There would be no place for the old groups in the developing new society; opposition to his party he attributed to malice rather than to genuine conviction. He was still resentful of the treatment he had received in the Storting: 'Everyone in the Storting sought to undermine my standing . . . in the end I had to leave the Agrarian Party as I could no longer endure its hypocrisy.'[22]

These attacks on his former colleagues made any united front against the Labour Party impossible, even had it been desired by the Agrarian and Conservative parties. Many of Quisling's most consistent opponents were members of one or other of these parties, Nils Trædal and Carl Hambro being two outstanding examples. At his trial Quisling claimed that in 1933 he could have co-operated in leading the Conservative and Agrarian parties; 'but after what I had been through I could not do it'.[23] This was entirely baseless; there was no greater likelihood in 1933 than there was in 1940 of Quisling being accepted as the leader of the conservative elements in Norway. His vague programme was as unpopular and distasteful to the right-wing parties as the left had ever been. They were utterly sceptical of Quisling's claim that the watchwords of his movement were 'peace, order and justice'. They disliked his insistence that NS 'shall not be a party in the same sense as the political parties, but a party beyond parties, an organised awakening'.[24] This implied that once NS gained control there would be no place for the other parties, and in 1940 this proved to be so. The suggestion naturally filled the other parties with alarm. The total effect of Quisling's pronouncements was to frighten off waverers and reduce his support to a small core of believers. As Hewins has expressed it, 'Quisling left himself with an insufficiently broad base on which to operate, . . . He virtually left himself where he started, namely with an amorphous following of intellectuals, do-gooders and windbags. Politically, this was hopeless.'[25]

If many of the supporters of NS had been disappointed by the campaign, they were even more disconcerted by the election results. Few political commentators believed Prytz's prediction that NS would win between 15 and 20 seats;[26] not a single one foresaw the disaster which actually followed. Nearly one and a quarter million votes were cast; the Labour Party obtained just over half a million, NS only 27,847.[27] This total – about 2·2 per cent of the votes cast – was not enough to win a single seat in the Storting, owing to the fact that the system (though based on proportional representation) gave no seats to small parties unless their vote was concentrated in one of the county's electoral areas. (The Christian

Popular Party, which obtained only 10,280 votes in 1933, won one seat.) In none of these areas was NS within striking distance of obtaining sufficient votes to entitle it to a seat. Its best performance was in Opland, where the party scored 31·6 per cent of the number of votes required.[28] The election was thus a serious reverse for Quisling and his party; Beniamin Vogt describes it as 'a gruesome defeat and a bitter disappointment . . . the party which was to stand above all other parties and unite them all on a national basis received fewer than 28,000 votes'.[29] In the days after the election the radical press was as triumphant as *Tidens Tegn* and *Nationen* were cast down. *Arbeiderbladet* rejoiced not only in the Labour Party's gain of 22 seats, giving them a total of 69, but in the humiliation of NS. Of all the parties which competed on a national scale in the 1933 elections only the Communists fared worse, polling some 22,762 votes, or 1·84 per cent of the total[30] – the sole satisfaction left for Quisling and his followers in their defeat.

But Quisling, optimistic as ever, did not take long to discover the reasons for the defeat of NS. Belatedly he and his circle agreed that the organisation of the party had not been strong enough to compete on a national scale; Aadahl had said as much six months before. They also recognised that if the party were ever to compete in national elections again, it must have much more money and a coherent, well-reasoned programme. These conclusions, based on a logical analysis of the causes of the disaster, were correct. But Quisling and his friends refused to learn the most important lesson of the campaign – that his own personality had played the major part in the defeat of NS. Instead they sought plausible excuses – there was a series of unfortunate events completely outside their control. Their meetings had been disturbed by rowdyism, part of a concerted plot between the Labour and Communist parties. Prytz and Fürst concluded that NS had not had enough time before the election to get its programme across – something for which, in truth, they were entirely to blame, having been determined to contest the 1933 elections rather than wait another three years. None of them was willing to admit his own misjudgements; they could only blame the malice of the press, which had obscured the policy of NS so successfully that throughout the six months' campaign it had had no chance of making converts. This, they maintained, could not have been foreseen.

The real reasons were rather different. The party's financial and organisational weaknesses played a major part, and its poor press reception, partly as a result of riotous meetings, made matters more difficult. *Nationen* and *Tidens Tegn* counted for little against the combined weight of *Aftenposten, Morgenbladet, Dagbladet* and *Arbeiderbladet*. Yet these disadvantages need not have been fatal. Responsibility for the party's defeat must be squarely placed at the door of Quisling and the small circle of his advisers, who utterly failed to appreciate that the Norwegian public looked for constructive solutions to national problems. This was the principal reason for the party's failure. Quisling's personality contributed to the disaster, for he tended to indulge in speculation rather than hard thinking about specific problems. His speeches contained too much philosophy and too little common sense for the ordinary voter, a failing recognised even by Hewins:

> Many regarded him as a very clever and experienced man, possibly great, but his ideas seemed airy-fairy compared with the everyday realities of life. Quisling had been alone too long – as a studious youth, as an independent humanitarian in Russia and as an isolated politician in the *Storting* – to get the feel of his countrymen and to come down to earth.[31]

These were the main reasons for the poor showing of NS in 1933, and by failing to acknowledge them Quisling merely created further problems for the party.

Having recovered from the shock, the party leaders set about preparations for the next year's municipal elections. These involved major changes in reorganisation. Early in 1934 these changes began to take effect, resulting largely from pressure by some of the younger party enthusiasts, such as J. B. Hjorth. Quisling's statement in 1945 that after the election he 'saved the remnants and built the party up again'[32] was quite untrue. The rescue of NS from immediate oblivion was achieved not by Quisling but despite him. During the winter of 1933–4 a new programme was drawn up, first adopted, according to Vogt, by a preliminary committee of thirteen members in December 1933.[33] The programme was then submitted officially to a full meeting of the executive committee of the party on 28–29 January. It was accepted and published under Quisling's name on 15 February. The aims of the party, as defined in the new programme, were 'national unity without class warfare or parties, a Norwegian popular union built up and based upon the work of all'.[34] The programme also contained detailed proposals on defence and foreign policy as well as on purely domestic issues. Although these changes proved to be of great importance, the organisational changes within NS were immediately more significant. The appointment of Hjorth as executive secretary was crucial; although Quisling retained the title of *Fører* ('Leader'), the really able men in the party made sure of some degree of control over his activities.

Hjorth had a purely practical outlook. Since large sums of money were not available to contest a national election, he held the view that NS should concentrate on two objectives – fighting certain local elections in 1934, and building up an election fund so as to have some real prospect of success in the national elections in 1936. There was no alternative, considering the poverty of the party, for which Quisling was largely responsible. Businessmen who had originally been interested in NS, such as Throne-Holst, had been alienated not only by its failure to approach problems in a practical fashion but also by the disorganised nature of the party administration. They regarded, quite rightly, the personal leadership of Quisling and a few of his cronies as a potentially fatal handicap, offering little inducement to invest heavily in the party. Without large gifts of money NS could not continue; accordingly, Hjorth set out to demonstrate that it deserved support. Quisling, whose attitude to money was very casual, was not much help.[35] He was not only very careless about money received for the party, but he also seems to have assumed that if money was needed it would arrive without any effort from him. It was no accident that Quisling constantly referred in his programme to the 'selfish materialism' of the other parties, and contrasted this with the 'moral basis of NS'.[36] Despite everything, however, Hjorth was moderately successful in refurbishing the image of NS and replenishing its coffers. His businesslike approach certainly led to a revival of confidence within the party.

By the time of the 1934 elections the party was in much better shape. Its central organisation was more effective and was wasting less money. Concentration on certain towns had given NS a chance in places where its local cadres had been built up. The party began to make more use of distinguished figures among its members, rather than relying almost exclusively on Quisling. Among these well-known people were Knut Hamsun, the Nobel Prizewinner in literature, Odd Nansen, son of the famous explorer, and three eminent scientists, Ragnar Skancke, Birger Meidell, and Gulbrand Lunde. Nevertheless, the one major defect from which the party still suffered was the lack of any party council to control Quisling. In 1934 this did not matter very much, as Quisling remained in the background. His attempts to rule his party as an autocrat were for the moment in abeyance, and it is notable that only in this year did NS enjoy any measure of electoral success. The municipal elections did not, indeed, bring about a major breakthrough, but they showed a substantial improvement upon the results of 1933. In all, NS won 28 seats on local councils, thus laying a solid base for further advance.[37]

The new party programme undoubtedly played some part in this revival. It was a surprisingly detailed and comprehensive document. It was originally brief, but had been supplemented by a series of explanatory pamphlets elaborating its main points. It outlined the defects in the Norwegian political system, especially the problems arising from unemployment and regional differences. Quisling also promised 'fundamental constitutional revision' in the shape of changes in the parliamentary and judicial systems. Another important pledge, called for by a number of unpleasant scandals in recent years, was his promise to 'eliminate graft and corruption'. There was emphasis upon the needs of defence, which was to benefit from 'particular attention to sea and air forces', and upon a new line in foreign policy, arguing the need to promote 'connexions between those nations of similar race, culture and interests'.[38] A special pamphlet addressed to farmers dealt in some detail with the particular problems facing agriculture. This was written by Hjorth with Quisling's approval. Underlined was the need to preserve the position of the farmers before the whole structure of society underwent change; subsidies were therefore proposed and the preparation of a land plan. Work for the unemployed was promised, and it was emphasised that methods similar to those used in Germany, where 'in two years unemployment went down from 6 million to 2·4 million',[39] could solve Norway's problem also.

The new programme thus provided something for almost every class of the community, and it was not surprising that NS was fairly successful in the municipal elections. None the less, the events of 1934 confirmed the public impression that NS was a Fascist party. This was derived mainly from three sources – the campaign in the press, the recurring violence at NS meetings and the implications behind many of the NS proposals. The effect produced by the press was very strong, and created an impression difficult for Quisling to counter. As Aadahl became less and less enthusiastic about NS, the case for the party tended more and more to go by default. The occasional issue of a newsletter entitled *Nasjonal Samling* was not sufficient to stem the tide of hostile propaganda. The violent outbreaks at NS meetings, in particular those addressed by Quisling, did the party no good. There had been notable scenes of violence in 1933, including a brawl at Tønsberg,[40] at which both Quisling and Knudsen were attacked. In 1934 these became much worse as NS was now prepared to meet violence with violence. Towards the end of the 1933 campaign, Quisling had come to rely increasingly upon the services of young enthusiasts acting as stewards at his meetings. In 1934 these stewards were organised into a regular bodyguard, numbering about 500, named the 'Hird', the name originally given to the personal bodyguard of the Kings of Norway. At Trondheim and in Oslo meetings degenerated into riots, and at Arendal there was a small-scale battle in which Knudsen's father was seriously injured. Quisling's forces were to some extent guilty of provocation; indeed, Knudsen records how the Communists could not prevent 'Nasjonal Samling from conquering the communist stronghold, the great market place in front of the "People's House" in Oslo, where the Red Front had sworn no one but they would get a hearing'.[41] Though the Communists and extreme Socialists were mainly responsible for the continuing disorders, the publicity to which they gave rise did not favour Quisling and his movement, and as a result the respectable middle class, to which he was appealing, was deterred from transferring their support to NS.

The programme of 1934 made clear for the first time the conversion of Quisling to a Fascist creed. Previously, his real views had been concealed by his vague allegiance to national regeneration, which had earned him support from certain sections of the community to whom any suggestion of Fascism would have been abhorrent. Once it became clear that NS had no chance of winning an election, Quisling's promise of fundamental constitutional revision was swiftly abandoned. In the place of this promise NS was now to carry out 'a *coup d'état* to transform the political institutions of the country'.[42] The proposals on economic and agricultural reform clearly envisaged the introduction of a corporate state; so did the promise to abolish the right to strike. Quisling's theories about the races with which Norway should co-operate introduced for the first time the Nazi theory of Nordic superiority. Although the programme of 1934 did not provide a full-blown theory of Fascism, it laid the basis for future development along these lines. It is hardly surprising that the vast majority of Norwegians, with the results of Hitler's first two years of power before their eyes, looked more closely into Quisling's programme and found it distasteful. None the less there were many who were deluded.

As if these embarrassments were not sufficient, Quisling continued his attacks on all the other parties. He insisted that NS was unique in its moral and religious mission. He thought of his campaigns almost as crusades against the unrighteous. In a newsletter of 21 June he attacked the Agrarian Party for pursuing party interests in the Storting, and arrogantly proclaimed: 'Our new party will easily deal with any crises between workers and farmers; it will be a party of national unity.' A week later he dismissed the Agrarian Party appeal for a national government supported by the four major parties; such a goal, he stated, could be achieved only by NS; the target of the party, as expressed 'in the first point of our programme', was a real national government untrammelled by 'the professional politicians'.

Quisling also attacked the Labour Party; he alleged that it was entirely dominated by Marxist elements and had no belief in democracy. 'Not one half of the supporters of the Labour Party know that the party is Marxist', he wrote on 8 November 1934, 'and 99 per cent of them have no idea what Marxism is.' Naturally, the Labour press reacted strongly to such assertions, and even more violently to Quisling's remark that 'the workers must be freed from their childish ignorance' so that they could learn how to pursue a labour policy which would be in the interests of Norway. Labour Party members saw this declaration as a challenge to working-class freedom and a warning of a fate similar to that of the German trade union movement. Quisling thus incurred unnecessary hostility to himself and his party, forfeiting his credibility as a politician. Ironically, a major statement of Quisling's programme declared that NS would no longer permit 'political dilettantes . . . to deal with important problems'.[43]

By the end of 1934, therefore, while Quisling's cause had advanced some way since the disaster of the previous year, its long-term prospects remained poor. During 1935 he slightly changed his approach, turning his attention largely to two problems – that of Norwegian defence and the failure of the Norwegian political system. Although both of these problems were central to his 1934 programme, in 1935 Quisling spoke of them to the virtual exclusion of other issues. In a new year address in January 1935 he asserted: 'We no longer have the fundamental law of Eidsvoll, but a dictatorship by the party machine.' The great struggle of the era, lay not between Marxism and Liberalism, but between Marxism and the 'spirit of a new age', in reaction to the gross materialism of western capitalists. Only through a new philosophy could the pernicious doctrine of Marxism be conquered – 'the bourgeois politicians will never overcome Marxism'; NS was the party to supply this new philosophy, and Quisling was to lead Norway back 'to the pleasant life found in the Norway of the past'.[44]

Quisling's criticisms of the Norwegian political system were based upon two main points – the failure of the party system to provide stable government or to preserve traditional values in a changing society. Although the second point was fundamental to his political beliefs it played little part in his practical political life. The failure of the parties, however, was a theme to which he constantly returned. To some extent his strictures were justified. During the inter-war years governmental instability had been chronic until 1935, when the Labour Party took office, tacitly supported on a number of important issues by the Agrarian Party. The rivalry between the Liberal and Agrarian parties, which were competing for the votes of the centre, had certainly contributed considerably to instability between 1928 and 1935, at a time when Norway was in the throes of an economic crisis. But Quisling's criticisms failed to take account of the fact that the parties represented fairly accurately the existing structure of society. It was foolish to blame the politicians for a situation which they had not created. Bitterness between the Labour Party and the bourgeois parties reflected rather than caused the class rivalry which bedevilled Norwegian politics in the inter-war years, and Quisling mistook the symptom for the cause of the disease. His idea of national unification had from the start little chance of success, and to identify it with his own person was to ignore the most elementary political facts. It was not that 'he was too nice for the job of national salvation which he had taken on',[45] but that he was so ignorant of political realities as to believe that such a task was possible or that he was the one to undertake it. A man who accused the parties of impelling Norway along the road to Armageddon was not the man to heal their differences.

Despite all the political disadvantages of a policy of no compromise, Quisling persisted in contending that his party, being, as he maintained, above party, alone held the solution to Norway's problems. Only if power were given to NS would the 'surrender of moral and political values . . . to a revolutionary and Marxist Communist party'[46] be prevented. Quisling accused the other parties of indirectly aiding the revolutionary elements by their 'crass materialism';[47] such a form of government could not long be maintained, for 'party political life is doomed'.[48] He also accused the parties of introducing corruption into politics – 'justice has become subject to party political influence'[49] – and insisted that these practices must be eliminated. No party was spared either direct attack or innuendo, and NS rapidly became anathema to the other parties; it constantly received a bad press, even for events, such as riotous meetings, for which it was not solely to blame.

In view of his ministerial record it is curious that Quisling chose to make an issue of the meagre provision made for the defence of Norway. At best the theme was not very attractive, and gained him votes only among the armed forces. As his own commitment to defence expenditure while in office from 1931 to 1933 had been equivocal, his enthusiasm for this cause after 1934 laid him open to the charge of hypocrisy. He demanded that Norway should be ready to defend herself, and the party adopted the motto 'Norway neutral – Norway prepared'.[50] Upon this issue Quisling was able to raise some support in the press, particularly in the conservative newspapers, so that he was not, as Hewins has stated, 'a one man opposition', 'crying in the wilderness and out-manœuvred'.[51] The bourgeois parties and the Labour Party were reluctant, however, to undertake an extensive programme of rearmament, preferring to put their trust in collective security. This remained so until 1937, when attitudes altered profoundly. Meanwhile Quisling vigorously attacked the parties for failing to spend more money on defence. In particular he attacked the Labour Party, which included a large number of pacifists and made disarmament one of its principal aims in its 1933 appeal to the electorate. After its coming to power Quisling feared that its theories would be put into practice. This helps to explain why he concentrated on this issue after March 1935. Instead of wooing the support of the other parties he attacked the Labour Party leaders so immoderately as to alienate those who thought him right in principle. He accused the Labour government of wishing to disband Norway's forces and thus make her easy prey for a Russian-supported Bolshevik *coup*.[52] Whatever the vices and follies of the Labour government of 1935–40, treason was not among them, and such accusations drew little support, even from those who could be described as 'friends of defence'.

During 1935 Quisling was taken up with affairs outside as well as inside Norway, but by 1936 he was concentrating entirely on the election due that autumn. Initially the prospects for NS seemed to be reasonable; the possibility of a bourgeois coalition against the Labour Party had been canvassed extensively, but negotiations collapsed and, much to the advantage of the Labour Party, no alliance was formed. In any event, the inclusion of Quisling's party in any coalition would have been doubtful, owing to the hostility of the three big bourgeois parties towards NS. Quisling's election campaign began as early as July 1935, at a national party convention held at Stavanger. In a speech to the representatives of some 15,000 NS members he stressed the importance of the next year's elections, and urged everyone to prepare for the struggle ahead.[53]

The party responded with elaborate preparations for the elections. Knudsen was put in charge of the propaganda department; Hjorth was reappointed executive secretary. An extensive programme of meetings was arranged for 1936, and early in the new year came the encouraging news that Hjorth and Prytz had raised a sufficient sum of money to start a regular newspaper. This would be invaluable in an election year, for, since 1933, both *Tidens Tegn* and *Nationen* had shown a marked reluctance to support NS and the party had had little publicity in its favour. The new paper was named *Fritt Folk* ('Free People'); the first issue appeared on 26 March 1936. From the start, however, it circulated only among devoted members of NS, so that as a means of mass communication it was an immediate and costly failure. On the other hand, its existence seems to have revived confidence among party members.

The newspaper began at once by attacking the government on the issue of neutrality and defence.[54] It highlighted certain campaign issues through a series of articles, many of them by Quisling himself, and of interviews with people sympathetic to NS. Among them were Knut Hamsun and Colonel Konrad Sundlo, who was to play such an ignominious role in April 1940. At the end of March, *Fritt Folk* compared the defence expenditure of Norway with that of Sweden, where the budgetary allowance was much larger.[55] In fact it was in the year 1936–7 that the disparity between the level of defence spending in the two countries was at its greatest. By 1937–8, when the gap had narrowed a little, there was still a considerable difference. Norway allotted 7·8 per cent of the budget as against Sweden's 13·2 per cent: this meant in Norway a level of 14·21 kroner per person, in Sweden a level of 27·15 kroner.[56] Here, NS had a very good case, but unfortunately it failed to attract much attention until the year after the election, when the whole matter was taken up by the Conservative group in the Storting.

The 1936 campaign was fought on several important issues; Quisling personally concentrated upon the defence question. From the outset he declared that the other parties had conspired to prevent NS winning the number of seats that it might legitimately expect. He complained that 'the Communist Party, in conjunction with the Labour Party, the Agrarian Party and the Conservatives, linked together against the real national party'.[57] To this theme he and his supporters returned after the election – 'the followers of NS can say that they have done their duty . . . but the other parties conspired against us'.[58] Knudsen writes of the impossibility of the task NS had attempted in face of 'collective opposition from both the "red" and the "blue" parties'.[59] In a sense, these complaints were justified, for the vast majority of Norwegians feared their long-standing political opponents much less than they disliked Quisling and his party; the obvious likeness between Hitler and Quisling made them fearful of voting for a party whose leader demanded *carte blanche* to solve the country's problems.

As in 1934, the party issued a number of pamphlets, usually based upon speeches or articles by Quisling, and explaining its policy in greater detail. One of these, entitled 'An appeal to Norwegian workers', consisted of a series of arguments designed to dissuade the working class from supporting the Labour Party. These arguments infuriated members of the Labour Party and had much to do with the disorders which accompanied Quisling's personal campaign. The pamphlet made an overt appeal to anti-Jewish prejudice, accusing the Labour Party of 'building the main points of its programme upon the teachings of the German Jew, Karl Marx'. Quisling also accused the Labour Party of wishing to destroy Christian civilisation, as the Communists had in Russia, and added: 'We must remember that of the ten chief figures in the Russian Bolshevik revolution seven were Jews.' He also asserted that the idea of international class solidarity was a 'Jewish trick' to prevent the development of 'national popular unity'. Marxism was merely another form of exploitation, which the workers should resist; he urged them 'to think for themselves instead of flocking to follow the Marxists'.[60] The tone of this appeal to the working class enraged many Socialists and Communists, who saw in Quisling another Hitler who would deprive the working class of its trade unions and its bargaining power. Many of these men thereupon set out to sabotage Quisling's meetings, and on the whole they succeeded. During the campaign a big rally was held at Gjøvik, one of the centres of Labour Party support, at which open fighting broke out between the Hird and Labour Party activists, and the scheduled programme had to be abandoned. As a result, Quisling went out of his way to provoke the Labour Party, holding a meeting in the Youngstorvet, a street in which the Labour Party had its headquarters.[61] Once again the rally became a riot, and the publicity which such incidents gave to Quisling and NS was scarcely favourable.

Towards the close of the campaign, Quisling returned to the question of defence. He pointed out, in the pages of *Fritt Folk*, the risk of war between England and Germany – 'which would be a catastrophic possibility'; each country should build up a rational defence system, for 'collective security will make . . . a world war out of a local conflict'.[62] On 30 June Quisling addressed a meeting at which he put forward a plan for a Nordic Defence League,[63] and in August he declared prophetically that Norway was 'entangled in a treasonable policy which will lead to war, without military preparation of any kind'.[64] He not only attempted to enlist votes from members of the armed forces, but also appealed to others likely to be receptive to nationalist pressures. Thus, in October, broadcasting shortly before election day, he predicted that 'Greenland would once again become Norwegian, and open to Norwegian fishermen and trappers'; he was not above using irredentist feeling in an attempt to promote his own interests. In a similar vein was his speech of 2 October, in which he insisted that 'we have arrived at a crisis in our nation's history',[65] and urged loyal Norwegians to rally round him.

Election year proved to be more than expectedly controversial. Quisling had managed to avoid personal incidents of the kind that had made life so difficult for him as a minister. A series of incidents, however, arising out of Trotsky's arrival in Norway, showed that he had in no way changed. In the previous June, the Labour government, despite pressure from the Soviet Union, had admitted Trotsky to Norway. It had been a difficult decision. If admission had been refused, the bourgeois parties and Quisling would have accused the Labour Party of bowing to the will of the Communist Party. On the other hand, if Trotsky were admitted, the same groups would undoubtedly denounce the government for encouraging revolutionary activity. The Labour government, despite warnings from the Communist journal *Ny Tid*, followed the dictates of conscience and allowed Trotsky to enter Norway, on condition that he abstained from political activity. Trotsky, however, having refused to bow to pressure from Stalin, was unlikely to allow himself to be curbed by a government of Social Democrats. Quisling immediately seized upon this point and accused the government, somewhat illogically, of anti-democratic leanings, suggesting that Trotsky had come at the special invitation of the Labour Party in order to foment revolution, to make Norway the headquarters of the Fourth International and to spread Bolshevism throughout Europe.

Quisling and his followers became particularly anxious at the large number of visitors Trotsky received; this proved that he was a centre of conspiracy. Since he was ill, his stay seemed likely to be prolonged, but Quisling asserted that this illness was merely a cover for illicit political activity. Knudsen asked why, if Trotsky were as sick as Trygve Lie, then Minister of Justice, believed, he needed a succession of secretaries to deal with his correspondence.[66] The Communist press also kept up a running fire upon the government for allowing Trotsky to remain. The Trotsky case made some strange bedfellows, but it was not to be the last time that Quisling found himself on the same side as the orthodox, pro-Moscow Communists.

After recovering from his illness, Trotsky retired to a friend's house some distance from Oslo, where he occupied himself in writing a justification of his policy (later published as *The Revolution Betrayed*). Having completed the book, he went away for a short holiday; in his absence his new home was burgled by NS members, who came away with papers proving, so Quisling claimed, that Trotsky was indulging in clandestine political activity. When these NS men were tried in August 1936, this was the basis of their defence. Quisling claimed on their behalf that, legal methods having failed to remove the menace of Trotsky from Norwegian soil, it was the duty of any patriot to take whatever action he deemed necessary. Not surprisingly this defence was rejected out of hand.

Currently with this blatant illegality, Quisling attempted a propaganda *coup*, convinced that the activities of NS in this matter had shown that there were 'tens of thousands of people outside NS who supported our action'.[67] In August he sent a letter to the King, urging him to dismiss the Labour government, on account of the outcome of the Trotsky affair. 'The existing government is guilty in this matter', wrote Quisling, arguing that the government was closely connected with Trotsky, and had some nefarious purpose in permitting him to remain in Norway. He suggested that the government was not fit to exercise its judgement in the matter, being composed of members of 'the illegal and compromised

Labour Party'. He therefore demanded that the King use 'his personal initiative' to solve the problem.[68] In asking the King to take such action Quisling must have known that he was asking him to exceed his constitutional powers. The King rightly refused to have anything to do with the matter, and referred Quisling's letter to the Minister of Justice. Trygve Lie, in turn, put it in the hands of the Attorney-General, whom he instructed to look into the advisability of prosecuting Quisling. The authorities, however, contented themselves with a short reply, refuting Quisling's allegations, on 6 November 1936.[69] The matter was then allowed to drop.

It is difficult to see what Quisling hoped to gain from this manœuvre. True, Trotsky left Norway for Mexico not long after, but this was owing to pressure from the Soviet Union[70] rather than from Quisling and NS. The Labour government handled the Trotsky affair badly, but Quisling could hardly claim credit for that. Only in one matter of importance was Quisling successful, and that was in drawing attention to himself and his party. When the letter to the King was published in *Fritt Folk* on 21 August, it became clear that Quisling hoped his *démarche* would attract to his party a large number of those who feared Communism. If so, his political judgement was once more sadly at fault. Notoriety rather than publicity was all that was gained. Quisling had simply confirmed the impression that neither he nor his party could be regarded as serious contenders for political office. He had succeeded in attracting to his cause a number of extremists, but in so doing he had lost some of his oldest party members.

The stage was thus set for a second electoral disaster. Although NS was much better prepared in 1936 than it had been in 1933, the results were even worse. Nearly one and a half million votes were cast; Quisling's party received 26,576.[71] This total represented an absolute decline in a much larger poll, a fall of about 0·36 per cent to 1·84 per cent. Even in Oslo, where he had made a special effort, NS was as far as ever from winning a seat; nowhere did it obtain even a quarter of the necessary votes. The Labour government, on the other hand, increased its total of seats from 69 to 70, and secured a vote of confidence. The Conservatives, who had vigorously dissociated themselves from NS (despite their advocating a similar defence policy), also did well, increasing their share of seats from 30 to 36. The election thus demonstrated clearly that Quisling could rely upon no significant section of the electorate; NS tactics had alienated many who held similar ideas, but who strongly resented Quisling's scurrilous attacks on respected politicians such as Carl Hambro. Thus, even on the issue of defence, on which Quisling had a reasoned policy, he spoilt his chances of success by vulgar appeals to prejudice or a campaign of abuse.

Quisling's explanation for his defeat was twofold. He claimed first that NS had been vanquished by a vast coalition, extending from the Conservatives to the Communists. Later he maintained that NS had been deserted by the ignorant bourgeoisie. But his final contention was that the defeat had really been a victory. In the period of depression immediately following the elections, Quisling wrote that the Norwegian people had rejected the way of peace: 'On Monday 19 October 1936 the Norwegian people chose the road which has led to the Spanish and Russian situations – to intensified class warfare.' At the same time he scotched rumours of the disbanding of NS by stating unequivocally that he and his party 'would continue the fight for a creative national policy'.[72] Not long after, he had recovered sufficiently from the shock of the results to report to the readers of *Fritt Folk* that, although NS had failed to win any seats, it had ensured that its constructive policies had been placed before the public; that 'was the true victory of the election'.[73] Quisling's self-deception, however, was not shared by certain other members of the party, many of whom realised that NS could no longer be regarded as a serious political force.

Some of the important leaders of the party soon decided that the explanations offered by Quisling for the defeat of NS would not hold water. Weakness at the top of the party was rightly seen to be a fundamental cause of the electoral disaster. Not only was Quisling as leader an insufficiently impressive figure, but he had attempted to dominate NS in such a way that he alone decided policy. Thus, he seized on issues irrelevant to the main campaign and frequently distasteful to the public, for example his attacks upon the Jews. For all his many articles and speeches, his arguments, generally, had little appeal. His method tended to be either high-flown and abstruse or a blatant manipulation of passion and prejudice. He thus appeared to many of his more able supporters as a political embarrassment, and soon after the election a concerted attempt was made to remove him from the leadership.

To the anti-Quisling group within NS his removal seemed to be a matter of urgency before further disasters overtook the party. Almost as soon as the election results became known members started to resign. Among these was Odd Nansen, to whom has been attributed the view that 'Quisling fell under the influence of undemocratic extremists ... and frightened people off'.[74] Men such as Hjorth realised that it was essential to act before the party fell to pieces. Already the party newspaper had virtually ceased to exist. *Fritt Folk* appeared on only a few occasions in the weeks following the election, and in December 1936 only one edition was published, marked 'December'.[75] Financial support fell off rapidly, and the party could not afford to maintain its own newspaper. Nor was Quisling wealthy enough to carry the cost of *Fritt Folk* himself. During the years 1933–39, his personal income was very low and he was obliged to sell a number of works of art which he possessed in order to supplement his earnings.[76] From the point of view of men like Hjorth there was little reason why Quisling should continue as leader; his contribution of ideas was limited, and so far as practical matters were concerned, he was a positive liability.

Nevertheless, there were obstacles in the way of his removal. In his attitude to the question of leadership Quisling always showed great consistency. For him it was all or nothing, and he had displayed some political skill in fending off attacks on his leadership after the disaster of 1933. Although his prestige was much less in 1936 than in 1933, he was no less successful in surviving the attacks of his opponents. His position had been strengthened by a meeting held at Oslo in 1936 at which 'his most active fellow combatants . . . solemnly took an oath of fealty to him – staking existence upon the issue – we promised – under his leadership – to continue with our struggle until we had won the victory'.[77] Armed with this oath of loyalty, Quisling was well protected. Furthermore, he enjoyed the loyal support of Prytz and Aall, both of whom realised that in any extensive re-organisation of NS their own positions would be imperilled. Despite the commitment of the majority of active party members to Quisling's leadership, Hjorth made a serious attempt to challenge his position and to impress on him the responsibility he bore for the electoral failures of 1933 and 1936. During the winter of 1936–37,[78] Hjorth had a long and acrimonious correspondence with him, in which he pointed out that Quisling had failed in his duty to the party and ought to make radical changes if he wished to continue to lead it. According to Hewins, Hjorth felt that

> after the 1936 Election, [Quisling] would not discuss what went wrong and get our best brains together to start afresh – professors, engineers, doctors and good people in the movement. He simply cut off the head of the party. He was too wrapped up in his own philosophy and was not really of this world. He was gifted, learned and well-read and should have been a professor of mathematics.[79]

Hjorth emphasised this point in particular; he constantly argued that Quisling was a much better theorist than practical politician, and he condemned the way he alienated potential supporters by his dictatorial attitude.

Hjorth's letters failed to change Quisling's views, and finally matters were brought to a head by Hjorth's resignation in February 1937. The loss of the executive secretary, whose organisational ability was greater than that of any other prominent member of NS, was disastrous. Hjorth had been instrumental in reviving NS fortunes in 1934 and in raising the money to start *Fritt Folk* in 1936. Quisling and the party were deeply indebted to him, and his resignation ruined any chance of recovery from the electoral catastrophe of 1936. Quisling once again found himself facing a party crisis. The volume of criticism increased sharply, and at a party meeting on 30 May 1937 the dispute was brought into the open. Quisling was able to crush the opposition largely owing to the 'young guard, who came to his rescue'.[80] This was the same section of the party later referred to by Halvdan Koht, Foreign Minister from 1935 to the outbreak of war, as 'a flock of juveniles'.[81] These young members, with their much more limited knowledge of Norwegian political life, certainly supported Quisling more enthusiastically than the older members of the movement. Much bitter criticism of Quisling was ventilated at the meeting, but in his bid to retain control he was assisted by the fact that both the party and its newspaper were registered in his name. Thus, frustrated in their attempts to change the party from within, many 'members left, and much bitter strife was caused'. After the events of the spring of 1937 only Quisling can be held responsible for the progress or failure of NS – 'the party, which stood or fell with the irremovable leader, fell with him'.[82]

After the departure of Hjorth and other like-minded members, there set in a steady decline in the fortunes of Quisling and his party. The party came increasingly to rely upon extremists and cranks. The number of genuine patriots involved in NS also declined. The group defined as 'solid and super-patriotic citizens, . . . men who were imbued with the traditional culture of the country',[83] with one or two notable exceptions, withdrew between 1937 and 1940. The party cadres came to consist largely of young enthusiasts rather than men of worth and experience. The newspaper appeared irregularly, though it was supposed to come out once a week. Quisling was not disheartened by these signs; he looked to the local and municipal elections of October 1937 to vindicate his policy. Even so, traces of bitterness occasionally appear in his speeches and articles, indicating that he was far from confident that he would ever receive widespread support within Norway. Just after the results of the 1936 elections, for example, he wrote: 'When the Norwegian people do not wish to hear, they will be obliged to feel. Such is the exacting decree of history.'[84] Revenge and anguish had already begun to dominate the thoughts and actions of the former idealist.

In 1937 Quisling was determined to demonstrate that NS could be an effective political force under his leadership. He made a great personal effort, including a tour of many areas of Norway. The most important result was to show those members of the party who were able to see events clearly that NS was politically in total isolation. Their leader was hated by the Labour Party and regarded by the bourgeois opposition as an embarrassment. The party had virtually no funds to draw on in its political adversity and Quisling could do nothing about it. Instead, he busied himself preparing a number of pamphlets for publication. The consistent theme of all his speeches and publications was that 'politics today is in reality a question of the very existence of the Norwegian people'.[85] Quisling gave out that the autumn local elections would be the last chance the electorate would have to correct its previous errors of judgement. But this did not mean the launching of a national offensive; he decided that NS must concentrate its efforts upon the municipal election in Oslo, even if this meant the almost complete neglect of other local elections; NS resources were very limited, even in those areas in which gains had been made in 1934. The results were disastrous, and Quisling's decision was undoubtedly a major factor in the débâcle. The proud boasts of his party were ridiculed; 21 of the 28 seats won in 1934 were lost, and in almost every district the fall in the number of NS votes was catastrophic. The percentage of votes cast for the party was nowhere near the 1·84 of 1936; in some of the municipalities it fell to ·06; in rural areas to 0·16.

Not even Quisling could ignore the magnitude of this reverse; within a week of the election he was forced to admit: 'Today has triumphed the wealth of the party politicians and also their distortions and misrepresentations.... Oslo has chosen Marx and Mammon.' Quisling was thus quick to accuse others of responsibility for his defeat, but he insisted that he would 'continue the fight' and that there was still hope for the party; 'we shall do our duty, and our cause will ultimately be victorious'.[86] If these statements were made sincerely, then he must already have recognised that the triumph of NS could come about only through external developments. The message given to NS by the electorate, both in 1936 and in 1937, was unequivocal, and to Quisling totally unacceptable. It is doubtful, however, if he fully grasped the extent of the political reverse suffered by his party. He realised that NS had performed badly, but his optimism was such that in any discouragement he could find crumbs of comfort. His capacity for self-delusion could expand to meet any demand. Others within the party were more realistic. After the 1937 elections, members of the party once again reviewed their allegiance to it. Some left, and abandoned the whole cause; others remained, and these gradually came to see that NS might have to rely on outside assistance to maintain an effective campaign. Thus, between 1937 and the outbreak of the Second World War in 1939, leading NS personalities began to approach the Nazis, hoping to reach some mutually satisfactory understanding. Prominent among them was Aall.[87]

Quisling himself was probably not one of the first to favour some connexion between NS and the German authorities, but constant pressure upon him from those who did advocate this step eventually converted him. The process was slow and cannot be traced to any particular event or precise date. The matter was further complicated by the different views taken by various members of his entourage as to the form any connexion should take. Some hoped for a wholesale commitment to Nazism and the adoption of appropriate articles of the Nazi creed. Others believed that NS should rather trade upon the Nazi desire to promote in other countries parties friendly to their regime, and that surrender to Nazi doctrine would be to abandon the nationalistic outlook claimed by NS as its own ever since 1933. The progress of events in 1938–39 largely determined the respective success and failure of these two parties.

The election results of 1937 put Quisling, to some extent, in the power of those colleagues who had a positive solution to the party's difficult situation. Aall was perhaps the most determined, and during these years he replaced Prytz in the role of chief adviser to Quisling. Also influential was the party secretary, Rolf Fuglesang, one of the youngest of the leading members of NS; he frequently acted as the channel of communication between Quisling and Aall, who spent much of his time in Sweden and Germany. Both Fuglesang and Aall appreciated that NS had been badly beaten at the local elections; in fact, Fuglesang wrote to Aall: 'The election result was very bad . . . and in the few places where we put forward a list we suffered a serious setback. The worst was the collapse in Oslo, where we received only about 800 votes as against about 6,000 in the Storting elections last year.'[88] Fuglesang and Aall realised that NS had not much chance of ever playing an important part in Norwegian political life; Quisling, however, refused to recognise this fact. In the years between 1937 and 1939 Quisling played a tragi-comic part. He acted as if NS was still a serious political organisation and he might one day be the saviour of Norway. He kept up a high level of political activity, and Knudsen writes: 'I arranged some 503 meetings during the years up to 1940.'[89] There were many other meetings, and for these Knudsen had no direct responsibility. The NS leader thus remained a busy man, busy in a hopeless cause.

During this period of almost two years, Quisling lost interest in many of the questions which had attracted him some years earlier, and concentrated increasingly upon the single issue of defence. In a short article in *Tidens Tegn*, published towards the close of 1937, he declared that the government was full of dishonest men: 'these criminals have involved Norway in a war policy'.[90] By this Quisling meant that the Labour government was pursuing not a policy of belligerence but one of surrender; if Norway remained weak, there was a much greater risk of involvement in war than if the country possessed adequate defences. Quisling turned out to be perfectly correct, and already some outside NS were recognising the truth of his words, while having no sympathy with his other beliefs or with his style of attack upon his political opponents. In debates on defence in 1937 the Conservatives had pressed for a large increase in defence expenditure,[91] but had been overruled by the other parties.[92] Hewins on the other hand insists not only that the Conservatives were not yet 'realistic', but also that 'Quisling was a voice crying in the wilderness, more isolated even than Churchill in England at this time'.[93] Both statements are totally untrue. Many others were aware of Norway's weakness and vulnerability, but as politicians they could not ignore the obvious wishes of the electorate. Quisling, as leader of a party little in touch with the feelings of the majority of the electorate, could afford to be more extreme in his comments.

Quisling was realistic enough to appreciate that the strength of NS had to be built up once again, if the party was ever to act as the mouthpiece of the 'friends of defence'. In *Fritt Folk*, on 8 January 1938, he wrote: 'We must strengthen the position of our newspaper in the country, or else we might as well surrender to the Comintern now.' Unless the party mouthpiece was healthy, the main body of the party would be ineffective; it was therefore decided by the party council that an appeal should be made to Norwegians living outside Norway, in the hope that they might be induced to give financial support to the party and its newspaper. About a year earlier, Quisling had already made such an appeal, on the advice of Fuglesang and a prominent nationalist businessman, Ellef Ringnes, formerly Austrian Consul in Oslo. So desperate then had the position seemed that Aall had received a letter reporting: 'The position is that *Fritt Folk* must close down next week unless some financial help is secured.'[94] The newspaper had survived that crisis, but after the 1937 elections the circulation again began to decline. An attempt was made early in 1938 to produce another journal, entitled *Samband* ('Union'), but although the list of intending contributors included Aall, Quisling and Sundlo, the new venture was an utter failure.[95] The party had to make do with *Fritt Folk*, although its value had already proved negligible. The paper suffered from the same defects as its owner; even when what it said was reasonable, the effect was destroyed by the immoderate language used to say it. The newspaper was of no more help to the party than its leader.

Fritt Folk came to reflect the personal opinions of Quisling even more closely after Hjorth's resignation. Only those whose views tallied almost exactly with Quisling's were allowed to contribute. So the standard of journalism fell to a level of absurdity equalled only by the Nazi newspapers. It ceased to take account of the news and concerned itself solely with items of party interest, either the ideas or the activities of NS. Defence became the principal issue, and the sole topic of interest to non-members of NS. In the issue of 18 December 1937, for example, Colonel Sundlo presented a long article about the decline in government expenditure on the armed forces which was not only very partisan but also tendentious. This set the tone for the next eighteen months, during which *Fritt Folk* repeatedly returned to the attack. On 26 March 1938 Quisling's editorial condemned the highly dangerous policy pursued by the government, stating that Norway was not prepared 'materially, morally or militarily to meet the requirements of a modern war'. All through the year 1938 Quisling assailed the government's defence record, and, as the pace of events outside Norway quickened, so he became ever more firmly convinced that he alone had the vision to foresee his country's needs. Defence had originally, in 1933, been a relatively small item in the NS programme. By 1936 it had become a major plank in the party platform; by 1938, the personal obsession of its leader.

While condemning the policy of his own government, Quisling praised that of those countries which had put their trust in the rejuvenating force of nationalism. In April 1938 he wrote: 'Over the whole world nationalism is on the advance. . . . Nationalism is the political belief of the twentieth century and is fated to be victorious.'[96] The diplomatic victories of Germany in 1938–39 did not cause Quisling alarm but pleasure, since they confirmed his theories. Encouraged by these portents, Quisling refused to believe that there was no future for NS. He continued to write articles and make speeches; according to Knudsen, his activity grew rather than declined, and, according to Quisling himself, 'in Telemark alone I spoke to half the population'.[97] Nor was the organisation of NS allowed to collapse. Regular meetings of the 'Råd' ('Council') were held, at which the problems before the movement were discussed in detail. The party organisation reached the peak of its efficiency during this period, when, in fact, there was little practical work to be done. Had the council shown such efficiency or enthusiasm in 1933 or 1936, the electoral disasters of those years might well have been reduced. The yearly 'Riksmøtet' ('Party Congress'), to which all party dignitaries came, was held in 1938 at Hamar on 1–3 July, and Quisling was very pleased with the quality of the debates and also with the degree of interest shown by those present. The rally, however, did not attract much attention outside the party; for the purpose of propaganda it was almost useless.

Political developments within Norway filled Quisling with alarm. The year of 1938 produced several political setbacks. Only minimal increases in defence expenditure were made at a time when the external situation was constantly becoming more serious and threatening. Prominent members of the government, such as Koht, Torp, and Nygaardsvold, believed it was their duty to forward the economic and social reconstruction of the country and not to spend large sums on rearmament. Quisling believed that Norway stood on the brink of a catastrophe, and that those mainly responsible were 'Mowinckel, Koht, Hambro and Nygaardsvold, together with the party system, the parties and the press. . . . They have much to answer for in the current situation.'[98] Quisling was equally concerned with the internal situation. In April 1938 a motion was put before the Storting to extend the life of the current parliament by one year, so that an election would be held in the autumn of 1940 rather than a year earlier. After some discussion and consultation the motion was carried by 123 votes to 24, with 3 members of the Storting absent. Quisling was enraged by this piece of legislation, which he believed deprived him of his chance of electoral victory. 'This Labour trick,' writes Hewins, 'designed to tighten their grip on office and to stifle opposition, naturally coloured Quisling's future behaviour.'[99] This comment betrays an almost total ignorance of the relevant facts. The decision of the Storting was no mere act of Labour chicanery, but, on the contrary, a calculated decision made by the whole parliament. The Labour Party held only 70 seats in the Storting at that time, so that manifestly it could not have obtained the majority of 99, had it not been supported by members of other parties. In fact, it was an all-party measure, and Carl Hambro, the leading Conservative, played a large part in drafting the bill.[100] The bourgeois parties, who controlled a majority in the Storting, would hardly have voted for such a measure had they believed that its sole purpose was to assist the electoral prospects of the Labour Party. The truth is that it was a reform long overdue.

Nevertheless, this fact does not acquit the Storting of an action that was unquestionably illegal. According to the Constitution (Section 112), changes made by the Storting had to be confirmed by the succeeding Storting – that is, after an election had been held. The reformers committed not only a constitutional but also a practical blunder, for it gave Quisling an excellent pretext for attacking all those concerned in the decision. There can be little doubt as to what the reaction of the mass of the electorate would have been, had an election been held in the autumn of 1939, and the party of reform was therefore foolish to rush the change through. Quisling assailed the change from the very first, claiming that he and his party had been heading for victory in the elections of 1939 until the Storting had postponed them in a deliberate attempt to deprive him of the fruits of his labours. This was a total misjudgement of the political situation. Quisling was to use this decision of the Storting as an excuse for all his future activities, in particular those after the autumn of 1939, by which time elections would normally have been held. Many were in agreement with Quisling about the illegality of the action of the Storting, notably the lawyers Castberg and Skeie, the former of whom had advised the Storting against the alteration; but, agree as they might, NS gained no increased support. The blatantly undemocratic nature of many of the proposals put forward by Quisling and NS was enough to alienate those who might have been attracted by the party's resistance to the constitutional changes. Men such as Castberg, with a high regard for the integrity of the constitution, found little to attract them in the programme of NS.

The year 1938 was a period of political disappointment for Quisling and his party. The expected recovery from the election disasters of 1937 did not take place; the elections of 1939 were postponed until 1940. Enthusiasm had begun to decline alarmingly among the youth of the movement. This was especially ominous for Quisling as it was this section that had supported him strongly in the years 1935–37 against those who had wanted a change in the leadership. Furthermore, the long-term effects of a prohibition upon the wearing of political uniforms, passed by the Mowinckel government of 1933–35, now began to be apparent. The *esprit de corps* found among all ranks of Hitler's paramilitary organisations was notably lacking in the Quisling forces. Forbidden by law to wear uniforms, and feeling itself the object of derisive comment on the part of the bulk of the population, the Hird, which had attracted most of its members from the under-21 age-group, declined both in numbers and effectiveness. Unlike the Nazi party in Germany, the movement never produced a martyr. There was violence at NS meetings, but no one was ever killed. Without organisation, without uniforms, without a martyr, the Hird gradually ceased to exert any significant political influence and became merely a body of stewards for party meetings. If Quisling had hoped that the Hird would develop along the lines of the SA in Germany, by 1938 all his hopes must have been dashed to the ground.

It is hardly surprising, therefore, that during the latter half of 1938 and throughout 1939 Quisling's propaganda took on a more bitter tone. He was both disillusioned and desperate. It seemed unlikely that his party would survive long enough in a form which would permit it to fight effectively in the 1940 election. His attacks grew wilder and more absurd. He blamed anything and anybody. Even Hewins agrees that 'by 1939, we find Quisling despairing of his Government, his people and the Western Democracies, and frantically searching for a Norwegian way out of the gathering storm'.[101] Extreme views and attitudes were not the solution to Quisling's problems; by behaving in this way he only alienated support. Occasionally, however, he argued and acted rationally. In early 1938, for example, he suggested that the best solution to international tension was reconciliation between Germany and Britain, though he believed that this would be achieved most easily by promoting Nordic union. On 9 April 1938 he announced that he and NS would do everything possible to create a lasting understanding between the two powers: 'To promote peace between England and Germany is our only task in international politics today.'[102] Yet, at the same time, Quisling was urging that Norway should not concern itself with power politics. On 2 April he had demanded 'an honourable and strong neutrality policy',[103] and on 27 August that 'Norway should leave the League of Nations and fortify the defence of national interests and neutrality'.[104] The government clearly could not at one and the same time withdraw from international politics and promote an understanding between Britain and Germany. But Quisling never fully worked out the practical aspects of the policies which he advocated, so that little attention was paid to his demands.

During 1938 Quisling began to emphasise more strongly the anti-Jewish elements in his policy. As far back as 1935 he had violently condemned the action of the Storting committee in awarding the Nobel Peace Prize to the German Ossietzky, who was at that time languishing in a German concentration camp. By 1938 his views had become even more extreme. At the time of the Czechoslovak crisis he declared that it was the goal of 'secret international circles, international Jewry, international democracy and international Bolshevism, to drag the British Empire and the Nordic countries into a fratricidal war on the continent',[105] which would lead to their mutual destruction. Quisling attributed the major share of the blame for this to the 'eternal Jew, who is once again on his wanderings'.[106] He accused the Jews of having representatives in every country in the world dedicated to promoting the interests of their race rather than of the country that had given them sanctuary. Such intemperate remarks earned him little or no support in Norway, where feeling was much incensed at the way in which the Jews in Germany had been treated. His habit of labelling his opponents as 'Jewish' or 'agents of world Jewry' enraged many Norwegians. Hitler's success in playing upon anti-Jewish prejudice in Germany encouraged Quisling to imitate the Führer's policy, but there was in Norway no general hostility to the Jews and Quisling's outlook was shared by very few.

At the same time he began to emphasise more strongly that the policy for Norway was one of neutrality; Norway must keep clear of 'the affairs of others'.[107] Yet neutrality in Quisling's sense involved close friendship with Germany. It also involved commitment against Communism. In December 1938, reviewing the events of the past year, he reported: 'The Communist movement has been driven back in Europe . . . and every day in 1939 will be a day nearer the attainment of our hopes.' Quisling's attitude was thus one of enthusiasm towards those countries, such as Germany, which were trying to resist the spread of Bolshevism, and of coolness toward those nations which appeared to be hindering such efforts. In 1938–39 his feelings toward Britain underwent a clear change. Whereas hitherto he had advocated the unification of all Nordic countries, Britain included, he now became suspicious of the aims of British foreign policy. The Czechoslovak crisis and its aftermath caused him some alarm, and by late 1938 his feelings toward Britain had so far altered that he was able to write that the new order had made some progress 'even in England'.[108] This was a far cry from his earlier enthusiasm. By the summer of 1939 he was convinced that Britain was the enemy, and he wrote that 'the Moscow pact has split the Jewish front. . . . It is a great blow to England, which will now look in vain for help from the Red Army.'[109] Statements of this kind make it clear that Quisling's concept of neutrality was no more conventional than that of Mussolini during the winter of 1939–40.

Quisling's public commitment to Germany reinforced the impression that he had now embraced the full range of Nazi doctrine. The progress of world events urged upon the Norwegians the necessity of strict neutrality; none the less, it had produced, especially in the press, a reaction against Germany and in favour of those powers which appeared most likely to resist Hitler and his regime. Quisling gained support only among those sections of opinion in Norway which believed that Hitler could not be stopped. Thus, by the autumn of 1939, Quisling and NS had already come to depend upon those who had much to gain from a German victory. From 1937 onwards, therefore, there had been a further serious decline in NS popularity. Quisling remained unconvinced that the number of pro-Germans in Norway was small. Throughout 1938–39 he solemnly spelled out the virtues of his own party and the vices of the rest. In his view, 'NS was the only party to maintain the ideal of nationalism'.[110] In contrast to its purity of motive he observed how the depravity of the other parties had 'opened the way for lies and corruption to reign in political life'.[111] The reforming zeal shown by him during this period was not reflected in the proposals put forward by his party, which continued to offer the same programme as in 1936–37. Nor did he come to grips with the realities of the political situation in Norway, where, despite the increasing tension in world affairs, popular concern was still focused upon domestic conditions. The interest in world politics shown by Quisling was not shared by the average Norwegian, who was much more concerned about national recovery from the economic depression. During the 1930s Norway steadily pursued a policy of non-involvement in European affairs, moving away from the concept of collective security. By 1939, Quisling's party had come to seem a political irrelevance.

Throughout the last year of peace, Quisling continued his attacks upon the dangerous political manœuvres of the Nygaardsvold government. He accused it of pursuing a 'disastrous financial policy . . . which was assisting the schemes of international capitalism'.[112] But he made no constructive suggestion as to what financial policy the government should follow. Similarly, he criticised the government's defence policy, and the inertia of Torp and Monsen, the successive Ministers of Defence since the Labour Party's advent to power. He condemned especially the failure of the government to prepare adequately for a deterioration in the international situation, and pointed to the minimal increases in defence expenditure in 1938. In this matter Quisling condemned the opposition as well as the government. He suggested that ever since the collapse of the Russian schemes in Spain 'the Bolsheviks had increased their interest in Scandinavia', adding that in Norway the leaders of 'both left and right are co-operating to betray their country'. In particular Quisling was furious at what he described as a 'vicious conspiracy', pointing to a publication written by Carl Hambro, entitled 'Defend the Nation from Fascism', which symbolised the extent to which the other parties were aligned against his policies. Was he to continue to be a 'voice preaching to the wind, or would the Norwegian people awake at the eleventh hour?' – a rhetorical appeal which made little impact on the political scene.[113]

As the normal date for the election approached, Quisling became increasingly agitated about the Storting's decision to postpone it. He recalled that the decision had been by no means unanimous and pointed out that it was a clear breach of the constitution, threatening that the politicians would 'later on have cause to regret this departure from legality'[114] and calling for an end to this 'quasi-democracy'.[115] He demanded to know what the King was about, to allow events to take such a course: 'It is clearly the King's duty to order a new election and not to support the existing illegal body.'[116] During the summer and early autumn of 1939 he was cherishing the hope that the King would refuse to open the new session of the Storting, rather than become the 'chief violator of the fundamental law of the constitution'.[117] By the winter of 1939–40 he had relinquished this hope, and was warning the King that he would henceforth be judged according to whether he 'took the side of the party politicians against the people or the part of the nation against party dictatorship'.[118] The rich variety of political abuse hurled by Quisling at his opponents during the previous year, however, had small effect, and amid the mounting tension following upon the outbreak of war the constitutional question was lost sight of.

Quisling and NS were now attracting little public attention. The strong current of anti-militarist feeling in Norway spelt political doom for any party which made increased expenditure on defence the main plank of its political platform. Once again the annual party congress was held at Hamar in August; to most Norwegians its deliberations, compared with the German–Polish crisis, seemed of little importance. Quisling was, as usual, the main star of the congress, and made a series of provocative speeches, later issued as a party pamphlet. For the first time he made public the very close sympathy between his views and those held by leading Nazis. For the first time he expressed views which could be accurately described as Fascist. He stressed the power of the forces of nationalism and hinted that the second world war, a war between nationalism and Bolshevism, had in reality already started. He saw the starting-point of this struggle as 'the march on Rome of 28 October 1922, when the European revolution began – against democracy, Bolshevism and the mastery of the Jews'.[119] He sought to defend German policy in words almost identical with those used by Hitler a few weeks later.[120] He suggested that England feared Germany's challenge to her world mastery and therefore wished to suppress the new and powerful Nazi state. Like Hitler, Quisling condemned the role of the Jews in seeking to start another European conflagration; 'world Jewry must dominate Germany, just as Bolshevism was a Jewish victory over anti-Semitic Russia'.[121] There was a gigantic international conspiracy against Germany, which was rightly attempting to free itself from encirclement and total destruction. The great crisis of the summer of 1939 offered Norway a unique chance to 'escape from the tyranny of England's sea power'.[122]

To those who cared to observe the political scene, Quisling's belief in Fascism was thus made clear. He laid great weight on 'the creation of a new order in the place of democracy',[123] and on the removal of decadent democratic dictatorship. By September 1939, his normal political career had run its course. Of his original followers few were left. Of his original ideas only his belief in his mission to help Norway remained. In the years 1931–39 he had moved steadily towards an acceptance of Fascism and away from his former conviction of the virtues of individualism and democracy. In muddled fashion, and with the assistance of Aall, he tried to reconcile these conflicting ideas within one conceptual framework. The apostle of the revival of Nordic individualism of 1931 had become the leading supporter of the New Order. Amid the tense diplomatic activity of the summer of 1939, few had the leisure to observe Quisling's activities; his eccentric views developed without attracting much attention, though within a few months they were to be of some importance. The failure of the Norwegian politicians to see the dangers inherent in this development must be attributed not to blindness but to the microscopic size of his party. Members of the government could hardly imagine that the tiny, totally discredited, Nasjonal Samling party could be any sort of threat to the elected representatives of the Norwegian nation. Having failed to mount a successful political campaign at any time between 1933 and 1939, Quisling could pursue his own policy unencumbered by any notion of responsibility or duty towards his supporters. Similarly, his secret and more sinister activities also went unnoticed; the politicians had long since written off both him and his movement.

It was now that Quisling's serious encounters with the Nazis began. They can only be understood in the light of the events of 1931–39. During those years Quisling had abandoned a promising military career for the sake of a dubious political venture, which he had then proceeded to ruin by his extremist outbursts. He had lived on the edge of poverty, and his party's repeated failure at the polls had made him the laughing-stock of Norwegian politics. By 1939 his early promise was for most Norwegians no more than a dim memory. Within Quisling's heart there accumulated bitterness and hatred. He could not understand that his own acts had been the ruin of his career, so he sought to blame others – Socialists, Communists, Conservatives, Jews, and even his former colleagues in office. He sought to blame institutions – the Storting, the monarchy and the electoral system, and even such nebulous concepts as world capitalism and Western democracy. From all this he turned towards Nazi Germany, full of rancour and vindictiveness. He was determined to be the saviour of Norway and believed that the chance of redeeming lost opportunities had come. By 1939 he had decided that if the Norwegians were not ready to accept his leadership then it had become his duty to save them in their own despite. So his conventional, though unusual, political career came to an end and his serious negotiations with Germany began.

Chapter 4 FIRST CONTACTS WITH GERMANY

THE PIECING together of the various fragments of information about Quisling's relations with Germany is a peculiarly difficult task. No detailed account can be given of the development of an intimate relationship. Contact was spasmodic, and was maintained through a number of different agents who were often ignorant of one another's activities. How did this relationship originate and how were the bonds strengthened between Quisling and various members of the Nazi hierarchy? Any objective assessment is made difficult by the German invasion of April 1940. The arrangement reached in the winter of 1939–40 was not foreseen in the mid-1930s when contacts were first made. Those who have sought for a fully developed plot in 1935 or 1936 have therefore been disappointed. About Quisling's intentions in these years we must remain cautious. He may have intended as early as 1935 to rely on German troops to instal him in power, though this seems unlikely in view of Germany's military weakness at that time. Even if this was his line of thought, it was never committed to paper, and has never been admitted to by any of his lieutenants. Probably, therefore, it may be ruled out. Yet it does seem clear that both Quisling and the Nazis, from the very beginning of their relationship, aimed at using each other for their own ends. Their first contacts were not very serious, but they became more important as the international situation worsened. Against this background the history of Quisling's relationship with Germany must be viewed.

Although Quisling's serious contacts with Nazi Germany began to take shape in the summer of 1939, his actual connexion with Germany may be dated much earlier. At his trial he declared: 'I had no connexion with Germany . . . though I did once receive a letter from Himmler which I did not answer.'[1] This statement was quite untrue, for he had met various members of the Nazi Party long before 1939. As far back as 1930 he had met Pferdekämper, and had renewed the acquaintanceship in 1932. Even at that time certain Nazis had hoped to use Quisling, and events after 1933 must have given them further encouragement. Quisling's period of political inactivity within Norway in 1934–35 coincided with intense external activity, in the course of which he must have met many Nazis and their sympathisers. In 1945 he recalled: 'I worked in Europe, I organised national parties throughout Europe. In 1934 and 1935 I organised national movements such as the Iron Guards, also in Spain and France and some other lands apart from Germany.'[2] If we can take this admission at its face value, it is hard to see how Quisling could have achieved anything without serious contact with influential members of the Nazi hierarchy, either directly or through their staffs. After 1933 Nazi organisations penetrated most nationalist parties in Europe, and his work could hardly have gone unnoticed by these various Nazi agencies.

Quisling's craving for publicity was also bound to mark him out for special notice. Soon after the foundation of NS he went to a conference of nationalist parties at Montreux. He made such an impression there, according to his own testimony, that he was elected 'world propaganda chief for 1934–35'.[3] In this capacity he toured the continent in the cause of a 'united states of Europe'.[4] He always maintained that his contacts were only with England and native nationalist parties, and that his work had no connexion with Germany. It is hard to judge the importance or success of this work, especially since his duties towards foreign nationalist parties seem to have attracted small attention. Taking his own Norwegian party as a yardstick, we can hardly regard his propaganda activities as much of a success. He had been unable to organise NS successfully, and there is little reason to suppose that he could have been any more useful to the Iron Guard or the British Union of Fascists. The incident, like many others in Quisling's life, remains vague and obscure. Only a few facts are undisputed – that he came into contact with a number of personalities connected with parties similar to NS, that these contacts were made during 1934–35, most of them outside Norway. Though it is by no means certain that they were made for dubious purposes, they may be taken as indicating the direction in which Quisling was travelling in the mid-1930s.

Perhaps as a result of these activities, Quisling was sought out by the man who was to be his closest collaborator during the war – Hagelin. Albert Viljam Hagelin (1881–1946) had been born in Bergen, although his family was Swedish in origin, and had lived in Germany for the greater part of his life. According to his own account, he first met Quisling in 1936, during a visit to Oslo – 'I went to find him at his office because he interested me.' Hagelin in his youth had known Christian Michelsen, and had been much impressed by a remark of Michelsen: 'One day there will arise a movement for national unification.'[5] He wanted to make contact with Quisling because he believed that NS could provide some degree of national unification. In view of Hagelin's background, this story seems somewhat improbable.

For much of his life Hagelin had maintained an intimate connexion with Germany, and it is more likely that Quisling's activities in Europe had attracted his attention and suggested the possibility of his acting as go-between and honest broker in establishing a permanent link-up between Germany and NS. Before the First World War Hagelin studied at the Technical High School in Dresden and later married a girl from Bremen. During 1917 he had worked for the German government as head of a food-buying commission in Sweden. After 1918 he had run his own export-import agency. Later he had been attracted by the nascent Nazi Party, and had even, according to the evidence of Dr Koren, who married his niece in 1936, become an eager supporter of Hitler, 'holding a membership number in the region of 300'.[6] He was frequently visited by high-ranking army and navy officers, and knew Rosenberg and Göring well. His wife had died in early 1935 and in the autumn of 1936 he had re-married. His second wife, who came from Oschatz in Saxony, was an enthusiastic Nazi, and his own sympathies were clearly very much with the Nazi Party. During a visit to Norway in the summer of 1936, he is reputed to have joined NS, though he always denied this – 'I did not join NS, for the reason that I lived abroad.'[7] This statement is inconsistent with his actions; he had interest enough in the movement to seek out its leader, and his later claim not to have been a full member of the party is even more improbable since his second wife, though foreign by birth and domicile, belonged to NS as well as to the Nazi Party.[8]

Thus it is probable that Hagelin was a member of NS from 1936 onwards. Residing in Dresden, he was in close touch with prominent Nazis. Through him, Quisling, without taking any initiative, had opportunities of contact with the German hierarchy. This seems to have been until 1939 his most important means of contact with the Nazis, and there is no firm evidence that the relationship was treasonable. He cannot, however, be acquitted of the desire to establish a much closer bond between NS and the Nazi Party, which would have involved him in dealings similar to those for which he condemned the Norwegian Labour and Communist parties in 1932. In 1945 Hagelin claimed that in no way had he acted as Quisling's agent in Germany. Denying that he had sought out Quisling at the request of friends in Germany, he claimed: 'I was interested in Quisling because I was against Bolshevism . . . and there were at that time many who felt the same way . . . for example, Churchill. I was wholly in agreement with Churchill and also in accord with Quisling.'[9] Despite these convenient protestations Hagelin had a somewhat closer connexion with Quisling than with Churchill.

The relationship between them was really much closer than might at first appear. Together with Aall they built up an intricate organisation resulting in 1939 in the fateful formation of a working arrangement between Quisling, his party and important members of the German hierarchy. Aall and Hagelin were the efficient organisers carrying Quisling towards his decision. To a certain extent his part was passive, but it would be wrong to assume that he was merely the tool of the other two men. Since he stood to gain by their activities he can hardly have been in ignorance of what was going on. Furthermore, Quisling's movement towards a pro-German attitude and pro-Nazi convictions during these years suggests that he was in full agreement with the actions of his collaborators.

While Hagelin was preaching the virtues of NS to his friends in Germany, and agitating for financial support, Quisling was being implicated by Aall in another direction. A pro-Nazi spy ring centred on Sweden had its headquarters at Malmö, where Aall owned some property. Its ostensible function was the propagation of the doctrine of 'Social Individualism' which had been invented by Aall, who had written a number of tracts on the subject. Like so many other similar movements it soon lost its original purposes and became closely connected with the activities of the Nazi Party. Aall, like Hagelin, had a long history of friendship for the German people and it was not long before he turned to the active promotion of German interests. The Germans desired to extend their influence in Norway in order to counterbalance the marked pro-British strain in Norwegian politics. Aall, closely affiliated to NS and friendly with Quisling, was the ideal person to act in this matter.

Aall's office at Malmö is referred to in correspondence as 'the Central', and during the years 1934–39 it was from Malmö that most of the important policy decisions emanated. The connexion between the Central and NS dates from 1934, when Aall visited a number of prominent NS leaders during a short tour of the principal towns of Norway.[10] The object of the tour seems to have been to collect information about well-known supporters or opponents of NS. Sometimes there was considerable delay in the Central obtaining the information required. It was not until 1935, for example, that Leiv Qvenild, an important NS member from Trondheim, was able to report any progress with 'the task of investigating the family background of Tranmæl' which he 'had undertaken the previous summer'; a reliable source had informed him that 'Tranmæl had a gipsy ancestry and possibly also some Jewish connexion'.[11] Thus it seems that long before Quisling overtly accepted the full implications of anti-Semitism Aall was encouraging that development of NS political theory, and was endeavouring from a very early date, certainly by 1935, to promote a close relationship between Quisling's organisation and his German friends. No point of similarity was too small to be stressed, whether it took the form of ideological agreement, political method or personal ambition. Aall constantly used his position as Quisling's trusted confidant to try to impose his desire for a strong connexion with Nazi Germany.

Through his office at Malmö Aall was able to maintain contact with friends in Germany and Norway, binding them ever more closely together, despite their lack of direct personal contact. He was greatly assisted by Hagelin, who, after 1936, in effect replaced Prytz as Quisling's principal adviser. Apart from infrequent visits to Norway, however, Hagelin was rarely able to contact Quisling directly. Responsibility for liaison was usually entrusted to Aall or one of his emissaries. In many ways this was a sensible arrangement, for the Central had resources at its command which Quisling and NS did not possess. Aall and his organisation provided the crucial link between Quisling and the Nazi leaders, while Hagelin provided many of the personal contacts within Germany.

However widespread its activity, and however many people were involved, the Central was firmly under the direction of Aall, or, during his long absences, of one of his deputies. Because of its international scope, communication between its agents took place mainly by letter or telegram, so that much of Aall's work in the period 1935–39 can be traced. One of the factors which make the investigation of the workings of the Central difficult is the habitual use by its agents of false names and codewords, a practice assiduously encouraged by Aall, who frequently appears in the correspondence in the rather transparent guide of 'Dr Alvaz'.[12] It is clear that the agents of the Central were fully aware that, wherever they were, their doings were unlikely to have the approval of the civil authorities.

A number of people on the fringes of NS were unwittingly involved in Aall's campaign. Among these was an American of Scandinavian ancestry, Professor Charles Stangeland, who lived and worked in Germany, and whose academic interests were economics and statistics. Stangeland's well-known advocacy of Nordic union was useful as a front for the more serious aims of Aall and his Nazi friends and Aall did not hesitate to use him. Several other sympathisers were similarly duped into co-operation. Thus although Aall, Hagelin and Prytz were chiefly responsible for the actions of Quisling and NS in 1940, others were involved in lesser roles and in varying degrees. Some were more conscious than others of where they were going – a factor which further helped to conceal the explicitness and unity of intention of the Central.

Very early in the negotiations Quisling left the promotion of good relations with the Nazis to Aall and Hagelin; nevertheless, his association with the project from the start was an important factor in attracting German attention. He had been an object of interest to the Aussenpolitisches Amt, the Foreign Political Office of the NSDAP (henceforward referred to as the APA), headed by Alfred Rosenberg, almost from the moment of its foundation. Aall and Hagelin were able to tie up the loose strands. Through the Central they gradually promoted policies of common interest to Quisling and the APA. This aspect of their activity was to be the most important in 1939–40, when the influence of the APA came to play a significant part in the formation of German policy towards Norway. We must therefore follow simultaneously the activities of Aall, Hagelin and the APA in order to see how effective the co-ordination of the Central was.

Like many other Nazi organisations, the APA began its activities in 1933. It concerned itself at once with Scandinavian affairs, though these were only one of its numerous interests. At various times agents of the APA appeared in such diverse places as America, the Caucasus, Japan and Rumania. Despite this diffusion of interest, the section known as Abteilung

Norden very soon became one of the most important. It was built up under Thilo von Trotha, who, as Rosenberg's private secretary, greatly influenced the formulation of policy.[13] Once established, the office looked for collaborators among the friends of Germany in Scandinavia, and soon found Norway a likely supporter in Quisling. As we have seen, he had come into contact in 1930 with Pferdekämper, who found him, even at that date, eager to enter into secret communication with the Nazi leaders. For some reason or other nothing came of this meeting – according to one historian, because the Nazis could not see that Quisling could be of any use to them.[14] After the foundation of NS in 1933 they had reason to investigate more carefully his sympathies and intentions.

With the exception of Quisling's relations with the APA details of his contacts with Nazis during these years are scarce. There was certainly some form of meeting, though no details are known as to time or place. Quisling also made overtures to the foreign department of the Reich-sicherheitshauptamt, the security organisation headed by Himmler (henceforward referred to as RSHA) and the Abwehr, the military secret service of the German High Command, headed by Canaris, according to notes made by those in close contact with the two Nazi chiefs. Any other approaches there may have been to German officials remain entirely un-known. Contact with the APA was made through the medium of the Nordische Gesellschaft (henceforward referred to as the Nordic Society), which had originated as an apparently genuine effort to encourage German–Scandinavian amity. Inevitably it had been infiltrated by the Nazis for their own aims. Its annual jamboree at Lübeck provided ready cover for those mainly aiming at the subversion of democratic govern-ment in Scandinavia. Dr Hermann Rauschning, once President of the Danzig Senate, who took part in the annual ceremony on several occa-sions, declared that from being 'the slightly romantic instrument of a valuable cultural mission, the society became the tool of insidious pro-paganda and crass espionage'.[15] The Ministry of Propaganda had tried to use the society, but without success, and had been replaced by the APA,[16] which in its turn had not been spectacularly successful; Dr Sahm, the German ambassador in Norway, later wrote that by 1938 the Nordic Society had the support only of a number of insignificant persons.[17] This estimate was probably fairly accurate, since the most constant source of worry to the Northern Department of the APA was the extent of anglophil feeling in Scandinavia, especially in Denmark and Norway. In both these countries, quite apart from any cultural ties, the national economy was very closely linked with that of Great Britain, and it seems improbable that the Nordic Society, even if properly conducted, could have con-verted Scandinavia to the German viewpoint.

In Denmark, there was a substantial German population in North Slesvig,[18] and the Nazis found a willing helper in Dr Fritz Clausen. Their task in Norway was not so easy, since the German population there was very small and no irredentist movement could exist. The task of the

Nazis, therefore, was rather to adapt a native party to their requirements than to create a pressure group based on a vocal minority, as in Denmark. The party selected by Thilo von Trotha was NS, despite its poor performance in the general election of 1933. He visited Norway in 1934, and, in order to gain first-hand experience of the organisation and methods of NS, he attended meetings at Trondheim and Stiklestad.[19] He was accompanied by Aall, and for the first time there was concerted effort by the APA, the Central and NS.[20] Thilo von Trotha was made very welcome in Norway and was introduced to Quisling. They subsequently renewed their acquaintance in Berlin. This second meeting was followed by a regular correspondence between them. Thilo von Trotha was, however, unable to achieve any close relationship between Quisling and Rosenberg; after an initial meeting in 1933, they do not seem to have met again for several years.[21] Thus NS was not financially assisted in the same way as Clausen's DNSAP. Nor was NS given anything beyond cultural support by the Nordic Society, except for the very occasional subsidies which Aall and Hagelin were able to extract. Although Rosenberg was not outstandingly practical, he seems to have realised 'how small a role NS played in Norwegian politics'.

The promotion of pro-German feeling in Norway between 1933 and 1938 thus fell largely to another organisation, called the Fichtebund (the 'League of the Pine Tree'). This was, like the Nordic Society, essentially a non-Nazi body, but it included many who in different circumstances might well have belonged to NS. This was especially true of Norwegians resident in Germany, many of whom, like Hagelin, might have been expected to be sympathetic towards NS and willing to support the party financially. Either by accident or preference, however, 'the Norwegians in Germany who supported the ideology of the Third Reich frequently held aloof from NS'.[22] The Fichtebund was therefore of some importance, particularly as it numbered in its ranks some potential Nazis, and thus indirectly diminished their prospects of recruitment to NS.[23] The existence of the Fichtebund, together with the lack of regular financial support from the APA, contributed in no small measure to the unsettled position of Quisling and NS at this time.

Yet the APA was by no means indifferent to the fate of NS or its leader. Quisling had, after all, many points of contact with his ideological ally Rosenberg, and this connexion was mirrored in the tone of *Fritt Folk*, from which emanated the same type of theoretical racial propaganda as marked the official outpourings of the APA. Indeed, many of Quisling's articles could well have been extracts from Rosenberg's own works. None the less Rosenberg failed to finance Quisling's movement regularly, contenting himself instead with encouraging Aall and Hagelin. Had Quisling been more successful in the general elections of 1933 and 1936, or in the municipal elections of 1934 and 1937, consistent support might have been forthcoming. It seems plain that until 1938 or 1939, because of his party's poor performance, Quisling was in German eyes merely the leader of yet another pro-German group, although NS was perhaps rather more pro-Nazi and consequently more promising than most of the others.

A further difficulty in the way of APA activity in these years was a total lack of understanding of Scandinavian life. This frustrated many of the attempts to promote pro-German feeling. Thilo von Trotha, whom Rosenberg had described as 'an assistant of mine, who was interested in Scandinavian culture and had written books about it',[24] could make serious, even disastrous, errors of judgement about the Scandinavian political situation. His annual survey for 1934 provides a typical example:

> the situation in the North can be regarded as follows. All five countries (except Iceland) are in a rapid economic decline. Politically Sweden and Denmark are governed by Reds, Norway is confronted by a similar decision. Finland and Iceland are governed by conversation . . . so called pure means of foreign policy are not suited to the North, which is little interested in pure foreign policy.[25]

Considering such radical misconception of Scandinavian political life, it is scarcely surprising that events took the course they did in the years after 1934. The amateur calibre of Rosenberg's staff and their diplomacy was revealed during the immediate pre-war years. The preparations for the manœuvres of 1939 and 1940 were badly conceived and worse executed. The pedantic emphasis on racial theory rather than practical development of pro-German feeling, combined with the elephantine clumsiness of the APA agents in Norway, made the situation of the Nazis in Norway more precarious in 1939 than in 1934, and contributed in no small measure to the failure of German wartime policy.

The relationship between Quisling and the APA up to 1938 therefore was by no means an unqualified success. The APA had neglected Quisling and NS for the Fichtebund and the Nordic Society. By the close of 1939 APA officials were working in close co-operation with those of NS. The reasons for this dramatic change in fortune are not hard to see. The basic reason of course was the change in the international situation after the Munich settlement. But a secondary factor was the enormous amount of work on behalf of NS done by Aall and Hagelin, which began to show results during 1938.

In making contact with important German officials during 1934–39 Aall and Hagelin hoped to build up a reserve of good will. On the whole they succeeded. Aall's correspondence demonstrates that in 1935 the connexion between Quisling and the Nazis was extremely tenuous, founded upon personal relationships rather than hard and fast agreements. By late 1938 things were very different. Aall's contact with the Nazi hierarchy was channelled mainly through Hagelin and Stangeland, both resident in Germany. He himself was spending a great deal of time in Norway and Sweden. Hagelin and Aall's deputies were doing the really hard work, and must be given most of the credit for the revival of German interest in Quisling in 1938.

Their campaign to attract the attention of highly placed officials in Germany was long and hard. In 1936, for example, Aall was complaining to Stangeland about the activity of Soviet agents in Norway, knowing that his complaint would eventually reach the right quarter. He suggested that NS must be strengthened, in view of the approaching election in which it would be pitted against 'our Marxist government'.[26] He hoped that this appeal might produce some financial assistance for NS; he was for the moment disappointed. Later his intentions become more clearly defined. On 22 November a German agent, Max Dinklage, wrote to another agent, named Görlitzer, about the importance of the iron-ore fields near Kirkenes. Dinklage revealed that 'Aall wished to visit certain ministries in Germany to persuade them to take an interest in this vitally important area'.[27] Dinklage's letter to Aall on the following day confirms the increase of German influence within all ranks of NS, involving now such figures as Olaf Fermann, the prominent Norwegian businessman.[28] On 11 December, Stangeland wrote to Aall that he 'had received copies of his memorandum . . . and had sent them to Beyer and Dinklage'.[29] Stangeland had then discussed with Ernst Beyer, a German civil servant, the possibility of Germany showing interest in this area. By Christmas Day, Stangeland, obviously excited by the pace of developments, was writing to Aall to tell him that Beyer 'had sent a copy of the memorandum to Dr Greiner, of the Propaganda Ministry . . . and had later had talks with the high-ranking official, Herr Funk, who was very interested'.[30]

By the end of the year, then, Aall's activities had clearly succeeded in directing German interest to the strategic importance of Norway. He had taken the first step towards his goal. The second step was to interest the Nazi hierarchy in NS and the personality of its leader. This was certainly a more difficult task, but Aall applied himself to it with great diligence. By 1939 his efforts would be crowned with success.

There is no evidence that connects Quisling directly with members of the Nazi hierarchy during this period, but it seems highly likely that he knew what Aall was doing. Certainly Aall at no time indicated that he lacked any support from members of the NS council. If Quisling was ignorant of his activities it could only have been through Aall's deliberate concealment of them, and this seems extremely improbable. Aall's correspondence shows how closely he was in tune with the wishes of NS and how much he knew about their difficulties. On 11 May 1937 he received an appeal from the NS secretariat begging him and his fellow Norwegians in Germany to support *Fritt Folk* financially; otherwise it would 'cease publication next week'.[31] Hagelin also was asked to help stave off this crisis; 'in 1937 or 1938 I agreed to try to help Quisling to obtain German advertisements . . . in order to support *Fritt Folk*'.[32]

These appeals to Germany for help, every time that NS fell into financial difficulties, were bound to give the impression, in Germany at least, that NS was a thoroughgoing Fascist organisation. Events soon confirmed this impression. On 22 June 1937 Fuglesang wrote to Aall thanking him for his offer to procure 'places for one hundred Norwegians in Hitler Youth camps', and adding that he would 'take the matter up with the Youth Organisation'.[33] Such an important step could obviously not have been taken by the General Secretary on his own initiative, without sanction of the NS Council and its leader. Fuglesang was Quisling's personal choice as General Secretary and could have no reason for concealment. The growth of ties between NS and the Nazi Party must not only have been accepted by Quisling, but was probably promoted at his request.

Nevertheless, Aall and Hagelin had to face a number of setbacks. Their contacts in Germany, believing that NS was a serious and effective political force, were sadly disappointed by the election results of 1937. On 29 October, Fuglesang wrote to Aall that 'in the few towns where we put forward lists we suffered a severe reverse';[34] he was intending to come to Germany, accompanied by Thronsen, an NS colleague, and he asked whether he could be given introductions to people 'with whom it would be useful for me to come into contact' and promised to 'make an address to R[osenberg]'. By coming in person Fuglesang hoped to correct the prevalent impression in Nazi circles that NS was dying. Yet it is clear that this electoral disaster made NS more dependent than ever upon German support. While Fuglesang was preparing for his visit to Germany Aall was busily engaged in trying to repair the damage done by the disastrous showing of NS. On 16 November he wrote to a German civil servant called Dräger, informing him of Norway's strategic importance and enclosing a pamphlet on the subject composed by himself. In this he suggested that there was still time to 'rescue Norway from the revolutionaries' through the agency of 'the party, Nasjonal Samling, and its leader, Quisling'.[35] A second letter, undated but clearly written soon after, informed Dräger that 'a political party dedicated to national improvement and to social and international peace in both Norway and the rest of Scandinavia is unthinkable unless it includes Quisling'.[36] Aall further pointed out that the task of leading a pro-German party in Norway was very difficult; only Quisling had the necessary qualities. Hagelin also tried to convince the Germans that Quisling, despite his electoral failures, represented the section of opinion in Norway best equipped to further the fortunes of a nationalist party. Later Hagelin was to claim that his sole purpose had been to help Quisling to obtain a German loan in order to sustain his neutrality policy.[37]

Thus, there is much evidence that through Aall and Hagelin regular contacts had been established between Quisling's party machine and the Germans at the latest by the end of 1937. Several of Aall's letters suggest that Quisling was far from unwilling to develop these contacts, since only through them could he expect any financial help. After the election results of 1937 all the important members of the NS hierarchy accepted the fact that the party was dependent upon foreign assistance. Fuglesang's visit, which eventually took place in early 1938, was therefore made for the express purpose of refilling the party coffers. NS dependence upon the organisation of the Central at this low point in the party's fortunes is evident from the fact that it was Aall who played the major part in stimulating a revival by arranging the visit made by Thronsen and Fuglesang.[28] Nor did recovery from the nadir greatly diminish this dependence. Aall's correspondence with the NS secretariat in 1938 shows that the disaster of 1937 largely deprived NS of any capacity for independent action it had ever possessed. Fuglesang became more anxious to consult Aall, even on trivial matters, before committing the party to a particular policy, especially if it was likely to involve major expenditure. In early 1938, for example, the party council decided to found the new periodical, *Samband*; Thronsen and Fuglesang had already been named as producer and editor. But no final decision could be taken without Fuglesang's seeking Aall's approval and his promise of financial support.[39] Aall's importance in NS can hardly be overestimated; his views were often decisive in the formulation of policy. The fact that Quisling entrusted Aall and Hagelin with the task of establishing a working relationship with Germany underlines their responsibility for the way things developed in 1939.

Events had begun to take a more hopeful turn for Quisling in 1938. The prospects of obtaining large-scale financial assistance for NS seemed firmer than they had ever been before. The important events of that year – the occupation of Austria and the destruction of Czechoslovakia – compelled the Nazis to concentrate their resources upon the fulfilment of these plans. There was thus very little scope for clandestine activity in Scandinavia, and such activity might in any event have alerted Britain to the danger of her position. Thus for Quisling and his party no practical assistance was forthcoming. But, as the international situation became increasingly unstable, the presence of pro-German groups in other countries became more valuable. NS, therefore, received much verbal encouragement, and the personal influence of Aall and Hagelin within certain circles in Germany developed apace. Hagelin regularly saw some of the prominent Nazis. Most important of all was Hermann Göring, to whom Hagelin had been introduced by his brother-in-law, Kurt Irgens.[40] Through Göring, Hagelin met Bürgermeister Dr Max Winkler, who handled a great deal of the Nazi financial transactions with illicit organisations outside Germany, and was thus an essential contact if NS were to gain any financial subsidy.

Aall contributed to the revival of interest in Norway by cultivating his friendship with Rosenberg. During one of his frequent visits to the APA bureau he met Hans-Wilhelm Scheidt, who had succeeded Thilo von Trotha as head of the Northern Department. The resulting friendship between Aall, Hagelin and Scheidt was to have fateful consequences. Scheidt was attracted by the positive attitude of Aall and Hagelin, who kept themselves very well informed about developments in Norway, and could thus make constructive suggestions about the policies Germany might wish to pursue in Scandinavia. Aall corresponded regularly with NS officials, principally Fuglesang, and also visited Norway on several occasions. He even found time to attend meetings of the NS council, at which important plans were discussed, and also the Riksmøtet.[41] Hagelin had less personal contact, owing to his many business engagements, which prevented him from visiting Norway so frequently. But he was equally busy in Germany, and in the summer of 1938 he admitted in conversation that he had 'made a number of visits to German authorities'.[42] Aall and Hagelin were hoping to obtain a subsidy for NS and to be recognised as representatives of the most reliable of the pro-German groups in Norway. In pursuit of these aims Quisling was induced to pay a flying visit to Germany at this time.[43] But the ground had not been sufficiently prepared, and he returned empty-handed.

International developments over the next few months brought about a significant alteration in German policy towards Norway. The events of September 1938 to March 1939 radically changed the outlook of the APA. The probability of war compelled the APA to revise its judgement on NS and its leader. The need for a powerful pro-German party in Norway had become imperative. An old project, now revived by Fermann and Hagelin, caught the attention of the APA at the right moment.[44] The scheme was simple. Quisling's small newspaper, *Fritt Folk*, had fallen upon evil days; if a loan could be obtained the newspaper might be expanded into a daily of at least twelve pages and used as a disseminator of pro-German propaganda. The venture was very ambitious, since newspapers in Norway tended to be rather smaller than their English counterparts, and is a measure of the enthusiasm which Aall managed to impart to his colleagues. It was Hagelin who had put forward this proposal. He apparently 'knew more about the press in Germany than in Norway', and had thought at first that it would be best to publish 'a Sunday newspaper with a somewhat greater number of pages'.[45] Aall, however, had persuaded him to set his sights rather higher.[46]

Despite the enthusiasm shown by Aall, Hagelin and Scheidt, nothing came of it. Hagelin and Aall had to fall back upon other schemes. They had met at Dresden shortly before Christmas 1938 to examine the coordination of their activities.[47] Curiously enough, although they had corresponded regularly, this was probably their first meeting. Aall informed Hagelin that he had succeeded in winning the support of Captain Walther de Laporte, who was attached to the Abwehr. This man was to become a regular correspondent of his, and one of the staunchest advocates of financial assistance to NS.[48] The contacts maintained by Aall and Hagelin were evidently widening.

Their first success was the arrangement of a visit by Scheidt to Norway in the winter of 1938–39. Scheidt was instructed by Rosenberg to travel to Oslo, where he was to meet a number of pro-German personalities. Hagelin had assured the APA that the critical time had come to establish contact with NS. This trip 'opened the way for Quisling to Rosenberg'.[49]

During his visit, Scheidt was introduced to Quisling by a teacher of languages named Günther Kern.[50] He seems to have been favourably impressed, and presumably told Rosenberg as much.

Hagelin and Aall were very satisfied with the results of Scheidt's visit. Although these two worked closely together they did so in spasms – periods of relative inactivity succeeded by brief intervals of energy. Hagelin was certainly working very hard in the spring of 1939. Not only did he deserve credit for promoting his friendship with Scheidt, but in these months he also made great efforts to attract the interest of Göring. He wrote regularly to Göring's nephew, Herbert Göring, an official in the Reichsbank, hoping in this way to influence Göring's policy towards Norway. Aall helped by renewing his contacts within Göring's Economic Ministry. His principal contacts were Winkler, with whom Hagelin was also acquainted, and Staatssekretär Paul Körner, permanent deputy to Göring as 'Commissioner for the Four Year Plan'. Both these men were intimately concerned with the formulation of policy at a high level. Göring's office therefore paid close attention to developments in Norway, and took some interest in the proposal for a loan to NS. Herbert Göring also showed some real enthusiasm, and asked Hagelin for details about Quisling so that he could inform his uncle more accurately. Quisling supplied these details in a letter to Hagelin on 19 April.[51] Herbert Göring's response was favourable and eventually Hagelin felt sufficiently bold to demand a subsidy of 6½m RM. In a letter to Herbert Göring, copies of which were sent to Winkler and the APA, Hagelin wrote:

> We are seeking a loan (in German marks, not in foreign currency) which would set us on the way to shortening our struggle, and would soon enable us to take over power in our country. We cannot guarantee with securities the repayment of the loan, we can only promise that repayment is automatic and will be undertaken as soon as we come to power.[52]

Hagelin made this demand on 18 May and it soon became clear that, before acceding to this request, the Germans were determined to discuss the matter personally with Quisling.

This was a decisive reversal of policy; only a few weeks before, Quisling had been personally snubbed by the Nazi hierarchy. In April 1939 the Nazis had held a great celebration in honour of Hitler's fiftieth birthday. Most of the important figures in pro-German parties throughout Europe were invited. Both Aall and Hagelin were present, but Quisling was omitted. The list of guests had been drawn up towards the end of 1938, and his claims for inclusion had been rejected as a result of the annual report from Norway, pointing out that NS had declined so much as a political force that it was hardly worth consideration. Quisling's omission was therefore scarcely surprising, and every effort to remedy it on Aall's part was in vain. But if the Nazis had forgotten Quisling, Quisling had not forgotten Hitler. He sent the Führer a telegram of congratulation in the name of himself and his party. The telegram referred to Hitler in flattering terms as 'the hero who has saved Europe from Bolshevism and Jewish domination'.[53] Aall, who had travelled from Sweden to be present,[54] felt that the way this message was received augured well for the future.[55] Hoping to reinforce the favourable impression made by Quisling's telegram, Aall had even tried to persuade the other Norwegian guests to sign a letter of introduction for Quisling to the Nazi authorities. The Norwegians were unwilling to co-operate.[56]

The birthday celebration did, however, focus attention on Scandinavia, and during the next few days Aall held a number of meetings at which the future of NS was the principal topic of discussion. On 21 April he met Ribbentrop at the Reich Chancellery.[57] He also had a long interview with de Laporte, whom he had known since 1934. De Laporte and Theodor von Hippel, who was attached to the General Staff of the army, were eager to persuade Aall to concentrate not so much on the political as on the ideological side of his movement's activities.[58] Aall, however, began to negotiate a project he had had in mind for some time; Quisling must come to Germany and deal with the Nazis direct. Hagelin also had been urging a meeting between Quisling and high officials of the APA; on 10 April, Quisling had written to him, expressing his 'hearty thanks for your indefatigable work for our cause'.[59] A few days later Aall left Germany, to consult further with Quisling.[60]

While Hagelin remained in Germany to keep up the pressure, Aall was concerned to build up an elaborate cover for his activities. All his recent actions were concealed under the guise of work for an independent political movement. False names were used and complicated financial transactions entered into in order to deflect attention from the real aims of the Central. The money for the peace movement was supposed to have been contributed by a philanthropic Frenchman named Bary,[61] though in actual fact it was supplied by Hippel from party funds.[62] Aall and Hagelin were certainly aware of all that was going on and were ready to take advantage of any benefits that might accrue to them. But Aall failed to reach Norway; he was delayed at Malmö, and instead wrote to Quisling, asking him to prepare for a visit to Berlin.[63] Ostensibly this trip was to be part of Aall's gathering to promote the foundation of the new peace movement. In fact it was to achieve the meeting for which Aall and Hagelin had worked so long.

On 5 May Hagelin wrote to Aall, who had now returned to Berlin, asking if they could meet on 15–16 May in order to discuss arrangements for Quisling's visit.[64] On 8 May Aall wrote to the finance secretary of NS about the plans which he and Hagelin had in hand for the revival of *Fritt Folk*.[65] Thus it is clear that both men had high hopes of the outcome of Quisling's visit and were counting on a German subsidy for NS. Owing to previous engagements Aall could not meet Hagelin on the dates suggested, so on 10 May Hagelin wired him that he would arrive in Berlin the next day.[66] At this meeting and at a subsequent meeting between Aall and Hippel on 18 May the arrangements for Quisling's visit were completed.[67]

During the next few weeks Aall and Hagelin kept in close touch. On 25 May Hagelin wrote to tell Aall that he had managed to make an appointment for Quisling to meet Herbert Göring,[68] and the next day Aall received a postcard from de Laporte promising full co-operation.[69] A few days later Aall opened an account with the Skandinaviske Bank in Malmö in readiness for the grant which he expected to receive soon.[70] On 31 May he prepared a memorandum on the difficulties of the German position in Scandinavia, to be sent to Werner von Grundherr, of the Foreign Office. Appropriately enough, the memorandum was entitled 'The promotion of German influence in the North'. In this short statement Aall was concerned to 'direct the attention of the German authorities towards the strategic interests of Russia in North Norway and of England in South Norway'.[71] He was also at pains to point out that it was Quisling who could best promote German interests, and that an arrangement ought to be made, if possible, between Quisling and the German authorities. Aall was in effect offering the full assistance of NS and its leader to the Germans in return for a subsidy large enough to keep the party in being.

Aall remained in Berlin at this critical stage, in order to be in a position from which he could control events. On 4 June he wrote to Hagelin, who was still in Dresden, telling him to come to Berlin as soon as he could.[72] Hagelin replied by letter the following day: 'Naturally I am coming to Berlin to talk with our friend. I would be glad if you would reserve a room for me at the same hotel as Quisling. I would also be very grateful if, as soon as you know when Quisling is coming, you would let me know by telegram. . . .'[73] On Wednesday 7 June Aall duly sent the telegram requested: 'Friend coming Thursday evening, Hotel Sachsenhof, room reserved.'[74] Aall had himself been informed only the previous day that Quisling was arriving on 8 June – 'Coming Thursday 8th. 18.13 Stettiner station. Can stay five or six days.'[75] Aall was at this time staying at Stangeland's home in a suburb of Berlin, and was therefore intending to leave Quisling to be looked after by Hagelin. On receipt of Aall's telegram Hagelin at once replied: 'Coming Thursday. 15.30.'[76] All arrived according to plan, and by the evening of 8 June preparations for Quisling's discussions with the German authorities had been completed.

On the same evening, shortly before Quisling's arrival, a briefing session between Aall, de Laporte and Hippel had taken place, at which it was decided to press on with arrangements for meetings with officials from both the Foreign Ministry and the APA.[77] Rosenberg himself met Quisling, but Quisling was tired after his journey and the first meeting had to be short. Rosenberg was impressed by Quisling's zeal and told Scheidt to introduce him to some of the other Germans interested in the Scandinavian question. He suggested an initial meeting between Quisling, Körner and Hagelin to co-ordinate planning between NS and the Economics Ministry. On 9 June accordingly Scheidt introduced Quisling to

Körner[78] at Sybelstrasse 40, a building in a side street off the Kürfür-stendamm. This office was disguised as a joint travel bureau and export-import agency, but it was actually a department of Section II of the Abwehr. Quisling was thus immediately introduced to people at the very centre of the Scandinavian section of German Intelligence. He seems to have seized his opportunity well. Körner discussed the economic and strategic position of Norway with him at some length, and was apparently much impressed by his schemes. It was provisionally decided that the NS funds should be given substantial support. Hippel was told of the progress made at the meeting, and later stated that

> Quisling had obtained financial support through me in order to further the Party's interests through the framework of N.S. The money was to be paid in two or three instalments. It was the first support Quisling received from the Germans. Quisling had explicitly and readily declared that these ideas were the foundation of his programme . . . and would eventually lead to taking over power in Norway's political system.[79]

At the meeting it had also been decided that Quisling should again see Rosenberg and other influential figures later in his stay, after they had had time to discuss the results of the meeting. In the meantime Quisling was to make contact with various acquaintances of Aall and Hagelin who might well be helpful. During the next few days he met a number of Aall's circle, and had a long debate at Stangeland's home with his host, de Laporte and a certain Dr Keller,[80] who was head of another quasi-Nazi organisation active in pan-Nordic affairs, called the 'Bund der Völker'. As a result, Aall's Central received a payment of £4,000 by 15 August from Keller's movement for the purpose of promoting the aims approved by the meeting in June. A further £4,000 was promised in due course.[81] This meeting clearly produced the kind of results looked for by Aall and Hagelin. A number of talks between Quisling and other acquaintances of Aall followed, but there were no important decisions, and this part of Quisling's visit seems to have been of a social rather than a business character.

On 15 June Quisling visited Rosenberg at his office.[82] Present also were Scheidt and Arno Schickedanz, chief of staff of the APA and very much in the confidence of Rosenberg. The conference was a great success. Quisling explained the political situation in his country, stating that Norway was favourably disposed towards Great Britain as a result of 'the extraordinarily clever, democratic and particularly anglo-saxon propaganda which had been accepted favourably by almost the entire nation'.[83] He feared that Norway, like the rest of the small neutral nations, would be drawn into the war which he saw as imminent, and that this involvement would lead inevitably to the triumph of the anglophil party unless NS received adequate support. Quisling lent force to this appeal by his enthusiasm for the pan-German movement which Rosenberg had tried so assiduously to foster in Scandinavia, and he added the suggestion that the long-term aim of any Nordic Union would be victory over Soviet Russia. Such an appeal, as can be imagined, was well received by Rosenberg.

Quisling owed his success at this meeting in no small measure to Scheidt and Schickedanz. These two at least appreciated the probable consequences of active APA participation in Norwegian affairs, and set out to promote the interests of the APA, and, indirectly, their own. Whenever the meeting had seemed likely to come to an inconclusive halt it had been Scheidt who had pressed on with the arguments for assistance for Quisling and his party. In the same way Schickedanz, much more intimately involved in the *haute politique* of the Third Reich than most of the rest of Quisling's contacts, was eager to settle the affair satisfactorily. It was he who appreciated the importance of some of Quisling's statements. In particular he remembered his conviction that 'in the case of a war between Germany and the western powers Norway could not remain neutral'.[84] Schickedanz realised that the implications of this would be very serious for Germany and was anxious to bring Quisling's remark to the attention of those members of the Nazi hierarchy who were concerned about these matters. He accordingly produced a report on the meeting,[85] for the information of Dr Hans Lammers, the head of the Reich Chancellery, to be submitted in turn by him to Hitler himself.[86] In this report Schickedanz provided not only details of the meeting but also an analysis of the Scandinavian situation together with a formal request by Quisling for a loan of about 6m marks. Quisling's meeting with Rosenberg thus had repercussions far beyond the APA.

Encouraged by their successful encounter with Rosenberg, Quisling and Scheidt visited Körner again the next day.[87] The implications of a loan to NS were discussed in full and Körner made various suggestions as to how the loan should be spent. This ended Quisling's mission to Berlin, the importance of which may be measured by the fact that, although he had intended to stay for less than a week, he had eventually spent at least eight days there. He was now free to go on to the annual congress of the Nordic Society at Lübeck. He left Berlin either on the evening of 16 June or early the next morning,[88] and reached Lübeck late on the 17th. Aall, well satisfied with his work, left for Malmö a couple of days later, and Hagelin returned to Dresden.

At the Lübeck congress of 1939 Quisling was one of the star turns. He succeeded in establishing himself as a leading expert on the proposed Nordic Union which was the avowed goal of the Nordic Society. His speech was crammed full of the ideological theories so often put forward by Rosenberg and his German colleagues. But Quisling went further. He did not confine himself to his habitual outline of racial and cultural theory, but expounded his own conception of the outcome of the critical situation in world politics. He told the congress of his fears about the role that Norway would probably play in the conflict. He drew attention to the decisive geopolitical position of Norway in the projected *Balticum*, and to 'the advantages that would accrue to the power dominating the Norwegian coast in case of a conflict between the Greater German Reich and Great Britain'.[89] He made these points with great urgency and emotion. Quisling's career contained few oratorical triumphs, but this speech must be singled out as one of his most impressive. It was received enthusiastically by the majority of his audience and attracted considerable attention both inside and outside Germany.

Quisling's success at Lübeck had an important bearing on his prospects in Germany. The appearance from Scandinavia of members of pro-German societies was a regular feature of the Nordic Society, but so vigorous a statement, from a man who had once held a key position in the Norwegian cabinet, seemed to promise from the Scandinavian peoples an entirely unexpected volume of support for Germany's aims. Quisling's performance was a propaganda victory of which Dr Goebbels himself might have been proud. Soon after his speech Quisling met Rosenberg, one of the most prominent and regular attenders of the congress. Rosenberg was delighted at his protégé's success and went on to elaborate some of the points made in the speech. The discussion which ensued ranged over the themes of politics and power, the desired expansion of Nordic and German influence and the inevitable diminution of Jewish–Bolshevik control. In Quisling Rosenberg had at last discovered a kindred spirit, and it is from this encounter rather than from the less emotional meeting of a few days earlier that their close alliance probably dates. Henceforth Rosenberg saw in Quisling the most suitable person to further pan-Germanic aims in Norway. This was the policy, however mistaken and costly, to which Rosenberg adhered inflexibly until the end of the war.

It was probably on 24 June, with this impressive speech as a background, that Schickedanz composed, at Rosenberg's request, the memorandum which he forwarded to Lammers two days later.[90] It is clear that it was ultimately meant for the attention of Hitler himself. Not only was Lammers then the Executive Secretary of the Secret Cabinet Council, a post he held from 1938 to 1945 and in which he was bound to draw Hitler's attention to any really important document, but Rosenberg's diary also emphasises that the memorandum was intended for Hitler's personal scrutiny. On 11 April 1940 Rosenberg wrote: 'I had already in 1939 given the Führer through the agency of Lammers a memorandum of the politico-strategic importance of Norway.'[91] Thus all the important figures connected with Nazi foreign policy were made aware of Quisling's existence. Prior to June 1939 only Rosenberg and, to a lesser extent, Göring and Ribbentrop, had paid much attention to Norway. After the events of June Hitler and the planning staff of the Oberkommando der Kriegsmarine (henceforward referred to as 'the OKM') became interested parties. Hitler had, as a matter of course, been informed of the scope of Rosenberg's activities in Norway previous to Quisling's visit, but it was the Schickedanz memorandum which aroused real interest. Of the suggestions made by Schickedanz the one which particularly attracted Hitler's attention was that NS should work simultaneously against Marxism and the Anglo-Saxon interests 'under the leadership of former Defence Minister Quisling'.[92] In this way the APA became committed to Quisling.

In order to examine the situation in Norway more closely, Scheidt was sent to Oslo, ostensibly on a holiday trip.[93] During his stay he was able to have talks with several other Norwegians. Among his friends were the head of the military academy at Halden, Captain Fritzner, and the commanding officer at the Norwegian army's largest drilling ground.[94] Reports from these soldiers confirmed that there certainly was a body of opinion within the Norwegian army which favoured Quisling's views. On learning this, Scheidt felt able to inform Quisling that Rosenberg had agreed to a request he had made during his brief visit to Berlin. Quisling had suggested that NS would benefit greatly by the sending of certain of its members, handpicked by himself, to Germany on a short but intensive course of training. Quisling now began making preparations for this scheme while Scheidt returned to Germany well pleased with the results of his visit. The exact dates of his trip to Norway are not known, but they may be tied down within quite narrow limits. He could not have arrived in Oslo before 10 July, since Quisling had written to Aall on 28 June to tell him that he 'would be on holiday in Telemark until about 10 July'.[95] Scheidt's visit must have ended before 24 July, for on that day he was back in Germany, receiving news from Quisling by letter that 'preparations for the NS party are now complete'.[96] Scheidt's trip had been short, but it had materially advanced the connexion between NS and the APA.

In the meantime Aall had been far from inactive. After his return to Malmö he had appointed a certain Winther-Hjelm to take charge of the running of the Central, since his own frequent absences made it impossible for him to cope with the greatly increased volume of secretarial work.[97] Thus he had more time for his propaganda activities and fund-raising schemes. On 27 June he was back in Berlin holding further discussions with Hippel,[98] but by early July he had returned to Sweden. On 7 July de Laporte sent Aall a postcard informing him that he would be arriving in Malmö on 10 July.[99] They duly met and talked over the progress made in Berlin. They then made a short tour of south Sweden in the hope of raising more money for the cause. But their efforts were unsuccessful and Aall had to subsidise Quisling himself. He personally guaranteed NS the sum of 250 kroner a month, which was paid through the Bergen Privatbank.[100] Such were the financial straits to which NS had been reduced in the summer of 1939.

Hagelin also was determined to take advantage of the favourable climate of opinion created by Quisling's visit. He was most anxious to maintain the interest shown by the APA and he therefore kept in constant touch with Scheidt, who was the member of the APA most enthusiastic about assisting Quisling. None the less it is at this stage that a cleavage of opinion as to Quisling's place in Norwegian politics first becomes apparent in Nazi counsels. Quisling's relationship with the Foreign Office had begun well, mainly as a result of Hagelin's contacts; but reports from the career diplomats in Norway were persistently adverse and caused him to fall out of favour with Ribbentrop's department. The rival ideas of the Foreign Office and the APA represented the two main schools of thought over Germany's foreign policy. The former believed in the value of Norwegian neutrality as in 1914–18, and consequently came to believe that Quisling would not only not aid Germany's interests, but by his very extremism and unpopularity would actually do them harm. The APA felt that the subjugation of Norway was essential to the creation of the 'New Order' and that as Quisling was the only prominent figure in Norwegian politics who supported this idea he should be helped. Hagelin, who had a very good grasp of the complexity of the process of determining policy in the Third Reich, was understandably anxious to ensure that the APA view would become official policy.

This is eventually what happened, and much of the credit must go to Hagelin. The adoption of the policy of the APA led directly to the development of German plans for the invasion of Norway. Hagelin realised that the German dilemma could be resolved only by a firm decision on Quisling's future role. The Germans must be made either to support Quisling wholeheartedly or to jettison him. On 12 July Hagelin wrote from his home at Dresden to Scheidt emphasising the difficulties facing Germany. Although Hagelin was mainly concerned about a loan he enumerated the dangers which threatened Norway in the event of war. He believed that Norway would become a Soviet puppet, and that south Norway and Skåne would be used as an air and naval base for an attack on Germany. To counteract such a disaster, Germany would be compelled to expend vast quantities of blood and money. The prospect of such a débâcle could be removed at once through the agency of Quisling. Germany could 'win a victory without firing a single shot'.[101] Hagelin therefore seems to have aimed at some kind of political action in Norway which would render any significant military operation unnecessary. His views on this matter were well ahead of thinking in Germany.

On 15 July Scheidt sent Rosenberg a report on the progress of his visit to Norway,[102] which was in essence a recapitulation of Hagelin's letter of 12 July. Not only did the general tone of Scheidt's report bear a close resemblance to Hagelin's letter but the similarity of phrase suggests that Scheidt transcribed most of Hagelin's information almost word for word. On only a few points was Hagelin more precise than Scheidt. The German had referred to the similarity of the relationship between Germany and Norway to that between Italy and Spain, thus implying that the justification for a potential German intervention in Norway might be very similar to that for Italy's intervention during the Spanish Civil War.[103] Hagelin was much more specific: 'Only a national government in Norway under the leadership of former Defence Minister Quisling can secure the threatened German flank. Such a government would take up the struggle on Germany's side.'[104] No wonder that the APA continued to support Quisling.

The significance of the correspondence between Scheidt and Hagelin can scarcely be overstated. The ties between NS and APA were progressively strengthened, and more people were committed to the line of policy advocated by Hagelin. The effects of the constant contact between Hagelin and Scheidt were significant also as far as both Quisling and Rosenberg were concerned. Quisling was convinced that the sole remedy for the failure of the Norwegian people to recognise the worth of his party lay in the receipt of German assistance, no matter what guarantees had to be given in order to secure that assistance. Rosenberg was persuaded by Scheidt that Germany would sooner or later be forced to choose between a 'coup engineered by pro-German Norwegians or full-scale invasion by German forces'.[105] Rosenberg naturally preferred the latter option, and acted accordingly. It is also worth noticing that Hagelin and Scheidt both played upon the fear of Communism shared by Rosenberg and Quisling. Despite the recent Nazi–Soviet pact, it was clearly anti-Communism which played the major part in Quisling's pro-German attitude during this period. Quisling and Rosenberg feared that, in the event of a war between Germany and the Soviet Union, Norway would become one of the principal battlegrounds, and would be swiftly sovietised. Norway in alliance with Germany would be much better placed. Hagelin and Scheidt thus carried Quisling towards the point of his fateful decision.

Hagelin was not alone in envisaging the military consequences of a full-scale Norwegian commitment to Germany. During July, Aall met Hippel on a number of occasions to discuss the same point. A letter from de Laporte to Aall, written on 20 July, makes it clear that Hippel had considered the possibility of giving military assistance to Quisling, should NS succeed in staging a political coup.[106] Nor was Hippel being unrealistic, for he had consulted Hans Clausen Korff, an expert on Scandinavian affairs.[107] Korff, however, understood that at the moment Hippel meant to leave matters to the civilians. If Hippel, de Laporte and Aall were seriously examining this contingency, then Quisling can hardly have been unaware of such a significant move. It was probably no mere coincidence that Quisling had asked for training facilities for certain of his NS followers only a few days previously. In fact it was in early August that a two-week course was held at the Aussenpolitisches Schulungshaus of the Nazi Party in Berlin.[108] This was attended by about twenty-five of Quisling's followers.[109] None of these items in isolation can be taken as definite proof that Quisling and his friends contemplated some kind of politico-military coup as early as July 1939, but together they strongly suggest that this was just what was in Quisling's mind.

Aall and Hagelin were eager to inform each other of their successes and they arranged to meet at Sassnitz in late July.[110] At this meeting it was decided that Quisling should mount a large-scale propaganda campaign in Norway; if he succeeded in attracting additional support at this juncture, his friends in Germany would be much encouraged. On Friday 28 July, Aall sent Quisling a circular on the political situation and called his attention to the views expressed at the Sassnitz meeting.[111] Aall and Hagelin then arranged for a second meeting at Sassnitz on 4 August in order to examine the progress of Quisling's campaign.[112] Quisling was immediately spurred on to great efforts, and began a tour of Norway in an attempt to rouse public opinion. He concentrated on the dangers of the international situation, and in particular on the stupidity of the British guarantee to Poland. He had attacked the British on this issue before. His editorial in *Fritt Folk* for 6 May had criticised Britain for 'encouraging the natural aggressiveness of the Poles to the extent of being ready to go to war for them'.[113] As the summer wore on, Quisling's attacks on Britain became more virulent and attracted a good deal of attention in Norway.

Quisling's campaign culminated in the seventh annual congress of NS, at Hamar on 11–18 August. In his speeches there, which were given some prominence not only in *Fritt Folk* but also in newspapers with wider circulations, he condemned the British scheme to encircle and isolate Germany, and accused the Norwegian government of seeking to ally Norway to the Soviet Union. 'We cannot trust England' was his repeated cry;[114] and the remedy was a wider Nordic combination (including Germany) capable of resistance to Britain's blandishments. In the prevailing anti-German atmosphere of the time his speeches were not well received outside NS circles, but they seem to have produced the desired effect on the staff of the APA, who were most impressed by Quisling's energetic espousal of a cause so dear to their own hearts. Hagelin and Aall had achieved their goal.

But there were other problems facing the conspirators. The most important was the divergence of opinion in Germany over the potential usefulness of Quisling. The APA continued the campaign to build him up as a powerful figure in Norwegian politics; the diplomats, both in their reports and their actions, persistently minimised his importance. The more pronounced this difference of opinion became, the more radically did it influence further developments. In the summer of 1939 there could be no doubt that the views of the diplomats still prevailed. The power of the career diplomats of the Foreign Office to influence German foreign policy seems, however, to have reached its zenith with the conclusion of the Nazi–Soviet pact on 23 August 1939. Thereafter the role of Ribbentrop and his staff appears to have declined; after the invasion of the Soviet Union on 22 June 1941 it was at an end. Despite the triumph of 23 August the influence of the Foreign Office over German policy towards Norway was short-lived. Even by the autumn of 1939 the reports of the diplomats in Norway were looked upon as the products of prejudice and ignorance, as the hostile influence of the APA and the OKM began to make itself felt. The events of August–September 1939 contributed materially to this development.

Hostility to the Soviet Union had been one of the basic elements in

Quisling's ideology ever since 1929; it had recommended him strongly to the APA. Throughout his summer campaign he had attacked the predatory policy of the Soviet Union; the dangers of Communism were much more serious than most Norwegians believed, and in his final speech at Hamar, on 18 August, he had declared: 'World Jewry will defeat Germany just as Bolshevism was the Jewish victory over anti-Semitic Russia.'[115] Such opinions, previously welcomed by the APA, suddenly became embarrassing after the signing of the Nazi–Soviet pact. Quisling's policy required immediate adjustment – the complete volte-face, in fact, performed by so many Fascist and Communist parties throughout Europe. After a short time in which to recover his balance Quisling responded to the demands of German policy; through *Fritt Folk*, he declared that the Moscow pact had split the Jewish front and removed the Red Army from the world conspiracy against Germany. Not even Quisling, however, could accept the ideological revolution implied by the signature of the pact, and in an editorial he stated that the pact did not represent a reconciliation of Nazism with Communism but a truce in the interests of both.

> The pact with the Soviet Union means nothing so far-reaching as an understanding between the ideologies, . . . between the National Socialist and the Communist outlook on the world. The differences are as fundamental as they have ever been. A neutrality pact between Germany and the Soviet government no more means that the Nazis have become 'brown Bolsheviks' than the Peace of Brest Litovsk turned Kaiser Wilhelm and Ludendorff into Bolsheviks.[116]

The difficulties Quisling encountered in trying to reconcile his views with this major shift in German policy had their counterpart in the relations between the APA and the Foreign Office over Norway. Early in the summer of 1939 it had appeared that the projected loan to Quisling would be expedited by the Foreign Office, but by August it was clear that the Foreign Office had decided to re-examine the position. Paul Körner had asked Dr Winkler to look into the financial aspects of Quisling's request. Neither was as enthusiastic as Scheidt or the rest of the staff of the APA, but the latter had no power to influence the course of events, since the responsibility for financing Quisling lay with the Foreign Office. The outbreak of war in September gave the Foreign Office a plausible excuse to delay forwarding the agreed subsidy. The Foreign Office was not slow to use the excuse and to announce that for the moment nothing could be done.[117] Quisling had to make the best he could of his rather limited Norwegian resources. As he was already dependent on gifts from quasi-official bodies such as the Bund der Völker and a monthly subscription from Aall, this was a bitter pill to swallow.

After the promising situation only a few weeks before, Quisling was very disappointed by developments as the summer passed by. So also were his two lieutenants and his supporters within the APA. All through August and the early part of September Aall and Hagelin strove to regain control of the situation. At the beginning of August matters had apparently been proceeding smoothly and Aall had written several letters to Max Tau, a friend in Oslo, telling him of the success of all his plans. He even made arrangements to see Tau in mid-August, expecting by then that all negotiations would be complete.[118] A few days later, on 10 August, Aall wrote to Köpke, a Foreign Office official, to discuss the best method of payment.[119] The next day Köpke replied, telling Aall that he had had an interview with Hippel and had found him 'a very sympathetic person'.[120] On 12 August Stangeland wrote to Aall about the visit which de Laporte was paying him at that time, and it is clear from the tone of this letter that Stangeland and de Laporte were still confident. They also hoped to be able to arrange a meeting with Hippel in the very near future at which the arrangements for transferring the money would be completed.[121] Aall's reply, dated 14 August, indicated that he expected all to go smoothly,[122] and two days later he wrote to de Laporte, giving some final instructions and sending fraternal greetings to Hippel, 'our friend in Sybelstrasse 40'.[123]

As late as 16 August, then, Aall and his colleagues had no idea that their plans were about to be disrupted. The first indication that all might not be well may be dated from 17 August, when, at Dr Winkler's urgent request, Scheidt sent him a copy of the whole of his correspondence with Hagelin. Scheidt was puzzled at the request and in his letter reminded Winkler that Rosenberg was very anxious that matters should go forward as speedily as possible. He also went to see both Rosenberg and Hagelin to try to discover if there was any hitch; neither of them had at this stage any inkling of the difficulties impending. Rosenberg had already seen Goebbels at least once about the whole affair,[124] to impress upon him the need for swift action to further the publication of pro-German propaganda in Norway. He now attempted to see him again, but if they did meet, nothing seems to have come of it.

On 23 August the situation was suddenly and brutally clarified for all concerned with the Quisling affair. It was readily apparent to Scheidt, Aall and Hagelin that there would be little hope of aid for Quisling at a time when Nazi foreign policy was newly adjusted towards co-operation with the Soviet Union. Aall had by this time arrived in Oslo where he had a series of rather gloomy meetings with Quisling and other important members of NS. Quisling was by this time fearful that nothing would ever come of all the work of his lieutenants, and Aall had hastened to Oslo to reassure him. Quisling's supporters in Berlin were hardly less stunned by the news. Writing to Aall, de Laporte expressed his surprise at the sudden change in German policy.[125] Rosenberg went to see Göring to remind him of the points originally set forth by Quisling. His pleas, however, fell on deaf ears. Göring, like the rest of Hitler's immediate circle, was firmly committed to the lines of policy determined by signature of the pact.[126] There seemed to be little that Quisling and his confederates could do except wait and hope that changing circumstances would alter German policy.

If the Nazi–Soviet pact marked the zenith of the influence of the Foreign Office in the world at large, in Scandinavia it marked the beginning of its decline. Opinion there, especially in Finland, was shocked at the conclusion of the agreement.[127] The political situation in Scandinavia was already tense, and the Nazi–Soviet pact made matters worse. German preoccupation with Poland permitted increased Russian activity in the Baltic area. The fears in most Scandinavian governing circles of intervention or political blackmail on the part of the Russians were intensified, and Germany, seen as the cause of this tension, became the target of increasingly hostile comment in the Scandinavian press. Despite this increase in anti-German sentiment, the Socialist government in Norway was so deeply committed to a policy of strict neutrality that it could not allow even the wave of popular feeling to influence its conduct of affairs. This attitude was maintained even after the outbreak of war. Trade negotiations with the German government continued without interruption.[128] Halvdan Koht, the Norwegian Minister for Foreign Affairs, went out of his way on several occasions to avoid any semblance of hostility to Germany. The difficulties facing the Scandinavian countries in such a situation had been accurately summed up earlier in the year by a Danish journalist: 'Our attitude is one of strict neutrality; which means, in practice, that it will have to be more favourable to Germany than to Britain.'[129]

The German diplomats in Oslo were convinced that the Norwegian government was determined to preserve a strictly neutral attitude. From their despatches to Berlin in this sense, Ribbentrop and his staff made the quite erroneous deduction that public opinion in Norway was not hostile to Germany. The fundamental cause of this error was the fact that the diplomats relied almost exclusively on reports received from governmental or quasi-official sources. These reports fully justified their belief that Norwegian opinion was still undecided as to the relative merits of the belligerents. Reports from Quisling expressed a totally different view. He stated flatly that the parties hostile to Germany had been greatly strengthened by the outbreak of war. On 9 September he wrote a long letter to Hagelin, who was keeping in close touch with the APA,[130] in which he fulminated against 'the Jew Hambro-Levy who is working with the anti-Nazi government . . . in order to bring Norway over to England's side'. At the same time Quisling realised that his task would be a very hard one; 'there exists here a fantastically well-organised anti-German agitation . . . which NS alone resists'.[131] Hagelin at once passed this letter on to Scheidt,[132] pointing out in an accompanying note that 'if Germany wishes to prevent Norway going over to the English side . . . it would be advisable to make the necessary payments'.[133] Although Hagelin's efforts were not immediately successful, it became clear in the following weeks that Quisling had been correct in many of his statements; as a result, his influence and that of the APA rose, while that of the Foreign Office fell.

This struggle for influence continued in Germany during the next few weeks, each side using the same weapon – despatches and reports from Norway. The APA received through Hagelin a stream of information from Quisling and other NS notables. The Foreign Office in defence of its policy pointed to correspondence received from Germany's accredited representatives in Oslo. Matters were further complicated by the death of Dr Sahm, the German ambassador, soon after the outbreak of war. While awaiting the arrival of his successor, Dr Bräuer, the Counsellor of the German Legation, von Neuhaus, acted as chargé d'affaires. Von Neuhaus fully recognised the pacific intentions of the Norwegian government. In one report he stated:

> The profound difference between public sentiment in Norway in this war and the World War has already been reported. It goes without saying that Norway is not wholeheartedly on the side of the Reich even today, but the country has cast off its former bondage to England to a degree that should be heartening to us. Norway no longer believes in the omnipotence of British prestige.[134]

While it is just possible to accept the accuracy of this part of the report, albeit with some reservations, it is impossible to take some of von Neuhaus's other statements at their face value. The irrationality and incongruity of much of the rest of his despatch casts doubt on the accuracy of his theory that Norway was no longer reliant upon Britain. Most notable among the curious theories of the chargé d'affaires was his assertion that the Norwegian Labour Party had radically changed its views on the independence of small countries since its strong disapproval of the rape of Czechoslovakia in March 1939. As evidence for his theory von Neuhaus had stated that representatives of the Labour Party had expressed in secret their 'unqualified pleasure that with Poland the last "feudalistic state" has disappeared from Europe'.[135] All the traditions of the Norwegian Labour Party indicate that such a statement could hardly have had official support. It conflicted not only with the policy of the Oslo Powers, to which the Labour government adhered, but also with editorial comment in *Arbeiderbladet*. In Germany several astute politicians, including Göring, doubted the reliability of these reports. Nevertheless the policy of the Foreign Office still took its stand upon von Neuhaus's despatches. Not surprisingly its credibility began to decline. The counter-version offered by the APA, based upon Quisling's views, began to gain wider support, since the gloomy reports put out by Scheidt had at least the merit of realism.

Von Neuhaus was not the only representative of the Foreign Office who failed to understand the strength of Norwegian public opinion. His sanguine views were supported by Reichsbankdirektor Ludwig and Emil Wiehl, director of the Economic Department of the Foreign Office from 1937 to 1944, who were the negotiators of the commercial agreement with Norway, and who seem to have mistaken the courtesy of the Norwegian government for official approval of German policy. They were in no way supported by Quisling's reports. While the Foreign Office and its Economic Department continued to receive memoranda minimising Norwegian hostility to Germany, Rosenberg's bureau received from Quisling a series of dismal and prophetic warnings. On 18 September, Quisling wrote to Aall outlining the complexity of the situation and welcoming the news that Aall would shortly be visiting Oslo. He was anxious 'that Norway shall not be betrayed'.[136] A few days later Hippel wrote to Aall urging the need for action: 'Many friends', he declared, 'are eagerly waiting to complete the matter taken up in June and July.'[137] Quisling was at the same time informing Hagelin that tensions in Scandinavia were aiding the efforts of Anglo-Saxon propaganda; he was so worried by this that he was ready to return to Germany for further consultations.[138]

During September, Quisling was very active in his attempts to counteract the influence of von Neuhaus. Not only was he ready to fight the official view of the Foreign Office through his agents in Germany but he was also politically very active in Norway. He was able to take advantage of the shock felt by the Norwegians at Germany's impressive victory over Poland. The political climate was favourable to the judicious advancement of pro-German propaganda, owing to the desire of the Norwegians not to offend their powerful neighbour; Quisling was, however, handicapped by lack of funds and by the public contempt in which he and his newspaper were held. Nevertheless he began a vigorous propaganda drive which did not suffer from the crudity which had so frequently marred his previous efforts.

Quisling decided that if his drive was to have any real success it must have the right starting point. Anti-Communism was the theme which would enable his party to capitalise upon anti-Russian feeling. Changes in the editorial policy of *Fritt Folk* during September demonstrate the gradual swing of his opinions back to their position prior to 23 August. On 3 September he had endorsed the Nazi–Soviet pact, but with some caution. By 16 September he was advocating a national union and consolidation of interests in a firm front against possible Soviet aggression. In the issue of 30 September, after his visit from Aall, who was in Oslo from about 24 September to 5 October, Quisling returned to his old theme of international union, referring particularly to the necessity of conquering Communism: 'Our civilisation, which for centuries has been proudly named Europe, now stands on the brink of a frightful crisis . . . and after the crisis has been resolved by a new World War between England and Germany then beware of Bolshevism which is already lurking within the walls and marching up to the very gates.' The dangers of a war between Britain and Germany were clearly outlined, and this marked the beginning of Quisling's attempt to recruit Norwegian support for his idea that the two countries should be reconciled and induced to work together. But the major emphasis of his propaganda was anti-Communist, and some of his predictions were uncannily accurate – 'Will not', he wrote, 'the victory of English policy reduce Germany to Bolshevism,

and invasion by the Red Army put an end to European culture and civilisation in Europe?'[139] Though his views were probably for the moment
unwelcome to Hitler, they certainly met with no hostility from the APA,
which had always been anti-Communist in belief and had regarded the
pact of 23 August as a temporary manœuvre.

The man behind this astute change in Quisling's policy was, in all
probability, Aall. At the end of September Aall had spent a few days in
Oslo and had promised Quisling that the matter to which they had devoted so much attention would soon be brought to a triumphant conclusion.[140] He advised Quisling not to trim his sails to every puff of the
political wind and assured him that his German friends would see to it
that his interests were not damaged by a temporary divergence from
official German policy. Towards the end of September, it became clear
that Quisling's was the only political group in Norway sympathetic to
German aims, and his claim that he alone was 'in a position to change
decisively in a short time the political situation of Norway, provided he
had the necessary, money',[141] began to be treated more seriously. His
estimate of Norwegian public opinion had, indeed, proved more accurate than that of von Neuhaus, with whose wild optimism he had not the
slightest sympathy. He had continually underlined the fact that, for all
Germany's successes, there were many difficulties still to be resolved. In
comparison with Quisling, von Neuhaus had shown amazing inconsistency. On 30 September he had stressed that the position of Germany
had become very strong and had attracted support for German policy.
Yet in the same despatch he had written: 'Here and there a certain fear
is creeping into the hearts of the Norwegians that the Northern States,
too, might be drawn into the orbit of power radiating from Berlin and
Moscow.'[142]

By the beginning of October it was clear to Aall, Hagelin and their
associates, though to few others, that opinion in Scandinavia was so
strongly anti-German and anti-Russian that a switch in policy was imperative. Within Germany also there were signs that those in control of
policy were not entirely satisfied with the situation in Scandinavia. On 2
October Hippel wrote to Aall suggesting 'a meeting in Berlin',[143] and it
is clear that from early October contact between Aall, Hagelin and the
staff of Sybelstrasse 40 had been fully restored.[144] In Norway, Quisling
had regained his confidence and was engaged once more in a massive
propaganda drive. He took up again his concept of European union and
modified his hostility towards Britain. His hope was that Germany's
swift and terrible conquest of Poland would affect opinion in the West as
much as it had in Scandinavia. He hoped that now the way was open for
Germany and Britain to reach a *modus vivendi*.

Quisling's great aim was to promote the cause of European unity. On
11 October he sent a telegram to Chamberlain urging him to guide the
statesmen of Europe back to the paths of reason. He warned Chamberlain
against the danger of Bolshevism as a *tertius gaudens* in the war,

insisting that peace should be established on the basis of Chamberlain's declaration of 30 September 1938. 'The only positive way to effect this is a fusion of British, French and German interests in a federalisation of Europe on the initiative of Great Britain in order to create community of interests and co-operation useful for all parties. . . . You are the only statesman who in the present circumstances can bring back Europe to peace and reason.'[145] It was only a few days earlier, on 6 October,[146] that that Hitler had made overtures to the Allies, and Quisling's appeal may well have been made on promptings from Germany. This point, however, lacks proof and with the rejection of Hitler's overtures on 12 October Quisling's own hopes of success must have been dashed; his telegram met with no more than a courteous acknowledgement.

After the rejection of his peace offers Quisling, like Hitler, did not seem to have any clear alternative plan. The possibility of such rejection without discussion does not seem to have occurred to Quisling any more than it did to Dahlerus or the other dabblers in international diplomacy. He was not an experienced negotiator and he concluded that the reason for Chamberlain's rejection of his overtures was the too general character of his approach. Accordingly he started to work out detailed proposals for a European settlement acceptable to all parties. On 4 November he drafted a treaty which he believed would be acceptable to Britain, France and Germany. It contained all his previous provisions, together with a few new proposals. The draft, however, was never forwarded to the governments concerned, with the exception of Germany.[147] The treaty was in the end given to Hitler for inspection, but as it did not reach him until December, it was not possible for the German authorities, even had they been so disposed, to use it to advance the prospects of peace in the late autumn of 1939. The draft treaty, therefore, achieved nothing useful except to keep Quisling in the limelight.

Quisling was very much dependent on the advice of Aall at this time. In a letter of 4 November he acknowledged that the draft treaty had been composed in conjunction with Aall;[148] Aall stated in 1945 that he had 'an idea that he had helped Quisling draft his proposals for an armistice'.[149] As the correspondence between Aall and Quisling contains no exchange of written drafts they must have met, and since Quisling did not leave Norway in October Aall must presumably have paid a second visit to Oslo in the latter part of that month. Aall kept in touch also with Hagelin, whom he met at Sassnitz on 6 November.[150] Correspondence, however, between Quisling and the APA during October and November was desultory. Quisling still submitted his reports on the situation in Norway and renewed his demands through Hagelin for financial support, which, owing to the unco-operative attitude of Winkler, had ceased to interest the APA.[151] Hagelin nevertheless persuaded Scheidt to put pressure on Schickedanz and Rosenberg to take up the matter once more. Hagelin's efforts did have one important consequence: Scheidt was given responsibility for all correspondence about the loan and was made Rosenberg's official deputy in the matter. This move had been suggested by Scheidt to Winkler as early as August, but at that time without effect.[152] Scheidt was more susceptible to the influence of Hagelin and Quisling than the rest of the staff of the APA. Hagelin saw as much, and made skilful use of it.[153]

After his unsuccessful attempt to intervene in international diplomacy Quisling occupied himself by renewing political controversy at home. During the month of November he was principally involved in a campaign against the Storting. As a result of the critical world situation the Storting had passed a bill extending its own life from three to four years. There had been considerable opposition to this bill within the Storting, especially among the Conservative members, and it had eventually been passed by 123 votes to 24.[154] This measure directly contravened sections 83 and 112 of the Constitution, though some lawyers thought it not to be illegal provided that an election were held on the issue first. Since the measure had been devised precisely to avoid an election, for perfectly proper reasons, the majority of the public seemed willing to acquiesce in a move of doubtful legality. Quisling, however, strongly opposed the measure for several reasons. Like many members of the Conservative and Agrarian parties he objected to the unconstitutional action of the Storting; if fundamental law could be broken once with impunity there would be no bar to further violations. But he had a further reason. His political efforts since the disastrous campaign of 1936 had been geared to a General Election in the autumn of 1939. The prolonging of the life of the Storting had completely disrupted his plans, and from October 1939, the normal date for the next election, his opposition to the government and the assembly became almost hysterical. In *Fritt Folk* he had expressed the hope that the King would declare the Storting to be illegal and dissolve it. The vanishing of this hope in November left Quisling very bitter against the King, and in an editorial of 2 December he described him as 'the heedless guardian of the Constitution',[155] who had failed to protect the rights of the people against the tyranny of the Storting. This attack made little impact on the Norwegian public, whose attention was largely absorbed in international affairs.

Thus Quisling's position was far from comfortable. His support for Germany had isolated him from the vast majority of his fellow countrymen. At the same time he had failed to gain enough German support to be sure of financial assistance. Moreover, his political credibility had suffered considerably from his continual switches in policy. Within a few weeks he had approved, and then condemned, the Nazi–Soviet pact; he had accused Britain of wishing to encircle Germany and then tried to bring about an Anglo–German alliance; and finally he had advocated NS rule in Norway, and yet posed as the champion of democracy. The APA had encouraged his overtures to the German authorities but had been unable to secure him financial aid. The efforts of Aall and Hagelin had not produced the results so confidently predicted in the summer.

instead, German relations with Norway had achieved no more than a precariously poised balance. Norwegian hostility to Germany had increased sharply since the outbreak of war, but there seemed little danger of Norway siding with the enemies of Germany. At the end of November 1939, therefore, Quisling appeared to be doomed to a career of utter political insignificance.

German–Norwegian relations might have been stabilised at this point, had the Germans been better served by their representatives in Oslo. But the Russian invasion of Finland on 30 November changed the situation in Scandinavia almost overnight. Public opinion, unfriendly towards Germany, but previously moderated by the attitude of the government, was now outraged. Germany, the traditional protector of Finland, was blamed as much as the Soviet Union. A storm of anti-German propaganda swept Norway, placing Quisling and his party in a very awkward position. The German government found itself in an even worse plight. The acquiescence of the Soviet Union in the invasion of Poland had been achieved at the expense of German interests and prestige in Scandinavia, a fact which von Neuhaus's optimistic reports had served only to blur. The Nazi–Soviet pact was regarded as a thieves' bargain to plunder their weaker neighbours. Opinion in Scandinavia, especially in the press, came down heavily on the side of the Allies; according to Hagelin, English propaganda scored its greatest success in the days following the invasion, when it seemed likely that the Allies might succeed in involving the Northern states in a conflict with Germany.[156] This information was forwarded to Rosenberg and Schickedanz, by whom it was circulated to other departments interested in Norway. The German authorities reacted strongly, especially as the despatches of von Neuhaus quite failed to alleviate their anxiety.[157] By the end of the first week of hostilities the Germans were ready for a complete turn-round in policy.

The effect of this sudden change in the political situation was dramatic. No one in the APA or the Foreign Office could be sure exactly how the Norwegians would react to a demand for transit facilities from the Allies in any attempt they might make to aid Finland. The only person whose estimate of the situation they felt they could trust was Quisling. It became imperative that he should visit Germany once more. Hagelin and Aall had for some time been urging a second trip by Quisling, and on 24 November Hagelin wrote to say that he had resumed negotiations for a loan. He also told Aall that he could not leave Dresden at once but 'hoped to come to Berlin next week',[158] in order to discuss matters more fully. On 27 November Aall wrote to Quisling urging him to come soon to Berlin.[159] That these two matters were connected is clear from the contents of the letters. In letters to Schickedanz, of 14 September and 26 November, Hagelin had insisted that Quisling must visit Germany.[160] Schickedanz told Winkler at the end of November that 'according to a communication from Quisling's representative in Germany, he is coming to Germany in the very near future'.[161] Hagelin's hope was that Quisling would be able to persuade Rosenberg to take active steps on his behalf. In order to make communication with the German authorities easier, Quisling would stay with Aall and Stangeland, as he had in June.[162]

The reaction of the staff of the APA to the proposed visit was very favourable. On 4 December, therefore, Aall sent a telegram to Winther-Hjelm asking him to contact Quisling as quickly as possible and tell him that a visit to Berlin was essential.[163] He had been worried at having had no reply to his letter of 27 November. His telegram to Winther-Hjelm and Winther-Hjelm's subsequent letter to Quisling[164] had in fact crossed with a telegram despatched by Quisling on 5 December. Quisling's reply was brief and to the point – 'Your letter of 27 November just received today. Coming Friday 8th, evening. Kindly inform Hagelin.'[165] On 7 December Quisling again telegraphed Aall to inform him that he had completed his application for a passport but had not yet succeeded in obtaining a visa; he asked Aall to seek the help of the Foreign Office in straightening matters out.[166] Preparations for the visit were almost complete on the German side, and Aall was anxious that the arrangements should not fall through. Some agitated letters and telegrams passed between Aall and Winther-Hjelm during the next few days, but Aall was able to settle the problem of the visa by direct application to von Weizsäcker, the Secretary of State to the Foreign Office.[167] On 9 December Quisling wired to Aall: 'Coming tomorrow, Sunday, Stettiner station.'[168] All was ready for Quisling's second visit to Berlin.

Quisling and his colleagues were quite clear about the aims of the visit. They hoped not only to obtain a loan for NS but also to establish the party as the principal channel of communication between Norway and Germany. Much had already been done in Germany towards the achievement of these aims. Rosenberg had made every effort to secure the support of Admiral Raeder.[169] He had told Raeder that Quisling enjoyed a considerable following in Norway, citing a letter which Konrad Sundlo, the army commander at Narvik, had recently sent to Quisling.[170] This letter had given dramatic proof of Scheidt's assertions regarding the extent of support for Quisling among the Norwegian officer corps. Aall and Hagelin had similarly lobbied their acquaintances and made sure that they were all aware not only of Quisling's visit but also of his purpose in making it.

On the other hand, among the German representatives in Oslo there was some uncertainty as to the real motives of the visit. Dr Noack, a German historian attached to the Legation in Oslo who knew Quisling well, had no precise idea of what was being planned, although he had had two long conversations with him just previously. Quisling was still much preoccupied with the Russian danger and Germany's need to be prepared against it; he told Noack that the future of Germany lay in the East and in the organisation of the conquered Russian territories.[171] Dr Bräuer, the new German ambassador, was also in the dark. In a report sent to Günther Altenburg, the head of Political Division IVB in the

Foreign Office, Bräuer suggested that, 'Quisling wishes to establish contact with leading German authorities to discuss certain plans relating to Russia. . . . Shortly before his departure, Noack apprised me of Quisling's ideas, which are ambiguous and based on his personal knowledge of Russia; they need not be taken seriously, however, and are completely contrary to our policy.'[172] None of Germany's diplomatic representatives in Oslo – Bräuer, von Neuhaus or Noack – seems to have had any idea of the imminence of German intervention in Norwegian politics. This explains the confusion and contradiction that prevailed in the relationships between the Foreign Office, the APA and Quisling.

In the minds of Quisling, Rosenberg and Raeder there was no confusion about the aims of NS or those of the Reich. Rosenberg expressed the real reason behind Quisling's visit thus:

> Firmly convinced that in the long run a genuinely neutral position in the great conflict would become impossible for the small nations and in his firm faith in the victory of Greater Germany in this conflict which also was an ideological one, Quisling considered it his duty – supported as he was by a small but determined minority – to tie Norway's fate to that of Greater Germany as the new centre of strength of a nordic–germanic life community.[173]

From this ideological position it was but a short step towards actively assisting the Reich in the fulfilment of its political ambitions. In this sense, therefore, this visit to Germany may be regarded as the decisive step in Quisling's career. Previously he had often expressed views which were in public disagreement with German policy; for example, in his opposition to the pact with the Soviet Union. After the visit, although he did not become a mere German puppet, he seems to have considered all his actions in the light of his responsibility to Rosenberg and the APA. This naturally led him ultimately to pursue a policy almost wholly German in outlook.

Quisling left Oslo late on 9 December and arrived in Berlin at 8.00 pm on the following day.[174] His stay in Germany was brief, of not more than ten days in all, but it was packed with activity. During these few days he discussed Norwegian affairs not only with Rosenberg but also with Hitler and Raeder. Rosenberg and his staff had paved the way. On 11 December Rosenberg informed Hitler of Quisling's arrival.[175] He had previously briefed Raeder, who wished to discuss the strategic situation in Norway first with Quisling and then with Hitler. Raeder's meeting with Quisling took place on the morning of 11 December;[176] Hagelin was present, and so was Lieutenant-Commander Karl Jesko von Puttkamer, then Marine Adjutant in the Adjutancy of the Armed Forces to Hitler. Quisling chose the occasion to express some of his more imaginative fears about Allied designs, including an intended invasion of Norway; 'the landing', he alleged, 'has been planned for the neighbourhood of Stavanger, and Kristiansand will be used as the English base.'[177] All the evidence indicates that Quisling gave a very alarmist account of events in Norway.[178] He stated that public opinion was very hostile to Germany and that the Russo–Finnish war had increased Allied influence enormously. In particular, 'England's influence is very great, above all through the President of the Storting, Hambro (a Jew and a friend of Hore-Belisha), who is at present all-powerful in Norway.' Quisling's ideas fitted in exactly with the ambitions of Raeder and Dönitz, and were well received.

Raeder reported this conversation to Hitler at a meeting on 12 December, with Keitel, Jodl and von Puttkamer also present. 'Raeder reported that Quisling, former Minister of War, and leader of the National Party, made a reliable impression.'[179] It is not quite clear exactly what this description was meant to convey, but Raeder's impression of Quisling seems to have been that he would be useful for German purposes. Immediately after the meeting Quisling had a short conversation with Rosenberg in which the role of Hambro – 'the Jew continually works against us' – was examined.[180] They also discussed Quisling's strength in key services such as the railways, the Post Office, the banks and the news bureaux, subjects on which Quisling had already enlightened Raeder. The principal result of this meeting was that Scheidt was officially appointed emissary for all future dealings between the Germans and Quisling.[181] Scheidt hoped thus to be able to co-ordinate the views of Raeder and Rosenberg.

Hitler, Jodl and Keitel had been very interested in Raeder's report; there was a long discussion,[182] in which the means of increasing German power in Norway were analysed at both the political and the military level, and the weaknesses of the German position at the moment were fully recognised. Hitler was particularly alarmed at the possibility of the Norwegian government's tacitly consenting to a British occupation,[183] and he felt that he would like to have a personal talk with Quisling. But before doing so he wanted to talk to Rosenberg, who had known Quisling for some time.[184] Raeder saw Rosenberg first, however,[185] and informed him that Quisling had provided the OKM with new and vital information.[186] Later the same day Hitler summoned Rosenberg to the Chancellery in order to complete the discussion on Quisling's initial *démarche* and Raeder's report. Hitler was not averse to receiving Quisling, but wanted first to hear something about his practical proposals. Rosenberg left with news for Quisling that Hitler wished to see him on the following day, 13 December.

In the course of a long talk with Quisling, Rosenberg seems to have given him some advice on the technique of appealing to Hitler through their common ideology; Scheidt was also present at this briefing session. Rosenberg had hurt his foot so badly that he could not take part personally in the discussions of the next few days, so Scheidt agreed to accompany Quisling to any interviews with high-ranking members of the Nazi hierarchy.[187] The meeting with Hitler therefore went forward as planned. When the Fører and the Führer met, certain other interested parties were present, including Keitel, Jodl, Scheidt and Hagelin. During the interview Hitler stressed that from Germany's point of view the most desirable attitude for Norway, and indeed for the whole of Scandinavia, to take would be one of complete neutrality.[188] This declaration, however, must be understood with some reservations, in the light not only of what followed, but also of Hitler's usual requirements from neutrals. Hitler's view of neutrality resembled the new non-belligerence of Italy and Spain, rather than the orthodox form of neutrality used in international law.[189] The kind of neutrality he demanded from Norway would, in all probability, have been unacceptable to the Norwegian government.

As was usual in interviews with Hitler, the most prominent part was taken by Hitler himself. He spoke for about twenty minutes on the Norwegian situation. Quisling was then permitted to make his suggestions for a change in German policy. He emphasised particularly the danger of the strangulation of Germany by a blockade by the British based on their domination of Denmark and Norway. The point was warmly received by Hitler, who in the course of his own harangue had declared that 'he had no intention to enlarge the theatres of war to draw other nations into the conflict. If, however, the enemy were preparing an enlargement of the zones of war with the aim to further throttle and threaten the Greater German Reich then, of course, he would be obliged to arm against such steps.'[190] Quisling could thus take advantage of Hitler's obsession with his fear of encirclement to commend himself to the Führer as a trustworthy ally. Certainly the meeting seems to have been a great success and Hitler informed Quisling that the long-awaited subsidy would soon be forthcoming. Quisling returned with Hagelin and Scheidt to the APA to discuss the progress of their schemes. In the evening they went to report to Rosenberg, who had had to stay in bed because of his injury. Rosenberg was pleased with their account of the meeting and noted in his diary that Quisling 'came back very contented'.[191]

On 14 December Raeder went to visit Rosenberg at his home in response to an invitation.[192] Rosenberg was anxious for Raeder's co-operation in counteracting the opposition he had met with from the Foreign Office. He told Raeder of the meeting between Hitler and Quisling and had asked him for his support. At their meeting Raeder and Rosenberg discussed the Norwegian situation in the light of Quisling's visit, and established a partnership which was to enable them not only to co-operate with each other but also to co-ordinate their efforts with Quisling's plans. Very little is known of the details of Quisling's movements during 14–17 December, but certain incidents stand out, showing how he missed no opportunity of deceiving those who patently opposed him or of ingratiating himself with people who might be induced to support him. During these days he was occupied in meeting lesser members of the Nazi hierarchy who wanted to know more of the purpose of his visit, and in paying social calls on a few old acquaintances.

It was probably on 14 December that Quisling went to the Foreign Office in company with Noack, who had come to Berlin expressly to promote his interests.[193] While at the Foreign Office, Noack inadvertently let slip the news that all the efforts of Altenburg and von Weizsäcker had not succeeded in preventing Quisling from having his interview with Hitler. Von Weizsäcker immediately responded by sending an urgent request to Bräuer for more information on Quisling.[194] The ambassador replied on 17 December,[195] but for the remainder of Quisling's visit to Berlin the Foreign Office was left in a state of utter confusion, since it was clear that Quisling had been very much more successful than had been expected in attracting the interest of influential figures. On 16 December Quisling conferred with von Puttkamer, who had been asked by Raeder to act as liaison officer between the OKM and the APA, and with Walther Hewel of the Foreign Office, who was from 1938 to 1945 Ribbentrop's personal representative attached to the Führer's staff. Two days later Quisling had another long discussion with Hewel, who on this occasion was accompanied by Colonel Rudolf Schmundt, Hitler's adjutant.[196] On both occasions Hagelin and Scheidt were also present. Practical arrangements for liaison were settled to the satisfaction of all concerned, and detailed arrangements for the loan promised by Hitler were completed.

Rosenberg was eager for Quisling to meet Hitler once more in order to cement their friendship. Hitler also wanted to make sure that Quisling was quite clear about his commitments to Germany. A second meeting between them was therefore arranged. It is not certain exactly when this encounter took place,[197] but in all probability it was on the afternoon of 18 December. Hagelin and Scheidt were present as well as the expected participants from the German side, Jodl and Keitel. As on the former occasion, the discussion was preceded by a long harangue from Hitler on the strategic importance of the North in his scheme for a 'New Order'. When he had ended, he was handed a memorandum entitled 'Reflections on the Faroes, Iceland and Greenland, the former Norwegian appanages'.[198] If there was to be any readjustment of the balance of power in the North, Quisling was anxious to stake Norway's claim to these territories. The memorandum seems to have produced a lively discussion on Nordic unity and kindred topics of interest to Hitler and Quisling. Hitler then made a definite commitment to NS and its leader. Financial aid for the promotion of pan-Germanic ideology and other propaganda was firmly promised. Military matters were to be transferred to a special staff, which was to assign a personal mission to Quisling. Political affairs were to be managed by Rosenberg, while financial aid would be provided by Ribbentrop. The appointment of Scheidt as liaison officer was confirmed, and it was agreed that he should be attached to the staff of the Naval Attaché in Oslo. Finally the strictest secrecy was enjoined upon all those involved in the scheme.[199]

The meeting, which lasted only for an hour or so, seems to have been very cordial.[200] The personal relationship established between Hitler and Quisling was clearly one of friendship as well as of business. Quisling 'received a strong impression that Hitler was very attached' to him.[201] One of the most important topics of discussion at this second meeting was exactly how Quisling proposed to counter the leaning of Norwegian opinion towards the Allied cause. According to the report of the meeting given by Quisling to Rosenberg, Hitler was fearful of the possibility of British intervention in Norway, relying on Norwegian co-operation, or, at least, passivity. His belief that Quisling might be able to resist such an intervention was an important factor in his final decision in Quisling's favour. He asked Quisling whether he realised that 'if you apply to me for help England will declare war on you', to which Quisling replied that he 'knew and reckoned with this, and also with the temporary dislocation of Norwegian trade'. Quisling, then, was aware of the consequences of attempting a political *coup* in order to rid himself of his enemies and the friends of Britain. Hitler and Quisling then discussed other questions of interest connected with the activities of the pro-British party in Norway, and the meeting concluded on a note of complete agreement. Quisling asked Hitler if he was sure that he would help NS and the Führer replied, 'Yes, that I will do.'[202] There can be no doubt that at the end of the meeting Quisling believed that he and his party had obtained a promise of assistance and was fully aware of the strings attached to such aid.

This meeting brought Quisling's duties to an end, as far as official visits were concerned. He was able to spend a few days in the company of his friends – Aall, Hagelin and Stangeland. Hagelin wanted to return soon to Dresden and on 20 December Quisling, Hagelin and Scheidt called on Rosenberg to bid him farewell.[203] Scheidt and Quisling soon after departed for Oslo. It is not clear exactly when they left Berlin, but it is known that Quisling was back in action by 24 December, [204] so presumably his departure cannot have been later than 22 December. He returned to Norway a happy and successful man. Admittedly he owed much of his success to the brilliant and tenacious preparatory work of Aall and Hagelin, but this must not be allowed to obscure the fact that during his trip he had achieved a great personal success. His visit was an irrevocable step forward, which was ultimately to lead to the fateful events of April 1940, when his fellow-countrymen would see openly the extent of his commitment to the German cause.

Chapter 5 BEFORE THE INVASION

DESPITE QUISLING'S commitment to the German cause in December 1939, it would be wrong to imagine that from that point the German invasion of Norway was inevitable. The central part played by Hagelin and Aall in sponsoring Quisling's visit to Germany indicates that in the shaping of German policy there had been other and more powerful influences at work impelling Hitler towards the decision to make an active intervention in Norwegian affairs. Thus the German invasion cannot be directly attributed to one specific cause, or to one particular person. Nevertheless Quisling played a key role in the determination of policy. Just as he convinced Hitler that it was in Germany's interests that NS should form the basis of any new government that might be set up in Norway, so did he assist in the conversion of the OKM and the Oberkommando der Wehrmacht (henceforward referred to as the OKW) to an aggressive policy. In this way, out of an optimistic political scheme there grew a military plan which in due course completely dominated discussions on Norway.

Although in early 1940 Quisling's contacts with Germany were more limited than in late 1939, his views still carried influence through the agency of Raeder and Rosenberg. While the early contacts with the APA and the Foreign Office provided the basis of an arrangement between Quisling and the Reich, it was duing the spring of 1940 that plans were more fully evolved, and eventually put into action. Their evolution was neither smooth nor continuous. Quisling's personal relations with Nazi Germany continued to be spasmodic, and, to complicate matters still further, enthusiasm for his schemes varied from week to week among his friends in Germany. The relationship thus came to display characteristics familiar to students of the working of the Nazi Party. Ruthless and brutal policies were adopted with amazing casualness and lack of consultation. Quisling's success in persuading Hitler to adopt a course of action favourable to his interests can be explained only by examining in detail the working of the German military machine in the light of the developments in international relations during the winter of 1939–40.

The situation in Scandinavia was modified by various changes in international politics during the spring of 1940. Early in the year the Allies were contemplating intervention in Finland, primarily to enable her to resist Soviet aggression, but also for an opportunity to cut off Swedish iron-ore supplies to Germany.[1] Finland's surrender on 12 March profoundly influenced the course of events, for it deprived both the Allies and Germany of a ready-made excuse for intervention in Scandinavia. The result was that during a vitally important period of the war neither German nor Allied policy was consistent. This factor alone bred mutual suspicion, and possibly contributed much to the events of April 1940. Certainly the fluctuations of policy strengthened the position of Quisling, who was at least consistent on the chief matter in dispute – the role of Norway in the war. The increased activity on the international scene reacted in contrasting ways upon the part allotted to Quisling by the Germans. The extension of activity on the part of the belligerents diminished his overall importance. Nevertheless, since support for Germany in Norway was very limited, his assistance, paradoxically, became more necessary. The clumsiness of German diplomacy alienated many Norwegians who had at first been favourably disposed towards strict neutrality, and this forced the Germans to rely more and more heavily on Quisling. It was a symptom of his new position that he became concerned with Norwegian–German relations on a much greater scale than before. Throughout the spring of 1940, his views and political activities were anxiously scanned by the Germans, for in many cases he provided the only satisfactory information available to them. Quisling always seems to have tried to tell Raeder and Rosenberg what they wished to hear, and this partly explains his importance.

In addition to modifications required by the developments on the international scene, German policy was able to evolve only in a limited way, on account of certain internal dissensions. The principal causes of these dissensions were differences of opinion as to whether to act in Norway, how any such action should be carried out, and further, when it should take place. Some of the disputants, such as Bräuer, held throughout to one viewpoint; others did not consistently support either the activists or the 'wait and see' party, and it was several months before a final decision was reached. The activist group included Rosenberg, Raeder and, later, the OKW. The opponents of intervention in Norway were to be found principally among the professional diplomats and the Army General Staff. The methods to be used created further divisions. Rosenberg and Quisling favoured a political *coup*, followed by German military backing on a limited scale. Raeder wanted the navy to lead a full-scale invasion, while the OKW wished to use the navy as only one part of a complex operation. Beyond these technical difficulties there was a third question – the date of the operation. Rosenberg and his staff advocated speedy action. The OKW wanted to postpone the operation until elaborate plans could be formulated. Raeder, while always in favour of planning, wavered between the two views. And over all their disputes towered the figure of the Führer himself, apparently uninterested in the problems facing his lieutenants. But since he alone could make the final decision, the central problem for his subordinates was that of persuading him to accept their plans. It was the pro-Quisling group which was finally victorious.

The OKM and the APA were, to begin with, the only bodies which supported Quisling against the traditional policy advocated by the Foreign Office. But in the end, the strategic requirements of the war and the accumulation of circumstantial evidence of co-operation between Britain and Norway led to the triumph of the OKM and the APA over their more optimistic opponents. The victory of the forward party did not, however, result in immediate action, for the OKW strenuously resisted all attempts to rush an invasion through without adequate planning. In the final dispute also over the date of the operation, the OKW restrained the impetuosity of the OKM. This caution derived partly from the optimistic reports received from the embassy in Oslo. Moreover, the OKW was less susceptible to Quisling's influence than the APA or the OKM and therefore less likely to embark upon a risky adventure. Quisling's influence, indeed, was not equally strong in all the top ranks of the Third Reich, and this contributed materially to the difficulties of the policy-makers. It was in this atmosphere of doubt and disunity that the attack on Norway was first mooted, then approved and finally put into operation.

Quisling's part in the original formulation of German policy is much more difficult to estimate. The basis of that policy had, after all, been laid long before his second visit in December 1939. It is clear from Raeder's testimony at Nuremberg that the invasion of Norway had been under consideration by the OKM planning staff almost from the outbreak of war.[2] On 3 October Raeder had framed a questionnaire entitled 'The gaining of bases in Norway', in which he had declared that 'the chief of the Naval War Staff considers it necessary that the Führer be informed as soon as possible of the opinions of the Naval War Staff on the possibilities of extending the operational base to the North'.[3] Dönitz also considered the matter and wrote a memorandum setting out the advantages and drawbacks of an invasion of Norway. In the concluding paragraph he proposed, '1. Establishment of a base in Trondheim, . . . 2. Establishment of the possibility of supplying fuel in Narvik as an alternative.'[4] Although Raeder and Dönitz were instrumental in promoting the Norwegian question to a position of importance in German strategic planning, the idea had not originated with either of them but with Admiral Karls, Commander-in-Chief, Navy Group North. Karls had written a letter to Raeder about Norway, from which Raeder had prepared his questionnaire and some notes for a report he made to Hitler on 10 October. Later in the war Raeder acknowledged that Karls had played an essential part in the Norwegian affair. In a letter to Admiral Assmann on the origins of operations 'Barbarossa'[5] and 'Weserübung'[6] he recounted how 'during the weeks preceding the report on 10.10.39, I was in correspondence with Admiral Karls, who, in a detailed letter to me, first pointed out the importance of an occupation of the Norwegian coasts by Germany'.[7]

Raeder's reasoning seems to have weighed heavily with Hitler from the earliest days of the war, and especially during the winter of 1939–40. A comparison between the intentions of Hitler before and after the report of 10 October illustrates Raeder's influence. As late as 9 October, in a famous memorandum on the direction of the war, Hitler had declared, with reference to the Northern states: 'Provided no completely unforeseen factors appear, their neutrality in the future is also to be assumed.'[8] After Raeder's report the possibility of invasion seems never to have been far from the Führer's mind.

The origins of Raeder's desire to consult with Quisling are thus clear, and it is surprising that contact was delayed till December. In fact at the trial of Raeder at Nuremberg an attempt was made to prove that he had been in close contact with Quisling through the agency of Hagelin long before their meeting on 11 December. It was believed that this contact would explain the pressure Raeder put on Hitler towards the end of 1939. The accusation was based upon an affidavit sworn by Erich Giese, an employee at Raeder's office in Berlin, who claimed that he had seen Hagelin visit Raeder. But Admiral Schulte-Mönting, Raeder's chief of staff from 1939 to 1943, conclusively refuted this charge.[9] Although Quisling did produce evidence of the type which Raeder needed to convince Hitler it does not seem to have been available until their meeting. It is not impossible that Hagelin may have met Raeder by chance at some Nazi function and spoken to him there, but he would surely have reported such an incident either to Scheidt or Aall.

The explanation for Raeder's anxiety about Norway, and consequently for his demands for action, lies simply in his foresight and the intelligent observations of Admiral Karls and Admiral Canaris. If no decision was reached in the autumn of 1939 it was because of the absence of substantiated evidence of Allied intentions in Norway. This gap Quisling later tried to fill, but the existence of Raeder's tentative plans removes from Quisling the responsibility for the initiation of discussions leading directly to the invasion. His willing co-operation thereafter suggests, however, that in time he also would have put forward conquest as Germany's only solution to the Norwegian problem.

Quisling's influence on the development of German policy towards Norway reached its peak during the months of January–April 1940. This influence did not assist in the evolution of a consistent and unified policy. After December 1939 the number of bodies closely concerned with Norway, and hence with Quisling's activities, rose to three. The interests of the OKM were added to the conflicting ambitions of the APA and the Foreign Office. The opinions of Quisling, previously almost unknown to the OKM, had thenceforth to be considered, even if not acted upon. Although Quisling's visit undoubtedly increased his standing in Germany it had serious side effects. German policy never recovered from the division in opinion over the desirability of the trip. While the APA and the OKM on the whole accepted Quisling's reports, the Foreign Office did not feel able to do so, chiefly because many of its staff were experienced in evaluating reports of the type which Quisling sent to his German supporters. Unlike the other two bodies, the Foreign Office had its own representatives in Norway, trained to report on political developments. These men, particularly Dr Bräuer, realised that Quisling's analyses of the situation were grossly inaccurate. Despite all its warnings, amply justified after the invasion, the Foreign Office remained a voice crying in the wilderness. Experience was ignored in favour of ambition.

Quisling's difficulties with the Foreign Office after the invasion stemmed from the poor understanding between them in early 1940. This disagreement may in turn be traced to a basic divergence of opinion as far back as 1936. The reports of the diplomats in Oslo did not often mention Quisling before 1939, though in 1936, after the General Election, Dr Sahm, the ambassador, reported that NS was unlikely ever to play any important part in Norwegian political life. Later Sahm wrote that both NS and Fedrelandslaget had 'almost completely vanished from the political scene'.[10] This opinion was repeated towards the end of 1938 – 'NS, led by Quisling, the former Minister of Defence, has almost entirely disappeared from the picture.'[11] Unfortunately Sahm died soon after the outbreak of war, and was succeeded in November 1939 by Bräuer. The new ambassador asked von Neuhaus, who had been chargé d'affaires during the interregnum, to send him a detailed exposition of the political situation. Among other things von Neuhaus told Bräuer about Quisling's latest scheme for ending the war.[12] After the failure of his approach to Chamberlain Quisling had decided that if he sent Prytz to London he could negotiate a peace between Britain and Germany. Even the optimistic von Neuhaus had been pessimistic and discouraging about this plan.

Bräuer faced his first meeting with Quisling with some trepidation, fearing that he would be dragged into the support of another crazy diplomatic venture. Their first encounter was on the evening of 27 November 1939, when a German book exhibition was opened in Oslo. During the course of conversation Quisling reviewed the Norwegian and international situations and informed the ambassador that he felt Germany would not in the long run derive much benefit from the Nazi–Soviet pact.[13] Bräuer, as a member of the body responsible for negotiating the pact, was not very impressed by this analysis. Quisling's prophecy, however, proved to be correct, at least as far as Norwegian–German relations were concerned, when, a few days later, Finland and the Soviet Union found themselves at war. Germany's prestige in Norway promptly receded still further.

The only member of the diplomatic staff in Oslo who had any sympathy for Quisling was Dr Noack, who was collecting material for a book on Norway and Nordic history, and had a desire to play an active part in politics. During late 1939 he acted as middleman between the Foreign Office and Quisling. His reports to Günther Altenburg were, however, treated with caution. From his contacts with various Norwegians, amongst them Aall, he had come to know Quisling. Despite Ribbentrop's orders[14] to Noack to refrain from meddling in politics, he struck up a friendship with Quisling, whom he had met through other Norwegian acquaintances, including Aall. Although Noack at first thought Quisling a crank,[15] he soon became a convert to his views and was convinced by him of the vital geopolitical position of Norway. In the first week of December he visited Quisling twice, and discovered that he believed the Soviet Union to be Germany's real enemy.[16] This was directly contrary to Germany's 'new course' in foreign policy, and Noack felt that Quisling's views were sufficiently important to be brought to the attention of the Foreign Office. After their second meeting he agreed to write a letter of introduction for Quisling to his contacts in the Foreign Office, Professor Fritz Berber and Günther Altenburg. This he did on 9 December, as Quisling was about to leave for Germany. On the following day Noack went to see Bräuer, before leaving himself for Berlin.[17] On his arrival there on the evening of the 11th, he telephoned both his contacts about Quisling. On the morning of the 12th he went to their department, but was received with little interest, being told merely to keep out of the whole affair.[18] Despite all his efforts to persuade von Grundherr and his colleagues the Foreign Office refused to take Quisling's views seriously. Quisling had no greater success when he met von Weizsäcker; this was probably on 14 December, and the State Secretary reported that it was 'impossible to conduct a political discussion with him on a serious basis'.[19] Thus the one man who might have been able to put relations between the Foreign Office and Quisling on a satisfactory footing was ignored, and his protégé was insulted.

Neither Quisling nor the staff of the Foreign Office was able to forget that in the opinion of certain senior diplomats and permanent officials this visit ought never to have taken place. Once Quisling had arrived, the earnest hope of the Foreign Office was that he would depart as soon as possible, preferably without having seen anyone of any consequence. On 14 December Altenburg wrote to Bräuer about the difficulties he had endured as a result of Noack's advocacy of Quisling's cause:

> As for the occasion of his present visit in Berlin – the trip of [State] Councilor Quisling – I immediately characterised the whole business to him as naïve and then put him in touch with the proper official, Herr von Grundherr. Their conversations had the desired effect, that Quisling gave up his plan to take his project to the Foreign Minister or even to the Führer.[20]

Altenburg believed that he had also succeeded in preventing Quisling and Noack from bothering von Weizsäcker with their requests for assistance – 'Even the easy solution of a conversation with the State Secretary was given up.'[21] This optimism was ill-founded. As soon as the news of Quisling's meeting with Hitler reached the Foreign Office von Weizsäcker sent off a telegram to Bräuer demanding details – 'Please telegraph immediately what else you know about State Councilor Quisling and his movement, as well as about Director Hagelin, who also is now in Berlin, and the standing of both figures. . . . Reply is requested by Monday morning, December 18.'[22] Despite this sudden change of front, its logical consequence, the acceptance of Quisling by the officials of the Wilhelmstrasse, in the role assigned to him by Rosenberg and Raeder, was never achieved.

Quisling's success of 11 December with the staff of the OKM was not repeated in his interviews with Hewel on 16 and 18 December. It proved impossible to reach any agreement over finance, though on the surface all parties seemed to be satisfied and at the first meeting, an open breach was avoided. The second meeting, however, failed to remove the explicit differences of opinion indicated at the first and the encounter ended without result. One of the reasons for this breakdown lay in the fact that by 18 December Hewel had been briefed with Bräuer's reply of the previous day, which so emphasised Quisling's anti-Soviet opinions as to persuade Hewel that Quisling would not be a very useful collaborator. In addition Bräuer's statement that 'Director Hagelin is not known to the Legation'[23] convinced Hewel that NS must be almost unknown and therefore insignificant. Altenburg and von Weizsäcker already opposed Quisling, the latter owing to his personal knowledge of Norway, where he had many friends. At the meetings between Hewel and Quisling, however, it gradually became clear to the staff of the Foreign Office that the Norwegian had the backing of both Rosenberg and Raeder, and probably that of Hitler himself. In these circumstances von Weizsäcker felt that it would be prudent for him to dissuade Ribbentrop from opposing Quisling openly.[24] The episode shows the lack of communication between the various German departments dealing with Norway. The day after Quisling's first meeting with Hitler it was still Altenburg's belief that Quisling had given up hope of such an interview. Similarly on the morning of 18 December Hewel had decided that Quisling was an insignificant figure who could be ignored. Yet later the same day, Quisling's momentous second meeting with Hitler took place, at which Hitler made financial arrangements with which the Foreign Minister was obliged to concur.

But although opposition to Quisling was not expressed as openly as before, it still existed within the Foreign Office. After his return to Norway reports from Oslo became even more conflicting. Quisling repeatedly emphasised the strength of the friendship between Norway and Britain, which he believed would permit the British to do much as they liked. The embassy, on the other hand, continually referred to the desire of Norway to remain neutral, and these reports, though inaccurate on certain issues, were far truer records of public opinion than those of Quisling, Scheidt or Hagelin. Bräuer's reports were usually factual and accurate, and seldom distorted by theory or optimism, as those of von Neuhaus had been.

Bräuer was mystified by the success Quisling had in Berlin. He felt that the Foreign Office had let him down by not drawing more attention to his despatches. On 15 December, for example, he had written:

I have pointed out in previous reports that Norwegian feeling regarding Germany is deteriorating in proportion as the Russo–Finnish conflict sharpens. Recently the rumor has been assiduously spread by word of mouth, especially via Sweden, that Germany would take advantage of Norway's increased involvement in the north to invade Scandinavia from the south. This rumor has been attacked with gratifying severity in the newspaper *Tidens Tegn* by Benjamin Vogt, who was for many years Norwegian Minister to London.[25]

Bräuer had also tried to stop the financial assistance to Quisling which had apparently been promised him in early December.[26] In his telegram of 17 December Bräuer had claimed: 'Despite his personal prestige, Quisling's political influence and prospects are . . . very slight.'[27] *Fritt Folk* had a maximum circulation of a thousand copies, and its influence in Norway was negligible. This state of affairs would continue even if the newspaper received a heavy subsidy. Bräuer felt that if proper notice had been taken of these views from the start, Hitler could not have conceivably been sanguine as to Quisling's prospects. Moreover he had done his best to kill the notion that NS was a powerful force comparable with the Nazi Party in Germany in the early 1930s. He dismissed the party contemptuously, declaring: 'This movement, which showed some modest growth at the outset, has suffered a great decline since the parliamentary elections of 1936, in the main probably because the social and economic conditions essential for the movement were lacking in Norway.'[28] Unfortunately this estimate also was ignored by the authorities in Germany. The foundations of covert opposition between the APA and the Foreign Office had thus been laid, and, during the German occupation of Norway this division of opinion came to the surface with disastrous consequences for all concerned.

The duality of opinion over Quisling's merits as the fount of pro-German propaganda in Norway was ignored by Hitler. After the consultations of December 1939 even those reluctantly connected with Quisling and Norwegian affairs were obliged to take an active part in pursuance of the Führer's aims in Scandinavia. Bräuer, Hewel, Altenburg, von Grundherr, von Weizsäcker – all might disapprove, but to no avail. It is hardly surprising that liaison between the various parties was one of the most difficult problems. Contact with Norway continued – in the hands of Scheidt in Oslo, in those of Hagelin and Aall in Berlin. Their system of communication did not really conceal the fact that no place had been left for the Foreign Office. Given a chance, the Foreign Office would have seen to it that active interference by Germany in Norway came to an end. The persistence of the pro-Quisling lobby saw to it that the Foreign Office never had the chance.

Rosenberg and Quisling were not so elated by their success that they failed to realise that much work still remained to do. Their relationship, like that in general between high-ranking members of NS and the staff of the APA, was very cordial. On one occasion Rosenberg recorded:

> Quisling thanked me warmly for my decisive help and for the immediate understanding of the whole plan. I laughingly answered that my supervision of the Nordic Society had been only in the nature of a psychological preparation. . . . We shook hands and looked forward to meeting each other again when the affair had been settled and Quisling named Norway's Prime Minister.[29]

Rosenberg's attitude was a great contrast to that of the Foreign Office.

The most important figure, Hitler himself, had already decided what must be done. After his discussion with Raeder, Jodl and Keitel on 12 December, the Führer had ordered a complete study of the Norwegian problem. In his diary Jodl noted that Hitler required 'the OKW to produce a case-study, thereby encouraging the former Defence Minister'.[30] A comparison of this with similar studies on Czechoslovakia and Poland must have suggested to Jodl that aggression and invasion were highly probable. Two plans were envisaged and prepared simultaneously. The less realistic of these 'depended on the political success of Quisling who was to be encouraged with coal supplies, propaganda and the infiltration of a number of Germans without recourse to military assistance'. The second plan, 'prepared in the event of the failure of the first', envisaged extensive military action; after some modifications it developed into the scheme actually adopted.[31]

There were serious structural weaknesses in these plans. Quisling's first and most urgent need was money. At this time the success of Hagelin and Aall in negotiating German backing for *Fritt Folk* was not yet assured; without massive financial aid Quisling was incapable of making the impression on Norwegian politics desired by Rosenberg. The question of finance was therefore the main concern of the staff of the APA during the weeks immediately before and after Christmas 1939. On 21 December Rosenberg and Scheidt visited Hewel in order to discuss an overture by the Foreign Office, which sought to obtain Rosenberg's agreement to a plan giving it control of any grant of money to Quisling. Rosenberg was annoyed by Hewel's inability to grasp the realities of the new political situation. He naturally opposed Hewel's proposal and declared that as soon as he had recovered from the injury to his foot he would go to Ribbentrop and demand full political control for the APA. Hewel pointed out that the management of the affair by the APA might upset the precarious understanding with the Soviet Union, since the APA was not famous for its delicate handling of complex situations. Rosenberg, somewhat incensed, countered abruptly: 'Norway is not a Soviet sphere of influence.'[32] Apart from the decision that matters would henceforth be decided by direct consultation between Rosenberg and Ribbentrop, the conference achieved nothing.

As might have been expected, the co-operation between the two men amounted to extremely little. This was due as much to their personal vanity and rivalry as to the wildly differing estimates of Quisling's effectiveness given them by their subordinates. The discussion between Hewel and Rosenberg was not without importance even though it produced no definite results. The question of finance was at least thoroughly examined. The Foreign Office, though unwilling to sponsor NS, was the better placed to secure money for Quisling. The APA, which had been his original backer, possessed only limited resources. Hewel, for all his disapproval of the scheme, knew well the dangers of defying a direct order from the Führer. He therefore suggested to Rosenberg that Quisling could easily be financed out of the many 'driblets of foreign exchange'[33] available to the Foreign Office. His department could thus keep a close watch on Quisling's activities while leaving nominal control in the hands of the APA. But Rosenberg was still suspicious of Hewel and demanded that details of financial support should be handled by the Reich Chancellery. Once again the question was left to be decided by consultation between Rosenberg and Ribbentrop.

Very soon the open breach between the opinions of the Foreign Minister and the Reichsleiter began to affect the actions of those directly concerned with the Quisling affair. In a letter to Lammers, written on 20 December, Rosenberg discussed the Scandinavian situation in general as well as his particular difficulties with the Foreign Office. He also asked that Scheidt be granted full diplomatic privileges and that money for Quisling should be made available as soon as possible.[34] Although no money was immediately forthcoming, the Reich Chancellery did issue a general order on 21 December which required that Scheidt and Hagelin should receive all the assistance they needed concerning customs and passport control as they were travelling on the Führer's business.[35] The question of financial assistance still continued to occupy the staff of the Foreign Office even after Hitler's orders had been passed on to Hewel by Rosenberg. Just before that meeting, Schickedanz had discussed the problem with Lammers at some length on 19 December, in an attempt to wean him from the official view of the Wilhelmstrasse.[36] Rosenberg's letter of 20 December had been an attempt to follow up the points put by Schickedanz on the previous day. However, on 22 December von Grundherr telephoned Schickedanz in order to try to discover how successful the efforts of the APA had been, intending to contact Lammers in order to counteract any progress that the APA might have made.

Von Grundherr was particularly anxious to discover what Scheidt was doing and told Schickedanz that he wished to see the Reichsamtsleiter. He was acting on orders from Ribbentrop, who hoped that Scheidt might be persuaded not to send inflammatory reports during the period of his visit to Norway. Unfortunately for their schemes, Schickedanz announced that Scheidt had left with Quisling that very morning for Oslo. He was expected, however, to be back early in the New Year, at the very latest, and would then be able to supply his personal report.[37] It was just this contingency which the Foreign Office had hoped to prevent, knowing the kind of report Scheidt might well produce after spending a few days under the influence of Quisling and his followers. The news of Scheidt's departure plunged von Grundherr into gloom. Scheidt had stolen a march on them. If his mission were allowed to succeed, all the efforts of the professional diplomats to prevent Quisling receiving a subsidy would go for nothing.

Von Grundherr's dismay was echoed throughout the ranks of the Foreign Office staff. At the head of the anti-Quisling faction was von Weizsäcker, who earlier in his diplomatic career had spent much time in Norway. He demanded that a close watch be kept on the activities of Scheidt and Quisling during their stay in Oslo, and informed Bräuer by telegram on 23 December that Scheidt was on his way to Oslo:

> Reichsamtsleiter Scheidt of the Aussenpolitisches Amt left last night at the instruction of Reichsleiter Rosenberg for several days in Oslo, in order to consult with Quisling, Hagelin and their circle. The purpose of the visit is observation, but not active participation in Quisling's plans. The Foreign Minister requests that you maintain discreet contact with Scheidt and come to Berlin for instructions shortly before or after the New Year. You will report in this matter only to the Foreign Minister, myself, and Grundherr.[38]

Von Weizsäcker expected that Bräuer's good sense, reinforced by his personal testimony, would provide a solid counterweight to Scheidt's influence and enable the Foreign Office to pursue an alternative policy.

Thus within a few days the façade of unity erected at Quisling's second meeting with Hitler had been completely dismantled; the APA and the Foreign Office had returned to their struggle for influence over the determination of policy regarding Norway. Despite all the efforts of the Foreign Office Rosenberg remained convinced of Quisling's importance. But he was surrounded by a tide of doubt and scepticism which threatened to sweep all his elaborate plans away. This atmosphere of uncertainty had some effect even upon Rosenberg himself; he began to question the urgency of the matter. After Scheidt and Hagelin had left Berlin the conduct of affairs rested very much in his hands. He was not a man of action, and his subordinates in the APA as well as his rivals in the Foreign Office remained for some days in a state of uncertainty about the purpose of Scheidt's mission; this uncertainty they attributed to Rosenberg's poor method of bureaucratic procedure.[39] After Christmas he still showed no sign of any effective liaison between the APA, the Foreign Office and the Reich Chancellery. Consequently Lammers felt that he must take responsibility for the project, as failure would reflect upon his own department as well as those of Rosenberg and Ribbentrop. On 29 December he took the matter up with Hitler himself, realising that the dispute between the APA and the Foreign Office over the management of political activity in Norway was assuming serious proportions.[40] At this interview the

Führer merely expressed his lack of confidence in the discretion of most of the parties concerned in the Norwegian affair, and suggested that Lammers might try to settle the dispute as quietly as possible.

Lammers's action did have the effect of focusing attention on the problems of the German bureacratic organisation. Lammers decided to turn this to advantage by attempting to impose a solution on the rival organisations. Hoping to arrange some kind of compromise, he summoned Schickedanz to his office on 4 January. At that very moment, Lammers's plans were being undermined by the actions of Bräuer and Scheidt. While Lammers, Schickedanz and von Grundherr, representing comparatively moderate viewpoints, were trying to arrive at a policy which would command the agreement of the various parties at the cost of some minor concessions, the activists, Scheidt and Bräuer, were preparing rival reports based upon their consultations in Norway. Aall and Hagelin were also concentrating upon the task of convincing Scheidt that it was important that a favourable report on Quisling should go to his superiors. On 30 December Aall met Hagelin at Sassnitz, and this matter formed a large part of their discussion.[41] Aall then travelled on to Oslo, where he hoped to meet Scheidt.

When Quisling and Scheidt left Berlin for Oslo, they were joined at the last minute by Hagelin, who had decided to ignore his business commitments for the time being in order to concentrate on the more important task of attracting the support of Scheidt. They broke their journey at Malmö, where Scheidt visited the German consul[42] and his companions visited Winther-Hjelm, and they reached Oslo on 24 December. Hagelin seems to have left Norway at latest by the end of the month, while Scheidt left on 2 January 1940. During his stay Scheidt made a number of important contacts, and was thus able to make a full report. At the same time Bräuer was keeping watch on his activities hoping to produce a document strong enough to counter Scheidt's observations.

According to diplomatic custom, Bräuer sent his New Year report on the situation. He wrote it in Germany whither he had come in accordance with his instructions of 23 December, and in it he stated that although Norwegian public opinion was pro-British, the actions of the government were unequivocally neutral. He was confident enough to declare:

> I vouch for the Norwegian Government's determination today to remain neutral. I believe I can vouch for my ability to give prompt notice if this attitude should undergo any change. The Norwegian Government's determination to remain neutral . . . cannot be seriously impaired by any British proposals to Norway that England be granted bases on the Norwegian coast. The Norwegian Government would resist such a move with the support of the Norwegian people.[43]

This report, delivered on 3 January, makes it clear that Bräuer hoped to expose the pretence of Quisling and his supporters that they needed aid in order to prevent the Norwegian government from selling out to the Allies. Bräuer was at pains to add that, while he could conceive of the

Norwegian government permitting arms shipments to Finland, none the less 'it wants to remain master in its own house and considers strict neutrality as Norway's only effective armament'.[44] Such a factual and balanced report should have influenced German policy strongly.

It is just possible that Bräuer might have succeeded and that the whole affair might have been allowed to rest for some time, had not Scheidt at this point returned from Oslo. The memorandum he submitted was pessimistic about German prospects in Norway, and urged the Foreign Office to take action. His return gave fresh stimulus to Rosenberg and changed the position entirely. Scheidt arrived in Berlin on 4 January, and his report, presented on 5 January, covered the whole period of his visit, from 24 December to 2 January. He had been astute enough to notice that Bräuer had already been informed about the bearing of German policy in Norway, and it seems likely that he constructed his report accordingly – stating his opinions in terms sufficiently strong to counter what Bräuer might say. Scheidt's account contained information of two different kinds. To the Foreign Office, the most significant part of his report was his general remarks on the state of Norwegian public opinion. To Rosenberg, on the other hand, the most interesting of Scheidt's observations were his detailed accounts of meetings with important Norwegians. Both parts of the report deserve close scrutiny, for they reveal a great deal not only about the workings of the German Embassy in Oslo but also about the methods employed by Scheidt and Quisling.

Scheidt's comments on the reputation of Germany in Norway were sombre indeed: 'the Finnish conflict', he reported, 'had excited public opinion to a truly disconcerting degree . . . although I was already prepared by Minister Quisling's description of the prevailing mood in Scandinavia'. This was, largely, fair comment. Scheidt pointed out that the Norwegian press was entirely preoccupied with the Russo-Finnish war and did not hesitate to use harsh words about the ignoble part played by Germany. To illustrate the way public opinion had moved against Germany he added: 'Two Norwegian publicists known previously to be extremely pro-German, M. Jakobsen in the newspaper *Ragnarøk* and Viktor Mogens in his weekly *Utenriks Chronik*, have dropped their previously pro-German course and are writing in an extremely anti-German way.'[45] This was especially discouraging since Mogens, an extremist of the right and leader of the political group Fedrelandslaget, had been a germanophil for many years. The position could be retrieved, in Scheidt's opinion, provided Germany refrained from making 'outspoken demonstrations of sympathy for Bolshevist Russia as have been seen over and over again since the Non-Aggression Pact'. He also suggested that if the German authorities were prepared to provide the money, the hostile trend of opinion might be reversed, and 'through a skilfully managed press policy'[46] Germany might equal what had been achieved by the Allies. The picture painted by Scheidt was very different from that of Bräuer.

The effect of Scheidt's report upon Rosenberg was to spur him on to fresh efforts. The general tone of the report was no more alarmist than several that the APA had received from Hagelin in the past, and Norway had in no case submitted to British pressure. The Foreign Office might therefore have decided to ignore Scheidt's warnings and pursue the policy preferred by von Grundherr and von Weizsäcker, had not Scheidt produced his trump card. He had been informed by Quisling that 'he would deal in these matters exclusively with Reichsleiter Rosenberg and me'.[47] Since Quisling had obtained the support of Hitler the Foreign Office could not afford to ignore this personal factor for fear that Hitler should penalise the anti-Quisling group. Quisling's guarantee enabled Scheidt to dismiss Bräuer's scepticism about the part assigned to him in Norwegian matters. Bräuer's observation that Scheidt's travels in Norway were infrequent and spasmodic and that therefore his political soundings were unlikely to be reliable, was ignored.[48] Von Weizsäcker suspected that Scheidt's alleged contacts with important Norwegians were figments of the Reichsamsleiter's perfervid imagination. But, dissatisfied as they were with the report, the Foreign Office none the less felt powerless to do any-thing about their suspicions. Rosenberg was alarmed at the report and was convinced that only immediate action could compensate for the apparent blindness and stupidity of the staff of the Foreign Office.

Scheidt supplied him with plenty of material for his political manoeuvres. His report expressed strong dissatisfaction with the attitude of the embassy staff. He objected to the attempts of the Foreign Office to subject the APA to its influence;[49] he even suspected breaches of security. The Führer had been right in thinking the principal agents in the Nor-wegian venture incapable of preserving security and secrecy; Scheidt had had personal experience of their negligence. Security precautions over his own visit to Oslo had been inadequate; Bräuer had known of his im-pending visit to Quisling and of Hagelin's projected return to Norway long before such information should have been released. Von Weizsäcker had, as we know, asked Bräuer to keep in discreet contact with the plotters. When Quisling discovered that the whole German Mission in Oslo seemed to know of Scheidt's visit, despite his requests for absolute secrecy, he was very worried. 'Minister Quisling pointed out', Scheidt reported, 'that the wider the circle of people knowing his plans, the harder it would be to keep them secret. I can certainly understand his wishes in this matter, for as a former Norwegian Minister of War his own neck is at stake with his policy.'

It may, indeed, be suggested without exaggeration that early in 1940 Quisling was panic-stricken. Not only had difficulties arisen over the money promised him by Hitler but there also seemed every likelihood that details of the arrangements so carefully negotiated in December might at any time be casually revealed by some careless Foreign Office official. It was Hagelin who alerted Quisling to the danger and pressed him to take up the matter strongly with Scheidt. Quisling realised that it was essential for Ribbentrop 'to be included in the total circle of those informed', but had strong reservations about the staff of the embassy, for 'his experiences with the German Mission in Oslo had made it seem advisable not to inform the Legation'.[50] To make matters worse, at least two members of the Legation staff were not particularly noted for their discretion – von Neuhaus and Noack. Scheidt, who had been greatly embarrassed by Quisling's anger, had difficulty in reassuring him that even Bräuer had been discreet.

On his trip Scheidt had seen also a number of prominent Norwegians other than NS members, and had discovered that on the whole their opinions confirmed those held by Quisling and Hagelin. Among them was Captain Irgens, senior captain of the Norwegian-American line, who was of the firm opinion that the British were invincible by sea, and that any German attempt to win a sea war was doomed in advance. The editor of the right-wing *Nationen* revealed in an interview with Scheidt 'the bane of Norwegian politics was Hambro, President of the Storting, chairman of its committee on foreign policy, and Norwegian representative in Geneva. This Jew is always spinning threads for England.'[51] This statement, however, might well have been made by Quisling himself. Scheidt also believed that the substantial measure of support for Quisling among the armed forces, not only among senior ranks, from men such as Colonel Sundlo, but also among junior ranks, should be built up – 'It is to be hoped that Quisling will extend further his relations with the officer corps, and he will be able to do this all the better the sooner German means for decisive propaganda are available.'[52] In choosing people to interview Scheidt may have been highly selective, but all their remarks reinforced his demands for swift and decisive action by Germany.

Scheidt returned, armed with his report, to find the staff of the APA somewhat despondent. After Bräuer's return to Norway, Schickedanz and Lammers had further discussions with Rosenberg, who seemed rather doubtful about the whole venture. These consultations had the effect of exasperating Lammers, who exclaimed to Schickedanz: 'When everything works it is fine, but when it goes badly it costs the heads of those responsible.'[53] The lack of purpose, activity and progress seems to have sapped even Rosenberg's enthusiasm; on 7 January he wrote, 'The Norwegian plan must now be slept upon for a little while.'[54] The real problem of the APA was that its leaders were not sure what their plans for Quisling were. They had still not decided whether to press for a full-scale military invasion of Norway and the installation of Quisling as Prime Minister or for a subsidy to enable Quisling to carry out a *coup* on his own. In the confused situation of early 1940 we can hardly wonder that the staff of the APA, always inclined rather to theory than to practice, had lost much of their determination. Scheidt's return had a salutary effect upon their attitude.

Scheidt was very angry when he returned, not only with the interference of the Foreign Office but also with the ineptitude of the APA in the absence of himself and Hagelin. He was also full of enthusiasm, and soon Rosenberg was busy arranging meetings between Scheidt and various Foreign Office officials. His flagging correspondence with Hagelin also acquired new vigour. Hagelin, urged by Aall and de Laporte,[55] pointed out that Berlin was the real centre for combined military and political plans and that Rosenberg must play a key part. The solution to the Norwegian problem must be found quickly, and only through a national government. The flattery in this appeal had its effect upon Rosenberg, and he once again took up Quisling's cause with energy. He asked Scheidt to talk to both Lammers and von Grundherr about his problems.[56] Scheidt had a talk with von Grundherr on 9 January, but not even an agreement to disagree resulted. Scheidt insisted that Norway might go over to the Allies at any moment; von Grundherr declared that Norway was doing her best to remain neutral under difficult circumstances and annoyed Scheidt with his sarcastic tone and thinly-veiled criticism.[57] A prolonged and acrimonious dispute on the management of foreign policy in Norway then ensued. Scheidt reported this quarrel to Hagelin, who drew up a memorandum on the subject, copies of which were sent to Rosenberg and Quisling. Hagelin urged that 'the political situation told heavily against continuing to maintain theories at the expense of practical policy'.[58] At this interview it became clear to von Grundherr that Quisling, Hagelin and Scheidt were firmly in league and had concerted a policy which it was almost impossible for the Foreign Office to combat. Von Grundherr having failed to change the course of Scheidt's policy, only Bräuer continued his attacks in the hope that they might eventually have some effect.

While the policy-makers of the Third Reich wrangled over the means and desirability of fulfilling their pledges to Quisling, the object of their concern was actively promoting his cause in Norway. He had been presented with a golden opportunity to attack the Norwegian government. Monsen, the Minister of Defence and a pacifist, had been the target of considerable criticism ever since the outbreak of war. So successful had his tenure of office been, and that of Halvdan Koht, who had been Foreign Minister since March 1935, that the Norwegian Defence Council had held no meeting since 1937. Incalculable harm had been done to the machinery for organising defence. Unity of direction no longer existed, with disastrous consequences in April 1940.[59] The outbreak of war gave the opportunity for certain necessary cabinet changes, including the reinforcement of the Ministry of Defence. Monsen, in very poor health at the time, thought this a good moment to resign. This was regretted by no one outside the ranks of NS. Monsen had been so inept and unpopular, especially among the officer corps, that Scheidt 'warned Quisling against proceeding too strongly against Monsen, for in the circumstances this might be [too] successful'.[60] The government's haste to remove the question of defence from the arena of party politics led it to commit a grave blunder. It was announced on 22 December that Monsen was to be replaced by Colonel Birger Ljungberg, a professional soldier, Commander of the First Infantry Regiment and the fortress of Fredrikstad. This provoked immediate controversy.[61] Despite the government's assertion that Ljungberg had been appointed because of his lack of political connexions, he was known to be very pro-British, like most of the King's personal entourage. Quisling informed Scheidt that the Norwegian government was moving still further along the road towards the complete accommodation of British plans. In fact the appointment of Ljungberg was doubly dangerous for the government. Not only was the government rendered more vulnerable to charges of giving way to British pressure but it was lulled into a false sense of security, believing that all its problems were solved by having a professional soldier at the Ministry of Defence. Until a radical change took place in the pacifist views of the Labour government such a belief was both naïve and foolish. As matters turned out, Ljungberg's appointment proved to be a mistake on technical grounds also; a few months later, the full measure of his incompetence was revealed. Meanwhile the appointment provided Quisling with plenty of ammunition.

Quisling was also extending his political activity; he intended to finance his actions from the funds promised him in Germany, depending heavily in the meantime on money received from Aall.[62] In order to avoid unfavourable comment and the possibility of an inquiry, he decided 'to camouflage his German sources of funds' by beginning 'a great money-raising drive for Nasjonal Samling',[63] the ostensible purpose of which was to buy out certain newspaper proprietors in order to set *Fritt Folk* on a better footing. Quisling also started another campaign for membership recruitment. The effect of Aall's subsidy was apparent even before the first instalment of German money arrived. The change in NS fortunes was noticed by Quisling's political rivals. Viktor Mogens wrote: 'Suddenly one saw an end to the party's financial difficulties. A great organisation was to be built up. In one of the modern palatial offices in Roald Amundsen Street the party rented a suite of fourteen rooms, which were furnished and fitted with the very best equipment.'[64] A centre for NS activity had been established in the heart of Oslo.

Along with this went a development of Quisling's pro-German propaganda. *Fritt Folk* received a large subsidy from Aall's Malmö office, and Quisling was thus able to put forward his views in greater detail. In an article on 6 January he defended the Nazi–Soviet pact, which he maintained had saved Norway from becoming 'a theatre of total war on land, sea and in the air, between England and Russia from the west and east, and Germany from the south'. In this way 'war, chaos and Communism had been averted'.[65] In the next issue Quisling returned to his attack on the extension of the Storting's life from three to four years. He attacked both the politicians and their newspapers, which in their reporting of the war had largely favoured the Allies. In order to counteract this dangerous trend, he wrote, 'We can now present our readers with a paper of eight pages in five column format. This is the result of a very prudent budget for the last two years and a great increase in subscriptions recently.'[66] In actual fact, the money came from Germany.

After his futile meeting with Scheidt on 9 January von Grundherr abandoned his attempts to prevent money being sent to Quisling. Shortly before seeing Scheidt, he had heard that von Weizsäcker had that very day been assuring a Norwegian diplomat of Germany's 'urgent desire that Norway should not become a theater of war'.[67] Moreover, Lieutenant-Commander Schreiber, naval attaché and representative of the OKM in Oslo, had visited Germany early in 1940, had told von Grundherr that it was essential to prevent British intervention in Norway, and on 8 January, in an interview with Scheidt, had given some support to the measures proposed by the APA.[68] Von Grundherr was powerless to resist the combined efforts of the APA and the OKM and when Scheidt saw Rosenberg soon after his meeting with von Grundherr this was made clear to the Reichsleiter. At Scheidt's urgent request Rosenberg acted at once and conferred with Ribbentrop, whose company he normally found utterly distasteful. Scheidt himself was given the money to deliver to Quisling, and in order to preserve security (apart from those directly concerned with the transfer of the money) only von Grundherr was informed of the transaction.[69] The exact size of the instalment is not known, but by 9 April 1940 Quisling had certainly received from Scheidt at least 200,000 marks.[70] The rest of the professional diplomats were left in ignorance of Germany's policy, and this greatly contributed to Scheidt's success in imposing his views on German policy later in the year. Well pleased by the outcome of his journey to Berlin, Scheidt returned to Oslo, probably on 19 January, taking the first instalment with him – 'Scheidt has taken the subsidy and is now travelling to Oslo.'[71]

The origins and purpose of the subsidy are clear. It was to be used to promote pro-German propaganda and the growth of NS. The explanation given in *Fritt Folk* of the new source of NS wealth was totally false. Quisling's attempt to relate the growth of *Fritt Folk* from a small weekly news-sheet to a proper newspaper, to his great drive for new members and new subscriptions seems to have been accepted by the rank and file of the party. On 17 January Quisling wrote to Aall about the happy position of *Fritt Folk* since money had become available,[72] and on 20 January the paper appeared in its new form. Instead of the normal small issue 25,000 copies went on sale. This expansion required an investment of approximately 5,000 kroner a day.[73]

Quisling was concerned not only with the future of *Fritt Folk* but also with that of his movement. His efforts to recruit support from the young officer-class had not had much success. He had told Scheidt that he was 'selecting from his shock troops a suitable number of reliable men who can be considered for a possible surprise action'. He saw this élite body, chosen from members of the Hird, as the Norwegian equivalent of the ss. He had also renewed contact with Colonel Sundlo, whom we now find

informing Quisling that 'on his own initiative he has made all preparations at Narvik and now only waits Quisling's order to attack'. Scheidt
advised Quisling to urge restraint on Sundlo, 'For any action by him
will be called for only if and when the German authorities consider the
moment for surprise opportune.'[74] Apart from Sundlo, none of Quisling's
contacts proved to be of much use, but Scheidt was impressed by these
energetic attempts to recruit key members of the armed forces.

Quisling summoned most of his chief collaborators to a meeting on 9
January. Only those in NS who were privy to the direction of Quisling's
aims were invited, and the meeting was a small one. Nevertheless in the
next issue of *Fritt Folk* it was described as a gathering of 'several hundred
fellow workers to hear the leader's interpretation of the position'. At this
meeting Quisling forbade his colleagues to assist Finland in any way; it
would be folly to send Norwegian youths to be slaughtered, particularly
when they would be needed for 'the struggle in which the Norwegian
nation will also be involved'.[75] These views did not meet with unqualified
approval. Even Quisling's personal secretary, Harald Franklin Knudsen,
expressed his dissent:

> I must admit that at the time I could not quite agree with his point of
> view, for, like everyone else, I had succumbed to the intense concern over
> Russia's attack on Finland, and could not forget that we of the Nasjonal
> Samling had been thundering against bolshevism for years. Here at last
> we had a chance of fighting them, and Quisling had said no. I could
> hardly believe it. However, I accepted his decision, and it was not long
> before I too realised that it had been the correct one.[76]

But the meeting had a wider importance than prevention of volunteers
going to Finland to fight against the Soviet Union. Quisling's speech
ranged over many topics and included the clearest warning he ever gave
his fellow-countrymen about his own intentions: 'First and foremost we
must prepare ourselves morally for the severe trial that awaits us. If we
hold firm, and remain courageous, then the New Year will be a good year
for us, and a year of victory.'[77] An election was due in 1940, but Quisling
could certainly not have been expecting an electoral victory. Not a single NS
supporter had been elected to the Storting either in 1933 or in 1936; by
1940 the party was much weaker than at either of those elections. For any
who cared to read the report in *Fritt Folk* the message should have been
clear. No democratic victory, even on a limited scale, for NS was possible; a
coup of some kind remained Quisling's only prospect. Coupled with the
great party reorganisation of early 1940, Quisling's statement could only
mean that NS was aiming at the seizure of power by some non-democratic
means.

The quarrel between Quisling and the Storting died down in January,
partly owing to a general feeling that in the existing state of international
insecurity an election would be inopportune, but partly also owing
to Quisling's illness; in the middle of January a kidney complaint had
put him out of action for some days. Nevertheless the activities of his

subordinates showed no decrease, and NS propaganda must have been having some effect, for the sales of *Fritt Folk* rose sharply. NS also started to distribute flysheets and leaflets examining political issues from the party's standpoint. A large political staff was recruited, at considerable expense, and Ragnar Skancke and Axel Stang were put in charge.

Some of the strain on Quisling was relieved by the return of Scheidt and Hagelin in the latter half of January.[78] They were able to shoulder the main burden of organisation pending Quisling's recovery. Hagelin's success in integrating himself into the NS party organisation was remarkable. He was not well known in the party, except among the inner circle of conspirators; while outside NS he was thought to be just another businessman with large trading interests in Germany. This gave him much latitude, and the credit for much of the successful planning during the vital period from December 1939 to April 1940 must go to Hagelin rather than Quisling. As well as being Quisling's deputy and chief liaison officer Hagelin was a competent businessman in his own right. His connexion with Quisling was not known in Norway, and he succeeded in penetrating certain circles of the Nygaardsvold government. He was thus able to learn their true opinions, and he confirmed Rosenberg's impression that the ministers 'conducted themselves like a secret Norwegian-Anglophile Society'.[79] A report made by Scheidt on 5 January paid tribute to Hagelin's brilliant performance in outwitting the Norwegian government: 'In the last few days, through Minister of Social Affairs Støstad, Hagelin has come in touch with [Trygve] Lie, the Minister of Supply, about Norwegian import licenses. After getting these licenses he expects to return to Germany to conduct further negotiations.'[80] Thus Hagelin, acting on behalf of NS, was able to travel to and from Germany on apparently legitimate errands.

Hagelin was at the same time the trusted agent of the Norwegian government in its negotiations for the purchase of German anti-aircraft equipment for the Norwegian navy. He could thus maintain open contact with the German Ministry of Marine and also gain useful scraps of information about the intentions of the Norwegian government and occasionally also of the Allies. He maintained his pretence of negotiating on behalf of the Norwegian government until the very end. Letters from von Brückner, the German negotiator, show that Hagelin was still engaged on official business as late as 2 April 1940.[81] Quisling was also employing Hagelin during these months to handle the shipments of coal and sugar he had asked for on 18 December.[82] The bulk shipments were to be shipped to Norway under cover of a new company to be established in Germany, or through specially selected firms in Norway which might be susceptible to Nazi influence. His own business intimates, such as Prytz or Fermann, were too well known, so Hagelin was appointed to act as consignee.[83] His role was central to the success of Quisling's ambitions, and the efficiency with which he managed Quisling's affairs must be fully recognised.

All the calculations, however, as to the relative positions of the Allies and Germany in Norway were upset by an astounding speech made by Foreign Minister Koht to the Storting on 19 January.[84] Koht declared that, if shipping was attacked, no individual power could be blamed but only the war itself. The speech betrayed Koht's anxiety not to fix on any one power responsibility for the war, or for any act of war. No prominent politician had given so clear an indication of the Norwegian government's intention to pursue a policy of strict neutrality. The speech revealed not only a degree of impartiality rare in politics but a naïvety even rarer. The Allies could hardly believe that Koht was serious. Sir Cecil Dormer, the British ambassador to Norway, was instructed to point out the bad impression created by this speech, and to tell Koht that 'if the Norwegian Government's conception of neutrality is that both belligerents earn equal blame for action known to be taken by one of them, the other will have less inducement to respect Norwegian interests'.[85] The truth of the matter was that the Norwegian government had been put under considerable pressure by the British government in early January over the question of the rights of ships in neutral territorial waters. Koht had hoped to relieve this pressure by an unmistakable affirmation of Norwegian neutrality. His gesture misfired completely. He was stunned by the reactions to his speech both inside Norway and among the belligerent powers. Britain and France were henceforth convinced that Norway was too frightened of the power of the Third Reich to follow a strictly neutral course, and accordingly prepared certain measures, the effect of which was to hasten the German invasion. To the Germans it seemed obvious that the Allies were preparing to intervene in Scandinavia, and the original purpose of Koht's statement was forgotten in the wave of anxiety which swept over those who were watching the Norwegian situation.

Reactions to Koht's speech were strong in Norway also. Many anglophil Norwegians were affronted at its failure to distinguish between Allied and German methods. Quisling was at first puzzled, later frightened and finally outraged. Realising that Koht's statement would only reinforce Bräuer's argument that there was no point in backing NS since Norway intended to stay neutral anyway, he redoubled his efforts to persuade the Germans that this declaration of neutrality was a pose, a Socialist trick designed to conceal from the Germans the government's true aim, which was to hand Norway over to the care of the Allies as soon as possible. Quisling and Scheidt, who also perceived the danger to his carefully laid plans, were now preaching to eager listeners. Accustomed to the tortuous patterns of European diplomacy, some members even of the Foreign Office were already regarding Koht's simple declaration with some scepticism. From this position little argument was needed to convince many of those connected with the Norwegian adventure, such as the Foreign Office official Luther, that Koht's language was simply an elaborate cover for some complex plot. Bräuer, a straightforward man, was nevertheless inflexible in his belief that Koht had meant what he said.[86]

There was thus no dramatic change in Germany's official attitude. On the contrary, German plans for Norway, which had been developing from the time of Quisling's visit in December, were stimulated by the events of January. The military experts, if not the political adventurers, were realistic enough to appreciate that in all probability a full-scale operation would have to be mounted. The staffs of the OKM and the OKW, in fact, contained the only people who had any long-term answer to the Norwegian problem, and the jarring sects in the Foreign Office and the APA were recognising the necessity of coming to some *modus vivendi*. It was pressure from outside rather than the acceptance of Quisling's importance that provided the real reason for the conversion of von Grundherr in early January. Only Bräuer still continued to strike a discordant note in the developing harmony, insisting, against Scheidt, that any supporters Quisling might have in the Norwegian army,[87] were small in number and negligible in influence. Bräuer believed that so long as the Norwegian Labour Party pursued national interests the opinions of a few officers did not really count. Two powerful deterrents prevented patriotic Norwegians from supporting Quisling – his ambiguous attitude in the past towards Bolshevism, and the foreign origins of the inspiration behind NS.[88] Moreover, the King had no respect for Quisling, though the Fører believed that the monarch held him in high esteem,[89] and Hambro, who was held in great respect by members of all parties in Norway, was known to oppose the aims of NS, and his influence was particularly strong in conservative circles, from which Quisling hoped to win converts. Bräuer's fulminations were not able to prevent a belated reconciliation between Rosenberg and Ribbentrop in January. Rosenberg recorded this success in his diary on 19 January: 'Ribbentrop is now much more judicious and better informed.'[90] In plain words, Ribbentrop had decided to ignore Bräuer's reports and to oppose Rosenberg's pretensions less determinedly.

Nevertheless, differences between the Foreign Office and the APA ran much too deep to be cured by any temporary co-operation. Rosenberg and the staff of the APA, assiduously encouraged by Quisling, continued to think in terms of a gigantic Norwegian-English conspiracy against the Reich up to the very date of the invasion. Long before 9 April, however, the plans for an initiative against Norway had fallen into stronger and more capable hands. The military staff dealing with the problem worked more conventionally, bureaucratically and thoroughly than Rosenberg's bureau, and its members were less subject to bouts of political fantasy. From the middle of January, preoccupation with the Norwegian affair spread throughout the higher echelons of the OKM and the OKW.

The principal advantage of the intervention of the OKM and the OKW was the gradual elimination of the wilder plans sponsored by the APA. Rosenberg had allowed Scheidt and Quisling to go their own way in formulating plans. He himself had taken a back seat, content to rest on his reputation as the German expert on Norway. During the course of

Scheidt's trip to Norway at the end of 1939, he and Quisling had developed a highly ambitious, and totally unrealistic, plan to forward the seizure of power by NS. A number of selected men were to be sent to Germany for a brief military training course in an isolated camp. They were then to be detailed as area and language specialists, and assigned to German troops, who were to be taken to Oslo on coal barges, in order to spearhead the invasion and assist the intended *coup*. Quisling hoped to seize by surprise all the key figures in Norwegian politics – including the King, who lived in or near Oslo for most of the year.[91] To the OKW the risks of such a plan were obvious. Preparations for the plan also needed absolute secrecy, and this was unlikely to be secured. The APA, however, supported the plan, despite its drawbacks. But as more and more of the Nazi hierarchy came to be involved, Quisling's plan came to look less and less attractive. Finally the excellent planning of the OKM superseded the political dreams of the APA and prevented the invasion of Norway from becoming one of the greatest disasters in German military history.

Looking back, one is bound to ask why Quisling should have been more successful than Bräuer in commending his estimate of the Norwegian situation to the influential decision-making bodies in Germany. The readiness of the OKW and the OKM to believe the reports sent them through the agency of Aall, Scheidt and Hagelin was perhaps decisive. Quisling's views did not really initiate thought or action in these bodies; rather they confirmed the prejudices and deductions of their staff and thus encouraged the policy-makers to proceed on lines already under consideration. The bases upon which both Quisling and Raeder worked were fundamentally the same. The ambitions of both men were equally large, their prospects equally unpromising. They both believed that Norway had an important strategic part to play in the war, and that some form of *coup* would be required to prevent the undue growth of British influence.[92] They differed mainly on the size of the forces to be employed. Quisling preferred the use of a small number of selected and trained Norwegians, backed up by a small force of German troops. Raeder naturally wished the German navy to play an important, if not the central, part in such a *coup*.

The plans of Quisling and of Raeder were not totally incompatible. The trained Norwegians could be transported, together with certain German troops, in German ships. They would then land and secure key points in Oslo and other important towns, such as Stavanger and Narvik. The army and air force could go into action in regular style after the important centres of communication had been captured and resistance disorganised. The invasion would then be legalised by the new government that was to be set up. Quisling believed that such a *coup* 'having been carried out with instantaneous success would immediately bring him the approval of those sections of the army with which he at present has connections'.[93] The plan seemed plausible to the ambitious Raeder, who, like most of his staff in the OKM, feared an Allied attack on the shipments of Swedish iron ore passing along the Norwegian coast. Raeder could not afford to disregard Quisling's reports of imminent Allied intervention in Norway; if they proved to be correct, Germany's war economy might at any moment suffer a shattering blow. It seemed to Raeder that his most prudent course was to assist Quisling in the hope that through this medium Germany would receive early news of any surrender to the Allies by the Norwegian government. Quisling was shrewd enough to take advantage of Raeder's refusal to trust Norway's alleged ability to preserve her own neutrality. Thus the way was paved for the catastrophe of April.

While Quisling and Scheidt were busy preparing their plans for a political *coup*, in Germany no final decision on the form of action had been taken. Both Raeder and Rosenberg were working hard to persuade Hitler that the invasion of Norway would be a decisive strategic blow. In his report to the Führer at the end of the year Raeder stated: 'It is essential that Norway does not fall into British hands. There is danger that volunteers from Britain, in disguise, will carry out an unobtrusive occupation of Norway. Therefore it is necessary to be prepared and ready.'[94] Norway was constantly coming up for discussion. Jodl's diary refers to the problem on 13, 18, 19, 20 and 30 December. Franz Halder, from 1938 to 1942 Chief of Staff of the Oberkommando des Heeres (henceforward referred to as the OKH), recorded discussions of schemes for invasion on 19 December and 1, 8 and 10 January.[95] Details of the study ordered by Hitler had been passed on by Jodl to Captain Freiherr Speck von Sternburg, the Senior Air Staff Officer in section 'L', the National Defence Section, of the OKW, and Jodl soon afterwards discussed the project with General Jeschonnek, Chief of Staff of the Luftwaffe. But when he reported on this discussion Hitler demanded that 'the Norwegian operation should be kept under our own hand'.[96] The task of producing Studie Nord (the name given to Hitler's study) returned to the OKW Operations Staff.

According to General Warlimont, at this time head of section 'L', there was henceforth no further mention of calling in Quisling, as Hitler had originally intended, nor was there any allusion to a possible Norwegian appeal for assistance as grounds for German intervention. From the time that the OKW took a hand in the planning, the part assigned to Quisling in a possible invasion was small. The case-study was being prepared by the OKW, but the detailed planning was referred to the Seekriegsleitung (henceforward referred to as the SKL), for the reason that it had been clear to the OKW staff from the very beginning that any operation would be essentially naval in design both strategically and technically. Plans produced by section 'L' and submitted to Hitler at the end of December 1939 was therefore ignored, at least as far as technical recommendations were concerned. Some of the organisational suggestions made by section 'L', however, were accepted.

In January, Studie Nord was received from the OKW. Jodl had hastened forward its completion, having since November 1939 perceived the real possibility that Norway would become a theatre of war. On 13 January Raeder discussed the plans for a full-scale Norwegian operation with Admiral Kurt Fricke, Chief of the Operations Division of the Naval Staff, and Admiral Otto Schniewind, Chief of the SKL from 1938 to 1941. Hitler had ordered a working committee to revise Studie Nord and had instructed Raeder that 'the chief of staff of this working committee shall be from the Navy'. The OKW also believed there to be a grave danger of Allied intervention in Norway and was glad to have the support of Raeder and Schniewind. Fricke, on the other hand, gave only qualified support to the theory; his division believed that 'it must be emphasised as unlikely that England could free from home such strong forces as the invasion of Norway would require, and still be able to meet the strong threat from Germany effectually'.[97] Fricke, and to a lesser extent Schniewind, were convinced that the maintenance of the *status quo* in the North would be the best solution. They both recognised the need for preliminary work on an invasion plan in case of a radical change in the Norwegian political situation. But on 13 January, according to Jodl, Hitler decided on a more aggressive course – 'the Führer makes up his mind to utilise the Danish and Norwegian space for the German warfare'.[98] This decision was reinforced by the events of the next few weeks in Norway.

By the middle of January, then, the stage was set for the dramatic events soon to take place. The APA and the Foreign Office had come to an uneasy truce. The OKM and the OKW were preparing plans for a possible invasion of Norway. In Norway Bräuer was still insisting that there was no danger of the government swerving from its declared policy of strict neutrality. Quisling and Scheidt, in receipt of German pay, denied the truth of Bräuer's reports and made absurd plans for an impossible political *coup*. The Norwegian government, in the face of mounting pressure from the principal belligerents, struggled on in its attempt to preserve neutrality. By the end of March Quisling and the German activists had finally won their battle with the Foreign Office, and preparations for a full-scale invasion were in train. Those ten weeks were crucial in the formation of German policy and the determining of Quisling's role in history.

The confused political situation in Norway was made more confused by the events of 20 January. In a rather injudicious speech Churchill had urged the neutral countries to join Britain in an attack on Germany.[99] The speech offended opinion in Scandinavia as a whole, and in Norway in particular, as it was construed as an attack upon Koht's justification of Norwegian neutrality. The Scandinavian governments showed marked hostility to Britain during the next few weeks, and the extreme anglophils in Norway split away from the large neutralist body of the population. Quisling, CBE and former friend of Britain, took advantage of the confusion amongst pro-Allied elements in Norway, making assiduous efforts to widen the split. In the first issue of *Fritt Folk* to appear after

Churchill's speech the leading article launched a vituperative attack on the policies of Britain. Quisling urged neutrality on his fellow country-men: 'We should take no notice of Churchill's childish broadcast de-claring it to be in the interest of the small nations to fight alongside England.'[100] This editorial was received moderately well in Norway, though not owing to any sudden conversion on the part of the Norwegian public to the policies of NS.

Koht's speech of 19 January and that of Churchill on the day following had a curious effect upon German opinion. A natural reaction would have been unqualified pleasure at such a strong stand by Koht and so stupid a response from Britain. This was Bräuer's reaction. On 24 January he had an interview with Koht which encouraged him greatly, and he reported some of Koht's thoughts on the situation:

> The speech was provocative and silly. . . . He had known Churchill for 30 years and considered him a demagogue and a windbag (sic!) . . . every time he ventured into practical politics, he got on the wrong track. He, Koht, had at the time been very much astonished that Churchill had been taken into the Cabinet just at so difficult a period and had been given a position of such importance in the British Government which called for the greatest tact and the deepest wisdom.[101]

Koht also asked Bräuer to obtain Germany's support in resisting British pressure for permission to undertake operations in Norwegian terri-torial waters.

Instead of accepting this report the German authorities chose to be-lieve Hagelin's account of developments. On 13 January, in a written memorandum Hagelin had reported the opinions expressed to him by two Norwegian ministers. The gist of their opinions was that Germany had already lost the war, and that Norway, if only because of its large mercantile marine, could not do other than favour Britain.[102] Quisling and Scheidt were quick to point out that as Churchill's speech had pro-duced an unfavourable reaction in Norway the British government had resorted to even greater pressure, and they cited Sir Cecil Dormer's strongly worded protest to Koht a few days after Churchill's speech. On 27 January Hagelin wrote to Aall that Koht's speech had been simply intended to deceive and that the government was still as pro-British as ever. Koht's duplicity had not fooled Quisling and Scheidt and they were confident that it would not fool the Germans.[103] The hopes of Quisling were not too optimistic. Opinion in Germany came down heavily on his side. Plans had been proceeding smoothly after the con-ference on 13 January, but the outbreak of Allied activity compelled a meeting of those closely concerned in Studie Nord. On 23 January de-finite suggestions for action were presented to Hitler. These were ampli-fied at a meeting three days later between Hitler, Keitel, Jodl, Raeder and von Puttkamer, at which Hitler repeatedly complained of the threat to German security posed by the unstable situation in northern Europe.[104]

This attitude was partly the result of recent meetings between Hitler and Rosenberg, at which Rosenberg lost no opportunity of impressing the opinions of Scheidt and Quisling on the Führer.[105] Though information on the meeting of 26 January is scanty, a memorandum written by Keitel on the following day shows that the invasion project was well advanced:

> The Fuehrer and Supreme Commander of the Armed Forces desires that work on Study 'N' be continued under his personal and immediate influence and in closest collaboration with the conduct of the war as a whole. For these reasons the Fuehrer has ordered me to take charge of the further preparations.[106]

Hitler was by this time much less interested in the political aspects of the Norwegian affair than in the military plans. The working staff at OKW Headquarters recognised this fact, and in the next few weeks was expanded into the nucleus of an operational staff for Norway. The project was given the official code name of 'Weserübung'. The intentions of those who supported the adoption of this plan were aggressive from the start. The plan was not based upon a defensive conception. Major Elwyn Jones, in his summary of events leading up to the Norwegian invasion, referred to the important part played by Keitel's memorandum –

> the issuance of this directive of Keitel's on 27th January, 1940, was the signal that the Supreme Command of the German Armed Forces, the O.K.W., had accepted the proposition of the group that was pressing for this Norwegian adventure, and turned the combined resources of the German military machine to the task of producing practical and co-ordinated plans for the Norwegian operation.[107]

Quisling had done much to persuade the Germans to adopt this policy. He and his colleagues had, for one reason or another, contrived to make a reliable impression on Hitler, Raeder and even Keitel, who, together with Jodl, determined military policy. Hitler, in fact, took a very strong personal interest in the whole operation. The origin of his interest in the fate of Norway must surely have been his conversations with Quisling. The implications of Keitel's directive were particularly serious, in the opinion of General Warlimont, for 'as subsequent events proved, [Hitler] meant by this nothing less than that he considered himself best qualified to command an unusual and particularly difficult operation of the type of Exercise Weser'.[108] The German reaction to events in January was therefore very positive and led to the formulation of plans for an invasion. Bräuer's reaction was not the reaction of high-ranking officers in the OKW and the OKM, nor the reaction of the Führer himself.

In Norway, while plans for its invasion were being drafted in Berlin, Quisling pressed on with his propaganda campaign and the reorganisation of NS. Despite the money given him by Aall and the subsidy brought over by Scheidt the new expenditure to which he was committed put a serious strain on his slender resources. He therefore instructed Hagelin to travel to Germany to attempt to obtain further capital advances.

Hagelin left Oslo on 31 January accompanied by another supporter of NS.[109] On the way he stopped briefly at Trelleborg, the Swedish port for the ferry to Sassnitz, where he had a short meeting with Aall and de Laporte.[110] He informed Aall of the excellent progress made by NS since December and outlined plans for further action. Once in Berlin, Hagelin visited Rosenberg and asked him to press for more money, or at least for an advance of the money promised, for the use of NS. Rosenberg agreed to do so, but any attempt he made was unsuccessful. Hagelin then travelled to his home in Dresden, to attend to certain business matters, and on 10 February he left Berlin for Oslo.[111]

Meanwhile Quisling and Scheidt had made great advances in Norway. From the new NS headquarters in Oslo a new intelligence network had been organised, modelled upon a similar German system in Denmark. Members of NS familiar with naval and mercantile marine affairs were incorporated in a complicated system of observation posts along the Norwegian coastline. The German naval attaché, Lieutenant-Commander Schreiber, confirmed that this branch of NS activity promised to supply much useful information. As, by Quisling's own admission, 90 per cent of the population was pro-British, the active co-operation of NS was essential. The gathering of information posed few problems for the widely scattered adherents of NS, and Quisling's realistic appraisal of the poor support on which NS could count and the degree of effectiveness of his small band of supporters went far to increase Scheidt's confidence in the accuracy of his other observations. These, however, usually showed much less realism or substance. Scheidt was nevertheless able to convince the APA that Bräuer's reports were conditioned by his continuous contact with the pacifists, Koht and Nygaardsvold, and did not provide an objective assessment of the situation. For once, Quisling's observations on the general tenor of Norwegian opinion were considerably more accurate than those of Bräuer. Even though public opinion had been roused by the clumsy manoeuvres of the British government, Quisling was right in thinking that this swing against Britain would not be permanent.

Thus, by early February the situation had become highly favourable, and Quisling's sole difficulty was the urgent need of NS for more money. He built up a campaign urging Norwegians to join NS or one of the subsidiary organisations connected with it and greatly expanded his party's activities, though at his trial he was to deny that this expansion was in any way due to his connexion with Scheidt. He even denied that he had established a working relationship with Scheidt at any time before the events of 9 April. He did admit, however, that during these weeks he had attempted to infiltrate independent organisations such as the Bondelag (the Farmers' Organisation) and the Seamen's Union. Both Scheidt and Schreiber approved of Quisling's activity within these bodies which they believed to be almost as useful as the intelligence network he had established. Quisling also denied forming any such network, though in this case, as the prosecuting counsel at his trial pointed out, the statements of

Scheidt and Schreiber 'must have been a complete fantasy'.[112] There can be little doubt, however, that Quisling was making extensive use of German funds. He mounted a violent attack on the pusillanimous pro-British character of the Nygaardsvold government and impugned the motives of the British government.[113] In another issue of *Fritt Folk* this immoderate tone was maintained in a slashing attack on the Soviet Union.[114] The effect of Quisling's propaganda was probably not very great, for the attitude of the Norwegian government was generally approved by the public. On the other hand it gave Scheidt and the APA the impression that his work was invaluable.

While Quisling was increasing his efforts in Norway, there appeared in Germany an unexpected obstacle to the Norwegian adventure. Regular communication between the APA and Scheidt was not speeding up the pace of preparation as Quisling had hoped, despite warnings from Hagelin that Germany might suddenly find Norway in process of Allied occupation. This lack of enthusiasm was almost entirely due to the influence of the Army General Staff, which was far from satisfied with the project.

> OKH were appalled at the risks and dangers inherent in the expedition, [wrote Sir John Wheeler-Bennett] and, braving their *Führer*'s wrath, they flatly refused to participate in the preliminary preparations. The Scandinavian operation was planned entirely by OKW, and the commander of the expedition, General Nikolaus von Falkenhorst, was selected personally by Hitler.[115]

Despite all the efforts of Hagelin, Scheidt and Rosenberg, then, there were certain military figures who regarded the project with disfavour. Considering the delicately poised political situation, the advocates of a 'wait and see' policy were almost certainly correct in their judgement, and might well have emerged victorious from their struggle with the activists, even at so late a stage, had not a very unfortunate sequence of events occurred, lending added point and justification to the attitude of Rosenberg and Raeder. Jodl's account of the development of preparations for 'Weserübung' shows how these plans were influenced appreciably by the transparent manoeuvres of the Allies.

On 5 February Jodl recorded: 'Special staff "Weser Exercise" meets and is welcomed' by Keitel.[116] Owing to the absence of a Luftwaffe representative constructive discussions could not go forward.[117] On 6 February the possibility of executing 'Weserübung' rather than 'Fall Gelb'[118] was examined. Pressure from prominent members of the OKH, including Halder, caused this plan to be dropped. Opposition to 'Weserübung' centred round Halder, who feared that Germany might be distracted from the pursuit of the most important war aims by the mirage of a cheap triumph in Norway and Denmark. None the less he felt obliged to release Major Tippelskirch for the 'Weserübung' planning staff. This special staff laboured under tremendous difficulties for it had no basis on which to work. According to Warlimont, 'Scandinavia had never been studied by the German General Staff in the past. Even maps were unobtainable.'[119] It is not to be wondered at, therefore, that for about a fortnight in early February the plan slipped into temporary obscurity. The OKW was very much occupied with the plan for the invasion of the Netherlands, and it was only a completely unexpected act of the Allies which revived interest in 'Weserübung'.

By mid-February most of those intimately connected with the affairs of NS were busily engaged with party affairs in Oslo. Hagelin had returned by 12 February, in time to resume contact with Aall, who was certainly in Oslo by 10 February.[120] All Quisling's advisers were thus on hand when the episode of the *Altmark* occurred. On 15 February the German supply ship *Altmark*, commanded by Heinrich Dau, was sighted by units of the Royal Navy in the Jøssingfjord, which was within Norwegian territorial waters. As it was known that she was carrying British prisoners from ships sunk by the *Graf Spee*, despite assurances to the contrary given by Captain Dau to the Norwegian authorities, the British government had given permission to the captain of HMS *Cossack*, which happened to be in the vicinity, to board the German vessel and rescue the prisoners. The boarding operation, executed on 16 February, was entirely successful, and produced an immediate and impassioned protest from Germany concerning the violation of Norwegian neutrality. The OKM was the first important German organisation to hear of this event and reported the matter to the Foreign Office. Ernst Woermann, the official in charge, Director of the Political Department (1938–43), at once telegraphed Bräuer, ordering him to protest strongly to the Norwegian Foreign Ministry.[121] This Bräuer did on 17 February, sending a strongly-worded note to Jens Bull, the Secretary-General of the Norwegian Foreign Ministry. The same day Bräuer was notified that Colban, the Norwegian ambassador in London, had presented a firm protest to Halifax.[122] Reaction in German official circles was strong, for the episode had greatly alarmed those who were already apprehensive of the possibility of British intervention in Norway. The British action had alarmed Quisling and his supporters also.

On 17 February, as soon as the news became known in Norway, Quisling launched a broadside against Britain for her failure to respect the rights of neutrals. This attack rebounded adversely on his own plans, since it highlighted the provocation to which Britain had been subject. If Britain was guilty of a flagrant breach of International Law so too was Germany. Nor was Norway free from blame, since the government should have instructed the appropriate officers to make thorough search of belligerent ships entering Norwegian waters. The charge was made by some Norwegians, as well as by the British, not without justification, that Norway, like other neutrals, made complaints selectively: a strong protest would be made at any incident in which Britain was in error, whereas complaint at the ruthless sinking of neutral ships and their crews by

Germany was, if possible, avoided, though Norway in particular had suffered heavy losses during the six months since the outbreak of war.

The official Norwegian reaction was almost as strong as that of the German government. The Norwegian Admiralty registered its anger and regret at the action of the *Cossack*,[123] and on 18 February Koht summoned the British ambassador to his office in order to express 'his strongest indignation'.[124] In the Storting he declared that the government was fully determined scrupulously to uphold its neutrality. The majority of Norwegians, however, were 'Jøssingers', as Quisling dubbed those who felt that the British had quite a strong case for their action. For all the protests of their government, the Norwegian people reacted, on the whole, rather differently. There were many, of this seafaring nation, who felt sympathy for the difficult position of the British. The smooth management of the whole operation undoubtedly did much to restore Norwegian confidence in the efficiency of the Royal Navy, which had been badly shaken by the affairs of the *Thomas Walton* and the *Garoufalia* earlier in the year. This revival of Norwegian confidence in Allied power was of great importance to Quisling, for it amply justified the statements he had been sending to the APA. In order to ensure that the dangers of the situation were fully understood in Germany it was decided to send Scheidt back to Berlin, where he would be able to keep in touch with the development of opinion within influential circles.

The most serious effect of the *Altmark* incident was that it drew the attention of the Germans to the Allied interest in Norway as the most likely springboard for action against the Reich. If the British were prepared to violate territorial waters to rescue a few hundred prisoners they might well be ready to do the same in order to cut off vital ore supplies to Germany. In military circles there was very sharp reaction to the *Altmark* episode. Jodl recorded on 19 February: 'The Führer urges on the preparation of operation Weserübung. Steamers to prepare. Troops to make ready. Will speak to the working staff.'[125] Rosenberg recognised that the episode might alter the plans so carefully worked out by the APA. On 19 February, therefore, he also went to see Hitler, who was very pessimistic about German influence in Norway. 'Today', wrote Rosenberg, 'I visited the Führer and spoke to him about the problem. As a result the *political* plan of the Norwegians has collapsed after our talk and proposals.'[126] Hitler than saw Jodl once more and approved his suggestion that a new commanding officer, designated by the army, should be charged with the future of the operation, which would come under the direction of the OKW. Bypassing the OKH, which would normally have detailed an Army Group or Army Headquarters for the task, the OKW chose a Corps Headquarters, 'the lowest level command organisation which could possibly have been considered',[127] more remote and less open to pressure from the OKH, which was still by no means happy about the proposed expedition.

Upon those who formed the backbone of the anti-activist party both

Scheidt and Schreiber urged the very real risk of the complete collapse of German influence in Norway. The opinions of Schreiber, recognised as a reliable and sensible officer, naturally had influence in military and naval circles, but he found Admiral Diesen, the Norwegian Commanding Admiral, 'very cautious and reserved'.[128] Schreiber used strong words to Diesen, expressing his 'utter failure to comprehend the attitude of the commanders of the two Norwegian torpedo boats, who could have furnished proof, despite the odds against them, that they could not only talk about neutrality but also die a hero's death for neutrality'.[129] Norwegian assurances about neutrality were worthless; they held good in theory but not in practice. Schreiber's words carried weight in Germany, and were, indirectly, confirmed by a report from Bräuer, who had a long talk with Koht on 21 February. Koht 'condemned the British action but regarded further violations of Norwegian territorial waters as unlikely'. This rather feeble assurance was regarded in Germany as proof of Norway's inability to resist British pressure. Matters were made worse by an interview on 24 February between Bräuer and Jens Bull, in which Bull 'asked that the ship be removed from Norwegian waters as soon as possible' and 'noted that Halifax had advanced the view that *Altmark*'s crew should be interned'.[130] By this time Hitler and his advisers had already decided on the policy they meant to follow, but Bull's attitude acted as reassurance that their decision had been correct.

On 20 February the OKH was informed that 'the Führer wishes to speak to General von Falkenhorst, since he is an expert on Finland'.[131] This was a somewhat exaggerated assessment of von Falkenhorst's qualifications; he had only been a Staff Officer in the Baltic–Finnish Area in the First World War, though he had subsequently risen to the command of XXI Corps. On the same day Hitler had a long conversation on the execution of 'Weserübung' with General Fromm, who, as head of the Wehramt, was best able to assess the technical requirements of the task force. The next day Hitler outlined the urgency of the situation to von Falkenhorst and gave him charge of the whole project, an assignment which the general accepted willingly.[132] Hitler did not inform him of the political background to the expedition, and this omission was to have serious consequences when von Falkenhorst came into contact with Quisling after 9 April. At this preliminary briefing Hitler merely informed von Falkenhorst that the Norwegian venture had been under consideration since the previous autumn.[133] Headquarters XXI Corps was promptly and arbitrarily placed under the command of the OKW 'to avoid difficulties with the Luftwaffe'. Halder realised that this was simply an excuse of Hitler's to justify the major part he and Raeder intended to play in planning the operation. Halder recorded his dissatisfaction that plans had reached such an advanced stage without proper consultation with the OKH; 'not a single word has passed between the Führer and the Commander-in-Chief of the Army on this subject. Get that on the record for the war historians.'[134]

Support for the action of the OKW came not only from Schreiber but also from Scheidt. Quite apart from the *Altmark* episode, Scheidt had good reasons for wishing to return to Germany. After the failure of Hagelin's mission early in February, Quisling was beginning to run short of money and Scheidt was anxious to obtain a further instalment of the subsidy for NS. He left Oslo on 20 February in order to report on the situation to Rosenberg. He was convinced that Quisling's campaign must not be allowed to fail or fade out through lack of funds, and to prevent this he was ready to exaggerate the dangers to the German position in Norway. On reaching Berlin, he gave Rosenberg a highly alarmist report, which Rosenberg did not hesitate to use to advance his policy.[135]

Scheidt's report was inflammatory. One of his agents, he said, had observed the reception of an extra release on the *Altmark* incident at the principal Oslo news office on 17 February.

> The fact that England had flagrantly violated neutrality had a surprising but by no means the alarming effect so frequently alleged in other quarters. The mob clustered outside the show windows greeted the fact that five German sailors (this was the number originally published but later changed) were killed in this British surprise attack with cries of 'What, only five! why weren't all of them killed!' I was very much interested in finding out whether only a few individuals had said this and whether others had protested, but to my regret I learned that these out-cries had evoked a general murmur of approval. During the next 2 days as well, the British act of piracy was characterised as an excellent job whenever no Germans were in evidence.

Influential people who accepted Scheidt as a reliable witness were not unnaturally alarmed at such reports, and their fears were not allayed by a passage in which Scheidt quoted a conversation overheard by Hagelin:

> On Monday, February 19, Hagelin was able to be at a tea attended by a number of members of the Norwegian Storting. On that occasion he overheard the conversation of two men, one of whom expressed the opinion that the Norwegians should at least have fired in the air, where-upon the other corrected him saying that this was entirely out of the question since the attitude displayed by the captains of the two torpedo boats, . . . was after all 'a matter of instructions'.[136]

Scheidt was not content merely to recount these improbable episodes. He was anxious to let Rosenberg know of the valuable work he and Quisling were undertaking.

> Quisling has now made further inquiries [he reported] and learned that a secret agreement between the Norwegian Government and England actually exists, by virtue of which the Norwegians are prepared to react to British encroachments merely with paper protests. All this occurred before the *Altmark* affair. The *Altmark* incident itself offers the first evidence that the Norwegian–British agreement is functioning.[137]

Scheidt believed that this made Quisling's aid essential to the pro-

German party and he persuaded Rosenberg to put pressure on von Grundherr and Ribbentrop to furnish the second instalment of the subsidy. This fitted in well with Rosenberg's own views. At his talk with Hitler on 19 February Rosenberg had emphasised that Germany should have some Norwegians at her disposal in case she was forced to protect her interests in Norway against British aggression.[138]

It is difficult to judge the extent to which Scheidt's memorandum influenced German policy at this critical time. Rosenberg had made it available to the principal participants in policy-making before 23 February, when another important conference took place. Present at this conference were Hitler, Jodl, Keitel, Raeder and von Puttkamer.[139] Some of the important details of the invasion were settled, such as the number and type of ships required for the operation. Raeder, however, was reluctant to push forward final arrangements for the invasion of Norway. Perhaps he had a shrewd suspicion that the reports he had received from Quisling's clique did not fairly represent the position. At the meeting he suggested that Norwegian neutrality still represented the most favourable state of affairs for Germany. Within a short time, however, this dissentient voice was silent. Perhaps the despatches of Scheidt and Schreiber convinced Raeder, for it was not long before he was once more at the head of the activist group, arguing that it was inevitable that Norwegian neutrality would soon become merely technical, owing to the pressure applied on the government by the Allies.

On 24 February von Falkenhorst arrived in Berlin and began to train XXI Corps for its novel assignment. Even at this stage no final timetable had been evolved, for, as late as 26 February, Hitler was not sure whether it was preferable to execute 'Weserübung' before or after 'Fall Gelb'. The Führer decided to defer his choice until the opinions of Göring, Jeschonnek and Milch, the Inspector-General of the Luftwaffe, could be taken. On 28 February Jodl managed to persuade Hitler and Keitel that 'Weserübung' would have to be set in train quite independently of 'Fall Gelb'.[140] Later the same day von Falkenhorst visited Jodl in order to brief him on the details of his preparations.[141] Thus, the German plans for the operation remained uncertain until a very late stage, delayed by the spasmodic interest shown by certain of the important military and naval experts and by the personal caprice of Hitler. Rosenberg's part in influencing the outcome of the Norwegian affair depended entirely on the degree of influence he was able to exert over the Führer. As Hitler himself had great personal influence in the determining of the Norwegian policy and was by temperament strongly in favour of direct action, the suggestion that the opinions of Rosenberg, and hence those of Quisling, Hagelin and Scheidt, carried considerable weight with him is probably not far wide of the mark. So great was Hitler's personal influence that Jodl was obliged to omit the normal procedure of consultation with the three High Commands, and against all the rules he detailed certain Luftwaffe units to serve under von Falkenhorst.[142] From this disregard of normal procedures it is easy to imagine that in the Norwegian venture personal influence was exerted to an unusual degree by non-military personalities.

Meanwhile Rosenberg and Scheidt had been examining afresh the part assigned to Quisling and his followers in the German *coup*. They were forced to conclude that nothing definite could be planned, but that it would be best to concentrate upon strengthening Quisling's position in Norway. This, Scheidt believed, could be best achieved by a further expansion of *Fritt Folk*, and he informed his chief that the investment already made had paid dividends: 'As agreed, I have so far given Quisling the equivalent of RM 100,000 in British pounds. Quisling has successfully launched his propaganda campaign and trebled the street sales of his periodical in Oslo within 4 weeks.' He also reported to Rosenberg the wide range of Quisling's activities:

> At my suggestion and at the request of the German Naval Attaché, Quisling is now organising an intelligence network along the Norwegian coast with the help of the members of his party. The arrangement is such that the country is divided into three major sectors and a party follower of Quisling familiar with maritime shipping is placed in charge of each sector (southern, central and northern Norway) on a full-time basis. Wherever possible, an effort is made to have an agent on every vessel, who will duly report to Quisling. The questions of interest to us will then be transmitted by Quisling to the German Naval Attaché through me. The German Naval Attaché promises himself a great deal from these facilities.[143]

A regular channel for the transmission of information to the Germans gave Quisling a considerable advantage over any who might wish to compete with him in conveying their impressions to the Nazi authorities.

Scheidt was astute enough to appreciate what an asset Quisling and NS could be. He referred to the usual difficulties of establishing agents in a foreign country, particularly emphasising expense and the unreliability of individuals.

> The method of hiring agents and supplying them with money is costly and unreliable, since only such elements agree to something of this sort as are predisposed by their own inclination. In Norway we have an opportunity to operate through a political movement, the followers of which act by conviction.

Scheidt realised that, whatever happened in Norway during the next few months, Germany could hardly lose by backing NS as heavily as possible: 'The more we support this movement now, the better it will be for us in the future.'[144] A number of prominent NS supporters had told him that funds were urgently needed; Professor Claus Hansen had tried to interest him in the purchase of *Tidens Tegn*, while Dr Mjøen had warned him of the extent of anti-German feeling within the government. Although Scheidt had been unable to make any definite promises of assistance, during his visit to Germany he campaigned vigorously for an increase in the subsidy. The most useful method would be for Germany to take over a daily newspaper. As they had missed one opportunity of taking over *Tidens Tegn*, the best thing for the Germans to do would be to expand *Fritt Folk* into a daily, though this would mean very considerable expenditure.

The problem of security had also been bothering Quisling, and at his request Scheidt raised the matter with Rosenberg. He had had a long talk with Quisling about a proposal, originally made by the Foreign Office, that a Reichsbahn office should be set up in Oslo. Such an office would be modelled on the branches set up in Czechoslovakia and Austria, which had been highly successful centres for espionage. Neither of them was in favour of the scheme. Scheidt felt that already 'too many offices in Germany are handling Scandinavian matters'.[145] Quisling recognised the threat to security involved in the proposal to inform still more people about the part that NS was playing. Scheidt believed that Quisling's services were much more valuable than any new espionage centre would be, and accordingly poured cold water on the plan.

Rosenberg, of course, was easily convinced by Scheidt's arguments, and at once began trying to reinforce Quisling's position. On 24 February he reminded Ribbentrop of their agreement that a sum of 200,000–300,000 marks would be made available for Quisling's use, adding that Scheidt urgently required the second instalment to take back with him to Norway.[146] Rosenberg's appeal succeeded and when Scheidt left for Oslo, he took with him another large sum of money. The more political aspects of Scheidt's memorandum Rosenberg wished to discuss with Hitler, with whom he had an interview on 29 February. But the political plans prepared by NS and the APA had become irrelevant as soon as the military crisis had supervened, and Rosenberg's failure to realise this partly explains the chaotic series of events which followed upon the German invasion. Rosenberg was unduly encouraged by Hitler's interest in the political activities sponsored in Norway by the APA and by Hitler's wish to speak to Scheidt, who had however returned to Norway.[147] Rosenberg and his associates therefore persisted in their encouragement of a political *coup* in Norway, long after any important advantage could be expected from it. Quisling's idea of a lightning political victory continued to receive the support of the entourage of the APA when there was no longer any practical possibility of success. Professor Skodvin accurately summed up the inadequacies of the APA when he wrote: 'Over Rosenberg's and his bureau's handling and attitude in this case there hung an atmosphere so remote and unpractical as to border on the fantastic.'[148] Nevertheless Rosenberg continued to play an important, though diminishing, part in discussions on Norway.

The decision fatal to Norway's hopes of remaining neutral was confirmed on 1 March. Thereafter there was little chance of the invasion being cancelled. Hitler laid great emphasis on speed and secrecy, especially as far as the execution of 'Weserübung Nord' was concerned: 'The shortest necessary space of time between the issue of the order for

"Weseruebung" and its execution must be reported.'[149] The reports from Norway indicated a strong possibility of immediate Allied action. If the Allies delayed too long, then he hoped to be able to forestall them. The plans of the OKM had been speeded up and were almost complete by the beginning of March. The attack was to be launched in six areas, ranging from Oslo in the south-east to Narvik in the far north. Transports were to be heavily escorted and the High Seas Fleet, in two groups, was to cover the flank of the long Norwegian coastline, devoting all its attention to preventing attacks by the Royal Navy. Once the troops had been landed and had made contact with Quisling's agents, no support would be given to the army by the fleet, since almost the entire German navy would be needed to defend the invasion areas from seaborne attack. Raeder realised that such an involved operation in an area where Germany had not absolute control of the sea would at best be risky. He believed, however, that the tactical surprise and speed of the invasion would defeat any possible Allied counter-attack.

There were protests against the plan. Halder objected to the lack of consultation;[150] Göring, to the lack of an independent command for the Luftwaffe.[151] Jodl managed to overbear both these redoubtable antagonists by telling them of Hitler's strong personal interest in the venture. On 3 March the Norwegian invasion was given precedence over 'Fall Gelb'. According to Jodl, the main driving force behind this decision was Hitler himself; 'the Führer was very insistent on the necessity of rapid and violent action in Norway'.[152] Despite Hitler's wishes the Luftwaffe still continued to object to the decision to subordinate some of its formations to von Falkenhorst. Jeschonnek and Bodenschatz, Göring's personal liaison officer to the OKW, raised further objections, to which Jodl made some concession on 4 March.[153] So confused was the situation that it was decided to hold a major briefing conference. On 5 March Hitler, Jodl and Keitel had 'a high-level conference on Exercise Weser with the three Commanders-in-Chief. The Field-Marshal vented his spleen, because of the lack of prior consultation. He dominated the discussion and tried to prove that all previous preparations were good for nothing.'[154] Some kind of compromise agreement was reached and on the next day Hitler signed the new directive.[155] He was preoccupied not only with the military preparations but also with the political possibilities following on a successful invasion. He had discussed this matter with Rosenberg on 6 March over lunch, but had come to no definite conclusion. Rosenberg pressed him to allocate a powerful political role to Quisling, pointing out the latter's recent successes, of which he had been told on the previous day by Hagelin,[156] who was again in Berlin.[157] Hitler pondered the matter for a few days and on 8 March informed Jodl that he wished revised orders to be issued for 'Weserübung'. Orders were to be divided between those of a military nature and those to deal with political contingencies, which were to be given to a Reich Plenipotentiary, who would be appointed later. Quisling was from this moment left out of the

German plan, unless Hitler meant to appoint him Reich Plenipotentiary, which seems unlikely. Hagelin's visit was not entirely fruitless, however, for he saw Raeder and told him more alarmist stories. Raeder at once went to tell Hitler that 'operation Weserübung is urgent'.[158] Two days after this warning, on 11 March, the detailed schedule for the operation was presented to Hitler, with the comment that preparations were proceeding smoothly. Plans for the invasion of Norway were in their final stage.

Meanwhile in Norway Quisling and his acquaintances were equally busy. Just as the *Altmark* incident helped certain members of the German hierarchy to make up their minds, so did it polarise feeling in Norway. The country was divided into two groups: one felt that the British action was totally wrong, the other sympathised with the British either openly or secretly. Quisling naturally flung himself into the fray on the side of the anti-British party. A regard for international law not hitherto conspicuous in his articles now became the dominant theme both in his speeches and his published work. He attacked the British action in issue after issue of *Fritt Folk*, culminating in that of 9 March, in which he referred to the 'flagrant breach of international law by the British' supported by the conspiracy of a 'camarilla of corrupt politicians in Oslo'.[159] This was a wide departure from his position in the early 1930s, when he had condemned the Hague Court and current notions of international law. He had recognised that, sooner or later, Norwegian neutrality would be irretrievably broken by violation of international law either by the Allies or by Germany.

Quisling, Scheidt and Hagelin put their subsidy at once to good use. Most of it was spent on the party organisation, the party offices and *Fritt Folk*. Propaganda became more intense, especially after the signature of an armistice agreement between Russia and Finland. The Russo-Finnish peace removed Quisling from a very embarrassing position. He even hoped to make political capital out of it; on 16 March he wrote: 'Now that peace has come to Finland we may hope that it will extend to the rest of Scandanivia, though we must beware of the intentions of the Allies.'[160] He was concerned to discover the intentions of the Norwegian government, which he hoped to do through Hagelin's contacts with official circles. He was sometimes reduced to the most trivial expedients in order to obtain evidence worth presenting to the Germans. In one instance the operation resembled classic comic opera rather than twentieth-century espionage.[161] The incident involved some bizarre activity within the French embassy, and the information seemed to Rosenberg important enough to pass on to Hitler on 6 March.

Yesterday [he wrote] Hagelin came from Oslo with the proof of the Anglo-French preparation for an attack on Norway. I immediately ordered the preparation of a memorandum by him, which I despatched to the Führer. He unburdened himself to me during the meal. 'I have read your paper', he said, 'it is a serious matter.' I gave him further particulars of French General Staff officers installed in the French embassy in the guise of customs officials. One of them fell in love with one of Quisling's secretaries. Quisling promptly interrogated her, but she had not discovered anything useful.[162]

Such information, small as it was in quantity and value, not only, in Quisling's opinion, impressed the Germans but also made Allied intervention in Norway seem much closer than it actually was.

Under Quisling's orders Hagelin had extended his previous contacts with representatives of the Norwegian government. Permission to import coal was secured from the Minister of Supply and Commerce. In Hagelin's absence from Germany this commercial transaction was arranged by Rosenberg himself, after long consultation with Göring and Helmut Wohlthat, the ministerial director of the four-year plan. Even Ribbentrop recognised the urgency of the operation and agreed to allow his officials to expedite the shipments of coal. As a result of a further report by Rosenberg to Hitler it was agreed that Quisling should be paid a sum of £10,000 a month for three months, beginning on 15 March. This was expected to provide sufficient stimulus for his pro-German activities.[163] While Hagelin was occupied with the task of raising money, Aall was engaged with the political aspects of the Nordic movement. In the period of 4–13 March he visited Berlin, Frankfurt an der Oder, Bremen, Hamburg, Kiel, Lübeck, Rostock, Güstrow and Stettin.[164] At most of these places Aall addressed members of the Nordic Society or similar bodies on the danger of allowing the northern states to fall under British control. His tour was something of a Roman triumph. He was very well received, and newspaper reports were uniformly favourable. The main topic of his orations was the freedom of the seas and the attempts of England to suppress the rights of other nations. A number of high officials from 'the Foreign Office, the OKW and the OKM'[165] were present at several of these meetings. Of special importance were Aall's speeches of 5 March, in Berlin,[166] and 6 March, in Bremen.[167] At the same time he was attempting to forward the political aspects of Quisling's plan for a *coup* in Norway, and from Bremen he was summoned by de Laporte 'to a conference in the Ministry of War'.[168] Later in March he may have met for a second time some of those concerned with the planning of the military intervention in Norway.

But German policy-makers were not entirely convinced that the Norwegian expedition was a purely defensive move in reply to Allied provocation. On 12 March Jodl wrote: 'The conclusion of peace between Finland and Russia deprives England, but also us, of any political basis to occupy Norway.'[169] The scheduled date for invasion had originally been 20 March, but this date had proved impossible for two reasons: firstly, because the persistence of ice and snow made the operation technically more hazardous, and secondly because 'Hitler is still looking for some justification'.[170] Any doubts which Raeder and his fellow conspirators may still have had at this late stage were dissipated by the middle of

March. Quisling's reports were read and studied at leisure. Once his version of affairs had been accepted, nothing, not even Koht's strident protests, could deflect Raeder and Rosenberg from their faith in him. In a speech made on 14 March, Koht vindicated all Bräuer's reports by administering a stinging rebuke to the Allies, whom he accused of attempting to embroil Norway in the Russo-Finnish war, and followed up this statement with an outspoken declaration of his country's firm intention to remain neutral.[171] It might have been thought that this speech would have entirely demolished Quisling's case. But by this time the German authorities either could not or would not see the truth. This may be largely attributed to the efforts of Hagelin, who suggested, in a report originally sent to the APA, that Koht's attack was a superb piece of bluff on the part of the Nygaardsvold government. Hagelin managed to visit Berlin only a few days after Koht's speech in order to dispel any lingering doubts. He left Oslo on 18 March,[172] and on his arrival in Berlin went to see Rosenberg. On Aall's advice,[173] Hagelin told the Germans that Koht had hoped to divert German suspicion, while the Norwegian government was completing its plans for an Allied take-over. He cited the fact that Allied intelligence officers were being allowed to check the Norwegian coastal towns for convenient landing-places. He had also learned that a certain Commander Kermarrec, who was in charge of this reconnaissance, had spoken to Colonel Sundlo about Allied intentions of landing motorised troops at Stavanger, Trondheim and possibly Kirkenes.[174] He alleged that it had also been prearranged with Britain that Norway would make no protest except on paper.

Hagelin's story was widely believed in Germany. Raeder's views had great influence, and at an important conference on 26 March with Hitler, Jodl, Keitel and von Puttkamer, he suggested that the British had been on the verge of occupying Norway in the middle of March. The danger had temporarily receded, but Raeder believed that

> sooner or later Germany will be faced with the necessity of carrying out operation Weserübung. Therefore it is advisable to do so as soon as possible, by April 15th at latest, since after that late date the nights are too short, and there will be a new moon on April 7th. The operational possibilities of the Navy will be restricted too much if Weserübung is postponed any longer.[175]

Raeder succeeded in convincing his colleagues of the need to fix a definite date for the invasion of Norway and Denmark.

As March drew to a close it was clear to all that a crisis was rapidly approaching. As the day of the invasion came nearer, there were constant comings and goings between Norway and Germany. Aall and de Laporte decided to travel to Oslo in order to make any necessary arrangements. De Laporte wished to see Bräuer in particular; and, after meeting Hagelin in Sassnitz, he and Aall arrived in Oslo on 20 March.[176] Thus, the principal conspirators, Quisling, Aall, Scheidt, de Laporte, Prytz and Schreiber, were all in Norway for a few days towards the end of March. Only Hagelin, who was engaged upon important work in Berlin, was absent from their consultations. Exactly what took place at these meetings is not known. The secrecy of them may be judged from the fact that Aall and de Laporte took rooms in a clinic, and both used their code names.[177] The conduct of affairs in Norway was entrusted to several different offices, and therefore only a muddled impression of the purpose of German policy emerges. At much the same time as the activists were in Oslo, Admiral Canaris paid a visit to Norway.[178] That the head of the Abwehr should travel to Oslo only a few weeks before the invasion suggests strongly his connexion with that matter. Certainly de Laporte, who was a member of the Abwehr, had a number of contacts with Bräuer, and the presence of Canaris was possibly connected with the activities of his subordinate.

During his visit de Laporte tried to familiarise himself with the somewhat complex situation in Oslo. The object of his visit may well have been to try to reconcile Bräuer to the fact that German policy was to be conducted on lines at variance from those he had advocated. To the intelligence departments in Germany the Norwegian situation appeared highly alarming. The OKW had no really good intelligence service at its disposal in Norway. The interest of the Abwehr probably represented a belated attempt to assess the situation accurately. As de Laporte was already committed to the pro-Quisling group any such attempt was doomed to failure. De Laporte stayed in Oslo from 20 to 28 March.[179] During that time he saw a number of key persons, exactly as instructed by the OKW.[180] On 25 March he met Schreiber, Scheidt and Lehmann, a civilian attached to the German embassy, where the meeting took place; Bräuer therefore could hardly have been unaware of it. The purpose of the meeting was to discover how much support NS could give the Germans in the event of an invasion, and what the reaction of the legation would be if Quisling were to stage a *coup* and ask Germany for help.[181] Such a discussion must have suggested to the participants that an invasion of Norway was a very real possibility, and de Laporte would hardly have discussed this matter with Lehmann and not with Bräuer. Neither Aall nor Quisling could have been unaware of the purpose of de Laporte's consultations with the embassy staff.

Admiral Canaris had also travelled to Norway, and was in Oslo on 28 March.[182] For security reasons he did not use his own name. He visited Schreiber at his office in Drammensvei, but did not 'say one word about the reason for his visit to Oslo'.[183] He did, however, discuss security and intelligence activities in Norway with Schreiber. Later in his visit he met Bräuer, and then returned to Germany.[184] The purpose of this visit is a mystery. It is known that he spoke to some Norwegians, but it is not known who they were. The motive of his visit can only be guessed at, but since the final preparations for the invasion of Norway were completed only in April, Canaris was probably asked to travel to Oslo in order to try to determine which, if any, of the reports sent to Germany revealed the true situation. And since the invasion took the form it did, Canaris must either have agreed with the version given by Quisling or, if he disagreed, must have been overruled.

The political position of the Norwegian government was still delicately poised at the end of March. Koht was still unsure whether Allied activity was directed to the laying of a coastal minefield or to an invasion.[185] The Allied intentions were even less clear to the Germans, and Koht naturally became fearful of the consequences of Allied activity. On 25 March, in an attempt to placate the Germans as well as ward off Allied intervention, Koht sent a firm note of warning to the Allies and made a determined and impressive speech in similar terms.[186] Lest this speech should affect German plans for intervention Hagelin acted swiftly, in a report on 26 March. The speech, he said, was part of an elaborate plot between the King, the Crown Prince, the Admiral-in-Chief and Colonel Ljungberg, who, as everyone knew, was an English nominee.[187] Quisling had told him to press for immediate action; any further delay would entail a grave risk for Germany. Rosenberg sent this report at once to the Führer, asking for action from the Norwegian task force as soon as possible.

Quisling's supporters had no monopoly of communication between Norway and Germany. Reports were still conflicting, and Bräuer was still swimming valiantly against the tide, which now ran strongly in favour of intervention. In a report of 28 March Bräuer stated 'that the English have no intentions of landing but that they want to disturb shipping in Norwegian territorial waters, perhaps, as Koht thinks, in order to provoke Germany'.[188] The views of the ambassador were conditioned, as always, by contact with Koht and other prominent members of the government. In particular he relied on an unequivocal declaration of neutrality issued by the government on 27 March,[189] and a denial by Agence Havas the next day that there was any prospect of Allied intervention in Norway.[190] While the statement issued by the French would obviously not be believed by the Germans, the Norwegian statement ought to have rung true. Once again Bräuer's efforts were neutralised by the pro-Quisling party. Scheidt at once perceived the danger and paid a flying visit to Berlin. In his diary for 9 April Rosenberg wrote: 'Scheidt was here ten days ago', which would date the visit 31 March. On his arrival in Berlin, Scheidt presented to Rosenberg a memorandum on the situation written on 28 March. This document was forwarded to Hitler, who promptly prohibited the OKW from taking part in political preparations for the Norwegian expedition. Scheidt returned to Oslo almost immediately 'in order to work with our attaché'.[191]

Raeder's view that the invasion of Norway should be undertaken early in April received Hitler's support on 26 March. None the less, technical problems continued to bother the study groups concerned with the detailed plans. On 29 March a top-level meeting was needed to settle the outstanding logistic difficulties, in particular the supply of oil and petrol.

On 30 March and 1 April Hitler had long discussions with von Falkenhorst. There was pessimism among many of the leading figures in the
military hierarchy. According to Jodl's diary for 28 March, 'individual
naval officers seem to be lukewarm concerning the Weser Exercise and
need a stimulus. Also von Falkenhorst and the other three commanders
are worrying about matters which are none of their business. Krancke
sees more disadvantages than advantages.'[192] At his meetings with von
Falkenhorst Hitler managed to allay some of these fears, and by 1 April
plans had been completed. On 2 April Hitler, Göring, Jodl, Keitel,
Raeder and von Falkenhorst[193] finally fixed the date of the invasion at 9
April, and the scheduled time as 5.15 am.[194] During the week following
this decision the leaders of the expedition remained in daily contact with
the Führer in case the date should be postponed.

The date originally favoured for the invasion was 2 April. What, then,
was the reason for the postponement? It may have been partly due to the
doubts expressed at a late stage by many of those concerned with the
enterprise. But the main reason was probably altogether different. Despite great attention to detail there were still certain points in the plan of
operations on which further information could be of use. It was decided
therefore to send an intelligence officer to meet Quisling in Copenhagen and
obtain this information. Hagelin was approached by Colonel Schmundt,
Hitler's adjutant, and asked if he would make speedy arrangements for
a conference between Quisling and a colonel attached to Military Intelligence; it would be best if they were to meet at some inconspicuous place.
Schmundt added that Hitler himself approved the meeting.

On hearing of Schmundt's request, Quisling readily agreed to travel to
Copenhagen. Scheidt promptly left for Oslo, confident that the meeting
would complete the process of co-ordination which he had begun. He was
followed by Hagelin on 4 April and remained in Norway until the date of
the invasion.[195] On 1 April Hitler chose Colonel Pieckenbrock, chief of
Military Intelligence I, to act as Germany's representative, and personally briefed him at the Reich Chancellery. He told him that the purpose
of the visit was greater co-ordination, and that in order to assist the smooth
running of the invasion Quisling would give him a considerable amount
of secret information about military dispositions in Norway.[196] Pieckenbrock was a good choice; he was not only fully aware of the complexity of
the Norwegian situation but he had also met Hagelin a few weeks earlier,
and therefore had some idea of the best way to appeal to Quisling.[197]

Pieckenbrock accordingly left for Copenhagen, arriving there late on
2 April. Quisling's journey to Copenhagen at this date, of course, had no
material effect on the progress of the invasion. It did, however, demonstrate that he was willing to do a great deal to help Germany. The ostensible purpose of his visit was to meet Fritz Clausen, leader of the DNSAP,
with whom he hoped to arrange a Nordic congress in the summer of
1940. In his statement of July 1945 Quisling asserted that his object was
'to draft plans for a rally in Aalborg to be held in the summer'.[198] Quisling

did have an interview with Clausen during his visit, as Clausen himself testified in 1945,[199] but this was merely a cover for his interview with Pieckenbrock. They met at the Hotel d'Angleterre at three o'clock in the afternoon of 3 April,[200] and had a very friendly talk, lasting about ninety minutes. A short conversation of a general kind followed, and they then separated. Jodl noted on 4 April: 'Pieckenbrock is back, with a good result from the conference with Quisling in Copenhagen.'[201] On the same day Quisling left by train for Norway.

It seems fairly certain that their discussion was on military matters. Quisling was certainly not informed of doings in the OKW or of the preparations for the invasion.[202] At Nuremberg Keitel confessed that he had been puzzled that there seemed no motive for the despatch of Pieckenbrock to Copenhagen.

> Pieckenbrock did not talk to Quisling about military operations. He just got some facts from Quisling . . . for instance, if the harbour of Oslo is fortified; if Narvik has fortifications and if it might be defended; if there are troops in Trondheim and so on.

Keitel also suggested that some of the information given by Quisling was not entirely accurate:

> Quisling was never informed of the plans and he never knew about the time, and he never knew about the amount of forces used. I recall him to have made wrong statements. I believe he explained that there were heavy guns installed in Narvik harbour. However, there were none.

The information given by Quisling was used by the working staff, which believed that it could have considerable relevance to the success or failure of the invasion. Keitel explained that their position was rather difficult, since 'there were just some questions put regarding the defence of Norway which had to be done specially. Questions which were very important for the operation and questions out of which Quisling could not get any information.'[203] From Keitel's testimony it is clear that the purpose of the meeting was that Quisling should supply Pieckenbrock with important military information. To the best of Keitel's recollection this is exactly what Quisling did.

This conference at Copenhagen may be deemed to mark in some ways the lowest point in Quisling's career. It was not only a betrayal of the nation which at that time he still idolised; it was the violation of an officer's code of honour. The conflict of loyalties in Quisling led him to perform an act in violent contrast with all his utterances for the past ten years. Henceforth Quisling had no real independence from German pressure. It was both a personal and a national tragedy.

On his way back to Oslo, however, Quisling did not think along these lines. He was pleased with the outcome of his journey, and was eager to pass on news of his success to his colleagues. Shortly before he left for Denmark it had been decided that a meeting of the NS Council would be held at once on his return. On 29 March, Fuglesang sent out invitations, including one to Aall,[204] who was unable to come, and one to Hagelin, who replied that he would be in Oslo by 6 April at the latest. The NS Council met on 7 April at noon; about thirty-five prominent members were present.[205] Quisling, however, did not tell the main body of the council about his meeting with Pieckenbrock but only about his contact with Clausen. According to Knudsen,

> as usual, Quisling summarised the general political situation, and he also mentioned the danger of war. It is obvious, though, that even he did not know how imminent the danger was. A great part of his address dealt with the ability of the North to support itself, in the event of being isolated from the open sea by the war. He also gave a report about a meeting he had just attended in Copenhagen, where the same matters had been discussed by the Danish National Socialist party, and he described a joint Nordic gathering planned for Aalborg in the summer. Fundamentally that was all there was to the meeting and, broadly speaking, I was disappointed with it.[206]

But other matters were discussed. Quisling gave some details of the progress of *Fritt Folk*, which appeared on 30 March as a daily.[207] The members of the council were delighted at the party's financial recovery, though Quisling did not inform the majority of them of the true source of its new-found wealth. Those interested in *Fritt Folk* should have guessed its source, as the newspaper had become little more than an organ of German propaganda. In the first daily issue, of 30 March, Quisling suggested in a personal article that 'Norway's and the North's vital interest is therefore the same as Germany's ... there must be immediate national revival, agreement with Germany and a breach with pro-British neutrality'.[208]

During the few hours that remained before the invasion Quisling was busy with the affairs of NS and engaged in observation of the international political scene, as the Allies put increasing pressure on the Norwegian government. On 8 April he issued a proclamation urging Norwegians to rally to NS in the hour of crisis which was at hand. He suggested that the King should dismiss the government and commission him to form a new cabinet. Flysheets bearing this proclamation were distributed in Oslo, but the general public was nervous and made no response. So as to be near the centre of events when the crisis broke, Quisling and his entourage took rooms in the Hotel Continental, where they would be accessible to NS members or anyone else who wished to contact them quickly.[209] They occupied at least nine rooms and were in constant communication with prominent NS members in other parts of the country. Quisling and Hagelin were asleep in the hotel when, early on 9 April, they were informed that the Germans had invaded. All that they had worked for had now come about; the opportunity for decisive action had arrived. Quisling's actions in the next few hours were to secure him a place in history.

Chapter 6 THE FIRST QUISLING
          ADMINISTRATION

THE GERMAN invasion of Norway on 9 April should not have taken the
Norwegian government by surprise. There had been plenty of warning,
both direct and indirect. It was, or should have been, obvious that both
British and German governments were showing undue interest in the
strategic role Norway might play in the war. This fact alone ought to have
alerted the Norwegians to the possibility of invasion. The Germans,
moreover, had given a crude warning of rather a different kind, for on the
evening of 5 April Bräuer had invited a number of notables, including
members of the government, to see a film showing the destruction of
Warsaw and the subjugation of Poland. The theme of the film was the
danger of relying upon British and French promises.[1]

There were also other warnings. It was on 5 April that the first hint
reached Oslo that Norway might be the target of preparations being made
by Germany.[2] On 7 April, an Admiralty communication to the Commander-in-Chief of the British Home Fleet stated that a German expedition to Norway was being prepared,[3] and the British communicated their
fears to the Norwegian ambassador in London. On 7 April also the Polish
submarine *Orzel* sank the German transport *Rio de Janeiro* off Lillesand;
about a hundred German soldiers were brought ashore by Norwegian
fishing boats, and after lengthy interrogation they disclosed that they
were on their way to protect Bergen.[4] Despite these clear indications of
imminent German action the Norwegian government remained paralysed.
Koht had his eyes firmly fixed on the minelaying activities of the Allies
rather than on the possibility of a German *coup*. For Koht, 'efforts to stop
whatever action the Allies had planned now took precedence, since he
believed that Germany would only act against Norway on direct enemy
provocation'.[5]

Late on 8 April German ships began to enter Norwegian territorial
waters and Koht's views were proved erroneous. By the early hours of
9 April the government had been able to summon most of the Cabinet
Ministers to a meeting at the Foreign Office. At 1.35 am a report from
Bergen established the fact that the invading force was German. Koht
and the rest of the government continued to discuss the situation in

irresolute fashion. In the meantime Hambro acted with commendable promptitude. Had his advice not prevailed over the vacillation of the government, the whole of the Storting and the Royal Family would probably have been captured by the invading forces. At 7.30 am a special train conveyed the 'Royal Family, the Cabinet, most members of the Parliament, and a small proportion of civil servants about seventy miles inland to Hamar'.[6]

The government's indecision was justly censured, after the war, as mainly responsible for the political vacuum which gave Quisling his opportunity.[7] The ignorance of most members of a pacificist government about elementary military matters can be understood, but the error of the Norwegian government lay in not transferring responsibility for military matters at as early a stage as possible to those competent to act. At 2.35 am Koht told Sir Cecil Dormer that Norway was at war with Germany, but at that stage he had still ordered only partial mobilisation. Koht also informed Dormer that he believed that the defences of Oslo were strong enough to resist any German attempt at occupation.[8] At 4.15 am Bräuer came to see Koht, in accordance with the instructions given to him only a few days before, and presented a long and complicated document, according to which Germany expected Norway to understand that the invasion had been mounted in order to protect the country from the Allies. The effect of this pronouncement was marred by the accompanying threat to crush any resistance offered by the Norwegian people. Bräuer's ultimatum also contained thirteen points to which the government was expected to agree. Among the most important of these demands were the transfer to the German authorities of all means of communication, control of the press and radio, military and naval installations, the armed forces and the coastguards.[9]

The acceptance of this ultimatum would have handed over complete control of the country to the occupying forces, and the government lost little time in rejecting it. The decision of the cabinet was immediately endorsed by the King, and arrangements were completed for the departure of the Royal Family and the government from the capital. The gold reserves were also a matter of concern, but arrangements were finally made for their removal to Hamar. The government decided to declare Oslo an open city in order to save its inhabitants from the horrors of another Warsaw, and so gave up all hope of retaining political control in the south-eastern part of the country. Thus, by the morning of 9 April Oslo had been abandoned and the way was open for Quisling.

Quisling and his immediate circle were very conveniently placed at the Hotel Continental at the moment of the invasion. On the evening of 8 April Quisling had spent most of the time in conference with his wife, Knudsen and Mrs Neegaard-Østbye, a prominent NS propagandist.[10] Early in the morning of the 9th he was wakened by the sound of planes and anti-aircraft fire. 'This is the German answer to the mines', he muttered.[11] As he was still unwell, from another attack of nephritis, he stayed in bed until about 8.00 am, when some important visitors called to see him. They were Scheidt and Hagelin.

By this time the shrewder members of Quisling's circle had realised that the government had been taken by surprise and had either abandoned or was about to abandon Oslo. It quickly became evident that the whole situation, both military and political, was hopelessly confused. Loyal Norwegians were unsure what they could do to aid their country. The government, having decided to leave Oslo, and being anxious not to advertise its destination to the Germans, was unable to broadcast its choice of Hamar for the time being as the new centre of administration. The morning newspapers, which had gone to press some hours before, were full of the *Rio de Janeiro* incident, not of the invasion.[12] In the confusion of the past night, the press, not surprisingly, could give no guidance to the millions of anxious citizens awaiting news of the latest developments. Thus, Quisling's chances of a successful political *coup* were much enhanced.

But if there was confusion among Norwegians, the position was much worse among the Germans who had to deal with the political aspects of the invasion. Their plans were wrecked by one idiotic supposition, namely, that the Norwegian government would submit to their demands without resistance, in order to escape the fate of Poland. In this they were mistaken, and, as a result, Bräuer was left with no clear instructions. Neither were military matters proceeding as smoothly as Jodl had hoped. This may have been partly due to a second foolish assumption. They believed that

a Norwegian fifth column was ready to help them. They overrated the importance of NS, since – and this must have been an unpleasant surprise for them – no Norwegian officers on active service, with one or two possible exceptions, acted as Nazis or traitors throughout the entire campaign. In part 6 of the operational orders it was added in parenthesis that the Norwegian commander at Horten was pro-German.[13]

This belief, as in so many other instances, proved to be totally unfounded. The sinking of the *Blücher*, which had contained many of the Germans assigned administrative duties, further complicated the situation. Thus on the German side, as well as on the Norwegian, there existed a political vacuum.

Scheidt and Schreiber had sufficient political awareness to realise what had happened, and were ready to take advantage of the situation. Schreiber had been informed of the date of the invasion some time earlier,[14] and he spent the evening of 8 April at home, discussing the situation with Scheidt. Early the next morning they both visited the German embassy, where they learned that matters had not gone forward as planned. They set out at once to find Quisling, and, according to Knudsen, arrived at the Hotel Continental at about 8.00 am. They eventually managed to contact Hagelin, and he took them to see Quisling, with whom they spent the next half-hour.[15] In view of what followed, it is not difficult to guess what they discussed. Scheidt and Schreiber were in favour of bold political action on Quisling's part and they were supported by Hagelin. Schreiber's report to the Foreign Office shows that he played a significant part in persuading Quisling to act; in his view 'there was only one sensible course to follow if there was to be organisation of a government friendly to Germany. The obvious choice was Quisling . . . he had the correct outlook with his pro-German political views.'[16] Scheidt was also a political activist, with the ambition to play a decisive role in Norway. Professor Skodvin has well summed up Scheidt's attitude: 'Scheidt saw Bräuer and the Foreign Office as opponents, Schreiber as an ally, Hagelin as a colleague and Quisling as a façade.'[17] Scheidt was eager to promote Quisling in order to further not only Rosenberg's designs but also his own career.

The aim of Scheidt and Schreiber was to persuade Quisling to form a national government on the lines of his proclamation of 8 April. Quisling should have been better prepared. Ever since the previous December he had reckoned that sooner or later a crisis in Norwegian affairs, owing to activity by one or more of the belligerent powers, would thrust him into prominence. The flysheet he had issued on 8 April, though it merely reiterated a number of appeals he had made in the past, had called upon Norwegians to support a truly 'national government which could save the independence and security of the Norwegian people'.[18] Was it a measure of Quisling's lack of confidence in the result of his appeal that when the moment arrived for him to nominate a government he had no notion what procedure to adopt? The invasion had, in point of fact, placed him in a very awkward position. He had hoped that Germany would be welcomed as a liberator; but after the events of the previous night even he must have realised that this was out of the question.

Quisling was not a resolute character. At their meeting the attitude of his friends was probably decisive. He was persuaded that his duty to the Norwegian people was to form a government that could rescue them from the confusion caused by Nygaardsvold's desertion. Like the rest of the Norwegian people Quisling was anxious to avoid bloodshed. Scheidt, Schreiber and Hagelin induced him to believe that unless the decision of the government to involve Norway in suicidal resistance were reversed, a catastrophe would ensue. So, with the advice of his friends, Quisling set about drawing up a list of prospective members of his new government. The next few hours were spent in scribbling various combinations of names on hotel note-paper and trying to think up a suitable form of proclamation with which to announce the new regime. His drafts were necessarily provisional, as he could not be sure what his nominees' reactions would be to the news that they had been raised to ministerial rank. He was unable to get into touch with most of them. He was also uncertain what type of government he should nominate; should it consist mainly of NS personalities or of men with a wider national reputation?

His confusion of mind was partly due to his own uncertainty as to the aim of his government. Scheidt had not made it clear how the German authorities would view his government. Quisling therefore did not know whether Scheidt wished him to fill a political vacuum or carry out a political *coup*.

This failure of comprehension on Quisling's part stemmed partly from his own irresolution, partly from the failure of the Germans to brief him adequately. His visit to Copenhagen could have given him a fairly accurate idea of the likely date of German intervention, but he had received no information of its details. The Germans in touch with him had in fact been consistently instructed not to reveal such matters to him.[19]

While Scheidt and Schreiber went out to discharge other items of business in Oslo, Quisling was left to wrestle with the problems of forming a government. By the time Scheidt returned at about 11.00 am,[20] Quisling had drafted his list of cabinet ministers. It consisted almost entirely of NS men: Professor Birger Meidell (Education and Church Affairs), Police Chief Jonas Lie (Justice), Dr Gulbrand Lunde (Social Affairs), Professor Skancke (Labour), Major Hvoslef (Defence), Tormod Hustad (Agriculture), Frederik Prytz (Finance) and Albert Hagelin (Trade). This was the list presented by Quisling later in the day, and there is no reason to suppose that it was different in any way from the list he had prepared in the morning.

This list indicates that Quisling had resolved some of the problems facing him. Since it contained hardly any well-known names, it is evident that Quisling had decided that it was his duty to 'take over the power of government'[21] rather than create a stopgap administration. This decision was to have fatal effects on his subsequent actions, as it meant that he and his party had forfeited much of their freedom of action. Scheidt's influence over Quisling's choice was considerable; it seems that Quisling did not disclose the names on his list to any of his collaborators until Scheidt had approved of them.[22] Scheidt by this time was able to give Quisling a fairly full account of the progress of the German invasion. He apparently possessed up-to-the-minute information of the thoroughness of the occupation and confirmed that nearly all the key towns on the Norwegian coast had been taken. He also stressed the very serious consequences of resistance to the German forces.[23] This warning undoubtedly influenced Quisling profoundly; he was anxious that the invasion should do as little damage as possible to German–Norwegian amity.

Quisling was worried about public reaction to the invasion and decided to investigate for himself. He went out and wandered around the city listening to conversations,[24] accompanied by Knudsen, who later recalled that Quisling 'wanted to see how the people were taking the situation. Broadly speaking, everything was calm and quiet, but a run on the banks had started, and there was an air of uncertainty which was hardly surprising.' Quisling and Knudsen then returned to the hotel, where they were joined at about 1.00 pm by Scheidt. They decided to visit the

Ministry of Defence in the hope that Quisling would be able to take some action which would prevent loss of life.

It is not absolutely clear who prompted this move. According to Knudsen's account, it was Quisling, who took Scheidt with him only in case the Germans should 'attempt to occupy the building'.[25] In view of Scheidt's actions earlier in the day this seems rather improbable. Scheidt was full of energy and, almost alone among those concerned with Norwegian affairs on 9 April, he had a clear idea of what he wanted. It therefore seems more likely that it was he who urged Quisling to go to the ministry soon after one o'clock.[26] There they discussed the situation with some of the high-ranking civil servants who had been left to cope with the problems of mobilisation. According to Knudsen, the permanent staff remembered Quisling from his days as a minister and welcomed his arrival. They were also 'in unanimous agreement that it would be an act of utter insanity to attempt to resist without ordering general mobilisation, considering what small forces there were available in the interior of the country. Organised resistance could only be thought of in North Norway.'[27] Yet Quisling did not immediately order the cancellation of the order for partial mobilisation. He contented himself instead with telephoning to the commanders of some of the coastal batteries, including those of Oslofjord Outer, Agdenes and Odderøya, and ordering that resistance to the Germans should cease, as it would only cause unnecessary bloodshed. In this matter he had certainly been advised by Schreiber, who was anxious that the Germans should not suffer a repetition of the *Blücher* catastrophe.[28] Knudsen states that Quisling then ordered the destruction of secret documents so as to prevent them falling into German hands.[29] There is, however, no external evidence to support this statement. Certainly Schreiber's report on the events of that day says nothing about such an important action.[30] Quisling's party then left the ministry and returned to the hotel.

A long meeting followed, at which Quisling, Hagelin and Scheidt were present. It lasted, with interruptions, including another visit to the Ministry of Defence, roughly from 4.00 pm to 6.30 pm. They discussed the situation in the light of the day's developments, being periodically interrupted by the arrival of prominent NS officials from towns within easy reach of Oslo, whose 'information conveyed a strong impression of the confusion prevailing everywhere, owing to the country's lack of leadership'.[31] Scheidt and Hagelin encouraged Quisling to broadcast to the Norwegian nation, announcing his assumption of power. After some discussion he agreed and began the task of drafting his proclamation. He was much encouraged by Scheidt's assurance that Hitler would look upon his assumption of power with favour, and that co-operation between Norwegians and Germans would go some way towards restoring relations with Germany to their condition before the invasion.[32]

At about 5.00 pm the discussion was broken off, and Scheidt, Quisling and Schreiber set off for the Ministry of Defence once more. By this time the Germans had seized control of a number of important administrative centres in Oslo, including the Ministry of Defence. A guard was posted at the entrance in order to ensure that resistance in the rest of Norway was not organised from the ministry.[33] This was probably a needless precaution, since by this time telephonic communication with the rest of Norway had become almost impossible. Quisling was anxious to seize legal administrative power in order to prevent forces of resistance from rallying around the King and his ministers. Schreiber and Scheidt were also anxious to capture the person of the King, and, if possible, the Crown Prince and the rest of the Royal Family. Quisling accordingly telephoned to Colonel Hiorth, the military commander at Elverum, not far from the Swedish frontier. The government had stayed at Hamar for only a few hours, during which it had taken plenary powers which would give its actions legal validity even if it were obliged to leave the country.[34] Believing that Hamar was insecure, the government had decided to move to Elverum. At this point Quisling intervened and telephoned Hiorth: 'The Marxist government is now on the way from Hamar to Elverum and will seek to flee to Sweden. I shall hold you personally responsible for the arrest of the government.'[35] This conversation took place between 5.00 pm and 6.00 pm, some hours before Quisling announced that he had taken over the leadership of the Norwegian nation, though he had already been announced to Hiorth as 'Chief of State'.[36] This disposes effectively of the reason given by Knudsen for the telephone call, alleging that Quisling wished to prevent the government from fleeing to Sweden as 'it would have been fatal for the country to have been left without a government at this juncture'.[37] Since Quisling had already prepared his list of ministers and steeled himself for the task of announcing his assumption of power, the return of the lawful government would have been nothing short of a disaster for him. On the other hand the incarceration of the government and the Storting would leave him with a free hand.

Quisling was now ready to make his broadcast to the Norwegian people. Unfortunately the Norwegian staff of the radio station were unwilling to let him do so. After Knudsen had met with a flat refusal from them, Scheidt managed to persuade the German-controlled radio staff to admit Quisling and his party.[38] The Norwegians in charge, Egil Sundt, the Director, and Olav Midthun, the Programme Organiser, were still reluctant, but were overruled by Scheidt, who seems to have obtained telephonic confirmation of his authority from the embassy.[39] Sundt later asserted that 'the embassy rang at once and verified Scheidt's representation orally. Scheidt was to be regarded as the representative for both civil and military German authorities.'[40] There was thus no possibility of further resistance from the Norwegians at radio headquarters. At 7.32 pm Quisling broadcast to the nation.[41] He stated that the cause of all Norway's misfortunes was the failure of the Nygaardsvold government to resist British violation of Norwegian territorial waters. He condemned the government also for ordering mobilisation and then decamping without making arrangements for any caretaker administration. This being so, he declared, it was the duty of NS to take over power. 'By virtue of circumstances and of the national aims of our movement, we are the only people who can do this and thereby save the country from the desperate situation brought upon us by the party politicians.'[42] Having announced that he would be the new Prime Minister and Minister of Foreign Affairs, he then gave the names of the rest of his cabinet. He ended by exhorting Norwegians to keep the peace and to remember that it was their duty to obey the orders of the new national government. This broadcast finally determined Quisling's role in history. Even he recognised that the course he had chosen was a perilous one. At the end of his speech he was congratulated by Knudsen, to whom he replied, 'It surely is no position to aspire after, Franklin. Let us hope, however, that the Germans understand our object.'[43]

Quisling's hopes were soon to be dashed. Whatever Scheidt's views were, it was clear that those of Bräuer differed from those expressed by Quisling. The German ambassador was in a very unhappy position. According to his briefing, Bräuer was from 5.00 am on 9 April technically Reich Plenipotentiary. It was not a position for which Bräuer had made any preparation, since the Norwegian government had not been expected to resist the invasion. Nor had it been thought likely that the government would escape capture or that the *Blücher* would be sunk. Not only had Bräuer been given no precise instructions about filling the political vacuum, but he also found himself having to perform a number of unexpected tasks. The absence of the military commanders assigned to the operation complicated an already difficult task. By 7.00 am Bräuer had realised that at that stage there existed no possibility of a compromise with the Norwegian government.[44] He therefore decided that drastic measures were needed. He determined to pursue two policies simultaneously in the hope that one or the other would meet with success. He alerted the German forces to the departure of the government to Hamar, hoping that a large enough force would be able to capture the refugees. Simultaneously he tried to open negotiations in the hope that eventually a compromise solution might be reached.

During the long day which followed, each of these plans was tried, but with differing success. At noon Bräuer made overtures to the government through the agency of Johannessen, a high-ranking official in the Ministry of Foreign Affairs. He assured Johannessen that the German government would respect Norwegian territory and independence, in the hope that the terms originally put to the government might, on reflection, prove more acceptable. Bräuer's message was passed on to the government and to the Storting, which was still in session. All but about five members of the 150-strong Storting were present; Bräuer's overtures were therefore thoroughly examined by a fully representative body. The ambassador was informed by Johannessen at 8.20 pm that the government intended to lay his proposals before the Storting, although no answer could be expected until late that night or early on 10 April.[45] But already the situation had changed, for Bräuer's second plan had been put into operation. The German Air Attaché had assembled troops and transport and had left for Elverum in the hope of being able to seize the person of the King, and so solving one of the Germans' more pressing problems. Fortunately for Norway, warning counsels given by General Ruge had prevailed and the Air Attaché's attempted *coup* was beaten off with some loss.

By this time, however, Bräuer's position had altered substantially. Before he heard of the failure to capture the King he had been informed that before the Storting had completed its session and dispersed from Elverum 'it gave its approval without a division to the renewal of negotiations . . . and appointed a small delegation for the purpose'.[46] Bräuer, then, might have had cause to believe that the worst difficulties had been overcome, had it not been for the news that Quisling had formed his own government. This once again complicated Bräuer's problems by rendering the task of negotiation much more delicate.

Bräuer had distrusted both Quisling and Scheidt, and on the evening of 9 April his fears were amply confirmed. Earlier in the day, he had given it as his opinion that there was no case for Quisling speaking to the Norwegian people.[47] When he heard of the broadcast he was not only annoyed; he was also puzzled. He could not believe that Scheidt would lightly ignore the opinion of the Reich Plenipotentiary, and came to the conclusion that Quisling had possibly received backing from Hitler himself. At the time Bräuer received the news he was in conference with Colonel Pohlman, who was operations officer for Group XXI and had brought Bräuer his original orders on the evening of 8 April.[48] Pohlman, as a member of von Falkenhorst's staff, knew of course of the unfavourable view of Quisling held by Military Intelligence.[49] He had received no instructions about Quisling and was even more perplexed than the ambassador. Certainly neither Pohlman nor Bräuer expected there to be any place for Quisling in the German plans. Their reaction was therefore hostile. Pohlman, on hearing the news, exclaimed to Bräuer, 'Who manages German foreign policy, the Foreign Minister or Reichsleiter Rosenberg?' The ambassador, accustomed to Rosenberg's interventions in foreign affairs, simply shrugged his shoulders.[50]

None the less Bräuer was determined to get to the bottom of the matter. It was essential that he should ascertain the amount of support there was for Quisling in Berlin, for he saw, quite correctly, that Quisling's declaration would complicate negotiations with the absent government. First, however, Bräuer telephoned Quisling, and asked him to come to see him at the embassy. Quisling told Knudsen to reply that the ambassador would have to come to the hotel.[51] This Bräuer did, but he was unable to get any useful information from Quisling. He decided therefore to telephone Berlin and contact Ribbentrop himself. He first got through to the office in the Wilhelmstrasse and then managed to find the minister at the Reich

Chancellery. When Ribbentrop came to the telephone Bräuer told him what had happened, and asked whether he should get into touch with the King. Ribbentrop was astute enough to appreciate that the ambassador had to choose between the King and Quisling. He was aware of the fact that Quisling had no influential backing in Norway, but he shrank from making such an important choice. He told Bräuer that he needed personal instructions from the Führer. Hitler promptly came to the telephone and told Bräuer that whatever happened he must support Quisling. He could negotiate with the King but was not permitted to discuss Quisling's position. Bräuer was also advised to see the king at a tête-à-tête.

Bräuer was not a little astonished at the support given to Quisling by Hitler. He had realised, however, that it was most improbable that the King would agree to accept Quisling's government. The reason for Hitler's support for Quisling is not difficult to see. The Führer had hoped that the King would decide to co-operate with the German forces and was annoyed that the King's resistance had endangered his plans. He believed that the Nygaardsvold government was really responsible for the King's resistance and therefore wanted it replaced by a more compliant administration. Quisling was the obvious candidate, and therefore Hitler supported him. Bräuer, however, saw no reason to tell either Quisling or Scheidt of Hitler's support for their seizure of power. He and Pohlman decided that the best course was to put up with Quisling until it became clear that his government was embarrassing any hopes of a settlement. In this they showed much clearer judgement than General Engelbrecht; he had clashed with Quisling earlier in the day,[52] and now at a meeting with the ambassador in the evening offered to arrest him.[53] But on the advice of Bräuer and Pohlman, Engelbrecht abandoned this plan.

The day had not yet ended for Quisling. After Bräuer's visit he began making plans for his administration in conjunction with some of the NS men who had managed to reach Oslo. His difficulties were considerable, since most of his nominees to cabinet posts were not in Oslo, and had still not been contacted. Later in the evening Quisling instructed Knudsen to call upon the president of the Shipowners' Association and ask him to come to the hotel to discuss the German demand that the Norwegian mercantile fleet should be ordered to neutral ports. Several other callers saw Quisling, and there were innumerable telephone calls. The self-designated Prime Minister eventually retired at about two o'clock on the morning of 10 April.[54] An eventful day was over.

The events of the next few days can be seen as a struggle between Quisling and Bräuer to dominate the Norwegian political scene. As might have been expected, neither was victorious. Quisling was not popular or realistic enough to make a lasting impression as Prime Minister. Bräuer was encumbered with too many conflicting instructions to be able to impose the kind of political settlement originally desired by Hitler. Of the two, however, Bräuer was the more successful. Unlike his opponents, he managed to maintain substantial contacts with influential Norwegians. Besides Johannessen, who acted as go-between for himself and the King, Bräuer was also able to use the services of Kristian Welhaven, the Oslo Chief of Police. Welhaven was in constant communication with Terje Wold, the Minister of Justice in the Nygaardsvold government, and during a long interview on the evening of the 9th he informed Bräuer that there was every prospect of arranging negotiations with the King and the government.[55] This opinion was confirmed shortly after midnight by news from Johannessen that the Storting had appointed a delegation consisting of Koht, Lykke, Sundby and Mowinckel, which had been given a mandate to try to achieve a peaceful settlement.[56]

Bräuer, pleased with this development, informed his Foreign Office at 12.45 am that the principal purpose of this commission was to assist in the restoration of order.[57] He added that Quisling was definitely *persona non grata* with many influential figures in Norway, including especially those who were otherwise not ill-disposed towards Germany.[58] A short memorandum taken from a telephone call on 10 April records that Bräuer informed his superiors that he hoped it would be possible for him to meet the King later that day, and had provisionally arranged to speak to him at 11.00 am at Elverum.[59] This was something of a surprise to the Storting delegation, the members of which had expected to travel to Oslo to see the ambassador there. Hitler's instructions, however, were followed faithfully by Bräuer, who insisted on seeing the King. Accordingly he left Oslo and arrived belatedly at Elverum at 2.45 pm. He spoke first of all to the King alone for about ten minutes, despite the King's wish that Koht should be present.[60] Koht was then called in for further discussions. Later, Bräuer saw the other three members of the delegation, and left at about 5.15 pm. The King and the delegation then conferred with the other royal advisers.

As Bräuer expected, the chief stumbling-block was the formation of Quisling's government. The King was outraged at the violation of his constitutional position. The politicians, particularly Hambro and Koht, were incensed at the assumption of power by a man whose support among the population was negligible. In his talk with the King, Bräuer was obliged to advocate a policy with which he did not fully agree. He had to stand firmly by his demand that Quisling must be a member of the government.[61] The reason he gave was that the existing government was known in Berlin as a pro-British administration, and Quisling would provide a counterweight, and he warned that the alternative would be the surrender of all governmental power to Germany.[62] His demand had a poor reception and Bräuer returned from his mission without much hope. Even before he left Eidsvoll, on his way back to Oslo, he telephoned the embassy to inform the staff that the King would not give his consent to a Quisling government and that Norwegian resistance would therefore continue. Von Neuhaus passed the message on, in code, to the Foreign Office, where it was received at 10.45 pm.[63]

On his return from Elverum Bräuer went to see von Falkenhorst, the commander-in-chief of the expedition, who had by this time flown in from Hamburg. Between them they represented the total German authority, civil and military, in Norway. Bräuer was convinced that Quisling was an encumbrance and told von Falkenhorst of his desire to form a government without him. Was it wise, he asked, to advise the Foreign Office to drop Quisling?[64] Von Falkenhorst realised that the little sympathy Bräuer had ever had for Quisling had been exhausted during the last two days. The ambassador's story was not new to him; Pohlman had telephoned him earlier from Oslo to tell him of Quisling's proclamation, only a few hours after the broadcast, and von Falkenhorst had then told Buschenhagen, his chief of staff, that he had no competence in political matters.[65] Nevertheless, he did want to end the fighting as soon as possible, and if Quisling stood in the way of a peaceful settlement then von Falkenhorst was against him. Bräuer could therefore rely on von Falkenhorst's sympathy, but not on his active support. After this discussion, at about 10.00 pm Bräuer tried to telephone Hitler in order to put to him the case against Quisling. He was unsuccessful, although he did manage to have a short talk to one of his colleagues in the Foreign Office. To him he explained that though he had been instructed not to deal with the delegation but with the King alone, in order to put more pressure on him,[66] this had proved to be impossible. The essential view of the King and his ministers was that Quisling could not be leader of a new government without a serious breach of the constitution, which they were not prepared to condone.[67] Eventually Bräuer was informed that he would receive further instructions the next day.

While Bräuer was busily engaged in these attempts to negotiate with the King and oust Quisling, the new Prime Minister was trying to consolidate his position. At about 3.00 am on 10 April, Quisling was awoken by the German naval attaché.[68] Schreiber asked him to use his influence to halt hostilities at Bolærne, a request to which he acceded.[69] Quisling and his party thereafter began to tackle some of the important problems facing the new administration.[70] He himself realised that his position was by no means secure; he had far too many influential opponents. Most of his energy was, therefore, devoted to the task of trying to eliminate opposition to his assumption of power. He became very soon aware that Bräuer was not only his most determined but also his most dangerous adversary. During their short talk on 9 April,[71] Bräuer had made it clear to Quisling that he had not approved of his broadcast. Later that night Quisling had received another indication that the German ambassador would try to prevent him from exercising any effective authority. In the evening Welhaven had been to see Bräuer, and on his return, at about 9.00 pm, had received a message from Quisling summoning him to a conference.[72] Welhaven had pointedly ignored this message and to Quisling this meant one thing only – Bräuer was already trying to undermine his authority.

Quisling's response was swift. He proceeded at once to the German headquarters in Akershus, where he discussed Welhaven's position[73] with the German commander, Colonel Nickelmann.[74] Quisling probably wished to have Welhaven removed from the political scene, for he provided an important link between Bräuer and the Nygaardsvold government, which Quisling was eager to discredit. Nickelmann, however, would not be prevailed upon. Quisling therefore returned to his hotel and at about midnight he summoned Askvig, the police chief of the Aker district. Askvig came as requested and was informed that Quisling wished him to take over the duties of police chief in Oslo as well as in Aker. In this way it was intended to eliminate Welhaven as a political force.[75]

Quisling was therefore more optimistic on 10 April. Askvig's politic reply to his summons made him feel that the danger from Welhaven was much reduced. Nevertheless he and his advisers knew that the best guarantee of his position would be either Hitler's personal backing or the successful negotiation of an agreement for the King's return to Oslo. Hagelin and Scheidt were among Quisling's first visitors on 10 April,[76] and they advised him to contact the King as soon as possible. Hagelin already had someone in mind for this difficult task, and, after a short discussion, Quisling approved. The man chosen was Captain Kjeld Stub Irgens, who was not only related to Hagelin but had also been on friendly terms with the King. Even more significant was the fact that he had not been a member of NS. It only remained to persuade Irgens to undertake this delicate task. At 10.00 am Hagelin rang Irgens and told him to come to the hotel at midday. Irgens, owing to various naval duties, was unable to come until about 2.00 pm. Quisling then had a long talk with him, and he finally consented. He was given detailed verbal instructions and a short written memorandum.[77] According to Irgens, Quisling's principal aim was to persuade the King to return to Oslo and to co-operate with the new government – 'The Quisling government calls upon the King and Royal Family to return to Oslo . . . in order to establish in Norway a system similar to that in Denmark and terminate the war.'[78] Irgens accordingly departed to see the King, though he was unable to see him until the next day.

In the meanwhile Quisling was eager to pursue the second line of policy – the direct appeal to Hitler. When one of Quisling's nominees for political position reached the hotel he found Quisling in earnest conversation with Scheidt and Hagelin. When they had finished, Quisling showed the newcomer, Birger Meidell, a draft telegram to Hitler.[79] A copy of this telegram was later found at 'Gimle', Quisling's official residence during the later part of the war, and on the draft, in Quisling's own handwriting, the time of despatch was noted – 10.00 am. The telegram informed Hitler that 'a national Norwegian government has been formed under my leadership' and asked for the Führer's support.[80] Had Quisling only known. there was no point in sending this telegram. Hitler had already instructed Bräuer to insist on a Quisling government. But Bräuer, opposed to the very idea of a Quisling administration, had not told Quisling of Hitler's support. Quisling's part in the decision to appeal to the Führer is not easy to establish. He was certainly strongly encouraged by Scheidt and Hagelin, and he himself claimed that the telegram was drafted by Scheidt.[81] But since Quisling was to be the beneficiary of this approach to Hitler it may be assumed that he was at least in favour of the scheme, especially as he believed that during his visit to Berlin he had established some kind of special relationship with the Führer.

Quisling next turned to certain details of administration; he took an office in the Storting building and there, according to Knudsen, he convened 'a series of meetings . . . with leading men and corporations within industry, trade and workday life'. It was then that he encountered the first signs of serious resistance to his government; these representatives were very reluctant to give him aid or comfort. Knudsen recalled that 'the attitude of the official representatives of industry to Quisling's address was rather cool, but otherwise I maintain that he had unanimous support'.[82] Knudsen's evidence is, however, somewhat suspect; he goes on to assert that 'the press also promised Quisling its support. . . . Every newspaper loyally quoted all the notices that Quisling sent, and it is no use saying that they were compelled to do so, because the new government did not possess any means of compelling anyone to do anything.'[83] According to a report of Bräuer's, written on 11 April, 'Immediately after occupation the direction of the Norwegian press was taken over by the Press Attaché of the German Legation.'[84] Von Tangens, the Press Attaché, seems at this time to have favoured Quisling's administration, and it seems likely that he was largely responsible for the compliance of the press.

After these negotiations with leading public personalities Quisling went again to the Foreign Ministry. There an attempt was made to prevent his entry, but after some argument he was admitted. Having spent some time there looking at various papers, Quisling and Knudsen started to walk back to the hotel. They were astonished to find that 'everyone was seized with wild panic, people were fleeing out of the town, in buses, trains, cars, carts and whatever means of locomotion they could lay their hands on'.[85] A rumour was abroad that Oslo was about to be bombarded by British warships; it was said that this story was being assiduously fostered by the police, on Welhaven's instructions.[86] Who exactly was responsible for the panic has never been established. Certainly not the Germans, for on 11 April the ambassador reported: 'Many inhabitants fled the city in terror, the most absurd rumors were circulating and found credence among these Phaeacians unaccustomed to war and the struggle for existence . . . even the police were infected by the panic. Everything pointed to a systematic incitement of the population.'[87] Quisling sought to take advantage of the confusion by giving orders for Welhaven's suspension and arrest.[88] Bräuer, on the other hand, reported:

'On the first evening representatives of the city administration and the Oslo Commissioner of Police came and made a declaration of loyalty to me personally.'[89] It seems unlikely, therefore, that Welhaven was responsible for creating these panic conditions.

For the rest of the day Quisling was occupied with administrative business, interrupted only by the unwelcome news that the King had informed Bräuer that he would name no government headed by the NS leader. Quisling and his advisers were put out at this, but they still hoped that Irgens's mission would change the situation. None the less another plan was now mooted – that Hagelin should journey to Berlin in order to contact Rosenberg and, if possible, the Führer himself. The day ended in an atmosphere of gloom. Quisling was at last realising that he had as many enemies among the Germans as among his own countrymen. Bräuer clearly desired to negotiate with the King without the embarrassment of a Quisling government, while opinion among the military was no more favourable. Von Falkenhorst and Pohlman agreed with Bräuer, while earlier in the day Engelbrecht had attempted to eject Quisling from the Hotel Continental, which he wanted to turn into the German headquarters.[90]

On the next day, 11 April, there were several important developments. At 7.00 am Irgens saw the King, who refused to accept the draft presented to him by what he termed an unconstitutional government. Irgens then took this uncompromising reply back to Quisling, whom he saw at 3.00 pm in his new office in the Storting building.[91] By that time Quisling was resigned to the failure of Irgens's trip; he had already heard some further bad news, suggesting that even in Berlin support for his government had begun to weaken. That morning he had attempted to get through on the telephone to Berlin, in order to discuss matters with Hitler. The Führer was much too busy with the military problems of the Norwegian invasion to speak to him. But he was informed that at 5.00 pm, if Hitler could not speak to him, someone else in authority would.[92] At 5.21 pm the telephone link was established, but Hitler handed the telephone over to Ribbentrop,[93] who in turn passed it over to Hewel. Quisling's conversation with Hewel could deal only with general matters, though he did assure Hewel that his government had a firm grasp on affairs and that the situation was slowly returning to normal.[94] He also informed him that he had decided that Hagelin should visit Berlin to settle matters on a more personal basis. Immediately, through the influence of Scheidt and Schreiber, a plane was placed at the disposal of Hagelin, who was in Berlin at latest by the evening of 12 April.[95]

While Quisling was making every effort to consolidate his regime the plot to remove him from power was slowly and clumsily gaining momentum. Bräuer, eager to undermine Quisling's position as quickly as possible, had the terms of the German ultimatum announced on the national radio network, which by this time was safely under German control.[96] He calculated that if the Quisling government were seen to be a stumbling-block to a settlement, other forces in Norway might make some attempt to overthrow or circumvent it. Bräuer's move received unwitting support from the Nygaardsvold government by the announcement from local stations under its control that the King had refused to accept any government headed by Quisling. In Berlin also there was support for Bräuer's attitude. At 9.40 am (Norwegian time) on 11 April, Friedrich Gaus, director of the legal department of the Foreign Office (1923–43), telephoned Bräuer and ordered him to 'secure the files of all Norwegian ministries, especially the Foreign Ministry and the Military departments'.[97] Bräuer took the opportunity of informing Gaus that, despite the previous day's rebuff, he would try to maintain communication with the King. Gaus promised to inform the Foreign Minister, which was exactly what Bräuer was hoping for; once Ribbentrop realised that Quisling was the main hindrance to a settlement, Bräuer's aims would be near fulfilment.

In order to reinforce his point, Bräuer sent the Foreign Office a telegram suggesting that the King might consent to form a moderately cooperative government provided that Quisling were removed.[98] Soon after, at 11.00 am, Gaus, who had seen Ribbentrop, informed Bräuer that he 'should at once endeavor to reestablish contact with the King . . . to give the Norwegian people one last chance of a reasonable agreement'.[99] Bräuer promptly tried to arrange another interview with the King, through the agency of Johannessen, but was unable to do so.[100] Within the next hour, the military forces attempted to cut the problem short by eliminating the King. At noon they bombed Elverum, and four hours later, hearing that the King had fled to Nybergsund, bombed that small town also. From both these attacks the King was lucky enough to escape unhurt. Bräuer, who was not in favour of this method, was still trying to arrange a meeting, on terms which he described in a telegram he sent to Berlin at 11.50 am. In this message he informed the Foreign Office that in the course of his talk with the King on the previous day the King and Koht had pointed out that 'while they appreciated that during a period of occupation the Norwegian Government must enjoy the confidence of Germany, it must also enjoy the confidence of its own country. This confidence was not, however, enjoyed by Quisling, the lone wolf without followers, who was rejected by the country.'[101] Bräuer, therefore, was aiming at a Norwegian government which could work with the Germans. Quisling must be replaced, but by whom? Most of the possible candidates had committed themselves too openly to take up the task of compromise, Bräuer's second attempt to contact the King, at 1.00 pm, failed, and he was again left in a difficult position.[102]

Bräuer's failure to contact the King caused him momentarily to reverse his policy towards Quisling. In a long report which he despatched later in the day he recognised, though without enthusiasm, that Quisling could conceivably play some useful peripheral part, despite the fact that 'the personality of Quisling renders the situation exceptionally difficult

for Germany'.[103] During this temporary phase of pessimism von Neuhaus, who now felt that the tide was flowing in Quisling's favour, recognised him as Prime Minister.[104] He was the first and the only member of
the embassy staff to do so. For the rest of the day Bräuer tried in vain to
think of some compromise to break the stalemate. In his report he wrote:

> In the Norwegian view it would be quite possible to form a government
> from the Storting acceptable to the Germans, and possessing in sufficient
> measure the confidence of the Norwegian people. There even seems to be
> some readiness to admit Quisling as a member of this government and to
> entrust him with the Ministry of Defense or of Foreign Affairs. Although
> matters have already gone very far, it is still thought possible that every-
> thing can be put right without disowning Quisling.[105]

This opinion, of course, conflicted not only with all Bräuer's previous
assertions but also with the views expressed by virtually every Norwegian he had recently consulted. He did, indeed, go on to point out that
there were good reasons for thinking that the post of Prime Minister did
not really suit Quisling's talents:

> Quisling is not a man of action, he is more critical than productive, and
> one is impelled to conclude that he is lacking in initiative. It is hard to
> believe that he will be equal to his task, and already the probability is
> becoming apparent that, under Quisling, the German occupying power
> will of its own accord have to take things more and more in hand if
> general anarchy is not to break out to the detriment of our armed forces.[106]

While Bräuer was thus showing some weakening in his attitude towards Quisling, the pro-Quisling party in Berlin had already suffered
reverses from which it was never to recover. Hitler himself, as Hagelin
was to see only too well, had lost confidence in Quisling, and this so depressed Rosenberg that on 11 April he wrote: 'The Foreign Office has
declared that Quisling has nobody backing him in Norway. The Führer
expressed his agreement with this viewpoint.'[107] Moreover, several of
those charged with planning the military and naval details of the invasion
were annoyed at Quisling's failure to supply correct information. Some
even felt he had been indirectly responsible for the loss of the *Blücher* and
the disorganisation that followed. Hitler himself, according to Warlimont,
'failed to realise that in any major operation there will be periods of
crisis and these duly arrived. They produced a spectacle of pitiable
weakness lasting more than a week.'[108] Accordingly, Hitler tended to
blame Quisling for the military errors of the invasion plan and therefore
deemed him unsuitable for the task of organising the political life of
Norway.

From Norway itself there was considerable support for Hitler's change
of attitude. Reliable German sources reported gathering protests against
Quisling's *coup*.[109] From Stockholm the German military attaché,
General Bruno von Uthmann, reported that in Sweden Quisling was
commonly referred to as a criminal and the members of his government

as gangsters. In Trondheim they were saying they would sooner have the Germans to rule them than Quisling,[110] and since it was imperative for the Germans to control Trondheim as quickly as possible propaganda of this kind had considerable effect. In a local Trondheim newspaper on 11 April there appeared further criticism of Quisling's assumption of power. A strongly worded article declared that three at least of the members of Quisling's cabinet – Lie, Skancke and Prytz – knew nothing of their nomination before their names were announced on the radio; Quisling's government could not rely even on the support of its nominees.[111] All these reports confirmed the opinions of Bräuer and Pohlman and the rest who had opposed the policy of backing Quisling.

Another day of intense political activity followed on 12 April. The situation was so unclear that *Fritt Folk* could allege that negotiations between the King and the Germans were not yet broken off.[112] Quisling's belief that this was true led him to try to despatch Irgens to see the King again.[113] At the same time he had copies distributed of a proclamation declaring that the national government had assumed power in accordance with law 41 of the fundamental constitution.[114] Emboldened by promises of support from a few prominent Norwegians, including Knut Hamsun, the famous author, he held a press conference in the morning, at which he stated that 'the political parties will be abolished and a corporative system erected in their place'.[115] He did not, however, rule out working 'in conjunction with the Royal House',[116] for he hoped to come 'to an understanding with the King, whom he personally liked'.[117] The statement was typical of Quisling's political insensitivity. It had become evident to almost everyone that the King was refusing to treat with his opponents except in consultation with the Nygaardsvold government and with such respected advisers as Hambro. For all his optimism, Quisling knew that his position was very far from secure and Hagelin was sent to Berlin in order to try to bolster the authority of his government.

Bräuer had now regained control of the situation and was convinced that in some way Quisling must be deposed. His contacts with prominent Norwegians, through his own acquaintances and those of his embassy staff, were extensive, and with those of them who were anti-Quisling he shared a community of interest. They wanted not only to depose Quisling but also to stop hostilities and set up a temporary administration to carry out governmental duties without offence or hostility to the majority of the population. Certain anti-Quisling Norwegians had first made contact with Bräuer on 11 April, when a barrister called Rivertz learned that the Quisling government had not yet succeeded in establishing itself securely in German favour. It is not certain who gave him this information, but it was probably a German businessman named Geldmacher.[118] Rivertz then conceived the idea that the High Court could serve as a central body for civil administration in Norway. In this way an alternative to Quisling could be found by the Norwegians themselves. It was this initiative which led to the fall of the short-lived Quisling regime.

Rivertz decided to put his ideas to Paal Berg, formerly a Liberal cabinet minister and now Chief Justice of the Supreme Court, who was known to feel concern at Quisling's threat to lawful government. At the same time he informed Noack, who was still attached to the German embassy, of his intentions. Bräuer was thus aware, at least by the evening of the 11th, of a powerful anti-Quisling lobby likely to emerge within the next day or so. Noack, besides informing Bräuer, had also told several Norwegian business acquaintances of his fears, suggesting that they 'go to the German ambassador and inform him of the Norwegian view of the state of things'.[119] By the next day the activities of Noack and Rivertz were beginning to take effect. The two men, together with Geldmacher, had a long interview with Bräuer from 2.00 pm to 4.00 pm. The discussion ranged over a number of topics, but the central purpose of the meeting was clear – to try to find some measure of agreement which would lead to the overthrow of the Quisling government.

Shortly afterwards Bräuer had a discussion with two other Norwegians, who were also interested in getting rid of the Quisling government. Fridtjof Heyerdahl and Gunnar Schjelderup were businessmen and friends of Noack, who had contacted them on the previous day and urged them to report their views to the German ambassador.[120] Closeted with Bräuer for some time, they both expressed serious reservations about the Quisling regime. This was music to Bräuer's ears. At last he had discovered some influential Norwegians who were not merely willing but positively anxious to depose Quisling. Bräuer's pleasure was reinforced shortly afterwards by a report from Pastor Günther of the German Lutheran Church in Oslo, suggesting that Bishop Berggrav, the Primate of Norway, might be ready to lend support to a government which excluded Quisling.

By 12 April, then, Bräuer had proof of the existence of a group of highly influential Norwegians willing to set up a temporary administration which would displace Quisling. This was a considerable relief, for he had tried hard to put into effect the impossible policy dictated by Hitler. He had recognised from the outset that the chief problem presented by a Quisling government would probably be its hindrance to any settlement with the Norwegian authorities. Bräuer consequently accepted the detailed reports presented in good faith by Rivertz and his friends and proceeded to investigate further the possibility of a new government. If such a government could be set up then he believed that it was

> even now possible that the settlement of the question point by point might cause such a revolution in popular feeling that acquiescence on the part of the constitutional representatives of Norway might create the state of affairs requested, and originally striven for, by us.[121]

The intervention of the Supreme Court had the added advantage in Bräuer's eyes that in certain circumstances such an acceptance of authority might be deemed constitutionally correct.

Rivertz, Geldmacher, Schjelderup, Heyerdahl and Noack all reported the progress they had made to Berg. Of these Rivertz was naturally the most influential, for Berg respected both his intelligence and his integrity. For Berg and Bräuer the problems facing their respective countries were fairly similar. Both felt that to support Quisling would be a disastrous obstacle to any political settlement. Military occupation involving the rule of the army should, if possible, be avoided. Both hoped for the creation of a civilian government which the King would at least tolerate, if not support. On these lines Rivertz and Berg discussed the situation on the evening of 12 April.[122] Berg was particularly anxious, as many Norwegians were, that the King should think well of any temporary administration set up, and hoped that he might even recognise it, so long as it consisted of honest men who respected the constitution. Berg finally agreed to take the initiative in trying to set up such a body provided that it was 'an administrative council for civil management in the occupied territories'.[123] This would make clear the temporary nature of such an institution and would forestall the accusation that it was just another, even if better disguised, Quisling government.

Bräuer was meanwhile drafting a telegram to Ribbentrop informing him of these recent overtures. He did not hesitate to criticise Quisling, assuring Ribbentrop: 'I consider it necessary to reexamine the question whether we should continue to support Quisling.' He described the difficulties created by the German espousal of Quisling's cause:

> We have the situation almost as in civil war of the Norwegian people fighting directly against the usurper and only indirectly against the power supporting him. I daily receive assurances from genuine friends of Germany here that the Norwegians would be quite willing to subordinate themselves to me or even to the German military authorities, but that they could never bring themselves to accept a Quisling government.

Bräuer went on to point out other weaknesses in Quisling's government. His list of ministers was only a government on paper; four of the nominees were not in Oslo, and two of them had decided to decline Quisling's invitation. Bräuer added that it was quite possible that 'if the fugitive members of the Storting do not give in, the Government will be taken over by the Supreme Court'.[124] He realised the urgent need of an agreement and was ready to make an open attack upon Quisling in the hope that this would destroy his place in the sun of the Führer's favour.

Bräuer's optimism received ample justification on the morrow, when Quisling's government suffered its first serious check. On the morning of 13 April Berg, Heyerdahl and Schjelderup went to see the German ambassador. They suggested that he should approach the military authorities with a request that Berg be allowed a free passage through German-held territory in order that he might see the King. After some debate Bräuer agreed,[125] assuring his visitors that the Quisling government would not be allowed to obstruct any possible understanding

By stating this policy, for which he had not yet obtained approval from Berlin, the ambassador had taken a decisive initiative. He no longer felt obliged to encumber his efforts at a settlement with the dead weight of a Quisling regime. His decision soon received confirmation from Berlin.

While Bräuer was pursuing his new course with energy, Hagelin was struggling to re-establish Quisling's position in Berlin. He had gone to see Quisling's most likely supporter, Rosenberg, but even from him he could obtain no more than lukewarm offers of support.[126] Hagelin assured Rosenberg of Quisling's strong backing in Norway; tne situation would soon be straightened out, if all his friends stood firm. He then went to see Ribbentrop, who had by this time had an opportunity to study Bräuer's telegram. The Foreign Minister had never been an admirer of Quisling, and received Hagelin very coolly. Hagelin then went on to the Reich Chancellery, where he was to meet Hitler. By this time he can hardly have hoped for much from the meeting. If Rosenberg, Quisling's most consistent supporter from a very early stage, took a non-committal line,[127] not much could be expected from Hitler. Hagelin was, of course, unaware that Rosenberg had belatedly realised that the responsibility for further decisions on Norway must be taken by others. He also was a typical politician of the Third Reich – more anxious to remain in Hitler's good graces than to make a decision which might turn out wrongly. He was well aware that during the past few days official opinion in Berlin had moved strongly against his protégé. Neither Hagelin nor Quisling was in a position to judge how seriously matters had developed.

Hagelin approached his interview with Hitler, therefore, under an entire misapprehension of the situation. The meeting lasted from 11.15 am until 1.15 pm, although Hagelin did withdraw for a short while when Arne Scheel, the Norwegian ambassador, came to see Hitler.[128] Hagelin's hope was to persuade Hitler that the most effective agency for the transmission of German wishes to the Norwegian public was the Quisling government. But even had he been able to carry conviction, he was given no opportunity to do so. From the outset of the meeting Hitler harangued him, reading out a Reuters report from Stockholm which stated that Major Hvoslef, one of the ministers nominated by Quisling, had refused to serve and had retired to Sweden. Hagelin, forced on to the defensive, could only retort that 'this must be a lie, for he himself had seen the telegram in which Hvoslef had placed his services at the disposal of the new Government. Hvoslef had been an officer in active service in Finland and had organised the SA of the Nasjonal Samling.'[129]

Hagelin had to admit also that the political situation was not yet under control. To some extent he blamed both the German military and civil authorities in Norway. The military should not have allowed the Nygaardsvold government to escape and Bräuer had ruined prospects of an arrangement with the King by going to see him before Quisling had been able to make preparations for negotiation. Knowing, however, that

Hitler was keen to come to an agreement with the King, Hagelin emphasised the anxiety of the Quisling government to make its peace with the King. Hitler, even more anxious about his military venture, then proceeded to lecture Hagelin on the complexity of the military situation. Jodl's diary for 14 April records: 'Hitler became terribly agitated. Every detail must be ordered from here',[130] and this preoccupation with the military crisis may well explain Hitler's desire to end the political strife in Norway. He had come to share von Falkenhorst's view that political strife must not be allowed to obstruct German military requirements. If Quisling's government proved to be a serious impediment to the conclusion of armistice or peace terms with the Norwegians, then it was expendable.

Hitler, however, was less despondent than Rosenberg. He asked Hagelin how much support Quisling could count on, to which Hagelin replied 'that this would amount to 15 percent of the population, including the most active elements'. Hitler then suggested that the 'Quisling Government would have to secure the active support of certain groups . . . such as the chambers of commerce, the merchants, the shipping interests, intellectual elements, professors, etc'.[131] Even then, it seems, Hitler had not given up hope that the Quisling government might yet be able to carry out proper administrative duties. He asked Hagelin whether a personal letter could be forwarded to the King. Hagelin replied that he could guarantee this through his 'personal contacts with good friends of the King'.[132] The Führer then decided that he must discuss the matter further with Scheel, and Hagelin left the room. After Scheel's departure Hitler saw Hagelin once more, though only briefly, and the whole matter was left undecided. But Hitler agreed to Hagelin's proposal that Major Richter should be appointed military liaison officer to the Quisling government, and this gave Hagelin the impression that Hitler intended to continue his support for Quisling.[133]

Hagelin's impression was wrong. Hitler felt himself in no way bound to support the Quisling government. He was merely unsure what course to adopt, and while making up his mind he decided to let the present situation continue. His conversation with Scheel seems to have convinced him that little could be expected from the King or the Nygaardsvold government.[134] The absence of reliable political information from Norway certainly seems to have worried Hitler, and, after Hagelin's departure from the Chancellery, he decided to send a special envoy to Oslo to investigate the situation there. Appropriately, the man he chose was Habicht, who had been present throughout the conversation with Hagelin. Habicht's relations with Rosenberg had been poor, but he had no strong opinions for or against a Quisling government. In this he was supported by Hitler, who ended his interview with Hagelin by stating that 'it made no difference to him who ruled up there'.[135]

If Habicht was to act as Hitler's personal emissary in Oslo, this was not made clear to Hagelin. In the afternoon of 13 April, at 4.30 pm, Hagelin had a long conversation with Scheidt, who was very uneasy about the whole business and stressed the fact that the opinion of the military authorities in Oslo was by then 'firmly against Quisling'.[136] Scheidt at least had realised that Quisling's position was very precarious and he was desperate enough to advise Hagelin to try to settle matters with Ribbentrop, whom he had previously, and correctly, judged to be totally hostile to Quisling's pretensions. Hagelin was not so pessimistic, and believed that he would be able to have a serious talk with Habicht on the journey to Oslo;[137] this, he thought, would ensure Habicht's co-operation with Quisling. It does not seem to have crossed his mind that Habicht would act as a troubleshooter. Scheidt, who had a better idea of the methods of the Third Reich, was much more pessimistic.

Bräuer was as confused as Hagelin. He was informed by Ribbentrop in a telephone conversation that evening at 8.30 pm that Habicht was on his way to Norway, but he was not told of the purpose of his visit. On the whole he was probably not displeased; he must have realised that a Foreign Office official would hardly be likely to add strength to Quisling's position. The permanent officials, such as von Weizsäcker, on being told of Habicht's projected trip, had certainly drawn that conclusion.

Ribbentrop's telephone conversation was quickly followed by a telegram informing the ambassador that Habicht's mission would mean several weeks' stay.[138] Plans had been changed, and Habicht's departure was delayed until Sunday 14 April. Hagelin, meanwhile, had set out on his return journey to Oslo. Ribbentrop then sent Bräuer another telegram, which arrived at 4.15 am on Sunday, informing him of the delay in Habicht's departure and adding that Habicht had

> instructions to organise propaganda in Norway and in particular to place himself at Quisling's disposal for propaganda purposes should the occasion arise. Without prejudice to the independent character of this task and to Under State Secretary Habicht's responsibility for its execution, your position as Minister and Plenipotentiary of the Reich will not be affected by this special mission. I request you to support Herr Habicht in his work by all available means.[139]

Not unnaturally Bräuer feared that, if Habicht's mission was really intended to strengthen the effect of Quisling's propaganda, this would prove a threat to the negotiations he had opened with Berg. His temporary alarm, however, was soon dispelled on Habicht's arrival in Oslo.

In Berlin, Scheidt was anxiously trying to prop up the Quisling government by every means in his power. As director of the German liaison staff with the head of the Norwegian government he sent Bräuer a memorandum on 13 April, informing him of a talk he had recently had with Colonel Schmundt, which had caused him alarm.

> To my mind the danger exists that these gentlemen [the staff of the German military forces in Norway] have gotten their information from those circles which claim to be nationally-minded and loyal, but are zealously pursuing the course of discrediting the Quisling Government.[140]

Scheidt was particularly eager to emphasise that what made Quisling invaluable to the Germans was his political reliability.

> All of us know from Germany how the work of a government can be sabotaged, when people outwardly protest their loyalty, but secretly sabotage every effort. Besides, a government built on a compromise would not be a fit partner to achieve certain of Germany's political goals for the future.[141]

The desperate straits in which Quisling's party now found itself may be judged by the fact that Scheidt felt obliged to make this personal appeal to Bräuer, a man who was known to be hostile to Quisling's pretensions. All Scheidt's fears were to be confirmed soon after Habicht's arrival.

This day, Sunday 14 April, proved to be critical in the short life of Quisling's government. For Bräuer the day began with a telephone conversation with Ribbentrop, at 11.00 am. The ambassador informed his chief:

> The situation is such that we must do something at once to pacify the population. . . . At the moment, I have summoned the Supreme Court and I intend to form a directorate with the Supreme Court. The question is whether this should be done with or without Quisling. The matter is very urgent as acts of sabotage have taken place and there are still people who are ready to put themselves at our disposal. These people, especially the administrative officials, have for the greater part refused to pledge their support to Quisling. Consequently, I must either take the matter in hand myself or put myself entirely on Quisling's side.[142]

But although such a decision might enable Bräuer 'to reach a peaceful settlement'[143] that day, Ribbentrop was bound by Hitler's decision to send Habicht to investigate the political problems in Norway, and could give no clear order to the ambassador. This fact, however, did permit Bräuer to continue with his existing policy.

At noon Pastor Günther came to see Bräuer and von Neuhaus in order to report on his own investigations. He had much encouraging information, including the news that 'Paal Berg, President of the Supreme Court, proposed to the King by telephone via the Norwegian Legation in Stockholm that negotiations be begun with the German occupation authorities at once and unconditionally'. Bishop Berggrav had also been in contact with the King's entourage, and had had a conversation with Hambro, who informed him that 'the King and he desired that an administrative body authorised by the King be set up'.[144] Berggrav had also expressed willingness to transmit to the King the conditions offered by the occupying power. Bräuer was enthusiastic about this further evidence of Norwegian goodwill; Ribbentrop was more cautious.[145]

Habicht had now arrived in Oslo. Accompanying him were Gauleiter Frauenfeld, a former colleague of his in Austria, and Legation Secretary Tafel, one of the Foreign Minister's protégés. From this moment events moved quickly. Bräuer suggested that Habicht would like to meet von

Falkenhorst and Engelbrecht. He could judge fairly accurately what those two inveterate enemies of Quisling would tell Habicht; there was no need for him to be present. It was at this point that Habicht became aware of the full political significance of his mission. A choice between Quisling and some kind of alternative administration was clearly necessary; the existing situation, beset with uncertainty, was damaging to German interests, and the generals informed him that in their opinion Quisling could not be used. Bräuer then saw Habicht once more, and discovered that he had been impressed by the generals' firmness. Feeling that the right moment had come, he told Habicht of his plans for a Norwegian Administrative Council.[146] The project appealed to Habicht; it seemed to offer a solution to most of his difficulties and he at once fell in with the ambassador's schemes.

Shortly after 1.00 pm Habicht and Bräuer met Berg at Bräuer's private residence,[147] and the idea of an Administrative Council was fully examined. The notion of handing over civil authority to respected Norwegians who were prepared to co-operate was accepted by the three men; the two main problems were the peaceful demission of Quisling's government, and the task of persuading the Supreme Court to accept Berg's decision. To a certain extent Berg's participation was a guarantee that his decision would be acceptable. The first problem, however, remained serious. In order to try to avoid too much trouble the negotiators agreed to compromise. They finally decided to base the settlement on four conditions:

(1) The government council shall pledge complete loyalty to the occupation authorities. (2) Each member of the council shall be personally responsible for maintenance of peace and order and for carrying out the instructions of the occupation authorities. (3) The President of the Supreme Court shall proclaim publicly that on April 9 Quisling showed himself to be a good patriot by stepping into the breach and then in renouncing the exercise of government authority. (4) Quisling will take take over certain duties connected with the winding-up of military affairs and, when dealing with such matters, he will have the rank of Head of Department.[148]

The success of the whole scheme turned upon Quisling's attitude. If he were to refuse the proffered compromise, then he would have to be forced out of office, and a very awkward situation would result. Fortunately for Bräuer, Quisling's own position was far from secure. His efforts to set up a government had had little success. His attempts to consolidate his position between 9 and 14 April had done no more than underline the meagre support there was for his government. Quisling's ministers had proved from the very outset to be broken reeds. When he had first announced his government, only two of the designated ministers had been in Oslo – Meidell and Hustad. Skancke and Prytz had been in Trondheim, Lie in Finnmark, Lunde in Stavanger, and Hvoslef in Finland. Thus, even including himself and Hagelin, the new Prime Minister had had only a ministerial staff of four upon whom he could call immediately. The reaction of those within Oslo was markedly different from that of those out of reach of his personal influence. Hagelin accepted Quisling's offer on the spot. Hustad was called to the telephone by Knudsen,[149] as was Meidell.[150] They were both summoned to the Hotel Continental and offered ministerial posts which they accepted. All the other ministers were informed of their appointments after they had been announced over the radio network. The ministerial list thus included five men who had not been consulted[151] when the list was sent to the Norwegian Telegram Bureau at about 6.00 pm.

The reactions of these five varied in hostility. Hvoslef, far away from the crisis at Torneå in Finland, had received a telegram on 8 April suggesting that he might accept the post of Minister of Defence in any government that Quisling might form in the future.[152] Such an invitation was rather different from the unwelcome news, that reached him on 10 April, that he had actually become a minister. In the afternoon of 11 April Hvoslef sent a message to the Norwegian Telegram Bureau stating that he did not wish to become a member of the government. He contacted Hambro soon after and joined the Norwegian army,[153] from which he was discharged on 13 June 1940. Lie, who was at Kirkenes, drove to Stockholm, rejected Quisling's offer, and claimed to have 'been appalled by the radio announcement'.[154] Prytz and Skancke, who lived near each other in Trondheim, were in communication almost immediately.[155] Prytz had in fact been informed of his new post by his servant, so little attention was he giving to the crisis in Oslo.[156] Skancke's first inclination was to dissociate himself from Quisling's political *démarche*, but eventually he and Prytz decided to await further developments. According to a conversation on 13 April between Sedlatzek, a German official in Trondheim, and the German Legation in Stockholm, both men would have preferred a pro-German administration without Quisling. 'There was not the least doubt that the two of them looked critically upon the *coup* mounted by Quisling',[157] declared Sedlatzek. Yet the situation was so confused that Sedlatzek was not sure whether he should arrest Prytz and Skancke or expedite their intended journey to Oslo. Lunde, in Stavanger, acted rather more equivocally, at first showing reluctance to be involved and later changing his mind.

Quisling's government had, therefore, a poor start, and all the efforts of those loyal to the aims of their leader were of no avail. In fact, so onerous had the task of forming a working government become by 14 April that it seems possible Quisling was rather relieved by the events of that day. The strain of operating in an almost totally hostile political environment had become wellnigh intolerable. Despite the absence of several of those he had nominated, Quisling, aided by Hustad, Meidell and Knudsen, had attempted to take over as head of the government on 10 April.[158] The faithful Knudsen had tried to rally NS support by calling party members to Oslo, to assist in the task of administration, but the response was very slight. The new ministers were largely ignored by the civil servants, so their orders could not be put into effect. In an attempt to counter this situation Quisling decided to press on with his plans for the formation of a one-party state. The general secretary of NS, Rolf Fuglesang, was appointed also to the post of government secretary. The party machine, however, was not equal to the additional burden of government administration. Similarly, a special government press agency was set up, directed by Arnt Rishovd, the editor of *Fritt Folk*. Other attempts, such as that to reorganise the police, had small success. On 12 April, Quisling issued an order replacing Welhaven by Christian Lange, but this was no more successful than his other manoeuvres. The whole edifice was to be headed by Quisling, with his liaison officer, Scheidt, taking second place. Quisling got as far as putting his plans on paper, but the time allowed him was too short to put most of them into effect.[159]

Much of Quisling's time, in fact, was spent in trying to solve the problems of his subordinates. Meidell managed to get involved in some complex negotiations with certain trade unionists, and Quisling saw in this an attempt to undermine his position. He also disagreed with Meidell over the part to be played by the King in the restoration of effective government in Norway. According to Hagelin, 'Quisling was very annoyed with Meidell and told him that he had nothing to do with political affairs.'[160] Trust was thus lacking at a very early stage. If Meidell spent his free time interfering in matters which Quisling regarded as his preserve, Hustad was able to do nothing at all. Hagelin had a disagreement with the chief civil servant in his department, Sellæg, who consequently refused to take orders from him.[161] Only Quisling himself seems to have exercised the slightest control over his department. On 10 April he drafted a telegram to all Norwegian diplomatic missions informing them that the Nygaardsvold government 'was under liquidation'.[162] The telegram was sent at 4.01 pm on 11 April, and was totally ignored. This was all that the Quisling government achieved, in its numerous attempts to carry out routine administrative functions.

The confusion in the government was partly due to the number of functions which Quisling arrogated to himself. The acting Prime Minister had also appointed himself Foreign Minister. The document giving Irgens instructions to negotiate with the King was signed by Quisling in his capacity as Foreign Minister. When Lie failed to take up his portfolio as Minister of Justice, Quisling was ready to fill the breach, and signed the order suspending Welhaven as 'acting chief of the Ministry of Justice'.[163] More commonly he described himself as 'Prime Minister' or just signed himself 'Quisling'. These titles really meant nothing, for there was no administration to carry out any orders that Quisling might choose to give. From beginning to end, Quisling's government was a fiction.

The arrival of Habicht was, in some ways, a relief for Quisling, since it led directly to the retirement of his government; but it was also an embarrassment. Quisling desired real power and hoped that Habicht would be able to relieve him from an almost untenable position. Before long, the pro-Quisling faction discovered what their leader's fate was to be. Schreiber, seeking some form of compromise, had suggested that Quisling be made chief for demobilisation in a new government. His suggestion was adopted as a sensible way out of the difficulty, and early in the afternoon of 10 April the meeting broke up, each party going to consult his own supporters. Paal Berg very soon obtained the consent of his colleagues of the Supreme Court, who submitted a memorandum in which they stated that the Supreme Court had undertaken to appoint a temporary civil administrative council for those parts of the country then occupied by the German forces 'for the reasons indicated in the proclamation by the Supreme Court. As is further stated there, the Supreme Court is doing this in the anticipation that the King of Norway will approve this step. The Supreme Court will inform the King about this as soon as possible.'[164] This agreement was to be the beginning of the downfall of the political independence of Berg and his colleagues, but for the moment it seemed as if it would provide an adequate solution to the problems which confronted them. The Supreme Court also agreed to the four points accepted by Berg.

While Habicht departed to see Quisling, Bräuer had a conversation with Scheidt which apparently 'brought out little opposition to this solution'. Bräuer was also under the impression that Quisling would accept the new plan, for he reported to the Foreign Minister: 'As . . . Quisling himself does not rate his prospects very high, he will probably accept the solution readily.'[165] Habicht, however, found his task more onerous than he had expected. Although Quisling had found the difficulties in the way of his administration virtually insuperable, he was unwilling to give up even the semblance of power without a struggle. At this turn of events he was handicapped by the absence of Scheidt, who was in conference with the German ambassador, and by the exhaustion of Hagelin, who had only just returned from Berlin. A long, and apparently bitter, argument ensued between Habicht and Quisling. Knudsen, who was present, suggested that the reason for the 'tumultuous meetings' Habicht and Bräuer had with Quisling was their belief 'that the King would yield and accept the German demands if only Quisling were removed'.[166] Quisling opposed this belief, and, in the event, proved a better judge of the character of the Norwegian King and the refugee government than Bräuer and his self-appointed Norwegian pundits. Habicht, who had spent most of the afternoon with Quisling, returned to see Bräuer with the matter still unsettled. Bräuer was obliged to report to Hewel later that evening that 'Quisling was not so willing as I had reported this afternoon'.[167]

After reporting on the progress of events at 6.00 pm[168] Bräuer then went to see von Falkenhorst in order to inform him of developments. The German military staff was glad to hear that the political situation was

at last to be stabilised and the ambassador left, confident of the full backing of von Falkenhorst and Engelbrecht. Immediately after, Bräuer went
to a full-scale conference at the Hotel Continental. Beside the ambassador
and Quisling, there were present Habicht, von Neuhaus, Graf, a legation
secretary, Hagelin and Scheidt.[169] This important meeting lasted from
about 6.30 pm to 9.00 pm. Bräuer and Habicht told Quisling that 'the
best solution for the situation in Norway after the occupation by the
German troops, in view of the serious consequences which further resistance by the Norwegian troops might entail, was the resignation of the
Quisling Government'.[170] Quisling was not prepared to accept this and
contested Bräuer's claim that his own resignation would make it easier to
set up a constitutional government. On this matter at least Quisling and
his supporters were correct. Whatever the legal basis of the Quisling regime, it seems clear that the legalistic arguments by which Bräuer and
Habicht tried to justify their actions and those of Berg were untenable.
The proposed Administrative Council could seek no comfort from the
approval of the Supreme Court, for in this matter it was acting *ultra vires*.

The chief weakness in Quisling's arguments lay in the fact that, to
operate effectively, his government needed a solid base of support. He
and his party did not enjoy such backing; indeed, according to Habicht
'in the opinion of the Germans the Government had only a very small
minority behind it'.[171] In such a situation constitutional niceties were
irrelevant. Quisling's verbal victory over the advocates of the legality of
the proposed Administrative Council could avail him nothing unless he
could demonstrate that his government could wield power effectively.
Here the events of the past few days told heavily against him and in
favour of the Administrative Council. Bräuer and Habicht correctly perceived that even if Berg's actions were constitutionally dubious they were
likely to win much greater support than those of Quisling some five days
before. Quisling and his colleagues, on the contrary, argued that 'apart
from the lack of a tenable legal basis, the appraisal of the situation in
Norway by the German gentlemen was incorrect and was based on false
premises and information. This information came from the circles of the
old party cliques.' Quisling went on to point out that the helpful co-
operation which he and NS had envisaged would be of immeasurable
assistance to the occupying power. Habicht retorted that 'there were
situations in which larger viewpoints justified a break even with political
partners. He mentioned . . . that the events in Austria in 1936, under
which he himself had suffered, also represented a similar fate.'

Quisling tried to counter Habicht's very cogent argument by suggesting that if Germany insisted on pursuing such a policy she ran the
risk of 'losing the only friends she had in Norway'. He was confident
that in the end he would be able to win the people over. This claim
was greeted with some scepticism, though Quisling was informed that

in the negotiations with the men of the proposed administrative council the condition would be laid down that Quisling's exit should occur in such a way as not only not to reflect on him but, on the contrary, make him a great figure, with the accompaniment of suitable publicity.[172]

Hagelin and his leader found themselves unable to accept the conclusions of Habicht and Bräuer. The meeting ended without any positive decision.

Later that evening the ambassador and the special envoy had a long telephone call to Hewel.[173] This took place at about 9.40 pm. Hewel was not entirely happy with the progress of events. Believing that the awkward question about Quisling's participation had not been resolved, Hewel did, however, inform Bräuer and Habicht that the Foreign Mnister agreed in principle with the proposals submitted to him, but 'would like to know how they envisaged continued participation by Quisling'. Ribbentrop had thus tried to insure against both possibilities – the failure of Quisling's government and the displeasure Hitler was likely to show if Quisling were to suffer humiliation. In fact, on 14 April, Ribbentrop seemed to be more worried by the second problem, for he told Hewel that he was 'particularly anxious that Quisling should not be compromised outwardly'.[174] Bräuer then informed Hewel that a purely decorative post had been found for Quisling with the title of Commissioner for Demobilisation. Despite the optimism of Bräuer, Hewel was more cautious, informing the ambassador that 'the Führer would in any case like Quisling to be held in reserve'.[175]

Thus while Bräuer and Habicht were trying to construct an administrative council which would enable them to get rid of Quisling their superiors in Berlin were preparing for the possibility that the new body would prove unsatisfactory. In this matter Hitler and Ribbentrop showed some appreciation of the real state of Norwegian opinion. They were particularly worried about the status of the new body and were eager to know who was to take on the burden of being chairman. Bräuer was able to tell Hewel that the chairman would be nominated by Berg and would be the President of the Oslo Council. He thought this appointment entirely satisfactory, especially as it would be backed by Bishop Berggrav. These assurances seemed to relieve Hewel's mind. When the vexed question of Quisling's attitude was raised, however, Bräuer was placed in a position of some difficulty and could only inform Hewel that 'when all is said and done he sees the necessity for it but he has, nevertheless, made various attempts to get round it'.[176] Scheidt was said to be in full agreement with the trend of German policy, and Hewel was left to infer that Quisling would raise no serious objections.

Bräuer knew, of course, that this was untrue, and Hewel does not seem to have wholly accepted the ambassador's report, for he then insisted on talking to Habicht. Habicht confirmed Bräuer's statement and told Hewel that he had found the Norwegian leader 'in a frame of mind which makes it seem absolutely impossible that he could assert himself. He is at bottom entirely unstable and weak. That is all I can say about it. Nothing can be done with him. He lacks all control.' Considering the time and money expended on him and his movement, the authorities in Berlin were not so willing to accept this new view of Quisling as a broken reed useless in the carrying out of German policy, and accordingly Hewel told Habicht: 'The Foreign Minister agrees to the proposal but expressly desires that Quisling be dispensed with in a dignified manner and that he will take part in sessions of the Government even though he has not a seat.'[177] Habicht was to inform Quisling that 'the Führer appreciates his attitude to the full and that the Foreign Minister will also send Quisling a personal communication in writing'.[178] Hewel also thought it desirable that the King should return to Oslo, thus removing a possible cause of embarrassment to the new council. If the King were to return, then the sacrifice of Quisling would not have been in vain.

Habicht and Bräuer can, therefore, have been under no illusion that the consent of Quisling to the surrender of his position was essential. They decided that there should be one further effort at persuasion, and a meeting with him was arranged for 11.45 pm that evening at the home of the ambassador. Bräuer, Habicht, von Neuhaus, Quisling and Hagelin were present but Scheidt was left out of the discussion entirely. Quisling was informed of the talk between Bräuer, Habicht and Hewel, including the fact that he was to be held in reserve in case of the collapse of the Administrative Council. The German negotiators made every attempt to placate the irate Norwegian, informing him that he would be given the task, outside the Administrative Council,

> of demobilizing the Norwegian Army and thereby receive an opportunity to exert a far-reaching influence on the demobilized soldiers. This would benefit his movement. No restriction of the movement through measures by the new administrative council would be tolerated; on the contrary, the assurance could be given that everything would be done to promote his movement.

Quisling was anxious about the status of his party and private guard, the members of which had been forbidden to wear uniforms by the Norwegian government. Bräuer stated that 'a prohibition against uniforms was out of the question',[179] and Quisling could be confident that, once the immediate crisis had passed, he could count on German support for his movement.

In the meantime Quisling felt it essential to maintain contact with those who favoured his political participation. He therefore 'expressly requested that Reichsamtsleiter Scheidt might remain with him in Norway for subsequent consultation and as liaison chief with the German authorities, while Hagelin would go to Berlin as his representative'. The ambassador saw that this demand would not involve dangerous complications for the Administrative Council and gave his approval to Quisling's suggestion. Even after this concession Quisling and his colleague were unwilling to accept Bräuer's solution. By this time the negotiations had become wearisome to all parties and, as it was about 1.30 am, it was decided to end the meeting on the understanding that 'Quisling and Hagelin would consider the proposed solution'.[180] Bräuer and Habicht wrongly concluded that this would mean capitulation by Quisling and, immediately after his departure, they telephoned Berlin to inform Hewel: 'Quisling agrees to the proposed arrangement. Further details will be settled tomorrow morning. After that a report will be sent from here.'[181] This report was somewhat premature, for Quisling had still not resolved to retire from office.

Talks were resumed the next day, 15 April, at 11.00 am in the German Legation. Only three people were present – Quisling, Habicht and Bräuer. Quisling continued to object to the proposed arrangements and suggested that he be allowed to submit his objections to the Führer, for his personal consideration. Bräuer was by this time thoroughly exasperated and retorted that 'the decision of the Führer had already been received and if Quisling refused they would just proceed with the business'.[182] Quisling once again stressed that the premises of the ambassador's arguments were false and his conclusions therefore faulty, and he gave Bräuer formal notice of his dissatisfaction. Quisling finally proposed a special directorate, consisting of himself, Berg, Bishop Berggrav and Ingolf Christensen, Governor of the county of Oslo. This was also rejected;[183] it was Quisling's last throw, and he had lost. He had to concede defeat with as much grace as he could muster, and was asked to prepare a statement for the press. He replied that 'he would place the chief emphasis in this statement on explaining his resignation as due to his inability to take responsibility for further bloodshed and that for him this was the decisive point'.[184] This reply apparently met with the approval of Habicht and Bräuer.

Bräuer's final important task was to arrange for the formal transfer of the authority of the Quisling government to the Administrative Council. On the part of the Administrative Council no objections were made. Indeed, some who had objected most strongly to Quisling's assumption of power were willing to be conciliatory in order to facilitate its transfer. Welhaven, for example, thought that 'Quisling should go with honour'.[185] Berg and his colleagues were of a similar opinion. Their difficulties were quite different, and concerned problems of status and recognition. The Supreme Court had suggested that the Administrative Council should not handle negotiations with Germany, but confine itself to internal functions.[186] The Germans, however, saw the new body as having rather more important responsibilities than those of mere internal administration. The Administrative Council had also to obtain royal assent to its actions, in order to secure legitimacy not only in the eyes of the Norwegians but also in those of the Germans. On 15 April neither of these problems had been solved.

In these two unsolved problems there was much fertile ground for future discord between the Germans and the Administrative Council. But Bräuer decided to press on with his policy. At 5.00 pm on the same day a formal announcement was made of the setting up of the Administrative Council. In addition to Berg and Christensen, who was named as chairman, the new body included some important figures in Norwegian public life: Didrik Seip, Rector of Oslo University, Judge Ole Harbek and Dr Andreas Diesen. Even more important was the support given by many public personalities and by several representative bodies, including most of the prominent industrial and labour associations. The new council was thus assured of a much broader backing than Quisling had ever had. Bräuer's announcement of the change of government was made in the conference room of the Academy of Sciences in the presence of 'the President of the Supreme Court, the chairman and members of the Government Committee, and representatives of the largest Norwegian organisations and of the press'.[187] The ambassador explained the events leading to the formation of this new body and hoped that it would soon be possible to return to a peaceful situation in Norway.

In order to ensure that the press was properly briefed, copies of the various pronouncements made were distributed. According to Bräuer the press was given:

(1) An announcement by me; (2) A proclamation by the President of the Supreme Court; (3) His statement of recognition for Quisling; (4) The text of the latter's radio address (statement to the Norwegian people); (5) An appeal by the Government Committee, and (6) A declaration of approval by the business and labor organizations.[188]

These statements were given to the press in the hope that the Norwegian public would be fully informed about the extent of the backing given to the Administrative Council. Bräuer's confidence in this method was fully justified by the fact that *Dagbladet* produced an extra edition which gave great prominence to all the important developments to which the ambassador had wished to draw attention.[189]

The meeting did not, however, end without one final protest from Quisling. He was both hurt and annoyed by the attitude of the Germans. According to Knudsen he vented his rage on the new chairman of the Administrative Council, who had offered to help him on with his overcoat. Quisling snatched it out of his hand and said:

No, Mr. Christensen, that I will not allow you. You have these thirty years been walking about acting [the] patriot and friend of the military defence of Norway, and now it becomes evident that you are willing to take over the government on German terms, which I had rejected in contempt. You have made yourself a vile hostage in the hands of the Wehrmacht. You will be forced to join in the plundering of our people, and when that is finished your new taskmasters will throw you out of office. It will be well deserved.[190]

On this note Quisling left. Henceforth he was to throw his weight against the Administrative Council. *Fritt Folk* the next day reported: 'Our country and party have taken a retrograde step.'[191] Quisling's disapproval of the Administrative Council was soon to receive support from a number of unexpected quarters, giving him some consolation for his political defeat.

From all the negotiations leading to the formation of the Administrative Council one clear conclusion may be drawn – that, in his eagerness to supplant Quisling, Bräuer did not fully investigate the complications that were bound to arise from the installation of the new regime. His superiors in Berlin were fully aware of them. At 5.50 pm on 15 April he received a telegram from Ribbentrop instructing him to ensure that

> neither the King nor the Crown Prince retain the possibility of establishing themselves anywhere in Norway with members of the old government, . . . It would therefore be politically desirable, if possible, to seize the persons of the King and the Crown Prince without endangering their lives.[192]

Bräuer was instructed to take this matter up with von Falkenhorst. From Ribbentrop's point of view the King's assent was absolutely essential to prop up the authority of the Administrative Council. The King must either be persuaded to give his assent to the events of 15 April of his own free will, or he must be held in captivity, and proclamations issued in his name. Otherwise there would be no advantage for the Germans in Quisling's removal from office.

It soon became apparent in Berlin that the reaction of the King towards the Administrative Council was likely to be hostile. Ribbentrop therefore decided to see Bräuer in order to discuss matters personally with him, and instructed him on 16 April 'to come to Berlin by the quickest route'.[193] In all probability a telephone conversation on the previous evening between Ribbentrop and Habicht[194] was the immediate cause of the recall of both Bräuer and Habicht. Bräuer reported that Habicht would arrive in Berlin at 4.00 pm and he himself at 8.00 pm on the same day.[195] A memorandum written that day by an old enemy of Quisling, von Weizsäcker, gives some clue to Ribbentrop's motives. In a message to the German consulates in Norway the State Secretary reported:

> In consequence of the attitude of the Nygaardsvold Government in Norway, German–Norwegian relations have not developed in the way we proposed in our memorandum. . . . Our ultimate attitude toward the sovereign power in Norway has not yet been clarified.[196]

On the morning of 17 April it became clear that the King and the Nygaardsvold government had rejected the Administrative Council on the ground that it had no basis in Norwegian law.[197] This decision vitiated most of Bräuer's efforts of the previous week, and proved a source of embarrassment to Hitler. According to later evidence Hitler was beside himself with rage and vowed that Bräuer would be punished severely – 'that man's career is finished'.[198] The same morning Bräuer was summoned to see an exceedingly displeased Ribbentrop, who informed him of the Führer's anger. He was instructed to prepare a memorandum setting out a clear statement of the premises on which his actions had been based.

Bräuer wrote a memorandum justifying his actions, in particular those with regard to Quisling. He asserted that his reason for taking a strong line against the Quisling government lay in the fact that it 'was regarded as unconstitutional. It was known that the King had rejected him; the 5 days following the formation of his Government had been allowed to pass unused without his having really established himself even in one ministry.'[199] The existence of the Quisling government was the main cause of unrest and resistance in Norway. In this view he was supported by von Falkenhorst. Bräuer therefore defended the political settlement of 15 April, for he believed that the Administrative Council had 'coupled its functions with the person of the King, which opens up possibilities for relations with him and for his return, which would not have obtained under either Quisling or any other usurper government'.[200] The ambassador had staked his claim to justification on two points. The first was that the institution which he had set up would be able to restore relations with the King in a way satisfactory to all parties. Secondly, he contended that the Administrative Council would be more able to fulfil the functions of government than the regime imposed by Quisling.

Bräuer clearly believed not only that his actions had been correct at the time but also that they would be justified by later events: 'The pacification which has ensued is more complete than was to be expected. . . . Resistance is manifestly slackening under the influence of the settlement reached in Oslo.'[201] The ambassador was not to know that the elaborate edifice of the Administrative Council had been built upon sands which were already shifting. Although the King had delivered a rebuff to the new body on 17 April, a still more decisive rejection was to follow a few days later when the King pointed out that the Administrative Council was not a free agent, being subject to the jurisdiction of a foreign power. After this pronouncement there could be no hope of co-operation between King and Council. The political *démarche* of Berg and Bräuer had been finally checked and their premises proved faulty. The fall of Quisling had led to no success for his opponents, but merely to an uncompromising rebuff to their pretensions.

The collapse of Bräuer's policy was followed by his dismissal. On 21 April it was officially admitted that he had been dismissed.[202] On 6 May he was called up by the army and on the 15th he was sent to the Western Front. Habicht was also dismissed and sent to serve in the army. Their political careers had ended in disillusionment and disgrace. Hitler could not afford the time to construct a new political solution, so, on 19 April, he conferred on von Falkenhorst 'executive power in the occupied territories of Norway'.[203] But the disgrace of his enemies was small consolation to Quisling. He had lost a position which he was not to regain for almost two years. He had to remove his headquarters from the Hotel Continental and retreat to the Grand Hotel, where for some time he and Scheidt remained unwanted and useless. The Administrative Council tottered to its inevitable fall some months later. With the exception of von Falkenhorst the rivals of 9 April had all, ten days later, been forced into political obscurity. Thus ended the process which had begun in December 1939. If Quisling had not profited, neither had those who had sought to remove him, often for dubious motives. Quisling's forecast of their political downfall had, as Knudsen pointed out,[204] been uncannily correct. Their opinions of Quisling's political incompetence had been no less justified.

Chapter 7 TEMPORARY RETIREMENT

THE DEMISE of the Quisling government of April 1940 was a Pyrrhic victory for Quisling's opponents. Those, like Berg and Bräuer, most nearly responsible for its collapse, reaped no political advantage. The rejection of the Administrative Council by the King confirmed Hitler in his conviction that he could no longer trust his Foreign Office with negotiations. His change of policy took place on 18 April, when he had been fully informed of the Norwegian King's actions. His first decision was to forbid further interference in Norwegian affairs by Ribbentrop or his staff,[1] much to the pleasure of some of the Foreign Minister's rivals. The Führer was then faced with the problem of finding or creating some authority in Norway which would pay regard to his requirements.

At this point Göring intervened by suggesting that Hitler send a Reichskommissar to rule in Norway.[2] Hitler agreed and chose Josef Terboven, the 41-year-old Gauleiter of Essen. The choice was not popular with Rosenberg, who had clashed with Terboven on several occasions,[3] but the appointment was generally well-received in Germany; Terboven 'was a proven and skilful administrator, well-suited to deal with the occupied lands in Norway'.[4] On 19 April, Hitler sent for him, and in a long, private talk with him that evening he told the new Reichskommissar that he was to knock some sense into the heads of the Norwegian politicians, and conferred on him powers of life and death.[5] Hitler also informed Terboven of Quisling's role in Norway, so that he would be equipped to deal with the Fører and his party.[6]

Hitler's decision to create Terboven Reichskommissar had far-reaching political implications. Both Rosenberg and Ribbentrop were in disgrace, and so was the leadership of the OKW on account of the military crisis in Norway. Those whom Hitler consulted therefore were Göring, Bormann, Ley and Lammers, and those in his inner circle who were interested in the Norwegian problem saw his decision as a victory for the party machine. But the appointment of Terboven over the heads of the leaders of the APA, the OKW and the Foreign Office was to have serious repercussions in the future.

On learning of Hitler's decision, Ribbentrop sent for Arne Scheel, the Norwegian ambassador, and told him that the embassy must leave

Berlin. Later that day, 19 April, the embassy staff left Germany for the duration of the war.[7] It was Ribbentrop's last important act in connexion with Norway, for on 20 April Hitler ordered a decree to be drafted defining Terboven's powers. This decree was eventually published on 24 April, and stated explicitly: 'The Reichskommissar shall be directly responsible to [the Führer] and shall receive his guidance and directives from [the Führer].'[8] Terboven was to be the guardian of German interests in Norway, which meant, in effect, that he outranked the military authorities there. By this decree the defeat of Bräuer and von Falkenhorst was finally sealed.

The 20th of April was a busy day for Terboven. He had not only to make the ordinary preparations but also to choose staff to execute his policy in Norway. Naturally he selected them from among those with whom he had been friendly. Those who were to be of the greatest assistance to him were Dr Hans Delbrügge, an administrative expert, and Paul Wegener, who acted as Terboven's deputy. After choosing these men, Terboven received a further briefing from Hitler. He was told not to regard the Norwegians as enemies, but as potential allies. He was, according to Raeder, instructed to co-operate with Quisling.[9] This was of some comfort to Raeder, who was fearful lest Quisling be forgotten; but it did little to assuage the fears of Jodl, who doubted Terboven's ability to take on the complex task of restoring order in Norway.[10]

On 21 April Ribbentrop informed von Neuhaus that Terboven was on his way to Norway to take up the post of Reichskommissar. The fate of the representatives of the Foreign Office was also indicated: 'Although the function of the Legation as such has ceased, you will remain on the spot for the present with the whole staff, place yourself at the disposal of Oberpräsident Terboven on his arrival, and assist him in questions of foreign policy. Minister Bräuer is not returning there.'[11] On the same day Terboven arrived in Norway, landing at Fornebu airport, where he was greeted by Milch, one of Göring's closest allies – a sure sign that the Field-Marshal was beginning to take an interest in Norway after his earlier opposition to the whole venture.

The advent of Terboven was a much more serious matter for Norway than was at first realised. The Administrative Council was allowed to continue to exist, but it could exercise no effective jurisdiction without Terboven's consent. For Quisling the situation was even worse. He and Scheidt had no idea what their position was after the débâcle of 14 April, and the events of the following week merely confused them further. Their first reaction was to try to prepare for the return of NS to power. In this they were encouraged by Schreiber, who entertained Quisling and Hagelin at his home on Bygdøy on 15–16 April.[12] Schreiber and his ally had no doubt that those in Germany who wished to work with Norway would be obliged, sooner or later, to seek out Quisling. Scheidt was much more pessimistic, and, as Schreiber later recalled, 'was very downcast by the failure of his schemes'.[13] Schreiber was at some pains to point out that

Quisling, as Commissioner for Demobilisation, still had a foot in the door. If he were able to participate in an effective demobilisation of the army and aid a pacification programme, then all might yet be well. Even Scheidt was persuaded to adhere to the view he had originally expressed on 14 April, that 'the post of commissioner was to be a political springboard'.[14]

With this encouragement, Quisling set to work forthwith. In the next few days a series of proclamations by the Administrative Council attempted to erect some framework for effective government. On 18 April Quisling's activities in the field of demobilisation were given official sanction.[15] But any chance of effective action by Quisling was ruled out by the landing of Allied troops in Norway and the resumption of full-scale warfare. Quisling's task became irrelevant before he had had a chance to begin. Despite this fact he was determined to prove his value to the Germans and *Fritt Folk* published on 19 April an article by him appealing for a ceasefire and peace for Norway.[16] He addressed a similar appeal to his colleagues on the Administrative Council calling on them to 'let England fight the war while Norway comes to an understanding with Germany, as had already been achieved in Denmark'.[17] The difficult position of the Administrative Council, which Berg ought to have foreseen, had not been solved by the time of Terboven's arrival.

Despite the setback of full-scale war between the official government, supported by the Allies, and the Germans, Quisling still hoped to be able to play a useful part. But his hopes of becoming the architect of Norwegian–German co-operation were fading fast even before Terboven's arrival.[18] Quisling and his party hierarchy had contrived to quarrel simultaneously with von Falkenhorst and the Administrative Council. The law of 13 May 1937 which banned the wearing of uniforms by political groups had been ignored by NS during the days immediately following the invasion and had resulted in chaos,[19] for the Germans were unable to tell friend from foe. To Quisling's chagrin, von Falkenhorst had referred the matter to the Administrative Council, which had declared that the existing law was to be enforced. Scheidt had tried to arrange for Quisling to make a broadcast, but this had been prevented by Commander Hahn; Bräuer had put Hahn in command of the radio headquarters and had referred the matter to the Administrative Council.

At every turn Quisling found opponents, and on 21 April he wrote to Bräuer in despair, telling him that the Administrative Council was destroying his life's work. He demanded German assistance against those in Norway 'who were laying obstacles in his way'.[20] Quisling was so out of touch that he had not realised that Bräuer had already been removed from office. He found that newspapers in Drammen, Sarpsborg, Fredrikstad and Skiensfjorden had been attacking him as a traitor, and that no attempt had been made by the authorities to counteract this propaganda. On 20 April he sent birthday greetings to Hitler, hoping thus to remind the Führer of his plight.[21] All his efforts were fruitless.

The problems facing Quisling during the week between the collapse of his government and the arrival of Terboven were to recur, though in a different form, throughout the next few months. Quisling did not know what role he was to play in Norwegian politics, nor what his status was to be, nor what standing his party might expect. The reasons why these problems were not satisfactorily settled until September 1940 are complicated, and revolve round not only the difficult military and constitutional situation which the Germans faced but also the clash of personalities in the German hierarchy. The principal cause of confusion was the entire lack of any clear chain of command among the German administrators. Although Terboven had been given sweeping powers, he was bound to refer matters to Hitler, lest his enemies in Berlin steal a march on him. Quisling and his party had many sympathisers in Germany who might well have done so. Thus, it took about six months before a stable situation emerged.

The first inkling of trouble came on 21 April, when Quisling met Terboven, and learned of the Reichskommissar's wide powers.[22] It is not certain who took the initiative at this meeting, but it was made plain to Quisling that Terboven did not envisage 'any special role for NS'.[23] Terboven asked the NS leader awkward questions about the numbers and quality of its membership, and according to Delbrügge, 'Quisling had no clear idea of how many supporters the party had; . . . including sympathisers, he thought perhaps 250,000.'[24] Delbrügge and Terboven were somewhat sceptical of this figure, and realised that NS had, in any event, far too small an activist core to be of much use.

The next few days did nothing to increase Quisling's confidence in Terboven. The Reichskommissar seemed to be more interested in dealing with the Administrative Council than with loyal friends of Germany. The fact was that Terboven, Delbrügge and Wegener were primarily concerned with the task of setting up their own administrative machinery, and had not much time to spare for Quisling or his querulous complaints.[25] Terboven came to believe that NS, as it was then constituted, would be a millstone round Germany's neck, preventing the establishment of a working relationship with the rest of the Norwegian people. Scheidt made an appointment to see Wegener on 23 April, and put to him the view that Quisling should be given a place befitting his importance and his loyalty. Wegener received these overtures coldly, and asked Scheidt to submit his proposals in writing. The next day, just before Terboven flew to Germany to consult with Hitler, he received a long memorandum reciting Quisling's services and grievances.[26]

By the time of Terboven's return to Germany his opponents had been able to rally. Rosenberg had recently been away on the Western Front; returning to Berlin on 19 April, he learned of Terboven's promotion. He had been unable to do anything, at that stage, to protect Quisling's interests, but had been reassured by Raeder's interview with Hitler on 22 April. On the other hand he was anxious to discuss with Hitler long-term plans for using Quisling's services, so he was reluctant to see Terboven seize too much power. On the day of his return, Rosenberg had received a latter from Scheidt attacking the duplicity of Habicht and Bräuer, which the liaison officer blamed for the confusion in Norway.[27] He intended to lay this document before Hitler at once, and to urge him to look at its contents carefully, but the moment was not favourable. On 25 April, however, Hitler drew Rosenberg aside and informed him of a big propaganda victory shortly to be achieved against the British, as a result of documents captured in Oslo. The Führer then expressed his appreciation of Quisling's services and assured Rosenberg that his Norwegian friend would not be forgotten.

Hitler had been thus far pleased with Terboven's work in Norway, but he advised the Reichskommissar to pay some attention to Quisling, and told him of Rosenberg's interest.[28] Terboven was, of course, already aware of the enmity between Rosenberg, as Scheidt's superior, and Raeder, as Schreiber's chief. He realised, however, that as long as he retained Hitler's confidence he did not need to worry too much about his opponents. Rosenberg and Raeder were aware of the delicate nature of their position; they did not wish to annoy Hitler, but each was equally determined to protect his own interests. On 25 April, Rosenberg was able to persuade Lammers, with whom Terboven dared not quarrel, to place Schickedanz in a liaison position attached to the staff of the Chancellery. Rosenberg recorded in his diary that 'Terboven greeted this news with a long face'.[29] The Reichskommissar left for Oslo on the evening of 25 April or early the next day; Schickedanz followed him on 27 April.

Terboven found that Rosenberg intended to fight to keep his influence; but he was confident that he could deal firmly with Quisling. During his visit he had persuaded Hitler to remove the last vestiges of Foreign Office power in Norway. On 3 May a circular was issued by the personnel department of the Wilhelmstrasse:

> In view of the designation of Oberpräsident Terboven as Reichskommissar for the Occupied Norwegian Territories, the German Legation at Oslo has been converted into the 'Representation of the Foreign Ministry with the Reichskommissar . . . Counselor of Legation von Neuhaus is designated as Representative . . .'[30]

Terboven had persuaded Hitler to give him full control over Foreign Office activity in Norway, and he was sure he could outmanoeuvre Rosenberg in the same way. Ribbentrop's humiliation was complete.

But Rosenberg's position was rather stronger than the Reichskommissar thought. He had the assistance not only of his own staff but also of Quisling and his party. Raeder also, through the agency of Schreiber, was now supporting Quisling. The enemies of Terboven, therefore, always had plenty of information at their disposal. The arrival of Schickedanz in Oslo was greeted with enthusiasm by the Quisling clique. According to Rosenberg he was hailed 'as their angel of salvation'.[31] He was just in time to give Quisling some badly needed advice. Schreiber, Quisling's main prop during the past ten days, was about to leave Norway, and had sent his last despatch on 24 April.[32] Hagelin had returned to Germany and Scheidt, since his interview with Wegener, had been a broken reed. Von Neuhaus had been politically impotent and was ordered back to Berlin on 8 May.[33] Without Schickedanz, Quisling would have been in a sorry plight.

Even Schickedanz was at first unable to prevent a successful political offensive by Terboven, who had decided to rid himself of some of Quisling's supporters. On 26 April Terboven arrived in Oslo to discover a further deterioration in relations between the Administrative Council and Quisling. Two days later he summoned Quisling and Scheidt to the Bristol Hotel, where his staff had established themselves. The Reichskommissar bullied Quisling without showing any regard for his past services. He told him that he intended to hold NS in reserve; if he pushed NS forward, it would become useless as a political weapon, as it would be regarded as a party for traitors. Reluctantly Quisling was forced to acquiesce.

Schickedanz had, however, other plans for Quisling. He told him that he was not to be thrown to the wolves; if they were careful, Terboven would soon run into difficulties. The plotters then decided that their best course of action was to prepare a document for presentation to Hitler at the earliest opportunity. By 1 May this document had been drafted by Scheidt.[34] It took the form of a letter to Hitler, stating Quisling's case; but it was forwarded through Terboven, in order to avoid the charge of going behind his back.[35] Terboven was not pleased with the letter but was obliged to send it to Berlin. Quisling's move had been carefully planned to coincide with pressure in Berlin, and by his own party, for his return. On 1 May, *Fritt Folk* produced a leader calling for the NS Fører's reinstatement and giving its own explanation of the events of the past few weeks; 'the first step in the national revolution ended on 15 April, after the old system had received its death-blow on 9 April. The 15th of April was not a reverse for us but the establishment of a base for the final victory.'[36] In Berlin Rosenberg had rallied support from Goebbels, who, though he had no very high opinion of either Quisling or Terboven,[37] agreed that 'it was a scandal that Quisling should be called a traitor'.[38] Thus the atmosphere for the reception of the letter was favourable.

The document itself had been drawn up with great care. Quisling realised that to claim that NS enjoyed the confidence of the Norwegian people would not only be futile but also dangerous to his hopes. He therefore declared: 'My political programme does not have majority backing, but behind me stands a determined group which represents the true interests of the people.'[39] On this basis he made three demands: (1) representation of NS on the Administrative Council;[40] (2) encouragement, including financial assistance, for NS; (3) a firm decision from Hitler about the date of the return of a Quisling government.[41]

Schickedanz, returning to Berlin on 4 May, carried a copy of the letter in case of accident. He gave Rosenberg a favourable report on Quisling's prospects, and was soon able to lay before his leader another letter from Quisling, in which the Fører laid particular emphasis upon the shabby way he had been used, and suggested that this was not the way Germany should treat loyal friends.[42] While the anti-Terboven faction was gathering its forces in Berlin, the object of its hatred was busily checking Quisling's ability to pursue a political offensive in Norway. While placing Delbrügge in charge of his Administrative Council,[43] Terboven decided that the political potential of NS must be thoroughly examined. The Reichskommissar applied to Bormann for a competent man who could look at the economic and political basis upon which NS was founded. Soon afterwards Gauschatzmeister Eck came to Oslo to undertake this task.

It was Terboven's hope that Eck would name Quisling as the main cause of the political weakness of NS, and so give him an excuse for getting rid of the Fører. Terboven believed that it would be a tactical blunder to use Quisling and his party to supplement the Administrative Council. Apart from considerations of political importance and size, NS was not recognised as a serious party by the other political groups. The admission of Quisling to power might precipitate another governmental crisis. There was also still a substantial body of opinion in Germany which hoped, however unrealistically, to bring the Norwegian King back into the picture, and the return of Quisling would put an end to such hopes for ever.

Terboven decided that before embarking upon the reconstitution of Quisling's party he needed Hitler's permission. On 8 May he arrived in Berlin and went to see the Führer.[44] His speed of action outmanoeuvred Rosenberg, who had tried to ensure that Quisling's letter to Schickedanz had not been forgotten. Terboven, his mission accomplished, returned to Oslo the next day. He at once announced that Scheidt's services as liaison officer to the government were no longer required.[45] On 17 May Scheidt was ordered to leave the country the next day; by 20 May he was in Berlin. Quisling had been deprived of a long-standing adviser.

The pro-Quisling party was furious and set about trying to reinstate the chastened Scheidt. Rosenberg and his circle were particularly annoyed with what they saw as Terboven's duplicity – 'It is apparent from Scheidt's letter that Reichskommissar Terboven has told Quisling – contrary to the truth – that Scheidt has now been given another assignment and will return to Germany.'[46] The head of the APA, for once, had reasoned aright. On 9 May, Terboven had informed Quisling and Scheidt that Rosenberg had 'a new assignment for Reichsamtsleiter Scheidt'.[47] In a letter to Rosenberg on the 11th, Terboven told him that Scheidt's activity had come to 'its natural conclusion'.[48] The Reichskommissar was determined to sweep all opposition out of the way, and the removal of Scheidt's influence was a necessary preliminary. On 12 May

Quisling wrote to Rosenberg commending Scheidt and asking that he be retained in Norway as a liaison officer with NS.[49] At the same time Quisling, hoping to embarrass Terboven, resumed his campaign for the removal of the Administrative Council, calling for a full-blooded NS government which would be capable of solving the tricky problem of Norwegian–German relations.[50]

Rosenberg took up Quisling's cause in Berlin. In a long memorandum outlining Terboven's mistakes, he not only accused the Reichskommissar of deliberate duplicity with which he felt it his 'duty to acquaint the Führer'[51] but also reported that he was alienating loyal friends of Germany.

> Quisling is doing what he conceives to be his duty toward pan-Germanism, but feels embittered and cheated. Nevertheless, he is working without voicing any complaint on the development of his scheme in unquestioning obedience to the Führer. All that which he with his co-workers, given different treatment, could otherwise be doing whole-heartedly and voluntarily, is now being done with inward aversion to a number of persons. This view of their treatment cannot fail to become known, nor can the knowledge of it fail to reach friends of Germany in all countries.[52]

This was a very powerful argument, and Rosenberg followed it up by reminding Hitler of Quisling's letter to Schickedanz in which he stated: 'The old anti-German circles are now cooperating with the German authorities.'[53] Failure to support those nationalist groups, after all the work they had done, would be a disaster.

Hitler took Rosenberg's point, and also that made by Quisling, when he pointed out that Germany was now relying upon Christensen, who had until very recently been strongly hostile to German interests and pretensions.[54] On 21 May Terboven flew to Berlin in an attempt not only to counteract Rosenberg's political offensive but also to remove Schickedanz. He saw Hitler on 22 and 23 May, but was only partially successful. He was probably asking for too much when he demanded strict control of Quisling's activities, but in any event Hitler reminded him of Rosenberg's interests,[55] and told him that any solution must make some provision for Quisling's future.

Terboven was not alarmed by these vague directives and was pleased with the confidence shown him by Hitler in quite a different matter. The Reichskommissar had decided that the smooth working of his administration required a revision of his relationship with the Administrative Council. In this matter Delbrügge was his chief adviser, for, apart from Bishop Berggrav,[56] Terboven had little contact with important Norwegian leaders. On 22 May Terboven had obtained Hitler's permission to proceed with these plans.

Some time during his first month in office Terboven had decided that he needed a co-operative Norwegian body with which he could work. This would mean the disappearance of both NS and the Administrative

Council in their present form. He wished to reform NS and give it a new leader; and, more important, to create a Riksråd, or State Council, to replace the existing body. Obviously the first target was the easier to hit, and, on his return from Berlin, Terboven renewed his attack. The activities of Eck had been supplemented by two other Nazi party officials, one of whom, Sturmbannführer Neumann, had been particularly active. In the opinion of Knudsen 'the intention of the Reichskommissar was that they should spy on the movement and trick the leaders into committing blunders, in order that the whole party should finally be delivered up to the tender mercies of the Reichskommissariat and liquidated'.[57] But Terboven's real aim was not to destroy the party but to put his own nominees in charge of it. Neumann and Eck were awkwardly placed. Neumann was believed by the Quisling faction to be a thoroughgoing supporter of Terboven,[58] but the Reichskommissar had in fact no great opinion of Neumann's abilities, mainly because he contrived to reorganise the Hird while still leaving it in the hands of Quisling's supporters.

Terboven approached the dismantling of the Administrative Council rather more cautiously. For some weeks he kept his ideas to himself and a close circle of colleagues. He was very anxious not to alarm those Norwegians who were co-operating through the Council. But the Council clearly pleased nobody. Quisling and NS disliked it since it had superseded their own short-lived government, Terboven disliked it since it had not been his own creation, and many Norwegians disliked obeying the instructions of a body which was unrecognised by a King still resident in his kingdom. Furthermore the Administrative Council could not avoid being associated with many of the worst aspects of German occupation, such as the currency inflation and the confiscation of property. Terboven might be cautious and discreet; NS was neither. On 23 May *Fritt Folk* condemned both the Administrative Council and the Nygaardsvold government.[59] Four days later a second editorial accused the Storting of being doubly insensitive; not only was it illegal, it was also failing to co-operate with the occupying power. The realities of the situation, however, were more realistically assessed at private meetings of the NS hierarchy than in their public utterances. The NS Council produced a short, private memorandum in which it was recognised that NS must, for the moment, fall in with Terboven's plans.[60]

Quisling's hopes for a recall were dashed at the beginning of June. On the 3rd the official gazette of the German administration published an appeal by Terboven to the Norwegian people to help him work towards the goal of a new government.[61] He was merely flying a kite in order to see what help he could obtain from sources outside NS. The same day one of his assistants reported that the Reichskommissar was being driven to choose 'between Quisling and Norway'.[62] Terboven hoped that if he were to receive widespread support for his ideas he could finally shake off the incubus of Quisling. A new State Council, once established, would make Quisling's co-operation unnecessary. The State Council would include representatives from the Storting, the Administrative Council, the political parties and other important organisations. Now that the war effort of the Allies was petering out and the departure of the King seemed imminent, it was clearly desirable for Norway to have some more permanent body than the Administrative Council, and Terboven's plan presented certain definite attractions.

Quisling and NS were not impressed by the Reichskommissar's arguments in favour of his scheme. At an important gathering of the party, on 5 June, Quisling announced that there were 'only two choices for Norway: either the people must rally round the national party or Norway must cease to exist as an independent state'.[63] This message was directly opposed to Terboven's plans and annoyed the Reichskommissar a good deal. On 8 June, the day on which the King left Norway, the party newspaper, fearful lest Terboven hand over control of NS to outsiders, launched an attack on Jonas Lie,[64] whose interest Terboven was thought to favour.

From the rest of Norway's politicians there was not the tremendous wave of enthusiasm for which the Reichskommissar had hoped. As the war in Norway drew to a close, Terboven imposed a more rigid censorship upon the press and radio. He summoned the editors of the major newspapers to his office on 9 June and informed them that they had a duty to lead public opinion as well as to give news. He therefore instructed them to publish editorials calling for a revision of the existing administrative arrangements. The reason he gave was that since the whole of Norway would be occupied, after the military surrender of 10 June, new policies were required. The King and the Nygaardsvold government had betrayed their patriotic duties and fled out of sheer self-interest; Norway now needed a government which would co-operate with the occupying power, not an Administrative Council restricted by promises previously made to the monarch.

Terboven's instructions achieved some success, for many Norwegians realised that the most likely alternative was another Quisling administration. Moreover there were many who sought to advance their careers by serving German interests once Norway's part in the war had temporarily ended. Terboven was gratified with the response; he also wished to avert Quisling's elevation to office and believed that the best solution lay in a re-shaping of the Administrative Council, with the aid of the Storting, into his favoured State Council.[65] This was also the opinion of several of his trusted deputies.[66]

On 11 June representatives of the four major political parties were summoned for negotiations, and discussions began.[67] Terboven's hope was that the new body would enjoy the appearance of legality, and would encourage realistic co-operation. This was one of the fundamental reasons for his distrust of Quisling's participation in politics. The Reichskommissar had, however, many other functions to perform, and the chief task of negotiation was delegated to Delbrügge. At their meeting the party representatives proposed a compromise solution. The Administrative Council was to govern the whole country, in the absence of the monarch, and must, therefore, be supplemented by the appointment of new members.[68] Delbrügge, unable to accept this proposal, reiterated Terboven's demand for the deposition of the King and the removal of the powers of the Nygaardsvold government. On 13 June an ultimatum to this effect, requiring an answer before midnight on the 17th, was presented to the meeting.

By this time control of the situation had passed out of the hands of the Administrative Council into those of the Presidential Board of the Storting, presided over by the Vice-President, Magnus Nilssen, in the absence of its President, Hambro, who had left Norway. For the purpose of these discussions the Presidential Board decided, on 15 June,[69] to appoint a special committee, presided over by Berg, to negotiate with Delbrügge. Berg soon withdrew and Christensen took over his difficult task. This new negotiating committee consisted of a number of representatives from the Administrative Council, the Storting, the political parties and certain large organisations, such as the trade unions, which played a prominent part in Norwegian life.[70] Acting on the advice of this body, late on 17 June, the Presidential Board agreed to appoint a State Council, conferring upon it extensive powers. It also agreed to the revocation of the special powers granted to the Nygaardsvold government on 9 April, and called upon the King to renounce his constitutional functions so long as the occupation continued.[71] As soon as he heard of these agreements, Terboven flew to Berlin, late on 18 June, to report to Hitler.

Quisling was alarmed at these developments. He saw his prospects of power rapidly slipping away, and, with the aid of Aall[72] and Hagelin, he quickly prepared a plan of resistance. On 11 June, *Fritt Folk* attacked the departure of the Nygaardsvold government to England,[73] demanding a few days later the transfer of its powers to Quisling and his party.[74] The Fører's demands did not fit into the Reichskommissar's plans, particularly as Terboven believed that he now stood on the verge of success. He wanted Quisling's total exclusion from the new framework of government; if his activities proved to be an embarrassment, then they must be stopped. Despite the curb imposed on his activities because of civil disorder at his meetings, Quisling was allowed to speak on 24 June to a selected party audience about the perils of the old system of political management. He called for 'the total destruction of the party political system and its replacement with a national government'.[75]

Quisling's political *démarche* enraged Terboven, who feared that it might endanger the delicate negotiations between Delbrügge and the Presidential Board. On 25 June he summoned Quisling and told him that he was expected to co-operate. As some compensation for political inactivity, a representative of NS was to be appointed to serve on the State

Council, but it could not be Quisling himself. Terboven added that unless he had Quisling's co-operation he would break his party and send him to Germany, where he would remain as an honoured, but powerless, guest. Quisling did not believe that Terboven had obtained Hitler's consent to these schemes, but until he could consult Hagelin and inform his allies in Germany, he decided to avoid a disastrous confrontation.[76] Terboven had of course no wish to destroy the party; he saw it as the readiest vehicle for introducing Nazism into Norway. But he was eager to be rid of Quisling, whom he found ineffective as a party leader.[77] To make sure that Quisling could cause no trouble or counteract his own influence, Terboven told him on 29 June that Jonas Lie would be nominated as the NS representative on the State Council.[78] This incensed Quisling and his supporters, with whom Lie had been in bad odour ever since his behaviour in April, and stirred Hagelin and his friends to great efforts on Quisling's behalf.

Nevertheless Delbrügge had meanwhile managed to come to an arrangement with the Presidential Board. On 30 June the King had received from them a letter urging him 'in consideration of the welfare of the nation and the future of the country' to agree to abdication.[79] But Terboven's hope to establish a State Council without rival legal authority was to be sadly disappointed; on 3 July, the King replied to the letter by refusing to recognise the validity of the Board's acts.[80] Terboven had at least started the process of splitting the anti-German front.

Quisling's reaction to these events was rather feeble. In discussions with Terboven he always came off second best, unless he had Hagelin or another of his advisers present to assist him. Hagelin had been suspicious of the Reichskommissar's intentions for some time, and on 20 June had written to Scheidt telling him of the difficulties under which NS was labouring.[81] The news of Lie's nomination confirmed all his fears, so he suggested that he should travel to Berlin, with Sundlo and Quisling, to put the NS case before the Führer.[82]

Terboven's many opponents in Berlin had already started to rally to Quisling's cause, though they were waiting for a suitable opportunity for action. Their chance was soon to come. The Reichskommissar had become increasingly critical of Quisling's potential as leader of NS and had come to the conclusion that he was no more than a figurehead for Hagelin, whom, according to Delbrügge, he disliked intensely. On 6 July Quisling had a stormy interview with one of Terboven's assistants, SS Oberführer Stahlecker, whom Quisling was pressing in vain for adequate official representation on the new State Council. Exasperated by Quisling's persistence, Terboven ordered his seizure and removal to Germany.[83] He followed this up by informing the NS party secretariat that Lie had been installed as official leader in Quisling's place. The disappearance of Quisling gave rise to fears on Knudsen's part that Terboven's 'original intention was to destroy him, in some reasonably decent way or other'.[84]

Terboven's action turned out to be the most serious mistake of his political career. It brought his covert hostility to Quisling out into the open, and his worst enemy, Hagelin, immediately took the offensive in Oslo, declaring that Quisling had nominated him as party leader.[85] By this method he was able to retain control of the party machine and the party funds, both of which Terboven had hoped to hand over to Lie. The Reichskommissar's attempt to separate Quisling from his party had rebounded on him. In Berlin, Quisling, staying at the Hotel Kaiserhof, prepared a thorough justification of all his acts and attitudes. Through the person of Schickedanz, to whom he dictated his letter, he set forth all the misfortunes that had overtaken NS since 9 April. He also complained of the unfair treatment he had received in return for his services and his loyalty, contrasting this vigorously with the preferential treatment given to 'that renegade Lie'. This letter was sent to Hitler on 10 July.[86] To coincide with Quisling's accusations against Terboven, his allies in Berlin, notably Raeder[87] and Rosenberg, were also making ready to attack the position of the Reichskommissar.

Terboven left for Berlin, well aware of his dangerous political position. His action against Quisling could only be justified if he succeeded in his attempt to set up a State Council. If he did not, then he would have incurred in vain the antagonism of Raeder, Rosenberg and Quisling. On 7 July his position was not secure; on the previous day he had been informed of the King's uncompromising refusal to agree to any of the Presidential Board's proposals.[88] Terboven's main task, therefore, was to persuade Hitler to give him more time to settle the vexed question of the administration of the occupied territories. In this he succeeded, for his treatment of Quisling had not yet come to the Führer's attention.

Terboven had, however, contrived to annoy Ribbentrop as well as those more directly interested in Norway, and this mistake was ultimately to bring about a general undermining of his position. Ribbentrop had had little love for Terboven throughout his mission; the Reichskommissar had, he believed, been mainly responsible for ending Foreign Office influence in Norway. But there was also a more recent source of conflict. According to a Foreign Office decision, neutral diplomats were to leave the areas occupied by Germany by 15 July,[89] as it was intended to transfer the control of foreign policy to Berlin. The Reichskommissariat had been officially informed of this decision on 29 June, and Delbrügge had formally contested the decision at a heated meeting on 4 July. Terboven and some of his staff believed that certain of the neutral diplomats might be of assistance to Delbrügge in his negotiations with the King and the Presidential Board, and were therefore reluctant to see these diplomats depart. As Terboven's deputy put his view in an arrogant fashion Ribbentrop remained firm, but later informed Terboven that although diplomatic relations were henceforth to be conducted through Berlin, the diplomats in Oslo could stay until 25 July, if the short extension would be of help.[90] Ribbentrop appeared accommodating, but Terboven had added another powerful enemy to the list of those bent on his humiliation.

Terboven's disagreement with Ribbentrop at once proved costly. Ribbentrop saw to it that Quisling's letter of 10 July reached Hitler. From that date, therefore, the differences between the Reichskommissar and Quisling were known to the Führer, and his confidence in Terboven was steadily eroded. Rosenberg and his allies lost no opportunity of revealing Terboven's duplicity. In the middle of July, Eck returned to Germany. Originally detailed to investigate the financial basis of NS, he had gradually come to believe that Terboven's determination to establish control was likely to ruin the party, and had said as much to Terboven. In Berlin, his story was taken up by Rosenberg.[91] Hitler became increasingly irritated with Terboven and began to express doubts about the Reichskommissar's ability to carry out his leader's plans for Norway.[92]

Terboven soon discovered that loss of influence in Berlin did nothing to help his negotiations in Oslo. He had returned from Germany in July with his discretionary powers intact, but he found very quickly that he had to fight on two fronts; against the Presidential Board in Norway and against Quisling in Berlin; although on 12 July Terboven's staff was so optimistic that Lie was assured that Quisling had definitely been out-manoeuvred on the 6th. Between 29 June and 7 September he was unable to negotiate seriously with the Board. The prospect of a State Council grew steadily more remote. Preparations had already been made by the end of June for its official installation in office on 15 July. But the dispute with Quisling caused its indefinite postponement, and Terboven knew that the chance would probably not recur.

The dispute between Quisling and Terboven was more than personal disagreement. It was an open struggle for power. Quisling and his followers had not given up the idea of a come-back even after Terboven's installation as Reichskommissar. Quisling wished to be premier and desired to associate his government with the hierarchy of his party. His claim to this, and the claim made by his friends, was that he had loyally supported German aims and had a clear notion of the future role of Norway in the new Greater Germany. His party was the obvious link between Norway and Germany. Terboven, on the other hand, knew that Quisling commanded very little confidence in Norway. He believed it would be disastrous for Norwegian–German co-operation in the long run for the Fører to be installed as head of government, and he therefore sought to negotiate with those groups in Norway which also wished to keep Quisling out of power. The views of the two men were incompatible; the decision could eventually be made only by Hitler.

Quisling's long stay in Germany may be seen as an attempt to influence Hitler's decision by his presence. He knew that Hagelin and Aall were well able to protect his interests in Norway, and he hoped that he might be able to persuade Hitler himself. During his stay in Germany he was very active. He was there ostensibly at the invitation of Goebbels,[93] but he was, in fact, the guest of Rosenberg. He was continually in the company of Scheidt[94] and other stalwarts of the APA. He made contact with Himmler, who was interested in the possibility of recruiting for the Waffen SS among Quisling's NS supporters. Most of the time, however, he spent in discussing theoretical matters of common interest with Rosenberg and his staff.

This prolonged contact with Quisling spurred the leader of the APA to take the initiative against Terboven, with whom he had come to recognise that there could be no compromise. For the sake of his Nordic interests, Rosenberg wanted the administration of Norway to be in the hands of a party totally committed to his own point of view. He had no time for renegades like Lie or dubious allies such as Stang. His object therefore was to see Quisling installed in office, backed by a cabinet majority of NS men. He contemptuously dismissed Terboven's theory that NS would only be of use if it were reconstructed and Quisling omitted from the party hierarchy.[95] But he did recognise that the very difficult situation which had arisen was not wholly Terboven's fault. The Reichskommissar ought to have been given clear instructions to work with Quisling from the moment he arrived in Norway.

Rosenberg was well placed to take advantage of Terboven. Unlike the Reichskommissar he had Hitler's ear, particularly on matters concerning racial developments, under which the Norwegian episode could legitimately be classified. Hitler's attention was constantly drawn to Quisling's letter of 10 July and to another memorandum, produced by Rosenberg on 21 July.[96] Hitler himself was already half-converted. He saw no reason why the victorious Third Reich should concern itself with the susceptibilities of its former enemies. He recognised also the justice of Quisling's claims. The Norwegian had given ample proof of his loyalty in the difficult days of April. His letter of 10 July had rung true, when he claimed that it was his intention 'to work for the goal of a Greater Germany and my fatherland'.[97] Why should not Quisling be an ideal collaborator?

In one sense, then, Quisling's triumph over Terboven was inevitable. He had the more powerful friends and Hitler was in his debt. Yet it was another three weeks at least before Hitler decided in his favour. The reason for the time-lag between Quisling's letter of 10 July and his meeting with Hitler on 16 August is not difficult to see. Hitler was fully occupied with several important military decisions, among them the preparations for Operation Barbarossa. It is not surprising that the Führer had no time to spend on the relatively unimportant political problems of Norway.

By 16 August Hitler had completed his preparations for a full examination of the Norwegian situation.[98] He then had a long talk with Quisling in the presence of Lammers, Bormann and Scheidt. Terboven, who had been specially summoned to Berlin, was not consulted at this stage. At this meeting Quisling reiterated his long list of complaints against Terboven's treatment of himself and his party, and was invited by Hitler to propose a solution. Quisling's answer came readily. He suggested that the government most likely to promote Norwegian–German unity would be one headed by himself and backed by a full complement of NS men. Hitler was prepared to accept this suggestion, for he had come to believe that the political impasse in Norway had been due to the failure of others to appreciate the use that might be made of Quisling and NS. The trouble was that 'Bräuer and the others had been badly led astray by the Norwegian lawyers'.[99] Quisling should have been backed from the first.

Hitler did not wish to make life impossible for Terboven, and he went out of his way to assure Quisling that the Reichskommissar had always wished him well, and had always held NS to be the only party worth attention. Where Terboven had been wrong was in believing that German help would have compromised NS. On the contrary it was essential to the interests of both Norway and Germany to have a strong NS party. Hitler fully recognised Quisling's part in averting the danger from the English, and finally Quisling was assured that he could place full reliance on the Führer's word.

The good news from Berlin was relayed the same evening to Oslo, where Sundlo was awaiting the outcome. In a document designed to give full information of the progress of Quisling's cause Sundlo expressed his confidence that Quisling would soon be returning to Norway to lead an NS government.[100] Terboven was told the news the next day, when he had a very brief interview with Hitler. The news was not welcome, for he had no wish to co-operate with Quisling. But since effective control of the country would remain in the hands of the German troops, he had little to fear. His hope that the Norwegian task would be a platform for more important duties later was, however, dashed once and for all, and he returned to Norway without great enthusiasm. Quisling returned shortly afterwards.[101]

Relations between Quisling and Terboven did not improve dramatically as a result of Hitler's decision. Each interpreted Hitler's directive in his own way. Quisling believed that Hitler meant him to form a government as soon as possible. Terboven held the view that a short transitional period must elapse before a Quisling government could be set up. Had Quisling been less short-sighted he would have seen that Terboven was bound to advocate the gradual introduction of a Quisling regime. The German needed time to disentangle the negotiations with the Presidential Board as well as to adjust to his new position.

A few days therefore elapsed before Quisling saw Terboven on 25 August.[102] It became clear at once that Terboven had not given up all his ambitious plans. Instead of the State Council he now advocated a government of commissars, directly responsible to the Reichskommissar; this should be given a trial run until the beginning of March 1941, and this would enable the transitional phase to be passed without difficulty. Quisling could not make much headway against the stronger personality of the Reichskommissar.

Terboven's plans, however, were not well received. NS believed that he was aiming at a protectorate, modelled upon those in Poland and Czechoslovakia, and they contrasted this solution unfavourably with that of a Quisling government. Opposition was by no means confined to supporters of Quisling. Even those Norwegians who advocated a State Council believed it to be a retrogressive measure. The bullying and threatening demeanour of Delbrügge strongly suggested that extreme pressure would be brought to bear on any dissenters.[103] If so, then further talks were superfluous. All Norwegians, whether supporters or opponents of Quisling, saw in Terboven's scheme for ministers directly responsible to himself a singularly unpleasant way of enforcing German commands, and were therefore eager to oppose it.

Aware of serious opposition to his plans, the Reichskommissar set about strengthening his own administration, so that, whatever happened, he would be in a position to carry out his own wishes. Meanwhile Quisling and Hagelin had decided that it was essential for them to take action. On 29 August they sent a letter to Terboven, making it clear that Quisling wanted power; the party had made great strides and it should be fairly represented in the new government.[104] If Terboven refused to comply with these demands then the letter would be laid before Hitler, and would show the Führer how untrustworthy his deputy was.

This tactless letter was totally unacceptable to Terboven. Soon after, Quisling was summoned to Berlin, and Terboven with him. On 4 September, Hitler saw Terboven first briefly and then Quisling. He felt it was time he gave some definite instructions. There was to be no question of Quisling remaining in Germany, he was to stay in Norway to advance the cause of NS, but he was not to represent NS on the State Council. Terboven was to do everything to ensure that NS could take over power as soon as possible.[105] According to Rosenberg, Hitler was critical of Terboven's methods in dealing with Quisling.[106] Undoubtedly Quisling had won the battle. On 6 September he wrote to Lammers urging 'an NS majority in the very near future'.[107] The same day Raeder asked Hitler what his future plans for Norway were and was gratified to learn that the 'OKM had been right from the very start'.[108]

On his return to Norway Terboven found himself facing a very difficult task, which was further complicated by internal disagreement between Stahlecker and Delbrügge.[109] But he still continued his policy of resistance to Quisling, with whom he had two talks, on 7 and 9 September, when they worked out in detail the departmental lists for the State Council. By this time Terboven had had considerable experience in drawing up such lists; this was about the twentieth since his arrival in Norway. This advantage, together with his usual dialectical superiority over Quisling, enabled him to secure considerable concessions. It had been agreed that Quisling's party should have a majority of seats on the temporary State Council; if the original number of fifteen were retained, this meant that they had to agree on eight names. By the end of the two meetings Quisling had had to be content with only nominal control. His first concession was that not all of the eight need be members of NS, and it was agreed that four should come from within the party and four from outside. From those who were non-NS members Quisling required a statement of loyalty.[110] The four NS nominees were to be under party discipline, and, if they left NS, were to forfeit their posts automatically.

By this device Terboven had got rid of the requirement of an NS majority. Among the eight selected were several of whom Quisling disapproved, candidates whom Terboven was most anxious to promote. On the original list were only two members of the NS old guard – Thorleif Dahl and Gulbrand Lunde, and even the choice of Lunde had advantages for Terboven, since he disliked Hagelin. The two other party representatives were Axel Stang and Jonas Lie, both of whom were in bad odour with Quisling. Once again Terboven had been able to nullify his rival's gains in Berlin.

Arrangements had been completed by 9 September, though as a last-minute concession Terboven agreed that Hagelin might be Minister without Portfolio.[111] Lunde accepted the terms offered him at once, and Dahl was instructed to agree by Quisling in a personal interview with him on 10 September.[112] Jonas Lie was accepted as Minister of Police after the personal humiliation of being kept waiting in Quisling's antechamber for five hours.[113] The only post over which there was still controversy was that of Foreign Minister: Quisling preferred Irgens; Terboven, Ellef Ringnes.[114] Terboven had reason to be satisfied with his achievements.

Hitler had given Quisling and Terboven a week to settle the details of their scheme, and on 11 September they both left for Berlin. There was really little to be pleased about, for most of the serious obstacles had been overlooked. There was no great reason to suppose that the negotiating committee representing Norwegian interests would agree to admit a majority of NS members to the State Council. Neither had those non-members of NS who were to be asked to state their loyalty to Quisling been consulted on that delicate matter. Finally, unbeknown to Terboven, Hagelin had advised Quisling to seek some adjustment of the settlement, once he arrived in Berlin.

Quisling had an interview with Hitler of about two-and-a-half hours on the evening of 11 September. According to Rosenberg the result was 'very good, and Terboven must follow a new course'.[115] The next day Quisling and Terboven were summoned together by Hitler, who informed them of further decisions. The State Council was to have the power to co-opt members, and Irgens was to be the new Foreign Minister. In any case of doubt between the negotiating parties the German text was to be binding. Finally, Terboven was to consult with Quisling very frequently, and Quisling was to be assisted to form his own government after a suitable lapse of time.[116] The result of this meeting was a victory all along the line for the pro-Quisling party.

This was recognised at the time; Rosenberg wrote that there had been agreement on 'a provisional government with an NS majority, to be followed by a Quisling government'.[117] Quisling was delighted. The replacement of Ringnes by Irgens was also a victory for Quisling, though a less important one, as Irgens had at one point been on the Reichskommissar's list.[118] What was important was the fact that Quisling and Hagelin had outmanoeuvred Terboven, who never trusted Quisling thereafter; he accused him of having broken his word.[119]

Quisling's victory caused Terboven some political embarrassment; it killed any idea of the formation of a State Council along the lines of the discussions of June. If Terboven disliked Quisling, Quisling was even more disliked among Norwegian politicians. But Terboven had to break off relations slowly. As a matter of personal prestige he wanted as few Norwegians as possible to know of Quisling's political victory. Terboven saw that if his negotiations could be brought to founder, then he could legitimately call upon NS as his last resort. During the next few weeks Terboven's task was to make agreement impossible, and this goal he achieved with some success.

Terboven knew that if he constantly pitched his demands higher, a point would be reached at which the Presidential Board could make no further concessions. Every time agreement looked possible there was just one more demand, and in order to stimulate resistance to his proposals Terboven harried the established political parties unmercifully. The Reichskommissar drove the Presidential Board remorselessly towards total concession, which he knew they could not make. After his return from Berlin it was clear that the Board would reject the proposal to suspend the King, would want to control co-option on to the State Council and to keep members of NS off it.[120] Terboven's brief from Hitler would not permit him to make concessions on these points but the negotiations continued.[121]

The breaking point came on 17 September, when Terboven had 'one last doubt'.[122] Late that evening he demanded that an NS man be created Minister of Justice instead of Judge Ole F. Harbek. Negotiations continued throughout the next day, but at 11.15 pm Terboven was informed that this concession was impossible.[123] Negotiations therefore came to an end. Quisling himself saw this as a political victory for his party, as he had made it clear in his letter of 10 September that Harbek's appointment would not be acceptable.[124] In five months Terboven was back where things had stood on his arrival.

By 19 September all those concerned with Norwegian administration were aware of the break. Terboven took no further initiatives, but informed Quisling that he must go ahead with his plans for preparing a new government. For the next few days Quisling was in an agony of indecision and was perpetually redrafting his list of ministers. Dahl had been removed on 16 September; Aall followed a few days later. Declarations of loyalty were obtained, after some argument, from eight of the proposed ministers.[125] Hagelin was particularly active and was deeply involved in the choice of names.[126] Quisling, who had been preparing a suitable proclamation for some time,[127] was delighted at the way the political climate had changed in his favour.

On 21 September Quisling's list of ministers was ready, though Hagelin still had hopes of attracting support from outside NS and would, no doubt, have arranged alterations had the opportunity arisen. On 22 September Terboven briefed his own staff and that of Quisling about his proposed action. The next day he flew to Berlin to obtain Hitler's consent. The final phase of his long struggle was about to end.

On 25 September Terboven spoke to the Norwegian nation.[128] He announced that a commissarial government would henceforth take over all the functions of the Administrative Council, which was deemed to have ceased to exist. The King was declared deposed and the powers of the Nygaardsvold government abolished. The names of the new ministers were announced, together with the news that all the political parties, except NS, had been dissolved. The Reichskommissar admitted that these measures were very severe, but added that 'these decisions would hurt only those who were ill-disposed'.[129] He ended by appealing to the more sensible elements in Norway, asking for their co-operation, and advising them that no solution of political problems was possible except through the agency of NS.

The commissarial government which had been appointed included thirteen ministers, of whom nine were members of NS and four qualified as experts in their particular field. The nine were: Stang, Minister of Sport; Lie, Minister of Police; Lunde, Minister of Culture and the Arts; Hustad, Minister of Labour; Skancke, Minister of Education and Religion; Hagelin, Minister of the Interior; Riisnæs, Minister of Justice; Meidell, Minister of Social Affairs; Irgens, Minister of Shipping. The four non-NS ministers were: Øystein Ravner (an industrialist), Minister of Supply; Erling Sandberg, Minister of Finance; Thorstein Fretheim (farmer and veterinary surgeon), Minister of Agriculture; Sigurd Johannessen (a civil servant), Minister of Trade and Industry. Needless to say, the nominated cabinet did not meet with the approval of the general public whose reactions were very hostile. Quisling's opponents believed that the government of commissarial ministers was just a step towards a full Quisling government. The dissolution of all political parties except NS lent support to this belief.

Quisling's victory of 25 September represented not only a triumph over Terboven but also a remarkable political revival. Just over five months before, his political career had seemed to be at an end. Now, although he had not become premier, he had a majority of the commissarial cabinet upon which he could rely. He saw the opportunity that presented itself. On 26 September he spoke to the nation in a very controversial broadcast. He told his listeners that the old parties were the dupes of colonial powers and international Jewry, and had not deserved to continue to play a part in Norwegian history. NS represented the only way by which progress could be made: 'We shall come to an understanding with our German brethren, so that in the new order and in the Greater Germany we shall have a leading place.' NS would not be just a passive body but would strive energetically to put its programme into practice. Finally Quisling reminded his listeners that although 25 September was the day of victory for his party, all Norwegians were comrades: 'The Norwegian race shall no longer form just a kingdom, but shall become a people.'[130]

Although Quisling had not yet attained the dignity of premier, in all but name he was leader of Norway. His party was in power and he was allowed to make regular broadcasts to the nation. As his German patron, Rosenberg, had written on 13 September, 'Now Quisling must prove himself.'[131] The next few years were to show how Quisling tried to rule Norway, with varying degrees of success, but it was 25 September, rather than 13 September, which was the dividing line. Until 25 September Quisling had been largely concerned with the mechanics of obtaining power, negotiating and contending with Terboven and his other enemies. Thereafter he was concerned with other political questions, how he should rule Norway and how he should try to come to terms with the trade unions. Until 25 September he could, in the last resort, fall back upon help from Rosenberg or Raeder; after that date he had to depend on his own judgement and that of his closest advisers. The Reichskommissar had cleared the stage; Quisling had now to show that he could act.

Chapter 8   RETURN TO POWER

THE MANNER in which Quisling intended to rule Norway was revealed in his broadcast on 26 September. NS was to be the tool with which national regeneration would be forged: 'Our ideas are those which will be a new foundation for the rebuilding of the Norwegian state and society, and that means a new order in the pattern of Norwegian life.'[1] Henceforth in order to participate successfully in public life it would be necessary to belong to NS. It was therefore Quisling's intention that NS should become the official party just as the Nazi Party in Germany and the Communist Party in the Soviet Union had become all-embracing organisations. The leader of NS had been driven to the conclusion that only through the imposition of a rigorous discipline could the goals for which he was striving be attained. His first task, therefore, was to build up the party and concentrate power in the hands of its members.

As soon as it was evident that NS was to play a central part in affairs, its ranks were swollen by a considerable number of timeservers, who hoped to profit from their late conversion. According to Hewins,

> By 1942 NS had certainly trebled its membership and had at least 70,000 paid-up members, apart from sympathisers and minors. Headquarters were inundated with applications. Surviving officials of the Secretariat claim as many as 100,000 members, which seems by no means improbable since almost that number of 'quisling' cases were investigated, and doubtless many more evaded detection.[2]

The most important asset of the party was its organisation, poor and small though it was. NS had a number of local branches which had managed to survive the electoral disasters of the 1930s and in the Hird there existed not only some means of self-protection but also a nucleus for political advancement. The aim of Quisling, and of Terboven, was to exercise control at a local level by the use of reliable men, and this could be achieved only through party members. Gradually local leaders, mayors and councillors who opposed Quisling's pro-German policies were to be replaced by NS followers. In this way it was hoped to place the reins of power in the hands of dependable adherents, or at least in those of men who professed loyalty to the regime. All kinds of inducements were to be offered to those who considered joining the party, and, conversely, pressure to retire or resign was to be put upon those who refused to join.

Quisling's hopes for the future flowed, of course, from his view of the present. In a report to Lammers, written on 24 September, Hagelin had made it clear that the commissarial government was only a stopgap administration, to exist 'until 1 March 1941 at the very latest'.[3] Hagelin, who was Quisling's principal counsellor throughout this period, believed that it was essential for NS to do two things – to build up its own organisation and membership, and then to set up a Riksting, or State Parliament, in which NS would play the central role.[4] In the autumn of 1940, therefore, Quisling and Hagelin had two distinct goals at which to aim, the short-term establishment of the party in local and national government, and the long-term winning of the full confidence of the Norwegian people. In their first aim they were, eventually, moderately successful; their second target was never to be reached.

The establishment of the party in government meant much political activity. Terboven's broadcast of 25 September had placed NS in a commanding position as far as the actual ministerial positions were concerned, but had left untouched a number of more serious problems. NS needed to penetrate and take over the major policy-making organisations in Norway, as well as governmental posts, in order to exercise effective control and satisfy the requirements of party ideology. This task was not simple, for it involved party penetration of the civil service, the trade unions, the farmers' organisation, the Church, and a whole host of professional bodies. Once these organisations had been made subject to party control, they could be reformed on such lines as to play a proper part in national affairs. After their loyalty to the party had been proved, the second stage of the plan could then be achieved by the calling of a Riksting (Council of the Kingdom) to decide important items of governmental policy. But the whole process depended upon the surrender of the organisations to the party, and, as Wyller has written, 'They solidly resisted the aggression of NS.'[5]

The history of the period from 26 September 1940 to 1 February 1942 is the history of Quisling's attempts to subdue the resistance of these organisations and to establish himself and his party more firmly in power. He knew he had a hard struggle on his hands but was convinced that victory was possible. He and his intimate advisers decided they must push ahead with their plans despite any resistance, convinced that Terboven would be obliged to support the party. Conquest rather than conciliation was their aim.

The attacks soon began. Quisling's first attempts at reorganisation was directed at the Farmers' Union, one of the most powerful pressure groups in the country, on 27 September. Fretheim, the Minister of Agriculture, was ordered to incorporate all industries involving agriculture, fishing and forestry in one organisation.[6] Fretheim himself was not very sanguine about the project, nor indeed very enthusiastic; he did not become a member of NS until May 1941. However, he began negotiations, which dragged on throughout October. Quisling's demands were simple; he wished to replace the organisation with one created by himself, to be called NS Bondelaug, and led by Steinar Klevar, a long-standing member of the party. But the scheme was unacceptable to the existing administration of the Farmers' Union, and eventually in mid-November the negotiations collapsed. In part the collapse had been caused by the failure of parallel negotiations, started in October, with the fishing industry. Here Quisling's aim had been to create a new body which would immediately affiliate itself to NS Bondelaug. But differences of opinion between Meidell and Johannessen had made resistance easier by the official body. Early in November it became apparent that the scheme was impracticable, although it was not finally abandoned until late November, and the Farmers' Union was sufficiently emboldened to refuse Fretheim's demands.

Hagelin and Quisling were very annoyed at the disunity shown by ministers over this important question. But Quisling could not intervene directly as he held no post save that of leader of the party. Hagelin, as Minister of the Interior, was commissioned to take charge of future initiatives and to smooth over differences between ministers before a *démarche* was made. Thus, for the first sixteen months of commissarial administration, 'Hagelin stood at the head, trying to build the Ministry of the Interior into a centre for the policy of the new order'.[7]

The next moves were made by Hagelin himself, in an attempt to seize control of the professional bodies organised by the doctors and dentists.[8] This attempt came to nothing, and Hagelin ordered some of the other ministers to embark upon attacks on organisations connected with their departments in order to distract attention from his own failure. There followed attacks on the press by Lunde and on the athletics federation by Stang.[9] Neither succeeded.

Thus, by the end of November 1940, it was clear to Quisling and Hagelin that piecemeal attacks on well-organised bodies were unlikely to be successful. NS had not members enough to take over the running of these organisations and was furthermore handicapped by hostility within the civil service. A start had to be made somewhere and the obvious place was in Oslo, where the administrative offices were concentrated. Hagelin's next initiative, therefore, was a move to purge the civil service. NS was faced with the problem that its orders had to be carried out by civil servants who disapproved of them, and most of whom believed the government to be illegal. Consequently Hagelin prepared a decree, which was issued by his ministry on 16 December,[10] authorising the replacement of senior officials by the simple device of lowering the age of retirement from 70 to 65.[11] In this way the leaders of NS hoped to be able to remove those who were reluctant to carry out party orders and replace them by men of their own choice. Strong protests against this action came from all over the country, and about 98 per cent of the entire civil service, led by Johan Refsdal, a civil servant from Bergen, sent in individual protests. By the end of January 1941 it was clear that NS would encounter the greatest difficulty in carrying out its wishes through the agency of the civil service.

Resistance to the commissarial government during the autumn and winter of 1940 grew in many quarters, notably among the teachers and the lawyers. An early attack upon the teaching profession by Skancke had met with an uncompromising refusal to support the aims of NS, in the form of a brusque rejection delivered on 23 November.[12] The lawyers had at first been passive in their attitude towards the government, principally because they believed that the Germans would not interfere with the law courts; Terboven had, indeed, given a public assurance that their independence would not be attacked. But here, as elsewhere, necessity knew no law and the occupying power was soon ignoring the legal safeguards of personal liberty. NS was not slow to imitate the Germans, and the Minister of Justice, Sverre Riisnæs, issued a decree authorising himself to dismiss and appoint jurymen. Another decree empowered him to appoint a new 'People's Court' which was to judge political cases and against whose verdict there was no appeal.[13] The Supreme Court made vigorous representations about these infringements of liberty, contrary not only to the Hague Convention regarding occupied territories but also to previous German commitments earlier in the year. On 3 December, Terboven, to whom the Court had appealed, replied by stating that 'neither the Supreme Court nor any other inferior court was permitted to raise the issue of the validity of decrees issued by him or the commissarial government'.[14] The members of the Supreme Court, frustrated by this disrespect for the law, resigned on 12 December 1940. Their decision was fully supported by the national organisation of the lawyers, though the result was unfortunate as it gave the government a chance to pack the courts with NS nominees. Riisnæs eventually selected Andreas Mohr, a lawyer of no great distinction, to fill Berg's place.

Having brought about the resignation of the Supreme Court, Quisling turned his attention to the teachers. He was well aware of the important place of the control of education in his plans. If indoctrination of the young could be promoted, then NS would be well on the way to victory. But he was deflected from his principal aim by an outbreak of unrest in Oslo University which demanded immediate action. On 30 September, Dr Johan Scharffenberg, whose influence was the greater for his being a well-known republican, addressed a gathering of students, urging them to support the King and his government-in-exile. This speech aroused great excitement; Scharffenberg was arrested by the Gestapo and the Students' Union forcibly dissolved. In order to regain control over the students a decree was passed permitting Skancke to promote academics from outside the faculties, in the hope that NS influence would thus be increased.[15] The first beneficiary under this unusual form of 'Buggins's turn' was Aall.[16] This action was followed by a futile attempt to organise an NS-dominated students' association. As in Germany, attacks were made on intellectual freedom. Skancke ordered books written by political opponents and Jewish authors to be removed from the university library. The works of Koht, Scharffenberg and Undset, among Norwegian scholars, were banned; those of Einstein, Orwell and Hemingway, among internationally famous names, received similar treatment.

Towards the end of the year Quisling's attention was turned to the role of the Norwegian Church. In the autumn pressure had been put on leading members of the Church to fall in with the wishes of the party. Opposition had been led by Bishop Berggrav, and on 25 October a special Church Council had been set up, to keep an eye on NS penetration of the Church and to act in defence of Christian values. As about 95 per cent of the population adhered to the State Church this Council was, potentially, very powerful. Quisling's attempts to install NS clergymen met, predictably, with stiffer resistance as his party's attempts to subvert other organisations were seen to have failed. On 15 January 1941 the seven bishops of the Norwegian Church sent Skancke a letter affirming their opposition to the infiltration of the Church by the party. This was followed on 6 February by a pastoral letter from the same bishops asking members of their congregations to refrain from attending services conducted by clergy who were members of NS.[17] This was an effective protest on two counts. In the first place Quisling had always claimed that his party enjoyed a moral basis, and now this belief had been demonstrably rejected by the Church. Secondly, the bishops had raised, in their letter of 15 January, the point that, as they were required to urge their flocks to obey the civil authorities, it was wrong for the government to condone violence and lawlessness from supporters of NS. Skancke's failure to produce an adequate reply showed just how far the government was prepared to tolerate a reign of terror against its opponents. The bishops' protest gave strength to those forces preparing to resist the government on other fronts.

By the beginning of 1941, therefore, Quisling's attempts to put his ideas into practice had not fared well. Resistance had come from farmers, shipowners,[18] teachers,[19] lawyers, the university, professional bodies and the Church. Nothing had been achieved in the way of subjugation of any of these groups. Quisling's sole success had been in the civil service, where the application of Hagelin's decree had resulted in a spate of resignations, thus easing the entry of a number of NS men into local and national government. Quisling and Hagelin were well aware of the shortcomings of their policies and, at the close of 1940, were preparing to revise their plans. This very reasonable decision was taken partly for fear of German intervention; Quisling dared not stir up too much unrest lest Terboven use this as a pretext for reimposing his authority. Partly it was due to an awareness that all the efforts made by NS would be futile unless the party managed to convert a significant section of public opinion to its views. As Quisling had few official duties, it was agreed that he should embark upon a propaganda campaign in order to whip up support for NS,[20] and a series of speeches was planned for 1941. In the meantime Hagelin's department was to press on with a scheme for the massive reorganisation of Norwegian public life. In this way it was hoped to avoid losing face over a number of side issues, as during the previous months.

It was Hagelin who took the first political initiative. On 20 January he wrote to Dahl, one of his administrative assistants, informing him of his intention to set up an office to register organisations (NSPOT).[21] Hagelin intended that NSPOT should base its activities on two decrees which were to be issued. The first was to legalise party control of all organisations; the second was to enforce the registration of these bodies. Thus Hagelin believed he would be able to control the membership, and hence the activities, of all important organisations. On 15 February NSPOT was formally set up and immediately began examining the credentials of the officers of leading organisations.[22] Protests were soon flowing in, and certain prominent men even suggested that a formal complaint should be lodged with Terboven. Early in March the new office had its first major success when Mellbye, the chairman of the Farmers' Union, was deposed. Hagelin and Quisling were elated, the latter in particular, as Mellbye had been a political enemy since his days in the Agrarian Party. Hagelin wrote to Terboven on 13 March, informing him that the work of unifying all important policy-making bodies was progressing well.[23] NS was obviously set upon the creation of a full-blown corporate state, and the Reichskommissar was obliged to co-operate, even though Hagelin's proposals were a grotesque parody of Nazi organisational techniques. But Terboven was not prepared to have his hand forced without seeking revenge; in late March he sent his legal consultant, Dr Schiedermair, to see Scheidt and discover whether Hagelin was really in control of NS policy.[24] Schiedermair reported, much to Terboven's chagrin, that Hagelin stood high in the estimation of both Quisling and his fellow ministers.

On 3 April the enemies of Quisling and NS counter-attacked with a letter to Terboven, signed by leaders of a number of important organisations, complaining about the illegality and irregularity of the behaviour of NS and Hagelin's office.[25] Terboven did not deign to reply and *Fritt Folk* ignored the existence of the protest. On 1 May, Terboven gave a special address urging Norwegians to obey the authorities, a message which gave no joy to the complainants and little to Quisling or his followers.[26] As a riposte, another letter was sent on 15 May to the Reichskommissar, protesting on behalf of 43 organisations, representing 700,000 citizens. The particular cause of complaint on this occasion was the unlawful behaviour of the Hird and party oppression by NS.[27] Once again the Reichskommissar vouchsafed no reply. Quisling and Hagelin were meanwhile pressing Terboven to act against the signatories. Terboven, however, anxious not to stir up a hornets' nest, did nothing. *Fritt*

Folk began to criticise the Reichskommissar with increasing severity, and at the end of the month launched two vigorous broadsides against his toleration of 'treasonable behaviour'.[28]

It soon became clear that Terboven would have to do something, if only to restore his crumbling authority. Quisling and Hagelin had each publicly attacked him for betraying NS. On 2 June, Quisling had outlined the hopes and plans of NS to a select audience,[29] and three days later Hagelin, at an official NS meeting, had confirmed Quisling's sentiments.[30] The necessity for the victory of the party over its opponents had also been greatly emphasised in an editorial in *Fritt Folk* on 29 May.[31] The party newspaper and the party leaders continued to attack Terboven until, on 12 June, three of the signatories were arrested by the Gestapo.[32] At the same time a meeting between Terboven and the leaders of the organisations was fixed for 18 June. On 16 June Schiedermair wrote to Hagelin informing him that Terboven earnestly wished to help NS to overcome its difficulties.[33] The next day a decree was prepared, giving the Ministry of the Interior full power to deal with the organisations. This was later published in *Norsk Lovtidend*, the official government gazette, and received the personal approval of Quisling and Fuglesang. At last Terboven had decided to support NS.

The meeting took place at noon on 18 June, in the Storting. All the important leaders of organisational resistance were there. They were addressed by Terboven, who refused to make any concessions, and were then informed of the new decree by Hagelin. Terboven's speech failed to win him any friends; he spoke as if he were 'a colonial governor addressing German slaves'.[34] After his peroration five more leaders were arrested.[35] Hagelin's decree placed all the organisations under commissarial ministerial control, and the next day Quisling, Hagelin and other leaders of the party summoned a formal meeting of the NS Council in order to discuss its implications for the party.[36] The matter was largely concealed from the general public until *Fritt Folk* published an official account of the affair, written by Hagelin, a week later.[37]

At this meeting of NS notables it was decided to set up a special branch of the Ministry of the Interior to cope with the problems of unification. This was known as the Foreningskontoret, or Office for Unification (FK) and came into existence on 25 June.[38] It worked in close contact with a number of German security organisations, so that it was easy for the FK to be rid of its opponents. Soon after its foundation the new office was able to seize control of several small organisations which could be managed easily by the party. None the less the party was unable to secure any major success, and as soon as it became apparent that NS controlled the official professional bodies large numbers of members began to leave. Nothing, therefore, had really been achieved except the formal elimination of the organisations from resistance groups. All that happened was that new, underground associations sprang up, which were even more difficult to control. Quisling and Hagelin had to fall back upon yet another restrictive measure. In July and August new plans were prepared by which compulsory membership was introduced in return for the granting of permission to professional men to practise their skills. Under this new scheme the doctors and lawyers were the first to suffer, the decree against them being put into effect in late August and early September. As this experiment proved moderately successful, the FK informed the office of the Reichskommissar on 17 September that a more comprehensive decree was being prepared.[39] On 1 October compulsory membership was introduced for a large number of professional organisations.[40]

Meanwhile, Quisling was busy making speeches and trying to rally the party. Only on a few occasions during the sixteen months of commissarial ministerial government did he personally take part in the campaign against the organisations, though Hagelin's actions had his full support. Quisling's efforts to rally support for the party had no great success. His campaign opened on 31 December 1940, when he addressed the nation in an end-of-the-year radio message. He reviewed the events of 1940, laying blame on the British and the Nygaardsvold government for the plight of Norway: 'If the Norwegian people wish to enjoy freedom and independence again there is only one way for them to travel, and that is the road of NS . . . it is now up to Norway to choose.'[41] Quisling followed up his speech by trying to raise a special regiment, to be called the Nordland Regiment, to fight against England. In his appeal he declared: 'Norwegian and German interests are the same. Germany's struggle is Norway's struggle. Germany's victory is Norway's victory.'[42] As the response to this appeal was very poor, he ordered members of the Hird to join the new regiment.[43]

Quisling returned repeatedly to the theme of Norwegian and German solidarity in the struggle against Britain, and on 1 February he emphasised the need for co-operation between the youth of both nations.[44] On 12 March, when he spoke again, it was clear that he had fallen completely under the influence of the advocates of total commitment to Nazism: 'A new Norway will arise, based upon the firm ground of National Socialism and Nordic principles, which will work together with our great German brothers.'[45] Later that month Quisling visited Germany, and on 28 March he spoke to a select audience at Frankfurt on the Jewish problem. He asserted that the inhabitants of Northern Europe were natural leaders as they had been 'least polluted by the Jews'.[46] He condemned Jews as parasites and asserted that 'English Jews were the new chosen people, and Norway was Benjamin'. Naturally, this speech was very well received in Germany; it attracted little attention in Norway, where a Jewish problem did not exist.

Quisling's next major public appearance was on 8 April, when he spoke about the events of the past twelve months: 'The Norwegian people had followed false prophets' with disastrous consequences. The people had been left to suffer while their guilty leaders had escaped to Sweden or

Britain. All the events which NS had feared and contended against had come to pass, with tragic results. The duty of NS had been plain – 'It was necessary to form a genuinely Norwegian government which could represent our country's true interests.' The Fører found himself in complete agreement with Hitler, who had stated on 16 March that the events of 9 April 1940 would form a dividing line in Norwegian history between subjection to corrupt politicians and a new awakening of the national spirit. The events of 1940 had given Norway a chance to recover from her mistakes in the 1930s. Since 25 September, the day of decisive defeat for 'the corrupt Marxist clique',[47] NS had tried to impose a socially just system in Norway, despite unthinking and selfish obstruction. The solution to all Norway's problems lay in holding fast to Germany.

This speech did not go down well with the Norwegian people. Resentment against the German invasion was strong, and so was feeling against NS for its clumsy attempts to incorporate national organisations into a party-dominated system. Quisling had failed to take these widespread feelings into account; his speech was a political disaster. None the less he was determined to preach the virtues of a permanent union between Norway and Germany. In an interview with a newspaper on 20 May[48] and in a speech on 23 June[49] he referred to the historic connexions between the two countries, and advocated close co-operation.

Towards the end of this summer, Quisling came to believe that the interests of NS would best be served by his playing a more active part in the struggle against the organisations. The events of June 1941 had shown that Terboven was reluctant to assist NS actively, and the party had been obliged to take up the aggressive policy of compulsory membership. NS had thus become the active force in Norway, trying to push through Nazification in all public bodies. Admittedly this was the only way the party could exercise effective power, but its actions did little to endear it either to the Norwegians or to the German administration. Terboven had little reason to hope for an NS victory, since it would imperil his own position. The Reichskommissar was therefore no friend to NS; in fact he did his best, discreetly, to hinder its progress. Successes by NS in the summer of 1941 were few, and there were several major setbacks. The party was unable to take over the Land Organisation;[50] a Directorate for Labour Organisation, set up on 19 June,[51] was an utter fiasco. As these failures became more widely known, so organisational resistance grew.

It was to this situation that Quisling returned in the early autumn of 1941. Terboven was reluctant to give NS the signal for an all-out offensive against trade unions and other bodies.[52] Quisling and his followers, however, hoped to force his hand. From their point of view the industrial and political situation had changed radically as a result of the German attack on the Soviet Union. Up to June 1941 the trade unions had been remarkably restrained in their dealings with NS. This restraint was mainly due to two factors: first, to Terboven's anxiety to keep industrial production high and his willingness therefore to turn a blind eye to some unrest, and, secondly, to the power of the Communist Party within the unions. Until the invasion of the Soviet Union industrial relations had not been too bad, although union leaders liked neither the government as a whole nor the Minister of Labour, Tormod Hustad. The Federation of Labour had been ordered to accept an NS-dominated executive council, but this had been rejected in May 1941. Until the invasion of Russia, however, the Communists had been ordered to co-operate with the Germans, so united resistance had been impossible. After June 1941 there was a dramatic increase in industrial unrest and sabotage, coming to a climax with a strike in early September at an Oslo shipyard. The organisers were Viggo Hansteen and Rolf Wickstrøm, both of whom were arrested and later executed by the German authorities. Quisling was not personally involved in these executions; indeed, the incident demonstrated his party's impotence to take any initiative in industrial affairs.

Quisling and his allies, while Terboven was still absorbing the lessons he had learned from this industrial unrest, pressed on with their plans. Quisling now began to play an active part in the industrial struggle. He was well equipped to do so, for all those in the commissarial government closely connected with the management of industrial and labour relations – Hagelin, Prytz, Fuglesang and Whist, the future Minister of Supply – were also close to Quisling. On 9 September he addressed a meeting of craftsmen, to whom he made a special appeal, assuring them it was his wish that they should be 'elevated to their proper place in society which is at present not recognised'. It was necessary to incorporate this group into the party's scheme for industrial reconstruction, which was, in fact, based upon Hitler's industrial measures. Quisling believed it 'was clear that these groups must work under the control of the state, just as the state must function under the control of the party'.[53] In the atmosphere of the recent executions this appeal fell on deaf ears, and was regarded as bad timing on Quisling's part.[54]

The increase in industrial unrest was not the only problem; there was also an upsurge of anti-government feeling in Oslo University. The decree of 9 October 1940, permitting the introduction of Aall to the academic community, had met with effective resistance from the professorial staff and the students. Aall and his cronies were boycotted and ignored. In September Dr Seip, the Rector, was arrested and deported to Germany. Thereafter NS concentrated on trying to infiltrate its supporters into the student body. Normal university life became impossible as the campus became not only an ideological but a physical battleground.

Quisling's main concern for the next few months was, however, the reorganisation of government. The commissarial government had originally been intended as a transitional administration, lasting about six months. Quisling was anxious to regain personal control. Although he intervened on a number of occasions, between September 1940 and February 1942 he devoted most of his attention to the reconstruction of the party[55] and the winning over of public opinion. By September 1941 it was clear that the provisional arrangements were no longer adequate. Quisling himself hinted at this in a speech on 5 September, when he stated that 'the fate of Norway must be placed in the hands of NS and its leaders'.[56] Quisling's wishes suited Terboven, who was exasperated with the inefficiency of his administration and considered a revision of the existing situation to be highly desirable. He knew that Quisling had long been meditating such a project. On 10 March 1941, for example, Quisling had written to Lammers, pointing out that the time for a transitional government was now past.[57] Terboven's only reservations were, firstly, his poor opinion of Quisling, and, secondly, his belief that if full power were given to NS that party might give the Germans more trouble than the existing regime.

These fears and reservations were now gradually overcome. Terboven was forced to admit that Quisling, if anyone, was capable of welding NS into an effective government. He was still far from enthusiastic at the prospect; but he had no alternative, short of direct German rule, and that possibility had been excluded by the arrangements of the summer of 1940. On 23 January 1942 the Reichskommissar finally gave in, and invited Quisling to form a government. The meeting between the rivals cannot have been wholly pleasant for either. Terboven was obliged to admit to a series of political errors; Quisling, in return for Terboven's concession, was compelled to postpone his plan for the signature of a peace treaty with Germany. He had hoped to have such a treaty signed on 28 January and to be admitted to office on 1 February. On instructions from Berlin, this part of the plan was postponed.[58] The wheel of political fortune appeared to have turned full circle.

But although Quisling believed that he had at last succeeded in returning to the position of 9 April 1940, the situation was really very different. During the intervening twenty-two months there had been many political developments. Norwegian hostility to the forces of occupation and to NS had grown steadily. A system of secret police and regimentation had been introduced. The leaders of important organisations had been forced to retire, but their work was continued secretly. The tide of war had at last ceased to flow in Germany's favour, and resistance movements were emboldened. Finally, during its sixteen months of office, NS had plainly been both unpopular and inept, incapable of exerting control over the processes of government. Quisling's position, then, was much weaker than when he and his party were unknown quantities.

On 1 February 1942, Quisling assumed office at the Akershus. Present were representatives of German authority, by whose grace the new Minister-President was being installed: Bormann, Terboven, Rediess and Admiral Boehm. At last the power which Quisling craved seemed to be within his grasp. One of his first acts was to reconstitute his ministerial team. Ten of the ministers from the commissarial government were retained. Sandberg was replaced as Minister of Finance by Prytz, and the Ministries of Supply and Trade, previously headed by Ravner and Johannessen, were combined under Eivind Blehr, formerly governor of Oslo and Aker. Sandberg, Ravner and Johannessen, however, continued as assistants and advisers to the new government. In addition, Fuglesang was brought into the cabinet to represent NS.[59] Quisling himself took over responsibility for dealing with defence and foreign affairs, though these were not likely to involve much work, as responsibility for them rested firmly in German hands. Quisling was not enthusiastic about all the members of his cabinet – in particular he disliked Lie – but he believed that he had brought together the best team possible.

Quisling's intentions were clear from the outset. He had in mind three goals – to conclude peace with Germany, to introduce a corporate state, to summon a Council of the Kingdom. None of these goals would be easy to achieve and Quisling was well aware of the difficulties. His views were reflected in *Fritt Folk* on 2 February, when a leading article declared, 'Mere installation is not victory.'[60] It would be no easy matter to conclude a lasting peace with Germany; there were many problems which had to be solved. It was this question of a peace treaty which was chiefly to concern Quisling for his first six months of office; in the meantime, he was largely content to let other ministers look after their own departments.

The appointment of Quisling as Minister-President met with varying reactions. Some Germans, including Goebbels, were critical of his pretensions, believing that he was not the man to bring peace to Norway.[61] On the other hand, the Wilhelmstrasse, which contained many enemies of Quisling, announced that now that he had been installed, 'peace negotiations would play an increasingly important part'.[62]

Quisling was fully aware that he had to put his government into working order before he could negotiate with the Germans. He was determined to eliminate opposition and hold real power. But Terboven's role continued the same, and while he and his office remained, Quisling could not initiate policy without Terboven's consent. Quisling sought to change this position by two separate methods. Through his friends in Germany he attempted to undermine Terboven's already tenuous position, while in Norway he tried to represent himself as the true voice of the Norwegian people. The latter campaign started almost immediately; a few days after the installation of the new government, *Fritt Folk* announced that 'majority or minority, NS represents the real will of the people'.[63] Quisling came to believe that any dissent from NS rule would be eliminated, once the Council of the Kingdom had been called and peace had been made. Accordingly he instructed his ministers to press on with plans for summoning the Riksting and introducing a corporate state, while he himself handled peace negotiations.

The first meeting of the new government took place on 5 February.[64] The cabinet was eager to establish the legal position of the government, and Quisling was able to report that approval had been given by the Supreme Court on 31 January.[65] The ministers then proceeded to declare that the government was invested with royal authority as well as parliamentary power.[66] Once this point had been established, it was only necessary for the cabinet to give its assent to a decree for it to become law. The ministers were anxious to take action against the organisations which had resisted their earlier efforts so successfully. Accordingly three decrees were passed. Compulsory membership of a new Teachers' Union was introduced;[67] so was compulsory membership of a Press Association. Finally, there was to be compulsory membership of organisations for youth service and training for all between the ages of ten and eighteen: these bodies were to be under the control of Axel Stang.[68] The new government hoped to be able to control education, news and youth through rigorous application of these decrees, thus showing how seriously the problems of introducing a corporate state were taken.

Quisling was not in Norway when the storm of protest broke. On 13 February he was in Germany where he was visiting Hitler in his new capacity as head of state,[69] and presented to the Führer a memorandum on peace talks, which he had composed a few days before.[70] Thereafter, whenever peace proposals came under discussion, Quisling always returned to this memorandum of 10 February. The new leader of Norway was very active while he was in Germany; he went to see both Göring and Rosenberg,[71] and presumably discussed his memorandum with them also, for it involved a review of domestic as well as foreign policy. After a few days Quisling returned to Norway to find that the decrees issued shortly before his departure had created a political uproar.

The decree which created most unrest was that relating to the teachers. In the autumn of 1941, Orvar Sæther, a former leader of the Hird, had pressed for action against the teachers, who had continued to agitate against the authority of NS.[72] In January 1942, Terboven had supported Sæther, declaring that it was time some discipline was introduced. The decree against the teachers had, in fact, been discussed by the cabinet at some length before they reached agreement. In retrospect the reasons are clear. The teachers were chosen as the first group to be compulsorily integrated into the corporate state, for several weighty reasons. NS had, in Sæther, a suitable candidate for the post of president of the new association. Furthermore, there were approximately 140,000 members of the Teachers' Union; for NS to take over such an important professional body would be an outstanding *coup*. Finally, the teachers were known to be very hostile to the ideas and programme of NS; considering their powerful position, this created a very dangerous situation. The teaching profession could make life uncomfortable for Quisling, and, in his absence, a number of prominent NS party leaders – Sæther, Hagelin, Skancke, Lunde and Riisnæs – decided to seize the initiative. The first move was made by Sæther, with the concurrence of Quisling, on 8 February, when, at a press conference, he revealed that it was the government's intention to link the new teachers' association with the party organisation for youth service.[73] This news raised a storm of protest, and succeeded only in uniting virtually the whole of the teaching profession. The hierarchy of the Teachers' Union prepared a standard form for rejection of the government's plans, and this was distributed to all members on 14 February.[74]

This was the situation which Quisling found on his return. The campaign against his government was in full swing, and by 20 February the letters of protest were flooding in to Skancke's department. Moreover, protests were not confined to the teachers. Before long, Quisling found that he had become involved in a series of acutely controversial actions. The month of February 1942 was to witness the beginning of a long and bitter struggle between Church and State. Although the Church was not directly allied with the teachers at this stage, the bishops were very hostile to the idea of a link between education and the NS youth organisations. There were also strong protests from university staff and parents. The bishops, however, had most effect, for on 14 February a pastoral letter condemning the action of the government was made public. Skancke and Quisling thus faced a formidable coalition between the Church, the teaching profession and the existing youth organisations.

The government was not in the mood either for retreat or for discreet withdrawal. Even though the sole effect of Quisling's and Sæther's actions had been to stir up strife, the government decided to press on with its plans. Quisling was firmly against making any concession to the opposition, although Skancke urged moderation on him. From 20 February, indeed, the Minister of Education pursued month-long negotiations with official representatives of the Teachers' Union, hoping to persuade them to agree to a declaration of loyalty,[75] which, he believed, would satisfy the more extreme party in the government. But this scheme was no more acceptable to the teachers than the other, and, in view of Quisling's opinions, it is also doubtful whether the government would have accepted it. After a month it was clear that the decree of 5 February had had no effect; Quisling demanded the use of force, and found that he had Terboven's support.[76] The Reichskommissar had been very irritated by the resistance to the new government and was, perhaps, fearful of being accused of undue leniency towards anti-Quisling Norwegians. Despite pressure from the military authorities, who believed that strong-arm action might imperil German control of the internal situation,[77] Quisling and Terboven decided to carry the war into the enemy's camp.

On 16 March Quisling wrote to Skancke provisionally authorising him to send recalcitrant teachers to forced labour in North Norway.[78] On 20 March over one thousand were arrested. On 15 April a large proportion were herded on to the *Skjærstad* at Trondheim, whence they were transported to Kirkenes to work on German fortifications in the far north.[79] Norwegian opinion was shocked not only by the appalling conditions on the boat but also by the government's recourse to plainly unlawful methods. During that two weeks' sea journey there was forged in Norway a temper of hostility to Quisling and NS which was never to cool. Quisling had disastrously miscalculated the effects of his tactics of terror.

Meanwhile, Quisling's other ministers were also demanding government action. Only Skancke, who had some idea of the trouble that was brewing, counselled moderation, and had a minor success in persuading Quisling to agree that those teachers left after the purge need not work with the NS youth organisation.[80] Laws on legal, social and cultural matters were pushed through regardless of the chaos which would have resulted from their enforcement. On 19 February Quisling was interviewed by *Morgenbladet*; the Minister-President made his attitude towards the press law of 5 February very clear: 'I shall order the Norwegian press to assist us . . . and those who write against us are condemning themselves to death.'[81] Despite these bold words the press law remained a dead letter. The activists were, however, in complete control. On 20 February Riisnæs, speaking at Lillestrøm, declared: 'We shall sweep passivity out of the way and resistance will be suppressed.'[82] It was in this atmosphere that Hagelin pressed Quisling to proceed with the reorganisation of labour.[83] Not only was the attitude of the cabinet favourable but in Whist they had a man capable of playing a leading part.

Whist had been promoted in November 1941 to be the party's leading policy-maker in matters of trade, labour, industry and economics.[84] Although he had not become a member of the government in February, he was a very powerful personality, in whom Quisling had great confidence. On 12 March, Whist wrote to Quisling urging him to revive the party's plans for an NS-dominated Labour Front.[85] Whist had been cast for the leadership of such a body at the time of his promotion, and it had been decided that the Labour Front should come into existence on 1 May 1942.[86] Whist had modelled his proposed system on that set up in Germany by Ley, though with certain features based on Ley's experience, among them a special organ of propaganda entitled *Norsk Arbeidsliv* (NAS), which was distributed from the middle of March onwards. It was Whist's belief that a favourable climate of opinion could be created well in advance of the formation of the Labour Front, so that formal inauguration of the body could take place at a meeting addressed by Quisling on Labour Day.

During April 1942 resistance to the proposals of Quisling and Whist began to take shape. The Church Council roundly condemned the NS proposals for setting up NAS, with the result that five of its seven members were arrested. Quisling became increasingly concerned about the future of his new proposals and in an article published on 8 April he defended the government's schemes and accused Berggrav of 'using conspiratorial methods to create unrest and faction among the Norwegian people'.[87] In Germany some were doubtful of the wisdom of Quisling's initiative on the labour front. After the reverses in Russia at the end of 1941 several important members of Hitler's military circle feared an Allied landing on the coast of Norway in the following spring.[88] Raeder sent a small fleet of battleships north, and the convoys to Murmansk were watched with great anxiety. It appeared to be of prime importance that the transfer of raw materials should not be interrupted. On two counts, therefore, the military authorities in Norway wanted Quisling to proceed discreetly. Firstly, they wished to keep production and transportation at a high level, and to retain voluntary labour if possible, rather than resort to conscription and labour camps.[89] In the second place they did not wish to increase the chance of internal unrest on the possible eve of an invasion. Von Falkenhorst and his staff therefore opposed Quisling's plan to set up NAS. The German military commander received support from an unexpected quarter, for Goebbels was highly critical of the actions of Quisling and the Reichskommissar.[90] The latter, however, held political power in Norway and their critics were unable to bring sufficient pressure to bear in favour of a revision of policy.

Thus at an early stage in the government's career a rift had opened between the Norwegian interests of Terboven and Quisling and the military needs of Germany. Quisling's labour policies were normally of secondary importance to the German government. Terboven, however, argued that the resistance of the teachers must be crushed if the general public were to be convinced that Germany would brook no opposition. According to *Fritt Folk* the Reichskommissar believed that there would be serious danger of the spread of unrest to industry if firm action was not taken against the teachers.[91] In this way Quisling's policies tied together neatly and conveniently. Quisling himself wished to persuade the public to be sensible and on 24 April, *Fritt Folk* warned that, if Norwegians did not heed the warnings of Quisling and the Reichskommissar, they ran the risk that 'all their interests would be sacrificed in the cause of German victory'.[92]

Despite these warnings, plans for resistance were still being made. Open declarations of dissent from the purposes of NAS alarmed Terboven a great deal, as he did not want any widespread industrial unrest. He grew less and less enamoured of Quisling's proposals, and urged that the plan to set up NAS be dropped.[93] On 16 April it became clear that the Land Organisation would not co-operate with NAS and on 25 April the leaders of the craftsmen also refused.[94] Their resistance was given great publicity in a rival newsletter to *Norsk Arbeidsliv*, published under the title *Fri Fagbevegelse*.[95] This illegal newsletter kept members of trade unions and other interested parties informed of developments on the industrial and labour fronts, and was very hostile to Quisling's government. Attempts at controlling it failed utterly.

Those who opposed NAS had their first major success when plans for the inauguration were dropped. This was partly due to Terboven, who, after a brief honeymoon with the Quisling government, was now veering round to the view that Quisling should be allowed to proceed with his plans only if he could demonstrate that support for NS was growing. If Quisling was firmly resisted, then, Terboven might well place restrictions on his activities. That Quisling decided none the less to continue with his policy is clear from the eulogy Blehr delivered on 22 May, in which he outlined Quisling's determination not to retreat, once victory was in his grasp.[96] The NS secretariat obeyed Quisling's directives by making plans for a new law on organisations and for the summoning of the Riksting in September 1942.

Quisling realised that the sole result would be confrontation, but he believed that he would win the struggle. On 22 May he met leaders of the Church and of the teaching profession at Stabekk school and vented his wrath on them for their part in obstructing the formation of NAS on 1 May.[97] The meeting should have convinced him that NS could achieve none of its aims; attack upon one organisation was now producing resistance on all fronts. The Germans were quicker to learn; they started drafting men to meet Sauckel's labour requirements, thus circumventing the vexed issue of NAS. Terboven was to pursue this policy with some success throughout the summer of 1942. Quisling did not learn so quickly. At the end of May, Alf Whist laid a new plan before him. Whist saw a very real risk of the outbreak of new conflicts and consequently pressed for a law conferring plenipotentiary powers upon himself. All previous attempts by NS to take over organisations had been very feeble. Whist was, in particular, critical of the law of 5 February,[98] and pointed out that, although the idea of compulsory membership was central to the whole plan, this had not yet been achieved. Quisling, however, could take no firm decision upon the points raised by Whist because the plans envisaged impinged upon other activities with which he was concerned.

It was at this point that Whist's plans became inextricably confused, and eventually fatally identified, with his leader's plans for the signature of a peace treaty and the creation of a Riksting. The idea of a peace offensive had long been maturing in Quisling's mind, and on 9 June he sent a memorandum to Hitler offering to conclude a peace treaty.[99] The document contained three basic proposals – that a temporary peace should be declared on 18 July, the anniversary of Havsfjord, that Norway should join the anti-Comintern Pact on 25 September, and that negotiations should begin as soon as possible for the conclusion of a permanent peace. Quisling had been considering these plans in detail for a few days before they were sent to Hitler, and there is reason to suppose that he had the support of several members of his cabinet.[100] The Minister-President was careful to inform Hitler that his reasons for wanting peace lay not in the weakness of his party but because 'NS government is the strongest Norway has enjoyed for many years'.[101] Quisling was under the delusion that he was negotiating with an equal. The themes of strength and equality were to run through Quisling's speeches during the next few weeks. On 22 June, for example, at Hamar, Quisling declared: 'There has never existed in Norway a party as strong as NS; there is no opposition too powerful for us to crush.'[102] The day before, at Sarpsborg, he had outlined the profit Norway would derive from a partnership with Germany.

Unfortunately for Quisling's aspirations an unfavourable answer to his memorandum arrived on 29 July. Lammers had written to Quisling informing him that Hitler had categorically rejected his proposals.[103] Quisling was rather depressed by this reply but came to the amazing conclusion that the way to success was to press on with the creation of a Riksting and the introduction of the corporate state. He was not putting the cart before the horse, for he had reversed his position of February and was relying on internal progress to produce peace. By staking his party's political future on the outcome of this decision Quisling made yet one more serious political misjudgement.

While its leader was awaiting Hitler's reply the government had proceeded with its other plans. In May there had been a series of inspired leaks from party sources about the proposals for a Riksting. These proposals had even attracted some attention abroad,[104] as well as a good deal of speculation at home. Quisling made a major speech on 25 May advocating the desirability of a Riksting,[105] and he was supported in a number of supplementary speeches by various colleagues during the next few weeks. In mid-June the cabinet decided to call the Riksting into existence in September, in the hope that it would be able to make binding decisions concerning the future of Norway.[106] At that stage, of course, Quisling was still optimistic about Hitler's reply to his peace proposals. Several members of the cabinet argued, however, that even in the event of the rejection of Quisling's proposals it would be best to proceed with the Riksting plan, as it would be possible for such an assembly to discharge a limited function.[107]

Even after the rejection of Quisling's overtures was known, the Riksting plan was still supported. Hagelin's and Quisling's interviews with reporters from *Fritt Folk* showed that the two leading personalities in NS were still optimistic about the status of a Riksting with limited functions.[108] But there was opposition within the party to Quisling's ideas, particularly from Fretheim and other moderates.[109] Hagelin was especially keen to proceed with the plans as he was becoming increasingly worried by the growth of German influence over matters which he considered were more properly the concern of the Quisling government.[110] He was able to appeal to Quisling on the grounds that the national welfare required a strong and unified leadership, which could be provided only through an NS administration supported by a Riksting. For both the Minister-President and the Minister of the Interior much was at stake.

On 5 August it was announced that the eighth national rally of NS would be held at Oslo on 25 September, following the first meeting of the Riksting on the previous day.[111] Once the public announcement had been made, discussion began of the organisation of the new corporate system. The idea eventually accepted by Quisling was very simple. There was to be a complete revision of the personnel and status of the existing organisations; the reformed bodies could then send delegates to the Riksting, which would thus be able to take important decisions, since it would have an acknowledged national basis. On 8 August a circular from the Ministry of the Interior made suggestions about the details of representation, including the numbers each organisation was to have.[112] The circular produced much activity in party circles, for it was expected that large numbers of party members would be required to act as delegates from the reformed organisations. Prytz, who was fully in the confidence of Quisling, went so far as to write to Dahl telling him that the purpose of the Riksting was to 'ratify a peace treaty with Germany'; the country could not afford to have 'Jøssinger as members of the new body'.[113] This viewpoint made it impossible for the Riksting to be representative. It was to be based on certain powerful groups which NS hoped to be able to penetrate and influence; all therefore depended upon success in this direction.

Hagelin's circular of 8 August created acute dissension within the party. His proposals were very simple, allocating representation as follows: 'agriculture and forestry 30, industry 20, crafts 7, fishing 10, shipping 6, transport 6, trade 10, tourism 2, banking 4, insurance 3, domestic industry 8, public service 7, and self-employed 7. In total this made 120 representatives for the 13 leading economic groups.'[114] Unfortunately for Quisling and Hagelin, the allocation of quotas was more easily announced than achieved. Nor was their task facilitated by the open discontent in the party. Whist was opposed to the whole project until he had been given plenipotentiary powers,[115] while Fretheim had objections of long standing. Even more serious was the fact that administrative officers were very pessimistic about the outcome of the plan. Hasle, a high-ranking official in the Ministry of the Interior, and an enthusiastic member of NS, dissociated himself from the proposals in a memorandum written on 20 August. Among his comments was the significant conclusion that it was simply not possible to introduce National Socialism in the way Quisling and Hagelin wished.[116]

Despite all these objections a new law on organisations was agreed on 20 August.[117] The differences of opinion between the NS labour organisations and the Ministry of the Interior concerning compulsory membership were settled amicably, but much to the advantage of Hagelin, who was, in practice, to have co-ordinating control. It was decided, however, that the law of 20 August would not be published until September, in an attempt to circumvent internal unrest. If this was the principal object of delay it was not achieved, for resistance to the Riksting plan steadily grew. Quisling and his party found the task of co-ordinating developments in both NAS and the Riksting impossible. Holding the Riksting became the first priority, but it was impossible to convene a meeting of that body while there was industrial unrest. During August it became clear that the proposals for a Riksting would meet with serious resistance. The leaders of the free bodies made preparations for a contingency strike,[118] in the case of the transfer of power to NAS. By early September the secret organisations had realised that it was equally important to discredit the Riksting, and preparations to oppose it were also made.

It had become clear to Quisling while the form of the new law on organisations was being discussed that a further effort to produce a peace treaty was necessary. He therefore flew to Berlin early in August in order to put fresh peace proposals to the Führer. On 11 August Hitler conferred with Terboven, Ribbentrop, Lammers and Bormann.[119] They discussed Quisling's latest memorandum, written on 3 August,[120] but found no reason to conclude the peace treaty which he so eagerly desired. There was to be no independent foreign policy for Norway and no formal end to hostilities. Quisling, who by this time was back in Norway, was not informed of Hitler's decision until 26 August, when Terboven brusquely told him that the Führer no longer wished to be bothered with the matter. In case Quisling refused to believe Terboven's report, Lammers wrote to him on 17 September, informing him that Hitler wished there to be no further discussion of the future of Norway. Should there be important political matters to be discussed, the Führer wished them 'to be forwarded through the Reichskommissar, who was his only personal representative in respect of the civil sector'.[121] Even Quisling had to recognise that his goal of a negotiated peace was now ruled out.

In the meantime the tempo of events in Norway had increased. The law of 20 August, published on 9 September,[122] was hailed by *Fritt Folk* as the answer to all Norway's problems, but was otherwise looked upon with hostility.[123] It was the Quisling government's last attempt to operate through comparatively normal legal processes, and it was as great a failure as all their preceding decrees. The law included savage penalties for industrial sabotage and other anti-government activities. On 10 September *Fri Fagbevegelse* advocated a mass withdrawal from trade unions and other bodies.[124] Within a few days there followed a tremendous response to this appeal, beginning with the Land Organisation and spreading rapidly. Within a week or so, between 100,000 and 150,000 members left their organisations and NS saw its policies in ruins. To Quisling it was crystal clear that these protests were directed, in the first instance, against NS rather than the German authorities.

As the scope of the disaster became apparent two further developments took place. Firstly, the Germans began to question the wisdom of Quisling's activities, and, secondly, opposition to the Riksting began to make itself felt. By 17 September it was clear that there was likely to be serious German opposition to the joint plans for NAS and the Riksting. This was hardly surprising, since early in September a special investigator had been sent by Heydrich's office (the RSHA) to report on the situation. Dr Stuckart had arrived in Oslo on 7 September and on the 14th had sent a long report to Berlin informing the RSHA office that 'getting on for 95 per cent of the Norwegian people are anti-Quisling and anti-NS'.[125] This was a damning indictment of Quisling's policy and was to have fatal consequences for it. To neutral observers at the time it seemed as if the mission of Stuckart had been at the request of Terboven and von Falkenhorst, so that an unfavourable report was bound to lead to the modification of NS policy.[126]

Whatever the reason, Terboven began to pay much more attention to internal affairs in September than at any point since Quisling's government had been placed in power. As time went by and Quisling was no closer to achieving his ends, the Reichskommissar became more sceptical of the soundness of the law of 20 August. He came to disbelieve that a Riksting could ever be organised, and his views received support within administrative circles; on 17 September, Dahl wrote to Lippestad, later the leader of NAS, informing him that it was 'quite out of the question to think of summoning the Riksting by 25 September'.[127] Terboven at first kept in the background, hoping that Quisling would give up the plan of his own accord. On 20 September, however, a united front against NAS and the Riksting was proclaimed. This declaration, coupled with the mass withdrawal of membership, was too much for the Reichskommissar, who feared there would be total chaos in industry, for which he might be held responsible by an irate Führer. Furthermore, there was the danger of civil disorder on a large scale, for already at the end of August there had been a bomb attack on police headquarters. Terboven was not the man to risk losing control of a potentially dangerous situation; unlike Quisling, he had the power to enforce his will. On 21 September he arrested a number of the leaders of the resistance and warned the rest that he would put certain people to death unless the mass resignations were withdrawn. On 24 September the first capitulation to Terboven's threats took place, to be followed by others, despite the fact that on 26 September *Fri Fagbevegelse* informed the German authorities that the protest had been directed at NS.[128] Terboven had won the round; Quisling had been knocked out of the reckoning.

During this critical week, Quisling discovered that he had very little control over events. As it became clear that the Riksting could not be summoned he began to make other plans. On 21 September he came to the conclusion that the answer was a 'Førerting', or an assembly nominated by himself which would, for all that, be representative. The same day telegrams were sent to leading members of the party, summoning them to a meeting on the 25th to discuss the situation.[129] As matters grew worse, so did Quisling try to save his own and his party's prestige. As late as 26 September, *Fritt Folk* was still assuring the public that the Riksting plan had only been 'temporarily postponed'.[130] But at the meeting on the 25th, Quisling and his colleagues were obliged to admit to themselves, if to no one else, that the proposal to set up NAS and the Riksting had failed. The special postage stamps which had been prepared for next day's formal inauguration had to be destroyed. The plan for a Riksting perished with them. On 25 September Quisling formally conceded defeat in a speech in which he advocated calling a Førerting, which would be 'a new and better Riksting, representing all that is best in the nation'.[131] But his promises of final victory convinced few, if any, Norwegians. His defeat was total and final.

After the events of September 1942, Quisling played a comparatively obscure part in Norwegian politics until the end of the war in May 1945. The collapse of his plans had irrefutably demonstrated that he did not, and was not likely to, enjoy the confidence of the Norwegian people. As a result, the German civil authority, Terboven, and the military commander, von Falkenhorst, carried out decisions which emanated from Berlin rather than Oslo. During the thirty-one months of power left to him, Quisling made few interventions in political affairs, and most of these were disastrous. Instead he concerned himself with party and personal matters, existing on the fringe rather than at the centre of politics. Occasionally he tried to raise questions which had already been answered, as in the case of a peace treaty, but most of the time he was content to ratify German decisions without close examination.

The process of withdrawal was gradual, however, which suited both Quisling and Terboven. On 5 October, a serious case of sabotage took place at Trondheim. German Gestapo agents went there immediately and ten prominent citizens were shot. Their decision was ratified without much thought by Henrik Rogstad, leader of NS in Trondheim. Quisling himself was not directly involved, but the repercussions seriously affected his personal standing and that of his party. A few days later, apprehensive of the effect of this atrocity upon his recruitment campaign, Quisling informed Hustad that 'those who have been members of the party, and who leave, shall lose their employment if they are in public service'.[132] In this way he tried to maintain the strength of NS in all posts involving administration, for he saw this as essential to any possible revival.

Instead of pitting himself against organisations which were able to resist his blandishments, Quisling moved against the small Jewish community. The German authorities had taken certain preliminary measures against the Jews in May 1940, when radio sets had been confiscated, but as there were fewer than 2,000 Jews in the whole country it was difficult even for the Nazis to take the threat of a Jewish conspiracy seriously. Not so Quisling. On 26 October he and his cabinet met to decree the confiscation and sequestration of all property owned by Jews; this came into effect on 10 November.[133] On the 17th it was further decreed that all those who were a quarter-Jewish or more were to register at the local police headquarters.[134] Owing to delay in enforcing this decree, about a quarter of the Jewish population of Norway managed to escape to join those who had already fled to other countries. About 800 remained, and these were interned in the Grini concentration camp. On 11 November protests against these acts were sent to Quisling by a number of eminent Norwegians, including bishops and professors. Quisling, however, declined to take up the case with Terboven, and in December the process of deportation began. In a speech made at Trondheim on 6 December, Quisling blamed the Jews for all the misfortunes which had overtaken the world since the Treaty of Versailles, and accused them of 'poisoning the blood of Norway'.[135] His solution was to remove them all. As he was instrumental, together with Hagelin, in devising the laws against the

Jews, he was largely responsible for the death of many of them in camps in Poland and Germany.

As 1942 drew to a close, Quisling became immersed in a new task, that of creating a reliable party armed force. There had been organisational weaknesses in the Hird from the beginning, and in July 1942 the 'Germanske SS Norge' had been formed to act as Quisling's new élite guard.[136] Recruitment for this guard had proceeded very slowly, particularly as many of those eligible were already fighting in one of the regiments Quisling had raised for service with the Germans on the Eastern Front. His obsession with the creation of a proper Norwegian army, which lasted for about nine months, arose, partly at least, from his relationship with Hitler. Quisling was desperately anxious to convince Hitler that he was a reliable ally and that he had the backing of the Norwegian people. By early 1943 he had come to believe that he could convince him only by raising large numbers of troops. After the Stalingrad disaster Quisling was reinforced in his belief that Hitler would be delighted to receive more volunteers. In February 1943 the danger of a Jewish–Russian onslaught loomed larger in Quisling's mind, and on 22 February he condemned the short-sighted policy of the Jew-corrupted Western powers in aiding the Soviet Union,[137] sending with Terboven on the same day a joint telegram to Hitler congratulating him upon the resolution of the German people in fighting on against the Russian menace.[138] On 9 March Quisling made an appeal to the nation, urging Norwegians to join in the titanic struggle being fought in the East. He suggested the formation of a special regiment, composed entirely of volunteers, to assist the German forces, reminding his listeners that

> either Germany will crush the red armies of Bolshevism and thus create a new order in Russia, or Bolshevism will conquer Europe, including Norway, which will be the end of our civilisation. In the contest in Russia is being decided our and the world's fate.[139]

Quisling's appeal met with a poor response in Norway. The new regiment was built up largely from the 700 survivors of the Standarte Nordland, which had been badly mauled at a battle near Leningrad in January 1942. In May 1943 it was dissolved and, soon after, those left were incorporated in Quisling's new regiment.[140] The Minister-President was still not satisfied that Norway was making sufficient contribution to the German war effort and began to make plans for building up a genuine Norwegian army. Quisling's concern is shown by his correspondence with Major Kjelstrup.[141] By the summer of 1943 it became clear that the Allies regarded the Norwegian government of Quisling as an enemy, so that Norway was apparently in the curious position of being at war with both the Axis and the Allied powers. Fears of Allied intervention in Norway were already great, and by mid-August 1943 Quisling was convinced that invasion was possible. On 14 August, he issued a decree proclaiming the existence of a Norwegian army, transferring to his new army a number of military and paramilitary units already in existence.[142] Among these were the Germanske SS Norge and the Hird, of the party's groups, and the regular Norwegian police force.[143] The Minister-President believed that by uniting all these forces in one body the task of defending Norway from an Allied invasion would be made easier. He was also under the misapprehension that a significant rise in the armed forces of Norway would commend his peace plans to Hitler.[144]

The immediate consequences of Quisling's decree of 14 August were disastrous for his government. Early that month a police inspector, Gunnar Eilifsen, had refused to carry out orders given to him by Askvig, the Police President, to arrest two young women who had offended against labour regulations. Eilifsen had been arrested on 9 August and charged with mutiny under the military code of 22 May 1902. Until 14 August the police had not been subject to the provisions of this code, so Eilifsen's actions prior to that date were not punishable under it. Nevertheless, on 15 August, Eilifsen was sentenced to death by a 'People's Court'. Quisling declined to exercise his right of reprieve; the next day he signed the death warrant and Eilifsen was shot.[145] Eilifsen's execution and the decree of 14 August were not only exceedingly unpopular throughout the country but also controversial within NS. The decree led to a split in Quisling's cabinet, as several of its members objected to the Minister-President's high-handed actions.

One of the fundamental causes of dispute was the declaration in the decree that 'a state of war exists in Norway as a result of the actions of the Soviet Union and its allies in attacking Norwegian territory and Norwegian citizens. Consequently, these countries must be considered legally as enemies of Norway, the German Reich and its allies.'[146] This caused considerable dissent. In a letter of 31 August Irgens condemned Quisling's actions as based upon faulty premises; Norway was not allied with Germany, nor was she at war with the Allies. Irgens, furthermore, believed that Quisling could act as Minister-President only when he was 'acting with the consent and co-operation of his cabinet'.[147] This view conflicted with Quisling's adherence to Hitler's principles of leadership. At his trial Quisling justified his action in refusing to save Eilifsen by saying that it was 'in order to preserve the position of the Norwegian government'.[148] Riisnæs, the Minister of Justice, agreed, on the grounds that a government had to be able to maintain authority among its own servants lest its right to govern be usurped.[149] Whatever the reasons, Quisling's decision was unpopular and led to a decline in confidence among even the members of his party and cabinet.

But Quisling was undisturbed by fresh evidence of dwindling support for himself and his party. After the events of August 1943 he preferred to leave the effective administration of the country in the hands of Terboven, and returned to his project for peace between Germany and Norway, which he had never entirely dropped. Quisling had seen 1943 as the year in which German victory would be achieved, and a long and glorious partnership between the Nordic races begin. In a speech on 1 February marking the first anniversary of his accession to power, he congratulated the Norwegian people on having 'driven Bolshevism far from Norway's frontiers', and advised them to pray 'for Germany's victory, which will produce peace'.[150] On 17 May, Norway's National Day, he looked back upon the ten years of achievement by NS and referred to the great work of education carried out by the party, which had only one further task to complete, and that was 'to lead Norway into a Germanic union, thus shaping a secure future for the Norwegian people in peace and plenty'.[151] During the summer, despite the reverses to German arms, he remained hopeful of a settlement between Germany and Norway. The Eilifsen affair he saw as an unfortunate episode in his campaign to convince Hitler of the worthiness of Norway's case.

On 26 September an assembly of the party was held at which Terboven discussed the role of the party in relation to Germany and the forces of occupation.[152] For the first time for some months he adopted a conciliatory and co-operative attitude. In part this may have been owing to increasing pressure from the Norwegian resistance on the German authorities, but is more likely to have been the result of a slight shift in German policy towards Quisling's wish for a peace treaty. During the summer Quisling had pestered Rosenberg and his other contacts in Germany, urging on them the necessity for proper regulation of the relationship between the two countries.[153] These efforts bore fruit when Hitler, on 26 September, declared that it was his 'unshakeable intention to permit the growth of a national, socialist Norway in conditions of independence and freedom after the conclusion of our present fateful struggle in victory'.[154] Quisling and his intimate advisers took this declaration as a promise that all difficulties between the two nations would soon be smoothed away.[155] On the 28th Quisling informed Hitler that he and NS were delighted at the declaration, as indeed were the people of Norway; he was certain that the fate of the Norwegian people was 'linked to a national and socialist programme of unification'.[156]

The autumn thus witnessed a revival of enthusiasm among Quisling and the members of his government. The belief that a profitable co-operation with Germany was about to begin restored self-confidence. Hagelin and Quisling began to talk in terms of ending the domination of Norway by Terboven and restoring the independence of Norway before the end of the war. These were, of course, only wild dreams. On 30 November the illusion of power was shattered. In response to increasing German pressure, the resistance of students and sympathisers had been growing ever more openly defiant. On 27 November, late at night, a fire broke out in the hall of the University of Oslo. During the next two days it became clear to the German authorities that this was the response of the Norwegian public to the appeals Quisling had been making for the last few months. Quisling's advice to the Norwegian people not to heed the 'activity of a treasonably inclined minority of obstructionists'[157] had been ignored. For a few days Terboven waited for some sign of activity from Quisling's government, for some indication that NS proposed to keep order in its own house. Quisling's government was no longer capable, if it ever had been, of facing such issues squarely. Quisling, Hagelin and Prytz knew that if they did nothing, responsibility would devolve upon the Germans. Quisling was content to endorse German measures while recognising that he was incapable of executing them himself. The result was predictable. On 30 November a large-scale raid was made by the Gestapo. Well over a thousand students were arrested, large numbers of whom were sent to Germany as prisoners.[158] The university was closed and the remaining students dispersed.

At this point Quisling should have resigned if he wished to preserve any illusion of independence. By remaining in office after the events of August and November 1943 he demonstrated to the world that he was a German puppet. Actions were taken in his name from which he made no attempt to dissociate himself. Instead, he threw his weight behind the Germans' measures. At the beginning of 1942 he had proposed a scheme of co-operation between the German forces and a projected Norwegian army,[159] and he now eagerly advocated increased naval co-operation.[160] Early in December he revived his plan for compulsory military service for all Norwegians, hoping thereby to create a corps which could fight by the side of German troops. Official discussions were held between the Minister-President and SS Obersturmbannführer Neumann, who was in charge of relations between the Reichskommissariat and NS.[161] Quisling proposed, in early December, that about 50,000 men should be mobilised 'to be used on the eastern front against the Russians'.[162] Like so many other Quisling schemes this came to nought. There were immense logistic and political difficulties involved, which NS was plainly incapable of overcoming. In a long reply, dated 18 December, Neumann pointed out the military, political and personal difficulties of Quisling's proposals.[163] Quisling was not so easily fobbed off. He urged Riisnæs to take the matter up with some of his contacts within the offices of the Reichskommissariat. On 17 January 1944 Riisnæs wrote to Berger, an SS General, suggesting the mobilisation of about 75,000 men, who were to be broken up into small units and dispersed among German troops.[164] Quisling, in fact, advocated this policy during a visit he paid to Hitler at some point in 1944. Once again his theories were listened to politely – and ignored.[165]

By 1944, therefore, Quisling could have retained little hope of full co-operation with the Germans. All his plans had been rejected, some brusquely, some after cautious consideration. The decline in the fortunes of the German armed forces ought to have induced in him a scepticism about German aims and plans for the post-war world. But although, according to Knudsen, 'as early as Christmas time 1943' he considered 'Germany's chances . . . as exhausted',[166] this produced no change of heart, nor any attempt to make his government more popular by resistance to Terboven's pressure. On the contrary, writes Knudsen, as 1944 advanced, his predictions about the imminent termination of the war assumed a more and more pointed tone, but he remained as imperturbable as ever. It was as if he were sitting on some lofty balcony looking down on humanity. He saw the tiny figures beneath him, but was insensible to their passions. He seemed quite uninterested in the fact that these passions might be aroused to acts of aggression which would recoil on him. He was not in the least anxious about his personal safety.[167]

Increasingly, Quisling withdrew his attention from the outside world and put his mind to the solution of other problems, problems of philosophy and political theory. Safe in his world of speculation, he was able to ignore the march of events.

Relations between Quisling and Terboven were rather better during this period than they had been for some time previously. The less Quisling interfered in the practical management of Norwegian affairs, the better Terboven liked him. For once their formal exchange of telegrams at the beginning of the new year bore some relation to the events which followed. Terboven's promise that Quisling would find him 'a good comrade'[168] was to a large extent borne out by events. Co-operation between the two men was increasingly important, for, as the war came closer to German soil, Hitler had less time to spare for the regulation of Norwegian disputes. The Germans lost interest in the promotion of good relations with the Norwegian people and became preoccupied with the task of extracting economic benefit from the occupation. Norway was robbed of large quantities of industrial and agricultural products, as no adequate return for forced sales and levies was made by the Germans.[169] Norwegian hydroelectric power was exploited for the purpose of pursuing atomic research. The Norwegians were increasingly regarded as expendable pawns, both in terms of labour and cannon fodder.[170] A strict regime of police supervision and Gestapo terror replaced the inefficient administration of Quisling and his government. In 1944 there was a whole series of cases involving executions as reprisals for the deaths of policemen or acts of sabotage. In none of them did Quisling exercise his power of reprieve.[171] Although Terboven would in all probability have overruled him in most instances, it is significant that Quisling made no attempt to ease the severe restrictions imposed upon the Norwegian people. In fact, in speeches made on 14[172] and 15 May[173] Quisling justified these harsh measures; they were necessary to purge Norway of her sins.

The year 1944 also marked the return of Quisling to religion for comfort. As the war went from bad to worse for Germany, Quisling confidently asserted that those who believed in God were on the side of NS, for it was 'the party of true Christianity'.[174] In this he was supported by Frøyland and other NS clerics who had been given episcopal sees after the imprisonment of the seven recalcitrant bishops. Quisling resumed drafting his political testament once more, devoting large amounts of time to the writing of a comprehensive politico-religious work which he entitled 'Universalism'. In May 1944 he took up the idea of buying the living of Moland, in Fyresdal,[175] and retiring there to act as the local priest. He had no time for the complex tasks of government or party, and, as a result, both began to fall to pieces. Despite all the penalties involved, the number of party members declined steadily. NS lost control of local administration, so the Germans stepped in. The government itself was split by personal rivalry between Whist, Hagelin and Lie. Knudsen, who had long been Quisling's secretary, retired in the autumn of 1943 and took no further part in Norwegian affairs.[176] To all these developments Quisling remained indifferent, wrapped up in his own interests and in elaborate plans for a future which even he saw was almost impossible.

Occasionally Quisling was roused from his torpor by some outstanding event. In May and June 1944 he devised a plan for giving land to those Norwegians who had fought in the anti-Bolshevik cause, despite the chaos this would have created in Norway and in the face of stiff opposition from Fretheim.[177] On 7 June, as a result of the Allied invasion of France, Quisling urged strong support for Germany in her desperate bid to save Europe from the 'Anglo-American and Russian conspiracy'.[178] On 20 July he sent Hitler a telegram assuring him that 'Norway stood by Germany's side in the struggle for the freedom of Europe'.[179] Yet, despite these brave words, Quisling was unable to give any help to the tottering Third Reich. Hitler needed men and munitions, not words; Quisling had neither troops nor guns to offer.

Quisling's indifference to the progress of the war seems to have annoyed many of his ministers. By the autumn of 1944, Hagelin was in disgrace and Lunde had been killed in an accident; thus two of Quisling's closest friends had been eliminated. In September a revolt was clearly brewing. At a ministerial meeting on 28 September Quisling was subjected to sharp criticism from those who wished him to take action against the stranglehold of German control. The ministers based their proposals upon a memorandum written by Prytz on 25 September and sent to Quisling a few days later.[180] It was signed not only by Prytz but also by Skarphagen, Whist, Fretheim, Riisnæs, Stang, Skancke, Lie, Lippestad and Fuglesang. They demanded that Quisling should accede to four important requests: firstly, the conclusion of a peace treaty with Germany; secondly, the assumption of full authority in Norway by Quisling; thirdly, a promise by Germany that the freedom and independence of Norway be respected; and, finally, that Norway and Germany exchange ambassadors, thus making the existence of a Reichskommissar unnecessary. The folly of Quisling was fully exposed by this document, for it was, in effect, an admission by members of his government that the Germans had used them for their own purposes without regard for Norwegian interests.

The document drafted by Prytz was full of good sense. The Minister of Finance was well aware of the difficulties which faced NS as a result of Quisling's lack of interest in political affairs. He pointed out that 'Norway is still in a state of war with the Reich'[181] and cited the treatment of Norwegian shipping by the German authorities as proof. Similarly, he reminded Quisling that the point of installing NS in power had been to build up a party sympathetic to the interests which bound Germany and Norway together. As long as Terboven and the Reichskommissariat remained in Norway this was impossible. Furthermore, Prytz feared an imminent invasion; the government-in-exile might well set up an alternative regime in Norway as soon as Allied troops had occupied some Norwegian territory, and that regime might well be more attractive to most Norwegians, for it would not be prevented from exercising power by foreign troops. The only solution to this problem was for the Germans to hand over all power to Quisling before it was too late to establish a genuinely national government.

But Quisling was deaf to these pleas by his colleagues. Perhaps he already realised that it was too late to try to set up a more representative government. In any event Prytz died soon after, and this removed the moving spirit behind the memorandum. By the end of the year, it was evident that, barring a miracle, the war was lost for Germany. In Norway, however, Quisling still tried to encourage his followers. On 16 December *Fritt Folk* outlined the dangers facing the Nordic powers but urged brave resistance as the best policy – 'in these gloomy days the valiant Hird must inspire the nation by its example.'[182] In private Quisling was less optimistic. According to Knudsen, who spoke to him at the close of 1944, Quisling stated that 'the defeat of Germany will be a defeat for Western Europe – and it will come quickly'.[183] Yet he was still full of optimistic schemes for the future of Norway. He told Knudsen that he did not believe the Russians would be able to dominate Europe immediately, despite the successes of the Red Army in 1944: 'I am casting about in my mind for some possibility, which I hope to lay before Hitler, before it is too late.'[184] Even at the end of 1944 he could not bring himself to face the facts of the situation. In that way he resembled his German idol.

In his message for the new year Quisling sounded a note of cautious optimism. He predicted that the Allied Powers would fall out with each other; it was only 'necessary to hold out to be victorious'. He criticised the *émigré* government for its pledges to punish NS for the part it had played during the past four years. He warned Nygaardsvold that it was he who would be punished, for 'the mills of God grind slowly, yet they grind exceeding small'.[185] Despite his optimism Quisling was very concerned about the outcome of the war, and devised a fantastic scheme by which the German troops in Norway, who numbered at least 300,000, would become Norwegian citizens, settling in the country and giving it adequate protection.[186] This plan was not supported by von Falkenhorst, nor by Rendulic, who succeeded him in early 1945. None the less, Quisling was determined to put his scheme before the very highest authorities, and, at the end of January, his chance came when he travelled to Berlin to see Hitler.

Quisling and Hitler met for the last time on 28 January 1945.[187] There seems to have been no rational attempt to plan for the future, nothing but long discussions of the past, interspersed by wild predictions of victory by Hitler, whose optimism was based upon the secret weapons at his command. The sole indication of their future plans for Norway was given in a news bulletin issued to the press on 29 January, in which it was stated that the freedom and independence of Norway would be restored after German victory. Like so many other promises this meant nothing at all, a fact which was clearly perceived by Finn Støren, who accompanied Quisling on his last visit to Hitler.[188] In March 1945 Støren wrote to Quisling, saying, 'I have a feeling that the German authorities are deliberately making fools of you . . . and of the *Nasjonal Samling*. . . . Under a pretence of friendship and co-operation, they manage to make our administration share their guilt as plunderers and oppressors.'[189]

Quisling returned to Norway at the end of January, and from then it was merely a case of waiting for the inevitable. But this did not prevent Terboven continuing to act as if victory were only a few days away. On 8 February, General Marthinsen, chief of the Secret Police since the summer of 1943, and of the Hird since the summer of 1944, was assassinated at Slemdal, on the outskirts of Oslo.[190] On the following day a number of Norwegians, some of whom had been under arrest for nearly two years, were executed as a reprisal. Quisling declined to pardon any of them.[191] It is doubtful if he could have exercised any influence over the Reichskommissar, but he did not even attempt to moderate the German attitude. Soon after, the Hird was mobilised and fully armed, being placed under the command of Rogstad. This transfer of power was made at the specific request of the Reichskommissar and was Quisling's last important ministerial act.

By the end of March it had become apparent that the defeat of Germany would not be long delayed. Quisling became more inaccessible than ever. His time was fully occupied with his own writings. The cabinet gave up the task of trying to administer the country and hardly bothered to meet during the last few weeks of the war. Toward the end of April rumours swept Norway that Hitler had transferred power to Göring or to Himmler. On the 28th Quisling called a special meeting of the government to discuss the situation.[192] It is not known what arrangements were made, but, according to Hewins, Quisling intended to proclaim 'a transitional government to maintain law and order';[193] he was overruled by Terboven. On 30 April Hitler committed suicide, and the next day Dönitz informed the world that the mantle of Hitler had fallen upon him.

At this point neither Terboven nor Quisling knew what course of action to pursue. Quisling was anxious to prevent large-scale fighting in Norway, which seemed only too likely unless a definite arrangement were reached. On 3 May Terboven flew to Flensburg, where Dönitz had established his headquarters, in order to discover the Admiral's intentions concerning Norway. He returned under the impression that Norway was to be defended to the last, and was not moved from this position by the news of Dönitz's surrender on 5 May. The same day Quisling went to see Terboven and Böhme, who had succeeded Rendulic, but they declined to take any initiative in negotiating with the Norwegian resistance movement. On 7 May Terboven and Böhme received formal notification from Dönitz that capitulation in Norway was expected. The official act of surrender took place at midnight on 8 May. The next day Allied troops began pouring into Norway.

Quisling had been fairly active during the last few days of his government. On 5 May an extraordinary meeting of the cabinet decided that he should negotiate with the leaders of the resistance in order to bring about a peaceful solution of their differences. On the 8th all the ministers except Whist, Lie and Riisnæs assembled at Quisling's home in order to negotiate the surrender of Norway with resistance representatives. In the absence of Whist, who was believed to be the best negotiator NS possessed, Lippestad[194] was appointed to make contact with the resistance. This he did, but negotiations were broken off abruptly late on the same day. Early on 9 May, Quisling reported to the Police Headquarters, and was promptly arrested despite all his protestations. His rule ended, as it had begun, in an atmosphere of confusion, ill-will and contradiction.

While Quisling was attempting to negotiate, other members of the government and of the German administration resolved their difficulties in other ways. Terboven and Rediess committed suicide. Weiner, the chief of the Gestapo, was captured, but contrived to kill himself later. Rogstad and Lie also committed suicide. Skancke, Aall, Hagelin, Riisnæs and all the surviving NS ministers were arrested and imprisoned. Prominent NS supporters, such as Hamsun and Smedal, were also seized and put in jail. By this time the government and administration of the country had collapsed. Quisling and his collaborators were under arrest, protected from the wrath of the populace, awaiting the return of a government which knew what to do. Confusion on 9 May 1945 was as great as it had been on 9 April 1940.

Chapter 9 QUISLING'S TRIAL AND POLITICAL IDEAS

AFTER QUISLING'S arrest on 9 May he was imprisoned, pending trial. The situation was both complicated and embarrassing for the Norwegian authorities, as there were numerous political, legal and constitutional problems standing in the way of a satisfactory resolution of the Quisling case. Immediately, the most important difficulty was the absence of an effective government, but this was resolved by the return of the government-in-exile from London on 13 May. Until a legal government was in being it was obviously impossible to institute judicial proceedings against the former Minister-President; but on 7 June the King landed in Norway and the way was clear for action.

During the period of the capitulation there had developed some political complications which made the task of bringing Quisling to trial even more difficult. There was the embarrassing obstacle of a provisional arrangement entered into on 8 May by Quisling and Bjørn Foss who had been delegated by the Home Front to negotiate the capitulation of the Quisling government.[1] The terms of the agreement were broken by Quisling's arrest the following day. Thus the obstacle was swept aside by the simple procedure of ignoring its existence. Doubts about the action to be taken against Quisling and his followers had not been allowed to prevent the authorities from mounting a full investigation into the events of the past five years. Almost as soon as the Norwegians took over power, a squad of investigators was ordered to research into the activities of Quisling and NS, presumably with the intention of bringing him and his colleagues to trial. While Quisling remained in jail, a furious hunt continued in the attempt to produce sufficient evidence to support the charges made against him.

Unfortunately for those who wished to try Quisling, the way was not clear. The government was beset by insoluble problems, the most serious of which were constitutional. The legal authority of the Nygaardsvold government was, to say the least, questionable. The extension of its life prior to 9 April 1940 had been a direct violation of the Constitution. So too had been its assumption of powers in the very confused days following the German invasion. Throughout the war the government-in-exile's constitutional, if not its popular, standing was in doubt. Furthermore, several of its actions were themselves legally suspect. Before the war the Norwegian penal code had included no death penalty. The government in London had sought to remedy this omission by promulgation of its law regarding treason on 15 December 1944.[2] For those who wished to dispose of Quisling by legal means this raised yet another formidable stumbling-block, for beside the other difficulties, there existed the question of the legality of the retrospective imposition of the treason law. This complicated the task of bringing Quisling to trial and delayed proceedings for some weeks.

It is to be regretted that none of these problems was faced adequately by the returned government. No doubt it was difficult for the members of the Storting who had just returned from exile to foresee the judgement of future generations, but the fact remains that the course they adopted was very unwise. In retrospect, the execution of Quisling is open to the same objection as that of the Nuremberg defendants – that it was insecurely based upon law. Like the German defendants, Quisling may have been guilty of the most serious offences against humanity and his country, but this cannot in itself justify the nature of the proceedings against him. The method adopted by the Norwegian government, although understandable in the emotional atmosphere of the summer of 1945, was little better in some respects than that of the 'kangaroo trials' in France the same year. The Norwegian government made a fair trial for Quisling impossible by allowing such controversial legal figures as Paal Berg, for example, to take part in the judgement of their former political enemy. The most impartial tribunal in the world would probably have reached the same verdict as the court did; all the more reason that the government should have excluded political figures from the bench of judges. By allowing Erik Solem, a former adversary of Quisling, to be presiding judge at the trial,[3] and Berg to be a member of the Court of Appeal, the government added political folly to the lack of a firm legal and constitutional basis for the proceedings against the former Minister-President.

The principal difficulty was that Quisling was an embarrassment to the government. Hewins has correctly observed: 'Few realists would complain if the "Home Front" had shot down Quisling in anger at the time of the liberation, as happened to Mussolini.'[4] To leave Quisling alive after the events of the preceding five years was unthinkable, yet by the canons of accepted legal practice it was impossible to impose the only suitable penalty. To leave Quisling alive, but imprisoned, would only have prolonged the situation of which the government so earnestly desired to rid itself. The action of the government in proceeding with a trial to which there could be only one conclusion was realistic, if of dubious propriety. Once the government had taken this decision, there still remained two questions to be answered; when, and with what, ought Quisling to be charged? The answer to the first was easy: As soon as possible. The answer to the second was found by charging him with all manner of offences, ranging from high treason down to the embezzlement of public funds.

In preparation for the trial, Quisling was subjected to a number of interrogations. On 26 May he appeared before a court of preliminary interrogation to whom he made a long statement in answer to the charges brought against him.[5] His line of defence was at once made clear by his concluding declaration: 'I wish to God that many of Norway's sons may be traitors as I have been, only that they might not be cast into prison.'[6] His statement, already modified in June, was modified further in July.[7] By this time Quisling had the assistance of Henrik Bergh as his defence counsel; much less time was spent on tedious justification, much more on rebuttal of the serious charges. Both Quisling and Bergh relied on the testimony of minor witnesses to refute the lesser charges made by the prosecution, and these tactics were largely successful.

Quisling was also frequently interrogated by the police. The most important of his statements was made on 24 July,[8] when the police were asking him about the events of April 1940. Time and again he was forced to take refuge in the excuse that he could not remember events in detail. As the weeks went by, his health visibly declined. The restrictions on his diet and the lack of exercise reduced him to a poor physical condition. Furthermore, he was increasingly taken up with the political and philosophical problems of his work on 'Universalism'. Some of his guards feared that he was becoming mentally affected, going mad under the strain, and on 8 August it was decided that he should undergo medical examination in order to test his fitness to plead.[9] Once Quisling had been brought back to reality, however, by the practical approach of his defence counsel, the problem of his sanity was soon resolved. The cause of his mental condition may have been the fact that his wife was in a difficult situation, both personal and economic; it was not until August that he was convinced that no proceedings were going to be instituted against her.

During these investigations, Quisling's lawyer had appealed against the decision to appoint certain persons to conduct the trial. On 25 July, the Supreme Court rejected Bergh's appeal. However unwise the decision, Quisling had inevitably to abide the judgement of his enemies. One of the principal difficulties, of course, was that in the atmosphere of 1945 it was hard to find anyone who had any sympathy for Quisling's point of view. Even Bergh had been a staunch supporter of the government-in-exile.[10]

The trial preparations had been completed by 20 August, and on that day the hearing began. The place chosen was Freemasons' Hall in Oslo. The presiding judge was Erik Solem, who had spent much of the war period in a concentration camp; he was assisted by two other judges and four assessors.[11] The prosecutor was Annaeus Schjødt, and Henrik Bergh acted for the defence. The court was well attended from the start, and it became clear during the trial that the attention of the world was focused on Oslo. The trial itself was short, lasting only until 7 September, but during that short space of time much was revealed about Quisling and his actions.

To a certain extent Quisling's defence was handicapped by the fact that some of the evidence derived from Colonel Amen's interrogations of leading members of the German hierarchy had only been introduced a few days before the opening of the trial. The total of this evidence, however, was slight in comparison to the vast bulk introduced by the prosecution from other sources. Quisling was much more seriously handicapped by another factor – the atmosphere of hostility around him. Bergh made this point with great skill at the very start of his defence plea:

> The indictment which is being presented for adjudication in this case is based upon a series of sections of the penal code, and the case is to that extent a criminal case. The background, however, and the numerous counts of the indictment, show that the case concerns the political viewpoint of the defendant. It is here that we encounter the peculiar situation that in this assembly, which fills the court, there is nobody who shares the political views of the defendant. No one belongs to the political movement of which he was the leader. Neither in the court nor at the bar is there anyone who shares his views, not even his own counsel, for all lawyers of his party are barred from pleading if they are not, as most of them already are, in prison.[12]

The lack of sympathy for Quisling was apparent throughout the trial,[13] and, although it can hardly have affected the verdict, it may well have affected Quisling.

The principal charges eventually brought against him were that his activities on 9 April 1940 were treasonable, and that his decision to proclaim a government on 1 February 1942 was treasonable. There were some lesser charges alleging persecution of the Jews and the execution of Norwegian citizens. Finally, but not least in importance, there was the charge of his having plotted to bring about the invasion of 9 April 1940. Quisling's defence to all of these charges was weak. The weight of documentary evidence was heavily against him, and as regards the offences of the period since the invasion there was a great deal of oral testimony. Henrik Bergh did his best, but his task was impossible.

The most interesting feature of the trial, and the episode which attracted the greatest attention at the time, was Quisling's own presentation of his case. It was made under conditions of some discomfort. Before the trial, Quisling had been subjected, as we have seen, to a series of medical tests. The physicians and surgeons had pronounced him sane.[14] None the less the examinations had exhausted him, and Solem decreed that

> although we are satisfied that there is nothing the matter with the defendant, in the meantime, as a result of these tests to which he has been subject, and in connexion with the polyneuritis from which he is suffering, his general health has declined. The court has therefore seen fit to decree that the defendant should enjoy a period of rest.[15]

Quisling was thus suffering from exhaustion and polyneuritis at the time of his speech in self-defence. In view of this, his final speech was an impressive effort. It began on 6 September and continued on the next day. In all, he spoke for about eight hours, relying on his wonderful powers of memory. He reviewed the whole of his career, including the war years, and justified his actions. At times his defence was moving; at others he was clearly trying to avoid the issue. He denied that he had been guilty of treason or of any of the other charges against him. He suggested that other men should be in the dock in his place, and that he should be rewarded for his patriotic efforts. To the very last he maintained that his objective had been to act as a Christian and a patriot, and concluded by urging others to follow his example. At the end he was clearly exhausted, which was hardly surprising, for, at the beginning of the trial, a journalist had written: 'He has grown much thinner, his suit hangs about him and his face is much more lined than it was before.'[16] His speech was his last major intellectual effort.

The court's judgement was delayed until Monday, 10 September. The verdict was inevitable. Quisling was found guilty of all the major charges and sentenced to death, under the terms of the military law of 1902. He bore himself well as the sentence was pronounced, although he was plainly astonished.[17] To the last he seems to have believed that the court would recognise the real significance of his actions. Immediately sentence had been pronounced, Bergh informed the presiding judge that Quisling would appeal to the Supreme Court. The principal grounds of appeal were concerned with legal matters rather than with an attempt to set aside the judgement of the lower court, although Quisling insisted on appealing against that judgement on points of fact.[18] The proceedings of the Supreme Court opened on 9 October and ended on the 11th. Judgement was delivered on 13 October.[19] The case was heard by the Chief Justice, Paal Berg, and four other justices, Stang, Bahr, Fougner and Klæstad. Once again Quisling made an impressive speech in concluding his defence:

> I am the same man I have always been, I remain unchanged. Can anyone point to acts of revenge in the last six years? There are many free men here in Oslo and other cities who have done me political harm, but I have never harmed any of them. Revenge is not a political motive, and I believe in leaving it to others. This case, then, is not just another judicial matter, but a question of politics.[20]

If Quisling exaggerated his political magnanimity, his view of the trial was none the less true. It was a political trial. Of all those in court, Chief Justice Berg, who had played an inglorious role in April 1940, should have been most conscious of the truth of what Quisling said. Perhaps this was Quisling's aim; if he succeeded, it was his final victory.

The Supreme Court dismissed the appeal and upheld the death sentence passed by the lower court. In order to stifle criticism of the illegality of the proceedings, Fougner, the judge appointed to deliver the verdict, went out of his way to establish the credentials of the court and the legality of its actions. There had been no death penalty in the code of 1902, but there existed such a penalty in the military code of that year. Quisling's behaviour in April 1940, and in his relations with the Germans before that date, came under the provisions of that act. But unfortunately, section 14 of that act required execution of the penalty before the close of hostilities. By an enactment of 3 October 1941 the government-in-exile had waived the provisions of section 14, and this had been confirmed by the Storting after liberation.[21] There only remained the question of retrospective imposition. According to section 97 of the fundamental constitution no law could have retroactive effect. With this provision the Supreme Court disagreed. In the opinion of the judges, anyone who was guilty of an offence prior to the enactment of 1941 might apply for relief, if he had not been sentenced and executed before the conclusion of hostilities. No offender, however, had an automatic right to such relief. In the case of Quisling, the Supreme Court believed that such relief would be inappropriate.[22]

After the verdict Quisling was taken back to prison, where he was placed in cell 34, the death cell, at Møllergaten 19. He did not wish to appeal to the King for mercy, although he wrote a letter protesting against the illegality of the proceedings against him.[23] On 18 October he made his final public appearance, when he gave evidence on behalf of Hagelin.[24] Quisling might refuse to appeal, but his wife refused to give up hope, and a petition was presented to the King on his behalf. This too was in vain, and on 23 October Quisling was informed that there would be no reprieve.[25] During his last days he saw few people. His meetings with his wife were very distressing to both of them, but his belief in his innocence helped him to retain his composure. There were no outward signs of self-recrimination. Quisling spent time discussing religion and philosophy with a succession of pastors who came to see him. In between visits he read the Bible and a religious work written by his father. Finally, he wrote a summary of his work on 'Universalism' for posterity.[26]

Quisling spent his last hours reading his Bible. To the very end he remained rational, but convinced of his innocence. According to Hewins, 'Even in the police car from Møllergaten to Akershus for the execution, he told the driver calmly: "I am guiltless and condemned unlawfully. My case was never thoroughly heard and was illegal. I go to a martyr's death." '[27] At 2.00 am on 24 October 1945 he was taken from his cell and driven to the old Akershus castle. He was then blindfolded and shot. His last request had been to shake hands with the firing squad. By 2.40 am the whole business was over.[28] Even his death caused controversy. According to Hewins, 'Quisling was kept waiting more than an hour in the cold autumnal air while scores of sightseers, including Judge Erik Solem, assembled on the ramparts.'[29] The evidence of Knudsen and those who were present indicates that this assertion is baseless. Similarly, Hewins has stated that 'his corpse was taken down to the Møllergaten 19 garage and put on view for all and sundry. Many "good Norwegians" came to see that the prototype "quisling" was really dead. For their bene-fit the covering was thrown back. People prodded the body and made ribald remarks.'[30] Once again there is no evidence for this statement, whereas there is much to suggest that Quisling met his fate with dignity, and that those responsible for his execution carried out their unpleasant duty in a decent and honourable way.[31]

Immediately after Quisling's death, Knudsen was installed in the cell so recently occupied by his master. According to his account, as he entered the cell,

> the jailer stepped on a rose-petal. There were more of them on the stone floor. Petals from his last bouquet. . . . On the table the Bible was open. . . . Some pencil lines showed what he had last been engaged in: '*He shall redeem their soul from defeat and violence and precious shall their blood be in his sight.*[32]

Quisling had taken comfort in the religion of his father. A remarkable life had drawn to a close.

What more can be said of this extraordinary man? How much is really known of what he thought? Why did he act in the way he did? The answers to these questions lie in his life and in his writings and in his statements at his trial. The prosecuting counsel established beyond all reasonable doubt that Quisling was guilty of the offences which related to 9 April 1940 and the years after. At the time, he was much less con-vincing concerning Quisling's alleged treason before that date. Yet this was the important charge, not, perhaps, as far as conviction was concerned, but for those who wish to understand Quisling. Did he commit treason? Former colleagues and more recent admirers have suggested that Quis-ling was not guilty, and that there was a grave miscarriage of justice on this charge. To a certain extent there is some justification in the criticism made, in that less evidence was available at the time when judgement was given. However, the more that has been uncovered, the more justified the sentence seems.

It is understandable that many of those who were associated with Quisling, those who loved or admired him, should seek to reverse the verdict of 1945. There was a good deal of hagiographical material pro-duced during Quisling's life,[33] and more since his death. The most im-portant of Quisling's apologists has been Ralph Hewins. His arguments are based upon several important assumptions. Some of these relate to the period after 1940 and do not affect argument about Quisling's role in preparing for the invasion of Norway. Hewins's principal argument, however, has been that Quisling's contacts with the Germans were inno-cent of treasonable intent, that he always sought to maintain Norwegian neutrality, in the best Norwegian tradition. How well does this assertion stand up?

The evidence seems overwhelming that Quisling did commit treason before April 1940. There is ample documentation to show that Quisling was in regular touch with Hagelin, Scheidt and Aall, all of whom had contacts with prominent figures in the Nazi hierarchy. Quisling may, indeed, have been ignorant of some of their activities, but he knew enough to visit important Nazis in Germany twice in 1939, and in Denmark in 1940. On each occasion he came into contact with Germans who favoured a policy of intervention in Norway. It can hardly be assumed that the possibility of a German occupation was never mentioned. The evidence shows that this subject was actually discussed in Quisling's presence. He knew, then, of German intentions. A true patriot would surely not have failed to inform his own government of this knowledge. Yet Quisling did fail to do so, and this in itself is highly suspicious.

To pass now from surmise to fact. In the first place, before the invasion, he gave information to men whom he knew to be members either of the Abwehr or of the OKW. This is confirmed by the evidence of Keitel, who stated that Pieckenbrock 'had a meeting with Quisling in Copenhagen and in a very careful manner asked certain questions concerning military matters we were not informed about'.[34] Secondly he prepared, together with Rosenberg and the APA, a plan for a political *coup* in Norway. As the military took over planning, however, so was Quisling's political plan forgotten. Quisling and his aides were also responsible for misleading German opinion about the true state of affairs in Norway. By so doing Quisling made sure that the activists would be victorious over those who abhorred the idea of German intervention in Norway.

The conjunction of Quisling's reports with Allied activity materially affected the views of Raeder in particular. The disorganisation of German intervention in Norway caused German efforts to appear much less effective than they were. It seemed as if the situation was out of the control of the various intelligence services, which appeared to work against each other rather than against the British. Reports from Hagelin and Bräuer during early 1940 showed that NS was not having the success expected of it. Quisling felt that his lack of success was owing to the insufficiency of German support, and the encouragement of people, who, whatever their feelings towards Germany, were strongly opposed to NS. It was this gloomy background of misunderstanding which conditioned the activities of Quisling and Bräuer and accounted for the divergence between their reports. Bräuer was much too optimistic to be easily believed by Raeder or Jodl. Although the contents of his reports were factual they were not reconcilable with what was known about Allied intentions. The reports of Quisling were. Jodl was not an optimistic man and Hagelin and Quisling were able to profit from his pessimism by painting the picture much blacker than it really was. Quisling believed that the Norwegian government secretly favoured the Allies, as perhaps it did. He was instrumental, however, in persuading the Germans that the Norwegian government was only waiting for a suitable moment to abandon neutrality and admit British troops into the country. This was a total misrepresentation, for the Norwegian government was exceedingly anxious to keep out of all involvement with any of the Great Powers.

In complete contrast to Quisling, Bräuer relied upon Norwegian good-will, citing the German–Norwegian trade agreement of 20 February as evidence of good faith. No one listened to Bräuer because of the successful attempts of Scheidt to discredit him. Scheidt even reported that the German Legation 'was unaware of the real state of Norwegian public opinion', and demanded to be given 'some regular position in Norway that would enable him to conduct his liaison and intelligence activities more effectively'.[35] The failure of Bräuer and the success of Quisling contributed to the reversal of German policy towards Norway. In no way should this be held to reflect on Bräuer's ability; he could hardly have made greater efforts. There was a curious psychology prevalent in certain quarters in Germany which prevented sensible evaluation of the rival reports. Bräuer could not penetrate this mental fog, while Quisling used it to cloak the furtherance of his own interests. Quisling was lucky to have the support of certain men close to Hitler – Rosenberg, Raeder and Jodl. Bräuer, on the other hand, was unfortunate enough to be a re-presentative of the Foreign Office, which Hitler never liked or respected. These factors, to some extent, mitigate the offence, for the pursuit of a moderate policy would never have permitted Quisling any opportunity for making mischief. Yet Hitler himself, when he spoke to Rosenberg on 25 April, after the success of the Norwegian invasion, declared that it was the warnings given by Quisling upon which he had based his decision to invade Norway.[36]

Quisling also received large sums of money from Germany, in direct contradiction of his own political principles. In the early 1930s he had been quick to condemn the Labour and Communist parties for receiving financial help from Moscow, but by 1939 he was agitating for a subsidy from Germany. Quisling was, therefore, prepared to mortgage his own political movement to the Germans in order to enhance his prospects of attaining power. Jodl stated in 1945 that it was even proposed at one stage to use Norwegian guides for the troops in Norway, but 'as far as I recall, this was not accepted because we were afraid that by accepting this plan the expedition would gain publicity in advance'.[37] It is worth noting that at no stage did Jodl believe that Quisling would refuse to supply guides, it was just that he felt that security precautions would not permit him to inform Quisling of the details of German plans. Important figures in Germany regarded Quisling as Germany's man; it is hard to believe that they were mistaken.

There is another point of interest which concerns Quisling's actions in Copenhagen in early April 1940. It seems clear that Quisling was not told of the German plans, and Keitel went so far as to state that 'if any-body had discussed this matter with Quisling, and the OKW had known about it, that man would have been court-martialled'.[38] Since several

306

prominent Nazis, including Ribbentrop, were only informed of the invasion a few hours before it took place,[39] it is most unlikely that Quisling would have been given details. This point has been strongly emphasised by Hewins, who has defended Quisling from allegations of treachery at the Copenhagen meeting by stating that

> it must be regarded as highly unlikely that Pieckenbrock, an experienced spy, would have committed an appalling indiscretion and divulged the current top secret of the war to a foreigner, and a stranger at that. Even Ribbentrop and Bräuer only heard of zero hour twenty-four hours before the event. Why should Quisling, who was summarily jettisoned from the plot in December, . . . suddenly be let into the secret now?[40]

Unfortunately, this spirited defence misses several important points. Quisling had a purpose in visiting Copenhagen, and this was the transmission of information. He must also have realised that the Abwehr believed that his information was of such crucial importance that it required his attendance at short notice. Quisling's logical mind must have appreciated the point of German questions about fortifications and harbours, particularly taken in conjunction with the fact that on his journey by sea to Copenhagen he must have noticed the ice in the Great Belt was breaking up. The climatic conditions indicated that an invasion was possible. The nature of the questions suggested that an invasion was likely and the urgency of the summons to an interview with an important intelligence officer showed that the Germans were in a hurry to do something, presumably in response to increased Allied activity. It would have been difficult for any intelligent man not to have made these deductions. No one who had served on the General Staff could have failed to do so. Quisling must have realised that a major military initiative on the part of Germany, and one involving his own country, was inevitable. Yet he made no attempt to warn any members of the government or to alert high-ranking officers to the danger, but kept his deductions to himself. The only possible conclusion is that Quisling was a willing party to any action the Germans might take.

There is thus strong evidence for upholding the verdict of the courts in 1945. Even after these arguments have been accepted, however, there still remains the important question, why did Quisling act in this way? The answer can be seen only in an examination of the way he thought, his political ideas and his political actions. Quisling's story cannot be complete unless the way he acted is related to the way he thought. In the documents available at his trial, in the great speech he made, and in the numerous pamphlets published by NS there is ample evidence of the working of his mind.

Perhaps the most important trait in Quisling's character was his sense of dedication. He believed that he was born to lead Norway, to guide the Norwegians (and the rest of the Nordic race) from darkness into light.[41] The necessity of this mission was only too clear to him and his small band of devoted followers. His convictions were easily confirmed by chance occurrences. For instance, the fact that he had been born on 18 July was especially important to him, since it was the anniversary of the battle of Havsfjord, at which Norway had been united by the victory of Harald Fairhair. For Quisling this was no mere coincidence but a clear indication and manifest proof of his destiny.

Believing that his role was to be historic, Quisling constructed his plans on a much larger scale than other politicians. His ambitions were readily communicated to his lieutenants, who often lacked the ability to see where Quisling was leading them. Blind faith in his powers replaced reason.[42] Despite his scientific training, Gulbrand Lunde was capable of writing complete nonsense about Quisling's mission: 'In our time our leader, Quisling, has tried to complete what Ibsen outlined so clearly – Norway has been a state, it shall yet become a people.'[43] Such an ambition was too nebulous and insubstantial to make a wide political appeal. Because his beliefs formed an article of faith, Quisling naturally refused to compromise with the beliefs of others. He was not prepared to give up a single article of his creed in order to attract support. He always believed that, provided he held to his task, he would in the end be victorious.[44]

Prophets, whether true or false, seldom seem to make successful politicians. Quisling was no exception. He was absolutely inflexible as a politician, and in consequence he never mastered the art of compromise which usually forms the basis of the successful politician's craft. His ideas were rarely adjusted to the needs of a situation, for they had been worked out in advance. Quisling took up a prepared position, whatever the circumstances, and, as a result, the vast majority of the Norwegian people found nothing of value in the sentiments which he expressed. But this made no difference to Quisling; he pursued his course resolutely, despite all setbacks. If he failed to gain wide popular support, at least his few followers were confirmed in their faith in him as an idealist, a visionary in pursuit of a lofty goal. For Aall, he was the man 'to lead the important crusade of the twentieth century'.[45]

Quisling's range of political interest was, as might be expected from such a man, exceedingly narrow. He was indifferent to issues which were of vital importance to others. He showed little concern for economic or social affairs, preferring to leave these matters to other ministers even when he was in power. His political programmes give slight evidence of attention to practical matters. Quisling was nearly always preoccupied by more abstruse questions, such as the conflict of ideologies, or the influence of religion on history.

Quisling attributed his lack of success, not to his failure to appeal to the people, but to a conspiracy between the other politicians to conceal his ideas from the public. His party's disastrous election results in 1936 were attributed to a massive front constructed by collusive party action ranging from Communists to Conservatives. Thereafter, bitterness against the parties and the politicians became a dominant factor in his attitude towards politics; he seemed to consider himself in some way above political life, though eager to enter and reform it. From his violent antipathy towards Norwegian politicians there gradually developed a profound aversion to the system which allowed these men to gain and cling to power. In 1937, for example, after learning the results of the Oslo Municipal Elections, Quisling denounced the evils of the financial power of the party bosses. He condemned the corruption and the greed which they brought to politics. He felt that the power of their money 'sapped true Norwegian national feeling'.[46] Two years later, he went even further: 'Democracy is a gigantic international system of exploitation.'[47] It was in this way that his practical experience of politics turned him away from the Norwegian parliamentary system. The fight which he henceforth envisaged had little connexion with electoral battles.

Nevertheless, he continued in his belief that one day he would be recognised by the Norwegian people as their saviour. A fundamental change had, however, taken place in his attitude towards his expected success. Observing the ability of the established parties to hold the support of the large majority of voters in Norway, he rightly concluded that he and his party were unable to compete on the same terms. The Norwegian people needed guidance until they could learn that Quisling's ideas would produce the best results. In other words, he decided that it was essential to have leadership from above, and particularly from himself. There lay before him in Italy and Germany two excellent examples of 'enlightened direction', and it was easy for him to conclude that Norway required a similar system.

It would be wrong to suggest that this development in Quisling's attitude towards Norwegian democracy can be traced entirely to the years immediately before the Second World War. Although circumstances favoured the adoption of new plans only in these years, Quisling had, in fact, held most of the ideas upon which they were based for many years. Many of his ideas were obviously derived from Fascist examples. When NS was founded, early in 1933, it was not long before Quisling took the title of 'Fører', in direct imitation of Hitler and Mussolini. He also attempted to raise a small private army, which was to have a dual function – guarding his own person, and providing a party élite. The similarity to the SA and, later, the SS is obvious. Quisling tried the procedures of democracy, but when these failed him he was equally ready to abandon conventional means of coming to power in favour of more drastic methods. These actions suggest that the affection which Quisling held, or professed to hold, for democracy when he first entered Norwegian politics at the end of the 1920s did not go very deep. Quisling was ready to abandon democracy when the verdict of the people went against him.

It was one of Quisling's blind spots that he could never understand the deep dislike which he so often aroused among his fellow countrymen. Though not wholly unfortunate from his own point of view, this factor did little to improve his grasp of political realities. Despite all setbacks and rebuffs, Quisling did not abandon his cherished hope that he would be called upon to lead his country when the hour of crisis was at hand. Eventually his genius would be recognised, and until that day dawned it was essential that he should not compromise with weaker spirits for the sake of arriving at his goal sooner than had been intended. Such ideas were wholly fantastic, but the evidence that Quisling held them seems irrefutable. Even in 1945 he had not given up hope that Norway would unite behind him.[48] The sad history of the events of the previous five years was conveniently forgotten. This total lack of realism was his strength and, at the same time, his greatest weakness. Quisling's immunity from political reality provided him with the power to ignore political reverses which would have crushed the spirit of a less introverted man.

The highly individual brand of Fascism which Quisling advocated had parallels in other movements, though in these cases the leader usually contributed less to the theoretical basis and more to the political activity of the movement. Quisling's political ideas were similar to those of Alfred Rosenberg. Both were composed of a strange amalgam of romanticism and authoritarianism, although Quisling's views were never as clearly defined as those of the German. Until he was actually awaiting trial, Quisling never completed a major political work explicitly stating his aims and intentions. His German mentor and patron, on the other hand, was an exceedingly prolific author. Although Quisling owed a great deal to Rosenberg in so far as putting his ideas into manageable form was concerned, the essentials were present long before he met the Nazi leader.

To a large extent Quisling's political ideas were moulded in his youth. His home and his country were two major influences in his life. The years he spent in Fyresdal taught him to love nature and to distrust mankind, which polluted nature in attempting to improve upon it. Quisling's ideal society was a simple association of peasant farmers working together to promote the good of the community, an idealistic blend of primitive Communism and the theories of Rousseau. This romantic image was somewhat modified by the second important influence in his life, love of his country. He was a patriot who believed that Norway had a useful part to play in the world, and he sought ways to enlarge his country's influence. Although he believed that this might best be achieved through the development of his simple society, he was realistic enough to appreciate that, as things were, it was impossible. But, if the structure of power in the world were to be changed in the right way, then the modification of society which Quisling desired would be possible. From an essentially traditionalist and conservative ideal of stability was born a doctrine of revolution that was inherently, and from the outset, self-contradictory. The confusion may be partly ascribed to the romanticism which was an essential part of Quisling's nature. He invariably enlarged the significance of events or personalities which had played a dramatic, though not necessarily important, part in history. The logical consequences of a particular belief were never as significant as the emotional content, but Quisling did not always realise that others might feel differently.

One of the most consistent elements in Quisling's political philosophy was his belief in the importance of the individual. He believed that mankind was best able to fulfil its potential through individual action, unregulated and unfettered by a strict, institutionalised society. This did not mean that he was in any sense an anarchist; actions needed guidance, but in a manner which left room for individuality to emerge. Perhaps the closest parallel to Quisling's ideas on this point was Himmler's views on natural leaders. Himmler wanted to develop the latent qualities of leadership which he believed existed in every man of Germanic blood, but was obliged to create the elaborate organisation of the ss in order to retain control. In other words, neither Quisling nor Himmler wanted undisciplined individuality. Quisling's speech at Hamar in August 1939 exposed another inherent and allied contradiction when the Fører declared that what he sought was 'a social individualism based upon national ideas'.[49] Aall was responsible for much of Quisling's muddled thinking at this important stage in his career.[50]

The sources of Quisling's belief in individualism are to be found chiefly in his childhood experiences. He spent his youth in the remote valley of Fyresdal, where children were quick to learn the value of self-reliance. In a community of individuals with strong personalities such a development was almost inevitable. The wild aspect of the countryside emphasised the need to develop a strong will if a man were to struggle successfully against his environment. It was there that Quisling developed respect for the peasant farmer who wrested a living from the soil. From respect it was a short step to the building of an ideal.

Other elements contributed to the growth of this belief. The long period Quisling spent in the Soviet Union during its formative years taught him how oppressive a bureaucratic state could be. At that time he was working under Fridtjof Nansen, and he came to dislike, and even hate, those who put obstacles in the way of his humanitarian work. Although Quisling occasionally grumbled about the malicious inefficiency of Western officials, most of his anger was directed at the Communists, for whose cause he had originally been most enthusiastic. He realised that only a strong man, such as Nansen, was capable of overcoming these obstacles. Leadership thus provided the best guarantee of human rights. The preservation of individualism was for Quisling the only barrier to the collapse of freedom. Democracy was no safeguard. 'Democracy', he proclaimed, 'is theoretically individualism – the right of each man. But in practice it is the right of the strongest.'[51] In this fashion yet another curious inconsistency was added to his personal beliefs, for he deduced from experience that individualism and democracy were incompatible. It did not apparently occur to him that in the absence of democracy, individualism in many of its forms was less likely to find tolerance.

Despite this enthusiasm for individualism, Quisling did not approve of unrestricted political choice for individuals. It was here that his bitter political experiences reshaped his earlier thought, with the result that his theories became an inextricable tangle of conflicting ideas. Although initially he was opposed to the concept of state control he gradually changed his views, and, by 1936, was advocating some form of guidance. If this guidance were given correctly then it would enable individualism to develop on desirable lines. There was a certain affinity at this point between his views and those of Plato. Quisling's 'guides' were intended to play the same moral, educational and political role as Plato's 'guardians'.

From this position he argued that education was essential to help people think clearly. Society required educated men to deal with, and eventually to eliminate, its undesirable institutions, an educated élite to assist in the completion of the development of the rest of society. They would all be individualistic, but would share a common purpose. As early as 1933 Quisling was making it clear that this purpose was more far-reaching than the creation of a personal bodyguard. The Hird was to be the spearhead of the new order.[52] These men would not form an oligarchy, for they would be dedicated, and not merely desirous of retaining power. The aim of the élite was to be service, not mastery. The implication behind Quisling's ideas was that it would be necessary to have different categories of citizens within the state. Since he made no provision for the withering away of the apparatus of benevolent administration, it is difficult to see how its permanence could have been avoided. Nor did Quisling ever attempt to define the exact relationship which should be maintained between these grades. Certain general suggestions were made, but none was in the smallest way relevant to the establishing of democratic government.

In the course of his search for a free society of individuals, Quisling had outlined a totalitarian system of government. He assumed that the actions of the élite would be correct simply because his élite could not take the wrong decision. The possibility of disagreement was ruled out from the very start. The people had no right of redress since, until they were educated, they were incapable of knowing what was in their best interests. It was the duty of the élite to protect the people from themselves.

The existence of an inferior class in Quisling's ideal society would have to be accepted for some time. Although education by the élite would, eventually, be almost completely successful, there were certain groups which would be unable to respond to the stimulus of the system because of their inherent inferiority: they were to have no place at all in the final structure of society. The problem with these groups was that they lacked the 'basic urge towards individuality',[53] which deficiency usually arose out of impurity in racial ancestry. The race which Quisling deemed to be particularly impure was that of the Jews, the existence of whom was consequently seen as an obstacle to the fulfilment of the ideal society. The logical elaboration of this principle was to lead Quisling to uncritical acceptance of Nazi doctrines.

The belief in Nordic superiority, and the contempt for inferior races had developed into a full-blown theory of race by the time Quisling came to power in 1942. Earlier, as Minister of Defence, he appears to have held different views; at any rate he did not express them openly. Nevertheless, their origins may be traced back to his youth and early manhood, and particularly to the years he spent in the Soviet Union. Quisling frequently stated that all his views had been formed before he entered politics in 1930,[54] but this may have been in response to accusations of inconsistency and double dealing which were frequently levelled against him in the 1930s.

It is difficult to understand why Quisling held his views on racial superiority so strongly. Norway was not a country where such sentiments were likely to engender enthusiasm. In central and eastern Europe there was a tradition of anti-Semitism, but until the establishment of Quisling's party there seem to have been few, if any, problems concerning the Jews in Norway. In 1851 the fundamental constitution of 1814 had been amended to allow practising Jews to enter Norway. Subsequently they were given full rights of citizenship. Even before 1851, however, there had arisen a relative concentration of the Jewish population in Bergen and other important ports on the west coast. In many cases these closely related families had been established in Norway since the heyday of the Hanseatic League. The fact that they had a different religion was often the sole characteristic which distinguished members of these families from the rest of the population. The immigration of Jews after 1851 was certainly not large, and the Norwegians found no difficulty in assimilating them. Complete equality had been achieved by 1870, and by 1900 all suggestion of prejudice seems to have vanished.[55]

By 1939 the Jews were virtually indistinguishable from the rest of the community, and played a full part in public affairs without a hint of prejudice. Their position in Norway was resented only by the small body of fanatics who followed Quisling, whose hatred of the Jews was unbridled. He usually referred to Carl Hambro (the leader of the Conservative Party, and later President of the League of Nations) as 'that plotting Jew, Hamburger-Levy' or some similar phrase.[56] Once Quisling came to power, the fate of the Jews was sealed. Yet, so far as is known, he had no unhappy encounters with Jews in his childhood or early schooldays, nor was his military career in any way affected. The earliest date at which his anti-Jewish sentiments were made manifest was after his return from the Soviet Union. His original enthusiasm for the new regime in Russia had been turned into a burning hatred, and, in seeking an explanation of Communist excesses, in particular the attack on the peasants at the end of the 1920s, Quisling concluded that the high aims of Communism had been perverted, and that this perversion was the work of the Jews. He certainly read anti-Semitic literature, for some of his speeches contain extracts, almost verbatim, from the notorious *Protocols of the Elders of Zion*. He clearly believed that responsibility for the decline of the idealism of 1917 rested with the leading figures in the Communist Party hierarchy, and that their corruption could be attributed to the fact that the majority of them were Jewish or half-Jewish.[57] Quisling's views on these matters coincided neatly with those of Rosenberg, whose racial theories, in later years, became the centre and the basis of most of Quisling's political plans.

Quisling's racial theory was much more elaborate than the mere advocacy of anti-Semitism. He believed in Nordic supremacy, and his definition of 'Nordic' included the inhabitants of most of Northern Europe. In addition there were the Germanic colonies in Austria, the Ukraine and Transylvania. There were also certain races of basically sound stock which had been polluted by the Jews. Among these he numbered the Dutch and the English. His aim was to purge these races of the inferior elements living among them, and then create a vast union of peoples of Nordic descent. War between Germany and Great Britain was to be avoided because it would decimate the Nordic race and ruin his vision of a 'Greater Nordic Peace Union, based on all the states bordering on the North Sea'.[58] It was here that Norway's statesmen, in particular himself, had a special task – 'to work together to promote peace between England and Germany is our chief task in international politics today'.[59] During the war his ideas on these points were drastically revised, and the participation of England in such a union was rejected. Quisling had discovered that the Jewish stranglehold was too strong, and that in consequence England had become hopelessly corrupt. Norway's new aim was defined as the need 'to come to an understanding with our Germanic fellow race; in the Greater German community we shall have a leading position in the working of the New Order'.[60]

Closely connected with this concept of Nordic unity were Quisling's ideas on nationalism. These were not aggressive in character, but symptoms of ultra-conservatism. It was the nationalism of a national revival which would lead to a new national order, both politically and socially. That his ideas on the reforms required to produce the new order were completely inconsistent did not matter to Quisling. He adopted any plan which took his fancy, and was equally ready to discard ideas if they involved any complex evaluation of policy. The details of policy were irrelevant – he would know which plan to adopt when the time came for decision. That these details might be of greater practical interest to people, and therefore of greater appeal, than his visionary schemes, did not concern him at all.

The need for a national revival in Norway was derived from Quisling's view of the difficulties of the years after the 1914–18 war. The bitter class struggle that followed its conclusion would, he believed, destroy all that he valued in Norway. 'The old parties are worked out . . . they are all more or less class parties.'[61] There has to be a new party which would rise above the old class struggles. Quisling, therefore, broke with the Agrarian Party, which he had joined in the hope that it would prove a suitable vehicle for his ideas, and founded NS. Some of the means which he proposed to use to promote national unity were far from new. They were often old conservative ideas decked out in ostensibly more radical clothes. 'Our party', declared its leader, 'will not be a party in the same sense as the other parties, but a party beyond party, an organised revival. In it farmers, workers, and burghers will be able to find a part to play in the national task. This will promote a national sense of purpose and will increase determination and strength.' The aim of NS was to unite Norway behind a new national government, the motto of which was to be 'peace, order, justice'.[62] To judge from the character of the wartime Quisling government, it seems unlikely that any of these lofty goals would have been reached in any national revival led by NS.

As a promising young politician, Quisling was given the Ministry of Defence in 1931. During his tenure of office he became the most unpopular politician in Norway. In the course of the Menstad affair he alienated the Labour Party, though he always insisted that his action was aimed at Communist agents and not at the workers. His quarrels with the Labour Party made him a hopeless liability to the Agrarian Party, many members of which were pleased to see him leave in 1933. Despite his protestations, it is evident from all that Quisling wrote or did that he had little sympathy for the urban working class. Certainly, when he became Minister-President, his main activity concerning the workers, apart from depressing their standard of living and signing the death warrants of some of their leaders, consisted in an attack on the trade unions. He proposed to replace them by a National Labour Front, as Ley had done in Germany. This was characteristic of his peculiar brand of nationalism. He made national unity the rallying call of his party, but was not actually ready to do anything to promote it.

Although traditionalist in his appeals to nationalism, Quisling was not unaware of the pressures which could be brought to bear on the working class on behalf of a new form of nationalism – National Socialism. 'Over the whole world nationalism is on the advance – nationalism is the political philosophy of the twentieth century and is pre-ordained to be victorious',[63] he wrote in 1938. It was, however, in vain that he sought to revive a more aggressive nationalism after the collapse of his scheme for national revival. He referred always in militant phrases to the need for a strong, prepared Norway. He even tried to create a national issue by reviving the dispute with Denmark over the ownership of Greenland, long after everyone else had lost interest. This appeal fell as flat as its predecessors, and as Quisling's chances of gaining power grew more remote and improbable, so the policies he advocated became more unrealistic. At the same time many of his early adherents were transferring their support to other parties, and NS fell into a decline from which it recovered only with the entry of a considerable number of timeservers in 1940 and 1941.

More and more, Quisling began to refer to the missionary task of his party – an implicit recognition that he was working in a hostile environment. His remedies for the serious state in which he found the Norwegian nation changed with every new event. By 1940 few Norwegians took him or NS at all seriously.

As hopes of power receded, Quisling came to emphasise that the first goal of his party was to exercise a moral influence. This theme had been apparent from its foundation, but did not emerge fully until after 1936, when the party was under pressure. In 1931 Quisling had demanded 'a political and religious party'.[64] During the war his ideas increasingly acquired a semi-religious content. In 1941, speaking of the German crusade on behalf of the Nordic races, he said: 'National Socialism must be united with Germanic radical thinking in a politico-religious party.'[65] As the war went increasingly badly for Germany, so did Quisling become more eager to establish his political position in Norway by claiming to be the guardian of moral and religious standards. In 1943 he claimed that his programme was 'a guarantee to the Norwegian Church that God's word will be preserved whole and undefiled'.[66] By 1945 all he wanted to do was to retire to Fyresdal as the local pastor. It was in that year that he completed his vast work on 'Universalism', which consisted largely of moral and religious, rather than political, dissertations.

It is hardly surprising that, armed with such a curious collection of conflicting ideas, Quisling's period as Minister-President was not a startling success. Quisling's government made little impact upon war-torn Norway. He and his movement failed their supreme test. The movement lacked real depth – it had no grass-roots support, the higher echelons of the party were not filled with men either of experience or of promise. At moments of decision, the party and its leader were not strong enough to resist German demands. Yet Quisling and NS retained office. Its high-sounding political 'activities, like those of its predecessors, degenerated into little more than day-to-day administration'.[67] The party of individualism and enterprise became a German puppet. Even a monopoly of news, from the summer of 1940 onwards, was unable to restore the prestige of the party. The party was fatally handicapped by the personality of its leader, and the ideas and theories he had imposed upon it.

What, then, did Quisling leave for his followers to admire? Where is his monument? His ideas were confused and diffuse, self-contradictory, unrealistic and obscure. He was cold and remote. He was not a successful politician. Apart from his unpublished treatise on 'Universalism' he left no *magnum opus*. Yet he had a great attraction for so many people, an attraction which has survived his death. He inspired tremendous loyalty from his friends, bitter enmity from those who came into conflict with him. He was not just 'the sad figure of a shadowy traitor'.[68] His strength lay in his self-confidence and his aloofness. He seemed strong when others were weak. Others followed where he led. The melancholy truth, however, was that he had no clear idea of the road he should follow. He was uncertain and hesitant.

The same traits are evident in Quisling's political ideas. It is impossible to detect any clear and unambiguous line of thought which can be followed through from the earliest days of his political career to its ignominious end. He was a political phenomenon rather than a politician; a collector of ideas rather than the creator of a new system. He was not a political thinker in any constructive sense; he introduced no new ideas and developed no coherent analysis of the state and its functions. The measures he occasionally advocated were designed for immediate adoption – of well-considered long-term plans he had none.

It has been a source of perplexity to many analysts of Quisling's character that it has proved difficult to reconcile his intelligence with his actions. How could a man with a brilliant academic record adopt such irrational ideas, and perform simple tasks so badly? The answer lies, perhaps, in two limitations of that intelligence. Firstly, Quisling found it impossible to make decisions quickly – choice was frequently imposed on him by the progress of events which he made no attempt to control. Secondly, although he loved to argue and speculate about intangible matters, he was always uneasy in his encounters with reality. He saw events in stark black and white, and his inability to compromise caused difficulties both in his personal relations and in his public life. He withdrew into a world of speculation, whence he expected to emerge as a *deus ex machina* at the critical moment. As the moment was deferred, so Quisling's faith in other men diminished, and his faith in his own mission grew. In this lonely and introspective world no healthy and constructive political philosophy could develop, and his ideas and actions thus became centred exclusively on himself and a few friends. He remained unaware and uncritical, and all his intelligence availed him nothing, for he never learned how to apply it.

Being this kind of person, an intelligent dreamer, devoid of political qualities such as perception and the ability to compromise, how did Quisling become famous as a man of action? The fact is that the world made its judgement on him in April 1940, and has not changed that judgement since. Major Quisling, like Judge Lynch and Captain Boycott, has been immortalised by giving his name to a word in the English language. Yet how strange is the decree of history! Whatever Quisling may have been, he was certainly not the most obvious candidate for that dubious honour. He was muddled rather than thoroughly corrupted. He loved Norway but he disagreed with the majority of his fellow countrymen on how best to protect his native land from the dangers threatening it in the 1930s. Other men – Seyss-Inquart and Laval, for example – played a far more destructive and sinister role in the history of the Second World War than the Norwegian collaborator. How ironical that it is Quisling who is remembered above all as the archetypal traitor!

Notes

Abbreviated references:

DA	Domsarkiv
DBFP	*Documents on British Foreign Policy*
DGFP	*Documents on German Foreign Policy*
IMT	*International Military Tribunal*
IUK	*Innstilling fra Undersøkelseskommisjonen*
NCA	*Nazi Conspiracy and Aggression*
UB	Universitetsbiblioteket
UDA	Utenriksdepartementets arkiv
UKA	Undersøkelseskommisjonensarkiv

Other works are referred to simply by the name of the author or editor; otherwise by the (sometimes shortened) title.

Chapter 1 EARLY YEARS

1 Stagg, 105.
2 DA. Quisling file.
3 Published in 1912 under the title of *Fra mine unge År.*
4 *Norsk Biografisk Leksikon,* vol XI.
5 The Hvide family was an old Danish family which included among its distinguished members Archbishop Absolon, founder of Copenhagen.
6 *Straffesak,* 327–8.
7 Hewins, 22: 'To the villagers she was inclined to be condescending and she brought up her children to keep their distance.'
8 *Straffesak,* 328.
9 *Straffesak,* 240. Ullmann was born in 1886 and was thus a contemporary of Quisling. He later became headmaster of the Oslo Secondary School.
10 Hewins, 22.
11 *Norsk Biografisk Leksikon,* vol XI.
12 *Straffesak,* 328.
13 Østbye, 55.
14 Myklebost, 41. This comment does not seem to be borne out by general opinion, but does reflect the extent of Norwegian bitterness towards Quisling.
15 *Straffesak,* 327.
16 *Straffesak,* 328.
17 *Straffesak,* 240.
18 *Straffesak,* 328. The reference is to Niels Henrik Abel (1802–29), the world-famous mathematicism, also a Norwegian.
19 Hartmann, 55. Quisling's solution appears in Eliassen's *Laerebok i Algebra.*

20 *Straffesak*, 328.
21 *Norsk Biografisk Leksikon*, vol XI.
22 *Straffesak*, 328.
23 Hartmann, 53.
24 *Straffesak*, 240.
25 *Norsk Biografisk Leksikon*, vol XI.
26 *Straffesak*, 328.
27 Hartmann, 66. The nearest comparison in British military terms is that of being the Cadet of Honour.
28 Hewins, 34.
29 DA. Quisling file. No R 2237–45. When Quisling was gazetted as a full lieutenant in 1908, he was assigned to Field Artillery.
30 *Straffesak*, 328. General Christian Theodor Holtfodt (1863–1930) was Commander-in-Chief from 1927 to 1930.
31 *Norsk Biografisk Leksikon*, vol XI. It is not clear whether Quisling chose or was assigned Russia to study.
32 DA. Quisling file.
33 *Straffesak*, 328.
34 *Straffesak*, 235.
35 *Straffesak*, 329.
36 DA. Quisling file. No R 2237–45.
37 Hewins, 37.
38 *Straffesak*, 329.
39 *Norsk Biografisk Leksikon*, vol XI. It is suggested that he was ordered to Petrograd, and there was no element of choice. Quisling's version, however, seems the more probable.
40 Hartmann, 68–9. There seems little doubt of the authenticity of this letter.
41 *Straffesak*, 329.
42 According to *Norsk Biografisk Leksikon*, vol XI, this story is merely a characteristic example of Quisling's inflation of casual, unimportant incidents. This may not be wholly correct. Quisling's attitude to Bolshevism at this time was rather sympathetic, and as a military expert he might well have been consulted by Trotsky.
43 *Straffesak*, 329.
44 *Straffesak*, 330.
45 Hartmann, 69.
46 Hartmann, 70: from a letter of 31.x.18 to his brother Jørgen.
47 In *Norsk Biografisk Leksikon*, vol XI, it is suggested that Quisling had exaggerated Russian instability. The existence of these contemporary letters would tell against this insinuation.
48 Hartmann, 70–1.
49 *Straffesak*, 330.
50 Hartmann, 75.
51 *Straffesak*, 235. It is not clear whether Ruge referred to 1919 or to 1920, but Quisling was attached to the General Staff in both years.
52 *Aftenposten*, Dec 1919; Jan and Feb 1920.
53 *Straffesak*, 330.
54 *Straffesak*, 238.
55 *Dagbladet*, 3.x.38: Portrait of the week by 'Beinset'.
56 *Straffesak*, 330.
57 The evidence of Fru Mollø Christensen, then on the embassy staff, is valuable, since she had known Quisling earlier in his life.
58 *Norsk Biografisk Leksikon*, vol XI. Quisling had paid a short visit to Norway at the end of 1920.
59 *Straffesak*, 330.

60 *Straffesak*, 239.
61 *Straffesak*, 330.
62 Xenophobia was of course widespread in Russia long before 1917, but rarely can it have been so intense as in the early 1920s.
63 Nansen's organisation, usually called (incorrectly) the League of Nations Mercy Commission.
64 Nansen, *Russia and Peace*, 29: quoting a letter of early May 1919 from Chicherin to Nansen.
65 Ibid, 36.
66 DA. Quisling file. Note concerning a memorandum by Nansen.
67 From Nansen's address as Rector of St Andrews University, 1927.
68 See Appendix A, p 349.
69 Nansen, *Russia and Peace*, 58–9.
70 *Norsk Biografisk Leksikon*, vol XI.
71 Hewins, 56.
72 Nansen, *Russia and Peace*, 65.
73 *Straffesak*, 330.
74 Østbye, 21.
75 Hayes, 'Vidkun Quisling: a short biography', in *History Today*, May 1966, p 333.
76 Mainly in regard to the amount of power Quisling was able to exercise and to the degree to which his evidence is reliable.
77 Høyer, 230–1.
78 From Nansen's Rectorial address of 1927.
79 Nansen, *Russia and Peace*, 150, 153–4.
80 Høyer, 235.
81 See Nansen's views in the 'Conclusion' to *Russia and Peace*.
82 *Straffesak*, 330.
83 Quisling also, at the end of his stay in the Ukraine, reported to the League of Nations headquarters at Geneva. An extract from this report is quoted in Appendix B, p 350.
84 *Norsk Biografisk Leksikon*, vol XI.
85 Quisling met her in Kharkov, where her parents had settled.
86 DA. Quisling file. No R 2237–45.
87 Østbye, 34.
88 *Biografiske Opplysninger til 25-aarsjubileet for Studentene i 1905.*
89 *Tidens Tegn*, 2.x.23.
90 DA. Quisling file: letter from Gudleik Støyen to the Advocate-General, 12.i.48.
91 DA. Quisling file. No R 2237–45.
92 *Straffesak*, 334.
93 Østbye, 41–4.
94 *Straffesak*, 334.
95 Østbye, 41–4.
96 *Straffesak*, 334.
97 Major-General Ivar Bauck was a teacher at the Military High School (1907–13), where he first came into contact with Quisling. He had become chief of the General Staff on 7 July 1919.
98 *Straffesak*, 334.
99 Østbye, 41–4.
100 Hartmann, 88.
101 *Straffesak*, 402.
102 Reynolds, 223.
103 Agreement between Russia and Bulgaria could not be reached as these countries had broken off diplomatic relations in the summer of 1923.

104 Høyer, 242.
105 Reynolds, 231.
106 Høyer, 242.
107 Nansen, *Armenia and the Near East*, 5.
108 Ibid, 6.
109 Ibid, 33.
110 Ibid, 53.
111 Ibid, 160.
112 Ibid, 170.
113 Ibid, 205.
114 Nansen, *Through the Caucasus to the Volga*, 16.
115 Ibid, 183–4.
116 Ibid, 7.
117 Reynolds, 252–4.
118 DA. Quisling file.
119 *Norsk Biografisk Leksikon*, vol XI.
120 Hewins, 60. The defence is based upon a talk between Hewins and an un-
     named Norwegian industrialist. Many of Hewins's controversial assertions
     depend upon evidence of this type.
121 *Samtiden*, 1947: article by Benjamin Vogt.
122 Hartmann, 100.
123 *Biografiske Opplysninger til 25-aarsjubileet for Studentene i 1905*.
124 Ibid: 'In 1928 I took my discharge as an officer and retired on half pay.'
     Links, however, were not finally cut until 1930.
125 *Norsk Biografisk Leksikon*, vol XI. Quisling's access to confidential informa-
     tion was only of a very limited nature.
126 See Hartmann, 100: 'Quisling was subjected several times to examination by
     the OGPU.' According to Quisling's own evidence, he was also in close contact
     with the OGPU in a rather different connexion. When in 1945 he was giving
     evidence about alleged overtures on his part to the Labour Party of Norway,
     he referred to a bizarre incident involving Tranmæl, the editor of the party
     newspaper. 'I knew the authorities in Russia well', he said; 'there was a
     meeting concerning Amundsen, so far as I remember, and there I encoun-
     tered Tranmæl. Later, I was talking to one of the most important men in the
     OGPU and he glanced at Tranmæl and said, "We will take him. He is a
     Trotskyite, he is working against Stalin, we will deal with him." I replied,
     "He is a Norwegian, and I think you can let him be." ' If this piece of evi-
     dence, from *Straffesak*, 154, is accepted at its face value, it might be inferred
     that Quisling had some influence with the OGPU, and that he was felt to be a
     person whom the OGPU could trust. Neither inference seems at all likely. The
     OGPU could have had little reason to trust a man who had worked for Prytz
     and had been friendly with Trotsky; nor, in view of the reputation of the
     OGPU, does it seem probable that any high-ranking officer would have re-
     vealed such opinions to a foreigner. The whole episode probably took place
     only in Quisling's imagination.
127 Unstad, (469), n 34.
128 Quisling, *Russland og vi*, 75.
129 Ibid, 70–1.
130 Ibid, 26.
131 Unstad, (468).
132 Hewins, 59.
133 *Straffesak*, 281.
134 DA. Quisling file: letter from Nansen to Quisling, 21.vi.29.
135 DBFP, ser 2, vol 7, no 24, p 37: 3.x.29.
136 DBFP, ser 2, vol 7, no 40, p 49: 13.xii.29.

137 Beloff, i, 17.
138 *Stortingsforhandlinger*, 19.v.31.
139 *Straffesak*, 153.
140 At Munkedamsveien 59 (misprinted as '5b' in *Straffesak*).
141 *Straffesak*, 150: letter of 10.vi.32.
142 *Straffesak*, 151: letter of 9.vi.32.
143 *Straffesak*, 152.
144 Hewins, 104.
145 Hartmann, 96.
146 *Straffesak*, 151–4.

Chapter 2   QUISLING AS POLITICIAN

1 Hewins, 72.
2 Hartmann, 101, writes that 'the affair of the roubles had torn away much of the glory from Quisling's name'.
3 See his article, 'Politiske tanker ved Fridtjof Nansens død', in *Tidens Tegn*, 24.v.30.
4 *Straffesak*, 333.
5 *Norsk Biografisk Leksikon*, vol XI.
6 Keilhau, 364.
7 *Stortingsforhandlinger*, 1928: vol 7a, 34–5.
8 Mogens, 44.
9 Unstad, (477).
10 *Straffesak*, 283.
11 It is worth noting that in 1930 Nansen's relatives made no protest at the association of his name with that of Quisling.
12 *Tidens Tegn*, 2.i.30.
13 *Tidens Tegn*, 31.i.30.
14 *Stortingsforhandlinger*, 1930.
15 *Tidens Tegn*, 24.v.30.
16 *Tidens Tegn*, 4.vi.30.
17 Vogt, 89.
18 *Tidens Tegn*, 26.ix.30.
19 Hewins, 96: 'The salvation, he maintained, was a corporate state.'
20 DA. Quisling file.
21 Hartmann, 112–13.
22 Hewins, 92.
23 Hewins, 100.
24 *Redegjørelse for Nordisk Folkereisnings Retningslinjer.*
25 Hartmann, 116–17.
26 Vogt, 96.
27 There were a number of contributory factors, but the actual cause of the fall of the government was the 'scandal of the Lilleborg concession'.
28 *Aftenposten*, 8.v.31.
29 Hewins, 102.
30 Hartmann, 122.
31 *Aftenposten*, 3.iii.31.
32 *Arbeiderbladet*, 9.v.31. Despite this accurate prediction, this was almost certainly no more than an inspired guess by the newspaper, possibly in the hope of ruling out the choice of Quisling.
33 Hartmann, 126.
34 Throne-Holst and Thommesen were close friends, being the leading figures in Frisinnede Venstre ('The Free Liberal Party').
35 According to a conversation between Hartman and Holten in 1959.

36   Hewins, 103.
37   *Vår Hær* was edited by Halvor Hansson, who was a member of the Central Committee of 'Nordic Folk Awakening'; see also *Straffesak*, 236.
38   Mainly because of Sundby's opposition to forming a government during the worst of the economic crisis: Hartmann, 121–2.
39   Lindboe, 19.
40   Though of course the names were well known by the time of this meeting. Unlike Hewins, Lindboe states that 'the reception of the government in the daily papers was somewhat mixed'.
41   *Arbeiderbladet*, 13.v.31.
42   *Arbeideren*, 15.v.31.
43   *Morgenbladet*, 12.v.31.
44   Vogt, 99.
45   *Stortingsforhandlinger*, 19.v.31.
46   Lindboe, 24. Mowinckel told the Storting that the attitude of the bourgeois parties to the government would depend on who its real leader was.
47   *Stortingsforhandlinger*, 19.v.31.
48   Lindboe, 24.
49   *Stortingsforhandlinger*, 19.v.31.
50   *Arbeiderbladet*, 28.v.31.
51   *Arbeiderbladet*, 6.vi.31.
52   *Redegjørelse* . . .
53   *Russland og vi*, 201.
54   Kolstad, it would appear, valued Quisling for his abilities as an expert on defence and ignored his semi-mystical ideas on politics, which obscured his virtues. He seems, moreover, to have appreciated that Quisling had not the resolution or insight to put into practice the ideas he held, with any hope of success; therefore he did not worry unduly about them. Quisling's opponents – and this is understandable in the situation – were less able to judge that Quisling would never be another Mussolini.
55   Lindboe, 25.
56   Hewins, 104.
57   Unstad, (479), n 59.
58   Lindboe, 32–3.
59   *Aftenposten*, 9.vi.31.
60   *Stortingsforhandlinger*, 8.vi.31.
61   Lindboe, 34–6. The evidence given by those who took part in the decision shows that Quisling's role was purely executive.
62   Hewins, 105.
63   *Aftenposten*, 9.vi.31.
64   Lindboe, 38.
65   Hewins, 105.
66   Knudsen, 25.
67   *Arbeiderbladet*, 10.vi.31.
68   Hartmann, 141.
69   *Aftenposten*, 19.vi.31. Within a month the affair had blown over.
70   Lindboe, 31.
71   *Straffesak*, 481.
72   Knudsen, 27.
73   Lindboe, 50–5.
74   *Arbeiderenes Enhetsfront*. It contained all kinds of improbable suggestions, such as an uprising by Young Communists.
75   *Straffesak*, 236–7.
76   Skeie, 487.
77   Lindboe, 60.

78 At this time the committee consisted of 3 Conservatives and 3 Agrarians on the one side, and 3 Socialists, 2 Liberals and Alf Mjøen of the Radical Popular Party on the other.
79 *Aftenposten*, 13.vi.31.
80 *Straffesak*, 235–6.
81 Lindboe, 64.
82 Lindboe, 62.
83 Laake's appointment had been a source of controversy, and critics of the appointment generally seem to have been justified by his later serious inadequacies.
84 Lindboe, 62.
85 *Stortingsforhandlinger*, 1931.
86 Lindboe, 62.
87 Lindboe, 81.
88 Lindboe, 95.
89 Hewins, 108–9.
90 *Aftenposten*, 22.i.32.
91 *Arbeiderbladet*, 30.i.32.
92 Hartmann, 163.
93 Lindboe, 118–19.
94 Lindboe, 119.
95 Hewins, 111.
96 *Straffesak*, 335.
97 Hartmann, 151.
98 Hewins, 112.
99 Official Police release, published in most newspapers.
100 *Aftenposten*, 5.ii.32.
101 *Arbeiderbladet*, 5.ii. 32.
102 Hewins, 111.
103 Nordahl Grieg put forward this theory in an article in *Veien Frem* in 1936.
104 Hartmann, 161.
105 Lindboe, 120, believed that the strain of constant crises involving Quisling, plus a number of vicious attacks by *Dagbladet*, had materially contributed to Kolstad's illness.
106 Hartmann, 169.
107 *Stortingsforhandlinger*, 6.iv. 32.
108 Hartmann, 175: Hundseid had ordered all ministers to prepare personal statements.
109 Lindboe, 126–7.
110 *Stortingsforhandlinger*, 7.iv.32.
111 Lindboe, 127.
112 Lindboe, 128.
113 See issues of *Arbeiderbladet* for week of 8–15.iv.32.
114 *Stortingsforhandlinger*, 15.iv.32.
115 *Stortingsforhandlinger*, 26.iv.32.
116 *Stortingsforhandlinger*, 13.v.32.
117 *Stortingsforhandlinger*, 7.vi.32.
118 *Innstilling fra Spesialkomiteen til undersøkelse av Quislingsaken*. The text is reprinted in *Straffesak*, 476–84.
119 *Straffesak*, 483.
120 *Straffesak*, 480–2.
121 *Stortingsforhandlinger*, 29–30.vi.32.
122 This number was made up of 41 members of the Labour Party, plus Hartmann, who found himself able to vote for the first point of the minority

report but no more. The second and third points therefore obtained only 41 votes.

123 Hewins, 118–19.
124 *Stortingsforhandlinger*, 6.v.32.
125 *Straffesak*, 237.
126 *Straffesak*, 321.
127 *Lindboe*, 139.
128 Not 1931, as Hewins suggests.
129 *Dagbladet*, 5.ix.32.
130 *Kullmannsaken*. Documents.
131 Hartmann, 193.
132 *Lindboe*, 179.
133 *Kullmannsaken*: Quisling's letter to the Ministry of Justice.
134 Hartmann, 198.
135 *Kullmannsaken*: statement to the NTB by Quisling.
136 *Arbeiderbladet*, 17.x.32.
137 Hartmann, 200.
138 Lindboe, 158–9.
139 *Aftenposten*, 25.x.32.
140 Hewins, 119.
141 Lindboe, 185–6.
142 Lindboe, 186–7.
143 Lindboe, 187–9.
144 Lindboe, 181.
145 Lindboe, 189.
146 Lindboe, 189–90.
147 Hartmann, 222.
148 *Arbeiderbladet*, 16.xi.32.
149 Letter from Pferdekämper to Himmler. Rijksinstituut voor oorlogsdocumentatie, Amsterdam.
150 Hewins, 120–1.
151 Lindboe, 179–80.
152 Lindboe, 180.
153 Hartmann, 230.
154 Lindboe, 181.
155 Lindboe, 191.
156 Hartmann, 242.
157 Lindboe, 181–2.
158 *Stortingsforhandlinger*, 30–31.i.33.
159 *Stortingsforhandlinger*, 10.ii.33.
160 *Stortingsforhandlinger*, 24.ii.33.
161 Lindboe, 207.
162 *Stortingsforhandlinger*, 7.ii.33.

Chapter 3 NASJONAL SAMLING

1 Lindboe, 181.
2 *Nationen*, 27.ii.33.
3 *Tidens Tegn*, 1.iii.33.
4 Lindboe, 185.
5 *Aftenposten*, 11.iii.33.
6 Lindboe, 185.
7 Hartmann, 259–60.
8 *Arbeiderbladet*, 4.v.33.
9 Hartmann, 269.

10 Hewins, 122.
11 Hartmann, 270.
12 Hartmann, 271.
13 The fourteen were Throne-Holst, Egeberg, Fürst, Prytz, Schyberg, Eggen, Hauge, Saeverud, Krag, Nissen, Falkenberg, Barth-Heyerdahl, Quisling and Havrevold. The last two were present on 9 May but not on 8 May.
14 UB: stenographic record.
15 Hartmann, 277.
16 Hewins, 124.
17 Knudsen, 44.
18 *Oppfordring til Nasjonal Samling.*
19 *Nationen,* June 1933.
20 Unstad, (485).
21 Knudsen, 44.
22 *Quislings Foredrag i Lillehammer.*
23 *Straffesak,* 337.
24 *Oppfordring til Nasjonal Samling.*
25 Hewins, 128.
26 DA. Aall file: conversation with Aall.
27 *Straffesak,* 484.
28 DA. Quisling file.
29 Vogt, 116.
30 *Straffesak,* 484.
31 Hewins, 129.
32 *Straffesak,* 337.
33 Vogt, 117.
34 *Nasjonal Samlings Program, 1934.*
35 DA. Quisling file.
36 *Nasjonal Samlings Program, 1934.*
37 Vogt, 118.
38 *Nasjonal Samlings Program, 1934.*
39 *Hvad vi vil.*
40 Knudsen, 44–5.
41 Knudsen, 48.
42 Unstad, (485).
43 *Hvad vi vil.*
44 *New Year Address,* 1935.
45 Hewins, 128.
46 DA. Quisling file: speech of 24.i.35.
47 *Hvad vi vil.*
48 DA. Quisling file: speech of 7.iii.35.
49 DA. Quisling file: speech of 17.v.35.
50 Knudsen, 50.
51 Hewins, 132.
52 DA. Quisling file: speech of 24.i.35.
53 DA. Quisling file: speech of 27.vii. 35.
54 *Fritt Folk,* 26.iii.36.
55 *Fritt Folk,* 31.iii.36.
56 Skeie, 504.
57 *Fritt Folk,* 19.ix.36.
58 *Fritt Folk,* 21.x.36.
59 Knudsen, 49.
60 *Opprop til Norske Arbeidere.*
61 Østbye, 102–3.
62 *Fritt Folk,* 27.vi.36.

63 DA. Quisling file: speech of 30.vi.36.
64 DA. Quisling file: undated note.
65 DA. Quisling file: speech of 2.x.36.
66 Knudsen, 53.
67 *Straffesak*, 337.
68 *Fritt Folk*, 21.viii.36.
69 *Straffesak*, 487–8.
70 Deutscher, 344.
71 *Straffesak*, 486.
72 *Fritt Folk*, 21.x.36.
73 *Fritt Folk*, 13.xi.36.
74 Hewins, 132.
75 Vogt, 128.
76 Vogt, Appendix.
77 Knudsen, 49.
78 Vogt, 122.
79 Hewins, 133.
80 Vogt, 122–3.
81 Koht, *Norway, Neutral and Invaded*, 98.
82 *Norsk Biografisk Leksikon*, vol XI.
83 Unstad, (489).
84 *Fritt Folk*, 21.x.36.
85 *Fra Partipolitikk til Fagstyre.*
86 *Fritt Folk*, 23.x.37.
87 DA. Aall file: Memorandum.
88 DA. Aall file: Fuglesang to Aall, 29.x.37.
89 Knudsen, 45.
90 *Tidens Tegn*, 23.xii.37.
91 Skeie, 501.
92 Holmsen & Jensen, ii.
93 Hewins, 140–1.
94 DA. Aall file: 11.v.37.
95 DA. Aall file: Fuglesang to Aall, 11.ii.38.
96 *Fritt Folk*, 9.iv.38.
97 *Straffesak*, 338.
98 *Fritt Folk*, 1.x.38.
99 Hewins, 140.
100 *Stortingsforhandlinger*, 1938.
101 Hewins, 141.
102 DA. Quisling file: speech in Oslo, 9.iv.38.
103 *Fritt Folk*, 2.iv.38.
104 *Fritt Folk*, 27.viii.38.
105 *Fritt Folk*, 17.ix.38.
106 *Quisling har sagt*, 72.
107 DA. Quisling file: speech of 9.iv.38.
108 *Fritt Folk*, 17.xii.38.
109 *Fritt Folk*, 2.ix.39.
110 *Fritt Folk*, 3.xii.38.
111 *Fritt Folk*, 18.ii.39.
112 *Quisling har sagt*, 78.
113 *Fritt Folk*, 25.iii.39.
114 *Quisling har sagt*, 81.
115 *Fritt Folk*, 18.ii.39.
116 *Fritt Folk*, 10.vi.39.
117 *Quisling har sagt*, 104.

118 *Fritt Folk*, 2.xii.39.
119 *Quisling har sagt*, 88.
120 See Shirer, 162.
121 DA. Quisling file: undated note.
122 *Quisling har sagt*, 90.
123 *Quisling har sagt*, 92.

Chapter 4 FIRST CONTACTS WITH GERMANY

1 *Straffesak*, 336.
2 *Straffesak*, 337.
3 Vogt, 133.
4 *Straffesak*, 337.
5 *Utdrag i Høyesterettssak*, Nov 1945.
6 DA. Hagelin file.
7 *Utdrag i Høyesterettssak*, Nov 1945.
8 DA. Hagelin file: evidence of Fru Hagelin, 25.x.45.
9 *Utdrag i Høyesterettssak*, Nov 1945.
10 DA. Aall file.
11 DA. Aall file: letter from Qvenild to Aall, 14.v.35.
12 DA. Aall file, 8.vi.39.
13 Skodvin, 22.
14 De Jong, 168. This is based on a letter of 19.xi.32, from Pferdekämper to Himmler (Collection Skodvin).
15 Rauschning, 141.
16 Skodvin, 23.
17 DGFP, ser D, vol 5, no 428, p 559: 19.v.38.
18 See de Jessen.
19 Skodvin, 24.
20 DA. Aall file.
21 See IMT, xi, 385: according to Rosenberg's evidence at Nuremberg there was a conversation in 1933 lasting some twenty minutes.
22 Skodvin, 24
23 DA. Hagelin file, in particular a letter from Fuglesang to Fermann, dated 19.iv.39, discussing the role of the Fichtebund, its 25th anniversary, and the world anti-Communist congress at Tokio.
24 IMT, xi, 385.
25 Report of 31.i.34: document 036–PS in the Nuremberg Trials file; see also *Kurzer Tätigkeitsbericht der A.P.A. der N.S.D.A.P.* for October 1935.
26 DA. Aall file: Aall to Stangeland, 7.x.36.
27 DA. Aall file: Dinklage to Görlitzer, 22.xi.36.
28 DA. Aall file: Dinklage to Aall, 23.xi.36.
29 DA. Aall file: Stangeland to Aall, 11.xii.36.
30 DA. Aall File: Stangeland to Aall, 25.xiii.36.
31 DA. Aall file: NS Secretariat to Aall, 11.v.37.
32 *Utdrag i Høyesterettssak*, Nov 1945.
33 DA. Aall file: Fuglesang to Aall, 22.vi.37.
34 DA. Aall file: Fuglesang to Aall, 29.x.37.
35 DA. Aall file: Aall to Dräger, 16.xi.37.
36 DA. Aall file: Aall to Dräger.
37 *Utdrag i Høyesterettssak*, Nov 1945.
38 DA. Aall file: Fuglesang to Aall, 20.xii.37.
39 DA. Aall file: Fuglesang to Aall, 11.ii.38.
40 Hewins, 147.
41 DA. Aall file: Fuglesang to Aall, 24.v.38.

42 DA. Hagelin file: Koren's evidence.
43 DA. Aall file: telegram from Quisling to Aall, 12.v.38.
44 DA. Quisling file: Fuglesang to Quisling, 19.ix.38.
45 Skodvin, 25; see also DA. Hagelin file: Hagelin to Herbert Göring, 18.v.39.
46 DA. Hagelin file: Hagelin to Quisling, 20.iii.39.
47 DA. Aall file: Hagelin to Aall, 30.iii.39.
48 Laporte was usually disguised under the name of 'de Laroche' in Aall's correspondence. He gave no evidence at the trial in 1945 as he fell into the hands of the Russians and then disappeared. He was, however, already then a sick man, and probably died soon after.
49 Skodvin, 25.
50 *Straffesak*, 27; see also Kern's testimony of 15.vi.45, in which he referred to the meeting taking place in January 1939.
51 DA. Aall file: Quisling to Hagelin, 19.iv.39. See also Appendix 1 of *Kurzer Tätigkeitsbericht der A.P.A. der N.S.D.A.P.*
52 DA. Aall file: Hagelin to Aall, 19.v.39. In this letter Hagelin quoted much of what he had written to Göring.
53 DA. Quisling file: Quisling to Hitler, telegram of 20.iv.39.
54 DA. Aall file: note of 18.iv.39.
55 DA. Aall file: note of 24.iv.39.
56 Hartmann, 14.
57 Statement of Aall to Sverre Hartmann, 1945.
58 DA. Aall file: Memorandum of 20.iv.39.
59 DA. Hagelin file: Quisling to Hagelin, 19.iv.39.
60 DA. Aall file: Hagelin to Aall, 25.iv.39.
61 DA. Aall file: Memorandum of 20.iv.39.
62 DA. Aall file: note on financial dealings, 16.v.39.
63 DA. Aall file: Aall to Quisling, 1.v.39.
64 DA. Aall file: Hagelin to Aall, 5.v.39.
65 DA. Aall file: Aall's memorandum to the NS council, 8.v.39.
66 DA. Aall file: telegram, Hagelin to Aall, Dresden, 10.v.39.
67 DA. Aall file: note of conversation, 18.v.39.
68 DA. Hagelin file: Hagelin to Aall, 25.v.39.
69 DA. Aall file: de Laporte to Aall, 26.v.39.
70 DA. Aall file: note by Aall, 30.v.39.
71 DA. Aall file: Memorandum of 31.v.39.
72 DA. Aall file: Aall to Hagelin, 4.vi.39.
73 DA. Hagelin file: Hagelin to Aall, 5.vi.39.
74 DA. Aall file: telegram from Aall to Hagelin, 7.vi.39.
75 DA. Quisling file: telegram from Quisling to Aall, 6.vi.39.
76 DA. Hagelin file: telegram from Hagelin to Aall, 7.vi.39.
77 DA. Aall file: note of discussion, 8.vi.39.
78 *Straffesak*, 35.
79 Evidence of Dr Hippel as given to Sverre Hartmann, 13.xii.48.
80 DA. Aall file: undated memorandum written by Aall.
81 DA. Aall file: undated note of receipt, in which it is clear that the money was to be paid by 15.viii.39.
82 DA. Aall file: note by Aall, 15.vi.39.
83 NCA, vol 3, no 004–PS, p 20.
84 DA. Aall file: note by Schickedanz of the meeting on 15.vi.39.
85 DA. Quisling file: pro-memoria from Schickedanz to Lammers, 26.vi.39.
86 NCA, vol 3, no 004–PS, p 20.
87 DA. Aall file: Memorandum by Scheidt for the attention of Rosenberg, 16.vi.39.
88 DA. Aall file: note written by Aall, June 1939.

89 NCA, vol 3, no 007–PS, p 33.
90 DGFP, ser D, vol 8, no 133, p 133, fn 3: 25.ix.39.
91 Seraphim, 127: entry for 11.iv.40. See also *Straffesak*, 28.
92 DA. Quisling file: pro-memoria from Schickedanz to Lammers, 26.vi.39.
93 *Straffesak*, 28.
94 NCA, vol 6, no 65–C, p 886.
95 DA. Quisling file: Quisling to Aall, 28.vi.39.
96 DA. Quisling file: Quisling to Scheidt, 24.vii.39.
97 DA. Aall file: evidence of Thorolf Winther-Hjelm, 7.ix.46.
98 DA. Aall file: note of discussion, written by Aall, 27.vi.39.
99 DA. Aall file: de Laporte to Aall, 7.vii.39.
100 DA. Aall file: note of 7.vii.39.
101 DA. Hagelin file: Hagelin to Scheidt, 12.vii.39.
102 DA. Quisling file: report on the visit of Reichsamtsleiter Scheidt to Norway, to Reichsminister Rosenberg, 15.vii.39.
103 DA. Quisling file: Scheidt to Rosenberg, 15.vii.39.
104 DA. Hagelin file: Hagelin to Scheidt, 12.vii.39.
105 DA. Quisling file: Scheidt to Rosenberg, 15.vii.39.
106 DA. Aall file: de Laporte to Aall, 20.vii.39.
107 Hartmann, 49.
108 NCA, vol 3, no 004–PS, p 21.
109 DA. Quisling file: Quisling to Scheidt, 24.vii.39.
110 DA. Aall file: de Laporte to Aall, 25.vii.39.
111 DA. Aall file: Aall to Quisling, 28.vii.39.
112 DA. Aall file: Aall to Hippel, 27.vii.39.
113 *Fritt Folk*, 6.v.39.
114 *Fritt Folk*, 19.viii.39.
115 *Fritt Folk*, 19.viii.39.
116 *Fritt Folk*, 2.ix.39.
117 Enclosure 3, no 004–PS, in the documents presented as evidence at the Nuremberg Trials.
118 DA. Aall file: Aall to Tau, 1 & 7.viii.39. Aall wanted to see Tau in Oslo or Malmö between 11 and 14 August.
119 DA. Aall file: Aall to Köpke, 10.viii.39.
120 DA. Aall file: Köpke to Aall, 11.viii.39.
121 DA. Aall file: Stangeland to Aall, 12.viii.39.
122 DA. Aall file: Aall to Stangeland, 14.viii.39.
123 DA. Aall file: Aall to de Laporte, 16.viii.39.
124 DA. Aall file: Scheidt to Winkler, 17.viii.39.
125 DA. Aall file: de Laporte to Aall, 29.viii.39.
126 NCA, vol 3, no 004–PS, p 21.
127 DGFP, ser D, vol 7, no 268, p 283: 25.viii.39. See also Kenney, 107.
128 DGFP, ser D, vol 8, no 165 (part 1), p 170: 28.ix.39. The negotiations took place in September over the question of supplies of vital materials for belligerents. Considering the circumstances, the Germans were able to conclude a very favourable agreement.
129 Kenney, 106.
130 NCA, vol 3, no 004–PS, pp 22–3.
131 DA. Hagelin file: 'Victor' (Quisling) to Hagelin, 9.ix.39.
132 DA. Aall file: note made by Aall, 14.ix.39.
133 DA. Hagelin file: 'Albert' (Hagelin) to Scheidt, 14.ix.39.
134 DGFP, ser D, vol 8, no 171, p 178: 30.ix.39. Von Neuhaus had telegraphed messages to this effect on 17 & 18.ix.39.
135 DGFP, ser D, vol 8, no 171, p 178: 30.ix.39.
136 DA. Aall file: Quisling to Aall, 18.ix.39.

137   DA. Aall file: Hippel to Aall, 23.ix.39.
138   DGFP, ser D, vol 8, no 133, p 133: 25.ix.39.
139   *Fritt Folk*, 30.ix.39.
140   DA. Aall file: various letters from Winther-Hjelm in response to missing letters from Aall, 25,26,29.ix & 1.x.39.
141   DGFP, ser D, vol 8, no 133, p 133, fn 3: 25.ix.39.
142   DGFP, ser D, vol 8, no 171, p 178: 30.ix.39.
143   DA. Aall file: Hippel to Aall, 2.x.39.
144   DA. Aall file: Perez and others to Aall, 5,8,10.x.39.
145   *Straffesak*, 288.
146   Hitler's overtures in 1939 are discussed in Woodward, 7–8.
147   *Straffesak*, 289, 492–6.
148   DA. Aall file: Quisling to Aall, 4.xi.39.
149   DA. Aall file: Aall's statement in 1945.
150   DA. Aall file: note of meeting, written by Aall.
151   IMT supplement, 1369–PS: correspondence between Schickedanz and Winkler.
152   DA. Aall file: Scheidt to Winkler, 17.viii.39.
153   UKA. Hagelin's letters to Schickedanz, 20 & 26.xi.39.
154   *Stortingsforhandlinger*, 1939.
155   *Fritt Folk*, 2.xii.39.
156   DA. Hagelin to Scheidt, 1.xii.39.
157   DGFP, ser D, vol 8, no 424, p 495: 7.xii.39.
158   DA. Aall file: Hagelin to Aall, 24.xi.39.
159   DA. Aall file: Aall to Quisling, 27.xi.39.
160   DA. Hagelin file: Hagelin to Schickedanz, 14.ix and 26.xi.39.
161   IMT supplement, 1369–PS: correspondence between Schickedanz and Winkler.
162   DA. Aall file: Hagelin to Aall, 24.xi.39.
163   DA. Aall file: telegram from Aall to Winther-Hjelm, 4.xii.39.
164   DA. Aall file: Winther-Hjelm to Quisling, 6.xii.39.
165   DA. Aall file: telegram from Quisling to Aall, 5.xii.39.
166   DA. Aall file: telegram from Quisling to Aall, 7.xii.39.
167   DA. Aall file: note written by Aall.
168   DA. Quisling file: Quisling to Aall, 9.xii.39.
169   NCA, vol 6, no 65–C, pp 885–7: Rosenberg's memo to Raeder.
170   Sundlo to Quisling, early December 1939; Quisling sent it to Hagelin.
171   Noack, 36; this section states that Noack had talked to Major Quisling 'on two occasions in the last few days'.
172   DGFP, ser D, vol 8, no 441, p 515: 11.xii.39.
173   NCA, vol 3, no 004–PS, pp 21–2.
174   DA. Quisling file: evidence from employees of the Travel Bureau.
175   Skodvin, 29.
176   *Straffesak*, 65, indicates that the meeting was Rosenberg's idea. It is clear from Seraphim, 110, that the date of the meeting was 11 December.
177   Skodvin, 30.
178   The best account is in 'Führer Conferences on Naval Affairs 1939 to 1945', printed in *Brassey's Naval Annual 1948*.
179   DGFP, ser D, vol 8, no 443, p 519: 12.xii.39.
180   Seraphim, 110.
181   DA. Quisling file: Sitzungsprotokoll of 11.xii.39.
182   IMT, v: Jodl's evidence, 5.vi.46. Jodl referred to 12 November; but this was clearly a slip of the tongue for '12 December'.
183   NCA, vol 3, no 007–PS, pp 33–4.
184   DGFP, ser D, vol 8, no 443, p 520: 12.xii.39.

185 Seraphim, 111.
186 *Straffesak*, 64.
187 Seraphim, 112.
188 NCA, vol 3, no 004–PS, p 22.
189 For Mussolini's original exposition of the theory of non-belligerence, see Hibbert, 115.
190 NCA, vol 3, no 004–PS, p 22.
191 Seraphim, 113.
192 DA. Aall file: notes on letter from Rosenberg to Raeder, 13.xii.39.
193 DGFP, ser D, vol 8, no 452, p 532: 14.xii.39.
194 DGFP, ser D, vol 8, no 453, p 532: 15.xii.39.
195 DGFP, ser D, vol 8, no 466, p 547: 17.xii.39.
196 For details of these meetings, see Skodvin, 33.
197 For a full discussion of the disputed dates, see Appendix E, p 354.
198 Skodvin, 114.
199 All these details are discussed in NCA, vol 3, no 004–PS, p 22.
200 Seraphim, 113.
201 Quisling's statement of 21.vi.45.
202 Seraphim, 114.
203 Letter written by Rosenberg to Lammers, 20.xii.39.
204 DGFP, ser D, vol 8, no 511, p 624: 5.i.40.

Chapter 5 BEFORE THE INVASION

1 For a full discussion of the way in which these issues were connected see Woodward, 20; also Appendix C, p 351.
2 IMT, xiv, 145–7: 17.v.46.
3 NCA, vol 6, no 122–C, p 928.
4 NCA, vol 6, no 5–C, p 816: dated Oct 9th 1939 and marked 'Most Secret'.
5 The code word for the attack on the Soviet Union.
6 'Weserübung Süd' was the code word for the attack on Denmark; 'Weserübung Nord' was the code word for the attack on Norway.
7 NCA, vol 6, no 66–C, p 891: this was a Memorandum for Admiral Assmann for his own information, not to be used for publication.
8 NCA, vol 7, no 52–L, p 803.
9 IMT, xiv, 304–5: 22.v.46.
10 Auswärtiges Amt, Länderakten Norwegen I: Politische Jahresübersicht 1937: dated 10.i.38.
11 Politischer Bericht, dated 14.xii.38.
12 Von Neuhaus to the Foreign Office, 26.x.39.
13 DGFP, ser D, vol 8, no 466, p 547: 17.xii.39.
14 Noack, 23.
15 Noack's diary: 27.xi.39. Reprinted in *Welt ohne Krieg*, Würzburg, February 1952.
16 Noack's two visits were on 4 and 8 December, when he spent all morning with Quisling. See *Straffesak*, 344; and Noack's pro-memoria, 'Bericht über die antirussischen Pläne Quislings'.
17 Noack's diary: 10.xii.39.
18 DGFP, ser D, vol 8, no 452, p 532: 14.xii.39.
19 Testimony of von Weizsäcker in the case versus the Wilhelmstrasse officials (Fall XI).
20 DGFP, ser D, vol 8, no 452, p 532: 14.xii.39.
21 DGFP, ser D, vol 8, no 452, p 532: 14.xii.39.
22 DGFP, ser D, vol 8, no 453, p 533: 15.xii.39.
23 DGFP, ser D, vol 8, no 466, p 547: 17.xii.39.

24 Testimony of von Weizsäcker (Fall XI).
25 DGFP, ser D, vol 8, no 459, p 540: 15.xii.39.
26 In his telegram of 17 December, Bräuer referred to a promise of financial aid in instructions dated 9 December and marked no P.VI.16981. The contents and whereabouts of this document remain unknown.
27 DGFP, ser D, vol 8, no 466, p 547: 17.xii.39.
28 DGFP, ser D, vol 8, no 466, p 546: 17.xii.39.
29 Seraphim, 114.
30 Jodl's diary: entry from 12.xii.39.
31 *Brassey's Naval Annual 1948*, 67.
32 DA. Quisling file: Memorandum of Schickedanz, 'Unterredung von Reichsleiter Rosenberg am 21.12.1939 mit Legationsrat Hewel'.
33 DA. Quisling file: Memorandum of Schickedanz.
34 DA. Quisling file: Rosenberg to Lammers, 20.xii.39.
35 From a transcript and letter sent by Legation Counsellor Luther, 8.i.40. Part of the file, 'Military Occupation. Norway. Foreign Office'. This included letters from Quisling, Hagelin and Scheidt, written in December 1939 and early 1940.
36 From Schickedanz's record of the conversation, no 139–PS.
37 DA. Quisling file: Memorandum of Schickedanz, 22.xii.39.
38 DGFP, ser D, vol 8, no 483, pp 569–70: 23.xii.39.
39 Skodvin, 43ff.
40 Letter of von Stutterheim, an official of the Reich Chancellery, to Schickedanz, 29.xii.39.
41 DA. Aall file: note written by Aall, 30.xii.39. Sassnitz was frequently used as a meeting place, as it was on the route to Malmö.
42 DGFP, ser D, vol 8, no 511, p 620: 5.i.40.
43 DGFP, ser D, vol 8, no 503, p 603: 5.i.40.
44 DGFP, ser D, vol 8, no 503, p 604: 3.i.40.
45 DGFP, ser D, vol 8, no 511, p 621: 5.i.40.
46 DGFP, ser D, vol 8, no 511, p 622: 5.i.40.
47 DGFP, ser D, vol 8, no 511, p 623: 5.i.40.
48 Skodvin, 47.
49 UKA: letter from Luther to the APA, 8.i.40.
50 DGFP, ser D, vol 8, no 511, p 623: 5.i.40.
51 DGFP, ser D, vol 8, no 511, p 626: 5.i.40.
52 DGFP, ser D, vol 8, no 511, p 627: 5.i.40.
53 Skodvin, 43ff.
54 Seraphim, 116.
55 DA. Aall file: de Laporte to Aall, 1.i.40.
56 DA. Hagelin file: Hagelin to Rosenberg, 13.i.40.
57 DGFP, ser D, vol 8, no 525, p 650: 11.i.40.
58 DA. Quisling file: Memorandum from Hagelin to Quisling, 13.i.40.
59 A committee set up by the Storting after the war found that Koht, Nygaardsvold and Monsen were equally to blame for this lamentable state of affairs.
60 DGFP, ser D, vol 8, no 511, p 624: 5.i.40. Brackets as in source quoted.
61 *Aftenposten*, 23.xii.39.
62 DA. Aall file: Aall transferred money totalling 25,000 kroner to Oslo, 4.i.40.
63 DGFP, ser D, vol 8, no 511, p 626: 5.i.40.
64 Mogens, 67.
65 *Fritt Folk*, 6.i.40.
66 *Fritt Folk*, 13.i.40.
67 DGFP, ser D, vol 8, no 503, p 604 fn: 3.i.40.
68 DGFP, ser D, vol 8, no 525, p 650: 11.i.40.
69 NCA, vol 3, no 004–PS, p 22.

70 DA. Aall file: undated note written by Aall.
71 Seraphim, 117.
72 DA. Aall file: Quisling to Aall, 17.i.40.
73 Mogens, 68.
74 DGFP, ser D, vol 8, no 511, pp 626–7: 5.i.40.
75 *Fritt Folk*, 13.i.40.
76 Knudsen, 73.
77 *Fritt Folk*, 13.i.40.
78 DA. Hagelin file: de Laporte to Aall, 19.i.40.
79 NCA, vol 3, no 004–PS, p 23.
80 DGFP, ser D, vol 8, no 511, p 626: 5.i.40.
81 DA. Hagelin file: letters from von Brückner to Hagelin, 6.iii & 2.iv.40.
82 NCA, 1369–PS, Appendix 2.
83 NCA, vol 3, no 004–PS, p 24.
84 *Aftenposten*, 20.i.40.
85 Woodward, 24.
86 DGFP, ser D, vol 8, no 566, p 697: 24.i.40.
87 Scheidt's report of 15.vii.39: no 004–PS, enclosure 2.
88 Bräuer's letter to von Grundherr, 23.i.40: a confidential memorandum to be found in 'Auswärtiges Amt. Military Occupation of Norway'. No 3081/613185 and no 3081/613186.
89 NCA, vol 6, no 65–C, p 886.
90 Seraphim, 117.
91 NCA, vol 3, no 004–PS, p 24.
92 NCA, vol 6, no 65–C, p 887.
93 NCA, vol 6, no 65–C, p 887.
94 *Brassey's Naval Annual 1948*, p 70; the report was dated 30.xii.39.
95 Hubatsch, Anhang B, pp 356–7.
96 Warlimont, 70.
97 Hubatsch, 391–3.
98 NCA, vol 4, no 1796–PS, p 374: 13.i.40.
99 Speech of 20.i.40: Churchill, i, 135–8.
100 *Fritt Folk*, 27.i.40.
101 DGFP, ser D, vol 8, no 565, p 696: 24.i.40. Parentheses as in source quoted.
102 NCA, vol 3, no 004–PS, p 23 (enclosure 9).
103 DA. Aall file: Hagelin to Aall, 27.i.40.
104 *Brassey's Naval Annual 1948*, 76–9.
105 Seraphim, 116–20.
106 NCA, vol 6, no 63–C, p 883.
107 IMT, ii, 187–8: Nuremberg, 7.xii.45.
108 Warlimont, 71.
109 *Utdrag i Høyesterettssak*: evidence of Erling Theodor Heide.
110 DA. Aall file: Aall's memorandum, 31.i.40.
111 *Utdrag i Høyesterettssak*: evidence of Erling Theodor Heide.
112 *Straffesak*, 63.
113 *Fritt Folk*, 3.ii.40.
114 *Fritt Folk*, 10.ii.40.
115 Wheeler-Bennett, 494.
116 Jodl's diary, in NCA, vol 4, no 1809–PS, 377–411.
117 Owing to Göring's jealousy of the greater importance of the role assigned to the Navy than that given to the Luftwaffe: Warlimont, 71.
118 The plan for the invasion of the Netherlands.
119 Warlimont, 71.
120 DA. Aall file: Winther-Hjelm to Aall, 10.ii.40.
121 DGFP, ser D, vol 8, no 615, p 776: 17.ii.40.

122 DGFP, ser D, vol 8, no 615, p 776, fn 1: 17.ii.40.
123 *Aftenposten*, 18.ii.40.
124 Norsk Telegrambyrå report, 19.ii.40.
125 Hubatsch, Anhang B, 357.
126 Seraphim, 123.
127 Warlimont, 72.
128 DGFP, ser D, vol 8, no 618, p 781: 17.ii.40.
129 DGFP, ser D, vol 8, no 618, p 782: 17.ii.40.
130 DGFP, ser D, vol 8, no 618, p 783, fn 2.
131 Halder's diary: entry for 20.ii.40.
132 Warlimont, 72.
133 *Preliminary Report on Germany's Crimes against Norway*, 10.
134 Halder's diary: entry for 21.ii.40.
135 DGFP, ser D, vol 8, no 626, pp 791–800: 21.ii.40.
136 DGFP, ser D, vol 8, no 626, p 794: 21.ii.40.
137 DGFP, ser D, vol 8, no 626, p 796: 21.ii.40.
138 Seraphim, 123.
139 *Brassey's Naval Annual 1948*, 81–3.
140 Jodl's diary: entry for 28.ii.40.
141 NCA, vol 4, no 1809–PS, p 388.
142 Jodl's diary: entry for 29.ii.40.
143 DGFP, ser D, vol 8, no 626, p 797: 21.ii.40.
144 DGFP, ser D, vol 8, no 626, pp 797–8: 21.ii.40.
145 DGFP, ser D, vol 8, no 626, p 799: 21.ii.40.
146 IMT, xxvi, 957–PS, p 411.
147 Seraphim, 123–4.
148 Skodvin, 37.
149 NCA, vol 6, no 174–C, p 1005.
150 Halder's diary: entry for 1.iii.40.
151 Jodl's diary: entry for 1.iii.40.
152 Jodl's Diary: entry for 3.iii.40.
153 Jodl's Diary: entry for 4.iii.40.
154 Jodl's Diary: entry for 5.iii.40.
155 Jodl's Diary: entry for 6.iii.40.
156 Seraphim, 125.
157 *Utdrag i Høyesterettssak*: evidence of Erling Theodor Heide.
158 *Brassey's Naval Annual 1948*, 86.
159 *Fritt Folk*, 9.iii.40.
160 *Fritt Folk*, 16.iii.40.
161 For fuller details, see Skodvin, 38.
162 Seraphim, 125.
163 Palmstrøm & Torgersen, 11.
164 DA. Aall file: Aall's travel plan, 4–13.iii.40.
165 *Berliner Lokalanzeiger*, 7.iii.40.
166 *Diplomatisches Bulletin*, 8.iii.40.
167 *Bremer Zeitung* and *Hamburger Fremdenblatt*, 8.iii.40.
168 DA. Aall file: note on evidence given by Raeder.
169 Jodl's Diary: entry for 12.iii.40.
170 Jodl's Diary: entry for 13.iii.40.
171 *The Times*, 15.iii.40.
172 *Utdrag i Høyesterettssak*: evidence of Erling Theodor Heide.
173 DA. Aall file: Aall met Hagelin at Sassnitz on 19.iii.40.
174 NCA, vol 3, no 004–PS, p 25 (enclosure 14).
175 NCA, vol 3, no 004–PS, p 25 (enclosures 15 and 16).
176 DA. Aall file: note made by Aall, 20.iii.40.

177   DA. Aall file: note made by Aall, 22.iii.40.
178   Evidence of Schreiber, as given on 22.v.46.
179   DA. Aall file: note made by Aall, 28.iii.40.
180   DA. Aall file: Winther-Hjelm to de Laporte, 14.iii.40.
181   DA. Aall file: report written by de Laporte, 25.iii.40.
182   DA. Aall file: note made by Aall, 28.iii.40.
183   Evidence of Schreiber, as given on 22.v.46.
184   DA. Aall file: note made by Aall, 28.iii.40.
185   See Appendix D, p 353.
186   *Aftenposten*, 26.iii.40.
187   DA. Hagelin file: report to Rosenberg.
188   DGFP, ser D, vol 9, no 17, p 35: 28.iii.40.
189   The text of the Norwegian declaration appears in *Le Temps*, 28.iii.40.
190   The denial of Agence Havas appears in *Monatshefte für Auswärtige Politik 1940*, 342.
191   Seraphim, 126.
192   Jodl's Diary: entry for 28.iii.40.
193   Jodl's Diary: entry for 2.iv.40.
194   *Brassey's Naval Annual 1948*, 90–1.
195   *Utdrag i Høyesterettssak*: evidence of Erling Theodor Heide.
196   *Samtiden*, vol 65 (1956), pp 317ff: article by Sverre Hartmann, based upon an interview with Pieckenbrock on 2.iv.56.
197   Admiral Bürkner testified on 8.xii.55 that he introduced Hagelin to Pieckenbrock a few weeks before the Copenhagen meeting.
198   DA. Quisling file: evidence of 25.vii.45.
199   DA. Quisling file: evidence of Clausen, 18.viii.45.
200   *Samtiden*, vol 65 (1956).
201   Jodl's Diary: entry for 4.iv.40.
202   Interrogation of Jodl by Col J. H. Amen, 15.viii.45.
203   Interrogation of Keitel, 15.viii.45.
204   DA. Aall file: Fuglesang to Aall, 29.iii.40.
205   Hewins, 217.
206   Knudsen, 74.
207   DA. Aall file: note by Aall, 30.iii.40.
208   *Fritt Folk*, 30.iii.40.
209   DA. Quisling file: evidence of staff from the hotel.

Chapter 6 THE FIRST QUISLING ADMINISTRATION

1   Kenney, 114.
2   Riste, 46.
3   Derry, 28.
4   Scheen, i, 140.
5   Riste, 47.
6   Derry, 38.
7   Report of the Storting Committee, 1947, Appendices, vol 2, p 212.
8   Derry, 37, 38.
9   Ash, 50.
10   Knudsen, 76.
11   Knudsen, 82.
12   *Aftenposten*, 9.iv.40.
13   *The Norseman*, i, 123: 'Aggression on Norway'.
14   Evidence of Schreiber, 5.v.46.
15   DA. Quisling file: evidence of Birger Olberg, 17.ix.45.

16 'Military Occupation. Norway': Foreign Office file.
17 Skodvin, 81.
18 IUK, 1945.
19 *Straffesak*, 50: pro-memoria written by Scheidt, 26.v.40.
20 Knudsen, 84.
21 Redegjørelse til siktelse fremsatt i Oslo forhørsrett, 21.vi.45.
22 *Morgenbladet*, no 72, 1950.
23 Knudsen, 84-5.
24 *Straffesak*, 82, 353.
25 Knudsen, 85.
26 *Straffesak*, 173.
27 Knudsen, 86.
28 DA. Quisling file: statement by Schreiber.
29 Knudsen, 86.
30 'Military Occupation. Norway': Foreign Office file.
31 Knudsen, 87.
32 Knudsen, 91.
33 Knudsen, 86.
34 Derry, 88.
35 *Straffesak*, 154.
36 *Straffesak*, 155.
37 Knudsen, 86.
38 DA. Quisling file: evidence of Gerhard Berghold.
39 Though it seems that this was a successful bluff on Scheidt's part.
40 DA. Quisling file: evidence of Egil Sundt, Knut Tvedt and Olva Midthun.
41 *Aftenposten*, 10.iv.40.
42 *Straffesak*, 75.
43 Knudsen, 89-90.
44 IUK, 1945: message from Bräuer to the Foreign Office, 9.iv.40.
45 UDA.
46 Derry, 38.
47 DA. Quisling file: evidence of Gerhard Berghold.
48 Moulton, 68.
49 Abwehr report from Bennecke: *Dagbladet*, 9.iv.54.
50 Hubatsch, 141, n 50.
51 Knudsen, 90.
52 *Straffesak*, 353.
53 Hubatsch, 141, n 50.
54 Knudsen, 91-2.
55 UKA, 1945: evidence of Welhaven, 29.xii.45.
56 UDA.
57 DA. Quisling file: stenographic record of telephone conversation.
58 IUK, 1945.
59 DGFP, ser D, vol 9, no 79, p 117: 10.iv.40.
60 Skodvin, 93.
61 Telephone conversation with the Foreign Office, 10.iv.40. *State Department Bulletin*, 1946, by J. S. Beddie.
62 IUK, 1945, Appendix 2.
63 Note in Foreign Office file (Abteilung Pol VII).
64 UKA: von Falkenhorst's evidence.
65 Hubatsch, 141-2, n 50.
66 J. S. Beddie: telephone conversation with the Foreign Office.
67 J. S. Beddie's account and DGFP, ser D, vol 9, no 83, p 124: 10.iv.40.
68 Knudsen, 92.
69 DA. Quisling file: Quisling's statement of 24.vii.45.

70 Knudsen, 94.
71 *Straffesak*, 80.
72 DA. Quisling file: Welhaven's statement of 31.v.45.
73 *Straffesak*, 173, 221.
74 DA. Quisling file: Nickelmann's evidence.
75 DA. Quisling file: Askvig's statement of 30.vi.45.
76 Knudsen, 94.
77 DA. Quisling file: Irgens's statement of 26.vii.45.
78 DA. Quisling file: note made by Irgens, summer 1940.
79 From the stenographic record of the case versus Meidell, p 58.
80 DA. Quisling file: Quisling to Hitler, 10.iv.40.
81 DA. Quisling file: Quisling's statement of 2.vii.45.
82 Knudsen, 95.
83 Knudsen, 96.
84 DGFP, ser D, vol 9, no 95, p 139: 11.iv.40.
85 Knudsen, 97–8.
86 Knudsen, 99.
87 DGFP, ser D, vol 9, no 95, p 138: 11.iv.40.
88 Hewins, 240.
89 DGFP, ser D, vol 9, no 95, p 138: 11.iv.40.
90 Knudsen, 104.
91 DA. Quisling file: note made by Irgens, summer 1940.
92 Seraphim, 127: DA. Quisling file: telephone call at 12.40 pm.
93 Seraphim, 127.
94 DA. Quisling file: telephone call at 5.21 pm.
95 Knudsen, 105.
96 DGFP, ser D, vol 9, no 95, p 139: 11.iv.40.
97 DGFP, ser D, vol 9, no 88, p 128: 11.iv.40.
98 This message has never been traced or identified. See DGFP, ser D, vol 9, no 95, p 137, fn 1: 11.iv. 40.
99 DGFP, ser D, vol 9, no 89, p 129: 11.iv.40.
100 DGFP, ser D, vol 9, no 89, p 129, fn 1: 11.iv.40.
101 DGFP, ser D, vol 9, no 90, pp 129–30: 11.iv.40.
102 Skodvin, 113: evidence of Koht as given to Skodvin.
103 DGFP, ser D, vol 9, no 95, p 137: 11.iv.40.
104 DA. Quisling file: note made by Quisling.
105 DGFP, ser D, vol 9, no 95, p 137: 11.iv.40.
106 DGFP, ser D, vol 9, no 95, p 138: 11.iv.40.
107 Seraphim, 127.
108 Warlimont, 76.
109 Hubatsch, 141–2, n 50.
110 DA. Quisling file: telephone conversation at 10.57 am, 13.iv.40.
111 *Adresseavisen*, 11.iv.40.
112 *Fritt Folk*, 12.iv.40.
113 Knudsen, 101.
114 DA. Quisling file.
115 *Aftenposten* (afternoon edition), 12.iv.40.
116 Case versus Meidell, 64, 79.
117 *Tidens Tegn*, 13.iv.40.
118 Knudsen, 104–5.
119 Knudsen, 106.
120 IUK, 1945, 133–5.
121 DGFP, ser D, vol 9, no 98, p 143: 13.iv.40.
122 IUK, 1945, 136.
123 Berg's Diary: 12.iv.40.

124 DGFP, ser D, vol 9, no 98, p 143: 13.iv.40.
125 IUK, 1945, 142.
126 Seraphim, 128.
127 Aktennotiz über Besuch des norwegischen Handelsministers Hagelin, 13.iv.40.
128 DGFP, ser D, vol 9, no 99, p 147: 13.iv.40.
129 DGFP, ser D, vol 9, no 99, p 144: 13.iv.40.
130 Jodl's Diary: entry for 14.iv.40.
131 DGFP, ser D, vol 9, no 99, p 145: 13.iv.40.
132 DGFP, ser D, vol 9, no 99, p 146: 13.iv.40.
133 DGFP, ser D, vol 9, no 99, p 147: 13.iv.40.
134 DGFP, ser D, vol 9, no 107, pp 152–6: 13.iv.40.
135 DGFP, ser D, vol 9, no 99, p 147: 13.iv.40.
136 DA. Quisling file: record of conversation between Hagelin and Scheidt.
137 Declaration made by Hagelin, 16.vi.45.
138 DGFP, ser D, vol 9, no 106, p 152, fn 1: 13.iv.40.
139 DGFP, ser D, vol 9, no 106, p 152: 13.iv.40.
140 DGFP, ser D, vol 9, no 110, p 158: 13.iv.40. Brackets not in the original.
141 DGFP, ser D, vol 9, no 110, p 159: 13.iv.40.
142 DGFP, ser D, vol 9, no 111, pp 159–60: 14.iv.40.
143 DGFP, ser D, vol 9, no 111, p 160: 14.iv.40.
144 DGFP, ser D, vol 9, no 112, p 160: 14.iv.40.
145 DGFP, ser D, vol 9, no 112, p 161, fn 4: 14.iv.40.
146 From a statement made by Bräuer to Skodvin.
147 IUK, 1945, 148.
148 DGFP, ser D, vol 9, no 113, p 161: 14.iv.40.
149 At about 3.00 pm: Hustad's declaration of 19.ix.45.
150 From the stenographic record of the case against Meidell.
151 *Straffesak*, 79.
152 DA. Quisling file: evidence of Rolf Pedersen and Ove Skabo-Brun.
153 Hambro, 83.
154 *Dagbladet*, 6.v.40.
155 Skancke's declarations of 24.ix and 13.xii.45.
156 *Straffesak*, 71.
157 DA. Quisling file: telephone conversation at 10.57 am: 13.iv.40.
158 Hambro, 18–20.
159 DA. Quisling file.
160 Declaration by Hagelin, 8.i.46.
161 IUK, 1945, 134.
162 DA. Quisling file.
163 IUK, 1945, 129.
164 DGFP, ser D, vol 9, no 114, p 162: 14.iv.40.
165 DGFP, ser D, vol 9, no 113, p 161: 14.iv.40.
166 Knudsen, 107.
167 DGFP, ser D, vol 9, no 115, p 163: 14.iv.40.
168 DGFP, ser D, vol 9, no 113, p 161: 14.iv.40.
169 DGFP, ser D, vol 9, no 118, pp 168–9: 15.iv.40.
170 DGFP, ser D, vol 9, no 118, p 169: 15.iv.40.
171 DGFP, ser D, vol 9, no 118, p 169: 15.iv.40.
172 DGFP, ser D, vol 9, no 118, p 170: 15.iv.40.
173 The full text was originally published in *Dagbladet*, 29.iv.54.
174 DGFP, ser D, vol 9, no 115, p 162: 14.iv.40.
175 DGFP, ser D, vol 9, no 115, p 163: 14.iv.40.
176 DGFP, ser D, vol 9, no 115, p 163: 14.iv.40.
177 DGFP, ser D, vol 9, no 115, p 163: 14.iv.40.
178 DGFP, ser D, vol 9, no 115, p 164: 14.iv.40.

179 DGFP, ser D, vol 9, no 118, p 171: 14.iv.40.
180 DGFP, ser D, vol 9, no 118, p 171: 14.iv.40.
181 DGFP, ser D, vol 9, no 115, p 164, fn 2.
182 DGFP, ser D, vol 9, no 118, p 172: 15.iv.40.
183 IUK, 1945, 158.
184 DGFP, ser D, vol 9, no 118, p 172: 15.iv.40.
185 Declaration of Welhaven, 31.v.45.
186 Pro-memoria written by Berg: IUK, 1945, 152.
187 DGFP, ser D, vol 9, no 124, p 176: 15.iv.40.
188 DGFP, ser D, vol 9, no 124, p 177: 15.iv.40.
189 *Dagbladet*, 15.iv.40.
190 Knudsen, 108–9.
191 *Fritt Folk*, 16.iv.40.
192 DGFP, ser D, vol 9, no 119, p 172: 15:iv.40.
193 DGFP, ser D, vol 9, no 130, p 193: 16.iv.40.
194 This message was at 6.50 pm, but has not been traced.
195 DGFP, ser D, vol 9, no 130, p 193, fn 2: 16.iv. 40.
196 DGFP, ser D, vol 9, no 131, p 193: 16.iv.40.
197 IUK, 1945, 168.
198 DA. Quisling file.
199 DGFP, ser D, vol 9, no 134, p 195: 17.iv.40.
200 DGFP, ser D, vol 9, no 134, p 196: 17.iv.40.
201 DGFP, ser D, vol 9, no 134, p 197: 17.iv.40.
202 DGFP, ser D, vol 9, no 147, p 215: 21.iv.40.
203 DGFP, ser D, vol 9, no 143, p 209: 19.iv.40.
204 Knudsen, 109.

Chapter 7 TEMPORARY RETIREMENT

1 Kordt, 243.
2 Seraphim, 128–9.
3 As a result of Terboven's disagreements with Meyer, the Gauleiter of North Westphalia, and Florian, the Gauleiter of Düsseldorf, who were friends of Rosenberg: Seraphim, 134.
4 *Hamburger Tageblatt*, 25.iv.40.
5 UKA, 1945, 4–5.
6 'Die politische Entwicklung in Norwegen in der Zeit seit der Besetzung 1940 bis zum Frühjahr', by H. Boehm (manuscript 1944), 11.
7 IUK, 1945, 295.
8 DGFP, ser D, vol 9, no 162, p 231: 24.iv.40. Words in brackets not in the original.
9 *Brassey's Naval Annual 1948*, 97.
10 Jodl's Diary: entry for 19.iv.40.
11 DGFP, ser D, vol 9, no 147, p 214: 21.iv.40.
12 Statement of Schreiber, 15.v.46.
13 Statement of Schreiber, 5.v.46.
14 DA. Quisling file: 'Memorandum zu den politischen Ereignissen in Norwegen vom 14 bis 15 April 1940'.
15 Administrasjonsrådets protokoll, 18.iv.40, p 13.
16 *Fritt Folk*, 19.iv.40: entitled 'Let the country have peace'.
17 DA. Quisling file.
18 There were two memoranda on Quisling's possible position, one referred to in note 14 above; the other is 'Aktennotiz über die Verhandlungen die zum Rücktritt des Staatsministers Quisling führten', which is in DA. Quisling file.

19 The NS men had worn Norwegian army uniforms with NS armbands, causing great confusion.
20 DA. Quisling file.
21 DA. Quisling file.
22 DA. Quisling file: Aktennotiz from Scheidt, 22.v.40.
23 *Straffesak*, 90.
24 UKA, 1945, 24.
25 On 23 April, for example, they were occupied in setting up the Norwegian section of the RSHA with the aid of Heydrich.
26 DA. Quisling file: Aktennotiz from Scheidt, 22.v.40.
27 Seraphim, 129.
28 Seraphim, 130. DA. Hagelin file.
29 Seraphim, 130.
30 DGFP, ser D, vol 9, no 147, p 215, fn 2.
31 Seraphim, 134.
32 DA. Quisling file: Schreiber to Weizsäcker, 24.iv.40. In this document Schreiber advocated full support for Quisling.
33 Telegram of 8.v.40, in response to a telegram of 4.v.40.
34 *Straffesak*, 357.
35 *Straffesak*, 92.
36 *Fritt Folk*, 1.v.40.
37 See Goebbels's diary for 4.ii.42; 13.ii.42; 15.iv.42; 9.v.43.
38 Seraphim, 132.
39 *Straffesak*, 93.
40 Quisling wanted NS to be given the Department of Police and Justice, and also control of the press and propaganda.
41 *Straffesak*, 93.
42 DGFP, ser D, vol 9, no 187, pp 265-8: 1.v.40.
43 Administrasjonsrådets protokoll, 1.v.40.
44 Seraphim, 137.
45 Memorandum written by Scheidt on 21 May, of which there is a copy in DA. Quisling file.
46 DGFP, ser D, vol 9, no 283, p 389: 20.v.40.
47 DGFP, ser D, vol 9, no 283, p 391: 20.v.40.
48 DGFP, ser D, vol 9, no 283, p 390: 20.v.40.
49 DA. Quisling file.
50 *Fritt Folk*, 14.v.40.
51 DGFP, ser D, vol 9, no 283, p 392: 20.v.40.
52 DGFP, ser D, vol 9, no 283, p 391: 20.v.40.
53 DGFP, ser D, vol 9, no 187, p 267: 1.v.40.
54 DGFP, ser D, vol 9, no 187, p 267: 1.v.40. Quisling was referring to an article in *Aftenposten*, 19.iii.40, in which Christensen had attacked German policy.
55 UKA, 1945, 28.
56 UKA, 1945, 21; also see Berggrav, 61-3.
57 Knudsen, 130.
58 DA. Quisling file: Aktennotiz from Scheidt, 23.v.40.
59 *Fritt Folk*, 23.v.40.
60 DA. Quisling file: dated 24.v.40.
61 *Die Deutsche Zeitung in Norwegen*, 3.vi.40.
62 Müller in 'Zwischen der Rede des Reichskommissars und der Parteiversammlung Quislings'. From the Foreign Office file.
63 NS propaganda publication: Quisling's speech at Oslo, 5.vi.40.
64 *Fritt Folk*, 8.vi.40.
65 *Die Deutsche Zeitung in Norwegen*, 14 & 15.vi.40.

66 See Müller's report.
67 Koht, *Norway, Neutral and Invaded*, 135.
68 Ibid, 136.
69 Ibid, 138.
70 DA. Quisling file.
71 Koht, op cit, 139.
72 DA. Aall file.
73 *Fritt Folk*, 11.vi.40.
74 *Fritt Folk*, 18.vi.40.
75 NS propaganda publication: Quisling's speech at Oslo, 24.vi.40.
76 *Straffesak*, 66–8: letter from Quisling to Hitler, 10.vii.40.
77 IUK, 1945, 184.
78 DA. Quisling file.
79 Koht, op cit, 140.
80 Ibid, 141.
81 DA. Hagelin file: Hagelin to Scheidt, 20.vi.40.
82 Stenographic record of Sundlo's case.
83 According to the evidence of Ellef Ringnes, as given on 28.v.46.
84 Knudsen, 115.
85 DA. Hagelin file: Hagelin to the Reichskommissariat, 9.vii.40.
86 *Straffesak*, 66–8.
87 Boehm, 11.
88 Sverre Steen, *Riksrådsforhandlingene*, 97.
89 *Handlingar rörande Sveriges politik under andra världskriget*, 41–4; referring to a document from Ribbentrop to von Weizsäcker, 25.vi.40.
90 Ibid, 63; Ribbentrop to Terboven, 10.vii.40.
91 *Straffesak*, 90; Knudsen, 130.
92 Notes on Delbrügge's negotiations in Berlin, in August and September 1940.
93 Quisling's declaration of 27.vii.45. Goebbels had some sympathy for Quisling, but stood outside the battle. He had good relations with Terboven also, and had been in contact with him on 22.v and 3.vii.40.
94 Quisling's declaration of 26.vii.45. Quisling would have preferred the companionship of Schickedanz.
95 Steen, 206.
96 Pro-memoria of 21 July: no 992–PS, from the IMT files.
97 *Straffesak*, 68.
98 IMT document NG 2948: 'Gedächtnisniederschrift der Besprechung zwischen dem Führer und Staatsrat Quisling am 16 August 1940'; written by Scheidt on 4.ix.40.
99 IMT, NG 2948.
100 *Straffesak*, 514.
101 From Sundlo's document, *Straffesak*, 514, it is clear that Quisling had not returned to Norway by 18 August.
102 DA. Quisling file: letter from Quisling to Terboven, 29.viii.40. It is just possible that they met on 24.viii.40.
103 Steen, 21; IUK, 1945, 148.
104 DA. Quisling file: letter of 29.viii.40.
105 UKA, 1945, 82: Delbrügge's evidence.
106 Seraphim, 140.
107 DA. Quisling file: Quisling to Lammers, 6.ix.40.
108 *Brassey's Naval Annual 1948*, 135.
109 UKA, 1945, 112.
110 DA. Quisling file: Quisling to Terboven, 10.ix.40.
111 DA. Quisling file: letter of 10.ix.40.
112 DA. Dahl file. Lunde's agreement is cited in Steen, 168.

113 Knudsen, 122.
114 DA. Quisling file: letter of 10.ix.40.
115 Seraphim, 141.
116 Steen, 177.
117 Seraphim, 144.
118 Pro-memoria of 21.vii.40.
119 Seip, 113.
120 'Partistillingen i Stortinget', note written by W. F. K. Christie on 11.ix.40.
121 Note written by Christie on 14.ix.40.
122 Steen, 185–7.
123 Steen, 187.
124 DA. Quisling file: letter of 10.ix.40.
125 On 16 September from Lunde; on the 18th from Stang; on the 20th from Hustad, Irgens and Meidell; on the 21st from Lie, Riisnæs and Skancke.
126 See Steen, 189; Ringnes, 215.
127 DA. Quisling file.
128 Text quoted in *Straffesak*, 514–18.
129 *Straffesak*, 518.
130 *Et nytt Norge kaller*, Quisling's speech of 26.ix.40.
131 Seraphim, 144.

Chapter 8 RETURN TO POWER

1   *Et nytt Norge kaller.*
2   Hewins, 306.
3   Seraphim, 225.
4   DA. Hagelin file: marked 'September 1940'.
5   Wyller, 312.
6   DA. Quisling file.
7   Wyller, 4.
8   DA. Hagelin file.
9   Wyller, 11.
10 DA. Hagelin file: Decree of 16 December.
11 Koht, *Norway, Neutral and Invaded*, 169.
12 Wyller, 15.
13 DA. Hagelin file.
14 DA. Quisling file: letter of 3.xii.40.
15 DA. Skancke file.
16 DA. Aall file.
17 Hewins, 299–300.
18 Wyller, 13. It was envisaged that Irgens might take over management of this group.
19 Wyller, 21.
20 DA. Quisling file.
21 DA. Krag-Brynildsen file.
22 DA. Hagelin file: Memorandum.
23 UB.
24 Wyller, 46.
25 DA. Hagelin file.
26 *Fritt Folk*, 2.v.41.
27 Wyller, 33.
28 *Fritt Folk*, 28 & 30.v.41.
29 *Fritt Folk*, 3.vi.41.
30 *Fritt Folk*, 6.vi.41.
31 *Fritt Folk*, 29.v.41.

32 E.-stabs arkiv.
33 UB.
34 *Norsk Tidend*, 24.vi.41.
35 E.-stabs arkiv.
36 DA. Quisling file.
37 *Fritt Folk*, 26.vi.41.
38 Ministry of the Interior circular, 26.vi.41: UB.
39 UB.
40 Wyller, 69.
41 *Quislings Nyttårstale 1941*: NS pamphlet.
42 *Quislings Oppfordring om regimentet Nordland*: NS pamphlet.
43 *Quislings appell til Hirden*: NS pamphlet.
44 *Norsk ungdom – Tysk ungdom*: NS pamphlet.
45 *Nasjonal Forfall og Nasjonal Gjenreising*: NS pamphlet.
46 *Kampen mellom Arier og Jødemakt*: NS pamphlet.
47 *8 April 1941 og 9 April 1940*: NS pamphlet.
48 *Fornyelsestanker i det norske folk*: NS pamphlet based upon Quisling's interview with *Die Deutsche Zeitung in Norwegen*, 20.v.41.
49 *Fenrisulven og Midgardsormen er sluppet løs*: NS pamphlet.
50 Wyller, 73.
51 UB.
52 Wyller, 74.
53 *Quislings tale til Norges Håndverkere*: NS pamphlet.
54 DA. Aall file.
55 DA. Quisling file.
56 *Morgenbladet*, 6.ix.41.
57 DA. Quisling file.
58 DA. Quisling file.
59 DA. Quisling file.
60 *Fritt Folk*, 2.ii.42.
61 Goebbels's diary for 4.ii.42.
62 *Morgenbladet*, 3.ii.42.
63 *Fritt Folk*, 4.ii.42.
64 *Fritt Folk*, 6.ii.42.
65 *Straffesak*, 542.
66 *Fritt Folk*, 6.ii.42.
67 *Fritt Folk*, 7.ii.42.
68 *Fritt Folk*, 9.ii.42.
69 DA. Quisling file.
70 *Straffesak*, 256.
71 DA. Quisling file.
72 DA. Saether file.
73 *Morgenbladet*, 9.ii.42.
74 DA. Saether file.
75 See Hoprekstad.
76 DA. Lundesgard file.
77 Wyller, 112.
78 DA. Lundesgard file: letter of 16 March.
79 *Fritt Folk*, 16.iv.42.
80 DA. Skancke file.
81 *Morgenbladet*, 20.ii.42.
82 *Morgenbladet*, 21.ii.42.
83 DA. Hagelin file.
84 *Fritt Folk*, 11.xi.41.
85 DA. Whist file.

86 *Fritt Folk*, 7.ii.42.
87 *Fritt Folk*, 8.iv.42.
88 *Brassey's Naval Annual 1948*, 259.
89 NCA, vol 3, p 830.
90 See Goebbels's diary for 3.iii.42; 15 & 23.iv.42.
91 *Fritt Folk*, 22.iv.42.
92 *Fritt Folk*, 24.iv.42.
93 DA. Skancke file.
94 *Aftenposten*, 25.iv.42; *Fritt Folk*, 27.iv.42.
95 *Fri Fagbevegelse*, 25.iv.42. This publication had been in existence for some time previously.
96 *Morgenbladet*, 23.v.42.
97 *Straffesak*, 115, 202.
98 DA. Quisling file: Whist to Quisling, 29.v.42.
99 *Straffesak*, 545.
100 DA. Quisling file: letters of Hustad and Prytz to Quisling, 1.vi.42.
101 DA. Quisling file: memorandum of 9.vi.42.
102 *Morgenbladet*, 24.vi.42.
103 *Morgenbladet*, 22.vii.42.
104 *Stockholms Tidningen*, 13.v.42.
105 *Fritt Folk*, 26.v.42.
106 *Fritt Folk*, 15.vi.42.
107 DA. Hagelin file.
108 *Fritt Folk*, 5.viii.42.
109 DA. Skancke file.
110 DA. Hagelin file.
111 *Fritt Folk*, 5.viii.42.
112 DA. Hagelin file: circular of 8.viii.42.
113 UB.
114 Wyller, 144.
115 UB: letter from Whist to Dahl, 12.viii.42.
116 UB: Hasle's pro-memoria, 20.vii.42.
117 DA. Hagelin file.
118 *Fri Fagbevegelse*, 8 & 19.viii.42.
119 Reich Chancellery Archives, 12.viii.42.
120 UB: 3.viii.42.
121 *Straffesak*, 546.
122 *Norsk Lovtidend*, 9.ix.42.
123 *Fritt Folk*, 11.ix.42.
124 *Fri Fagbevegelse*, 10.ix.42.
125 Reich Chancellery Archives, 14.ix.42.
126 *Nya Dagligt allehanda*, 30.ix.42.
127 DA. Hagelin case; Dahl to Lippestad, 17.ix.42.
128 *Fri Fagbevegelse*, 26.ix.42.
129 DA. Hundseid file.
130 *Fritt Folk*, 26.ix.42.
131 *Quislings tale pa Førertinget*: NS pamphlet.
132 DA. Quisling file: Quisling to Hustad, 10.x.42.
133 *Straffesak*, 548.
134 DA. Quisling and Hagelin files.
135 *Fritt Folk*, 7.xii.42.
136 Riste, 74.
137 *Morgenbladet*, 23.ii.43.
138 DA. Quisling file: telegram of 22.ii.43.
139 *Opprop fra Ministerpresidenten til alle Nordmenn*: NS pamphlet.

140 Riste, 73.
141 *Straffesak*, 551–2.
142 DA. Quisling file: Decree of 14.viii.43.
143 Riste, 74.
144 DA. Quisling file.
145 *Aftenposten*, 16.viii.43.
146 DA. Quisling file: Decree of 14.viii.43.
147 DA. Irgens file.
148 *Straffesak*, 131.
149 DA. Riisnæs file.
150 *Quislings tale den 1 Februar 1943*: NS pamphlet.
151 *Quislings tale den 17 Mai 1943*: NS pamphlet.
152 *Straffesak*, 552–4.
153 DA. Quisling and Aall files.
154 *Straffesak*, 555.
155 DA. Quisling and Hagelin files.
156 DA. Quisling file: telegram of 28.ix.43.
157 DA. Quisling file: speech of 18.x.43.
158 DA. Skancke file.
159 The memorandum of 10.ii.42.
160 *Aftenposten*, 4.xii.43.
161 DA. Quisling file.
162 Riste, 80.
163 DA. Quisling file: memorandum of 18.xii.43.
164 DA. Riisnæs file.
165 Riste, 81.
166 Knudsen, 159.
167 Knudsen, 159.
168 *Aftenposten*, 3.i.44.
169 *Straffesak*, 558–9.
170 *Aftenposten*, 22.iv.44.
171 *Straffesak*, 560–1.
172 *Ministerpresident Quislings tale den 14 Mai 1944*: NS pamphlet.
173 *Fritt Folk*, 16.v.44.
174 *Fritt Folk*, 15.v.44.
175 DA. Quisling file: note dated 16.v.44.
176 Knudsen, 159.
177 *Aftenposten*, 5.vi.44.
178 *Aftenposten*, 7.vi.44.
179 DA. Quisling file: telegram of 20.vii.44.
180 Text given in *Straffesak*, 563–4.
181 *Straffesak*, 563.
182 *Fritt Folk*, 16.xii.44.
183 Knudsen, 181.
184 Knudsen, 182.
185 *Ved Terskelen til det avgjørende år*: NS pamphlet.
186 Riste, 81; Hewins, 336.
187 DA. Quisling file.
188 *Aftenposten*, 29.i.45.
189 Quoted by Riste, 79.
190 *Fritt Folk*, 9.ii.45.
191 *Aftenposten*, 10.ii.45.
192 DA. Quisling file.
193 Hewins, 339.
194 DA. Quisling file.

Chapter 9 QUISLING'S TRIAL AND POLITICAL IDEAS

1 Hewins, 349-50.
2 DA. Quisling file.
3 According to the independent magazine, *The Norseman*, for 1945, 'It was a fair trial, though it was certainly not impartially conducted.' With the criticisms of this magazine about the political aspects I am in full agreement. The verdict and the method of reaching it seem to me to have been perfectly fair.
4 Hewins, 362.
5 *Straffesak*, 570.
6 *Straffesak*, 591.
7 Modifications were made on 21 June and 11 July 1945.
8 DA. Quisling file.
9 *Straffesak*, 244.
10 *Expressen*, 6.viii.45.
11 *Straffesak*, 382.
12 *Straffesak*, 278.
13 See *Aftenposten*, 18.iv.47.
14 *Straffesak*, 244.
15 *Straffesak*, 245.
16 *Aftenposten*, 20.viii.45.
17 *Aftenposten*, 11.ix.45.
18 DA. Quisling file.
19 *Straffesak*, 466.
20 *Straffesak*, 459-60.
21 DA. Quisling file.
22 *Straffesak*, 461-6.
23 DA. Quisling file.
24 DA. Hagelin file.
25 DA. Quisling file.
26 DA. Quisling file.
27 Hewins, 371.
28 Knudsen, 7.
29 Hewins, 372.
30 Hewins, 372.
31 DA. Quisling file.
32 Knudsen, 8-9.
33 As in Østbye.
34 DA. Quisling file: interrogation of Keitel by Col J. H. Amen, 15.viii.45.
35 DGFP, ser D, vol 8, no 626, p 795, fn 3: 2.ii.40.
36 Seraphim, 130.
37 DA. Quisling file: interrogation of Jodl by Col J. H. Amen, 15.viii.45.
38 DA. Quisling file: interrogation of Keitel, 15.viii.45.
39 DA. Quisling file: interrogation of Ribbentrop by Col J. H. Amen, 15.viii.45.
40 Hewins, 217.
41 *Straffesak*, 460.
42 DA. Hagelin file: comments on Fuglesang.
43 *Quisling har sagt*, Introduction to Vol 1.
44 *Ved terskelen til det avgjørende år.*
45 DA. Aall file.
46 *Fritt Folk*, 23.x.37.
47 *Demokratiet går til grunne – en ny tid bryter fram.*
48 *Ved Terskelen til det avgjørende år.*
49 *Demokratiet går til grunne – en ny tid bryter fram.*

50 DA. Aall file.
51 *Quisling har sagt*, 93.
52 *Quislings foredrag i Lillehammer*.
53 DA. Quisling file: speech made during the 1937 municipal elections.
54 DA. Quisling file.
55 Hilberg, 355: 'Henceforth, the Jews were not merely undergoing emancipation, they were being absorbed into the Scandinavian way of life, and that was a process from which the North was reluctant to retreat even under Nazi pressure.'
56 DA. Quisling file.
57 DA. Quisling file.
58 *Straffesak*, 572.
59 DA. Quisling file: from a talk in Oslo, 8.iv.38.
60 *Et nytt Norge kaller*.
61 *Oppfordring til Nasjonal Samling*.
62 DA. Quisling file: Introduction to an NS pamphlet, 1933.
63 *Fritt Folk*, 9.iv.38.
64 DA. Quisling file.
65 *Norsk ungdom – Tysk ungdom*.
66 *Quislings tale den 1 Februar 1943*.
67 Hewins, 323.
68 Skodvin, article in *The Times* (1965).

Appendix A
(see p 24, n 68)

THE FIGURES used are derived from *Russia and Peace*, which in turn drew heavily upon a League of Nations statistical survey of 1923.

1   Transport
- (*a*) Goods transported by river, canal and lake in 1913 totalled 37 million tons, which by 1922 had fallen to 8·6 million tons. The figures for rail transport were almost as serious.
- (*b*) The number of ships plying on the Volga declined from 588 in 1913 to 336 in 1922 and 146 in 1923.

2   Crops
- (*a*) The area sown with corn declined from 90·8 million hectares in 1916 to 49·5 million hectares in 1922. The yield for those years, respectively, was 65·9 and 33·6 million tons.
- (*b*) The area sown with flax declined from 1·5 million acres in 1913 to ·4 million acres in 1921. The yield for those years, respectively, was 416,000 tons and 94,000 tons.

3   Industry
- (a) Coal production declined from 1,824·4 million poods* in 1917 to 592 million poods in 1922.
- (*b*) Petroleum production declined from 523 million poods in 1917 to 283 million poods in 1922.
- (*c*) Textiles declined from 23·6 million poods in 1913 to 3·1 million poods in 1922.

* One pood weighed approximately 36 lb.

Appendix B
(see p 27, n 83)

THE TERRIBLE conditions in Russia were fully reported in a publication of the League of Nations entitled *Report on economic conditions in Russia with special reference to the famine of 1921–1922 and the state of agriculture.* (Document No C.705.M.451. 1922 II.) Much of the reporting was based upon Quisling's observations, and according to the report (p 37), 'The Ukraine, which has a territory as large as Italy and a population of 26 million had been peculiarly affected by the movement of warring armies; and, even after the Civil War, Captain Quisling states that until the end of 1921 the country suffered on a very large scale from roaming companies of bandits. These difficulties, as well as continued requisitions, had left the country peculiarly bereft of stock, and, as in the Volga, it suffered from a particularly severe drought in the critical months of 1921. Captain Quisling gives the total harvest of that year as 350 million poods, as against the 298 millions of the Ukrainian Committee and Popov's 580 millions, and 1,000 millions before the war. More than 30 million poods were exported to Russia for the assistance of the famine regions.'

Appendix C
(see p 166, n 1)

THE MUTUAL economic dependence of Sweden and Germany as a result of the iron ore exports is clearly demonstrated by the period between the wars. Germany was Sweden's biggest customer for iron ore during the First World War. The effect of her discontinuance of armament manufacture in 1918 upon trade figures is demonstrated by a comparison between the figures for the last full year (1917) and the first year after the war (1919).[1]

	Productions of Swedish Ore in Metric Tons	Exports in Metric Tons
1917	6,217,172	5,613,000
1919	4,981,110	2,419,000

The high phosphorus content of the Swedish ores formed a necessary supplement to the high calcium content ores which Germany imported from France. Germany's imports from these two trading areas totalled nearly 70 per cent of her iron ore.[2] In fact just before the outbreak of war it was clear that 'Germany has become increasingly dependent on the high-grade Swedish product which is so admirably suited to the metallurgical process she employs'.[3] This was confirmed by Fritz Thyssen, the industrial magnate, from his retreat in Switzerland whither he had fled to escape Hitler, in a series of memoranda to the Allies. The figures for 1930 to 1935 (overleaf) show Germany's dependence on Swedish ore imports.[4]

These figures become even more impressive when it is remembered that almost all of the Swedish ore exported to Germany was the highest grade phosphoric ore, and that Germany was almost exclusively dependent on Sweden for this type of ore. This important source of imports became even more essential after the outbreak of war when imports from overseas were cut off by the Allies. On 22 February 1940 the Defence Economy Staff of the OKW notified the Operations division of the Naval

Notes
1 Rickman, 150.
2 Rickman, 163.
3 Rickman, 158.
4 Rickman, 150, 159: Tables.

Staff of the OKM of the status of Swedish and Norwegian ore deliveries to Germany. The report, which was an annex to Raeder's report to Hitler of 23 February read as follows:

'Iron ore deliveries to Germany for 1940 as specified by the German–Swedish agreement – 10,000,000 tons. (Swedish authorities consider it necessary to ship 2–3 million tons via Narvik.) However, if arrangements could be made for storage during the winter months the following amounts could be shipped:

(1) via Luleå up to 6 million tons;
(2) via Oxelösund at least 3 million tons.

Thus the ore to be shipped via Narvik would not exceed 1 million tons. However, we cannot depend on shipment of this amount during 1940 for the following reasons:

(1) Owing to unfavourable weather conditions shipments to Luleå will begin later than usual this year.
(2) Accumulated stocks do not exceed normal figures.
(3) The ore railroad Luleå–Narvik will have to carry the additional load of supplies for Finland.

(All figures in Metric Tons)

Year	(a)	(b)	(c)	(d)	(e)	(f)
1930	11,236,428	9,476,598	6,662,519	13,889,867	70·3	48·0
1931	7,070,868	4,496,275	2,497,776	7,070,842	55·6	35·3
1932	3,298,989	2,219,309	1,552,885	3,451,608	69·9	45·0
1933	2,698,750	3,150,636*	2,253,435	4,571,641	71·5	49·3
1934	5,253,058	6,870,134*	5,157,759	8,264,605	75·1	62·4
1935	7,932,854	7,718,892	5,509,300	14,061,077	71·4	39·2

(a) Swedish Production
(b) Swedish Exports
(c) German Imports of Swedish Ore
(d) German Total Imports of Ore
(e) Percentage of Sweden's Ore to Germany
(f) Percentage of Swedish Ore in Imports

* (These figures are larger than production figures owing to the exports of stockpiled ores.)

Swedish ore shipments to Germany since the beginning of the war have been as follows:

September	590,000 tons
October	795,000 tons
November	873,000 tons
December	661,000 tons (including 118,000 tons via Narvik)
January	490,000 tons (including 260,000 tons via Narvik)'

These figures show more clearly than ever that Germany required the route via Narvik to be kept open at all costs.

Appendix D

(see p 206, n 185)

IN DETAIL, Operation Wilfred and the associated military plan R4 involved the laying of two minefields in the approaches to the Vestfjord, north of Bodø, so as to close the passage south from Narvik and off Stadland (between Ålesund and Bergen). There was also to be a simulated operation off Molde. These operations, though not previously announced to the Norwegian government, entailed the double risk of Norwegian counter-action in defence of neutrality and of action of German warships which fortune or foresight might bring into the vicinity. In order to protect the minelayers, therefore, various units of the Home Fleet were to cruise in the operational areas. There would be initially one cruiser and two destroyers in this covering force. Two other cruisers and three destroyers at Rosyth, and at longer notice three more cruisers from Scapa Flow, were to be available as a striking force against any German sortie that might occur. The plan also provided for a military expedition to take advantage of the moment when 'the Germans set foot on Norwegian soil, or there is clear evidence that they intend to do so'.[1] Narvik and its railway as far as the Swedish border formed the primary object.[2] A force of one infantry brigade was assigned to Narvik, together with one light anti-aircraft battery, of which the first battalion was to set sail in a transport escorted by two cruisers a few hours after the mines had been laid. The forces to occupy Bergen and Trondheim, and to raid Stavanger, were much smaller, totalling a mere five battalions plus technical troops. This plan was supported by Reynaud, who, in his account of the technical details of the task force wrote that 'England had in February, from the time of the first appeal by Helsinki, prepared seven battalions with the occupation of Stavanger, Bergen and Trondheim in view.'[3] This was the plan which, if executed, might have driven Norway into war against the Allies.

Notes

1 Derry, 14–15.
2 The importance of Narvik was its use as a centre for the shipment of iron ore: see Appendix C.
3 Reynaud, 389. Reynaud's 'seven battalions' refers to the original force envisaged; after the surrender of Finland, this was reduced in strength to five battalions.

Appendix E
(see p 163, n 197)

The disputed dates of Quisling's meetings with Hitler in December 1939

THE MOST probable date of Hitler's first encounter with Quisling seems to be 13 December; that of the second, 18 December. Evidence on these meetings, however, conflicts considerably. According to *NCA*, Volume 3, No 004–PS the date of the first meeting was 16 December. This is supported in *NCA*, Volume 3, No 007–PS. It is further supported by the letter sent from Rosenberg to Raeder on 13 December 1939, for if this letter had been the cause of Hitler's interviews with Quisling, the initial meeting could hardly have taken place the same day. On the other hand it seems more probable that Rosenberg's letter was just a general memorandum for the information of Raeder. It may well have been supplementary to a meeting rather than a briefing. This is confirmed by the diary of Alfred Jodl. The entry for 13 December states that the Führer received Quisling and later that day suggested 'that investigations on how to seize Norway should be conducted by a very restricted staff group'; 13 December seems, therefore, likely to be the better choice. Not only is Jodl definite when the other diarists are not clear, but he was also present at all Hitler's important conferences, thus giving him a reliable over-all picture of Hitler's policies. Further, Hitler's directive of the evening of 13 December makes good sense if he had had a meeting with Quisling earlier that day.

A similar difficulty exists in the case of the second meeting. Rosenberg thought that this took place on 18 December, if his memorandum of 15 June 1940, as given in *NCA*, Volume 3, No 004–PS, is to be believed. However, this is contradicted by Raeder's memorandum to Assmann of 10 January 1944, which states that the decision on Norway was taken by 14 December. As Raeder was usually accurate about such matters it is no light matter to reject his opinion. It is stated in *NCA*, Volume 6, No 66–C that 'on the grounds of the Führer's discussion with Quisling and Hagelin on the afternoon of 14.12.1939, the Führer gave the order that preparations for the Norwegian operation were to be made by the Supreme Command of the Armed Forces'. This would of course confirm

Jodl's record of 13 December for the first meeting. Other dates which have at some time been suggested are 16 and 17 December. However, Rosenberg's diary contains a record of a second meeting on 17 December. There are two entries – for 19 and 20 December – which erroneously contain information which points generally towards 17 December as the important day. The most decisive evidence, however, is indirect. In his communication of 15 December von Weizsäcker demanded information about Quisling from Bräuer at latest by 'Monday morning, 18 December'. As at the time this was written Quisling's interview with Hewel had not been arranged it seems most probable that the information was required for a briefing for a meeting with Quisling on 18 December – probably therefore for Quisling's second meeting with Hitler.

Bibliography

FOR THE sake of clarity the works used have been divided into seven different categories. In some cases it has not been entirely clear which was the correct category and there an explanatory note has been added.

1 Material from Archives

(*i*) Domsarkiv: the official collections of evidence prepared for use in the trials of the leading collaborators. The files which have been of particular assistance are those relating to Hagelin, Aall, Quisling, Skancke and Riisnæs. Reference has occasionally been made to those concerning Hundseid, Sæther, Whist and a few others of lesser importance. This material has not been published previously.

(*ii*) Universitetsbiblioteket: records of the trials of the lesser war criminals and collaborators, including a great deal of unpublished material.

(*iii*) Utenriksdepartementets arkiv: the files of the Norwegian Foreign Office.

(*iv*) Reich Chancellery Archives: records of the activities of Lammers and Bormann at critical moments in the Second World War.

(*v*) Undersøkelseskommisjonsarkiv: the documents and testimony presented to the commission which investigated the part played by a number of Norwegians in early 1940. Part of these investigations have been published in *Innstilling fra Undersøkelseskommisjonen* (Oslo, 1946).

(*vi*) Kurzer Tätigkeitsbericht der APA des NSDAP: an important document presented for consideration at the Nuremberg trials but which was not printed in the standard collections.

2 Printed records, including official publications

Innstilling fra Undersøkelseskommisjonen. See section 1.

Ny Norsk Kvitbok (London, 1940). The official record of events in 1940 as seen at the time.

Preliminary report on Germany's crimes against Norway (Oslo, 1945). Edited by Palmstrøm and Torgersen, this collection gave a very selective account of events between 1940 and 1945.

Straffesak mot Vidkun Abraham Lauritz Jonssøn Quisling (Oslo, 1946).

The invaluable official record of Quisling's trial; a useful collection of documents is appended.

Stortingsforhandlinger. The records of the proceedings of the Norwegian Parliament. Particularly useful for 1931, 1932, 1933 and 1939.

Innstilling fra Spesialkomiteen til undersøkelse av Quislingsaken (Oslo, 1932). The report of the committee which looked into Quisling's allegations, and those of the Labour Party, in 1932.

Kullmannsaken (Oslo, 1932). The case prepared against Kullmann in 1932.

Utdrag i Høyesterettssak (Oslo, 1946). The record of Hagelin's appeal to the Supreme Court.

Brassey's Naval Annual 1948 (London, 1948). Records of the Führer's conferences on naval affairs.

Documents on British Foreign Policy (HMSO).

Documents on German Foreign Policy (HMSO), Series D.

Nazi Conspiracy and Aggression (Washington, 1946). A collection of documents relating to the policy of the Third Reich.

International Military Tribunal (HMSO). The account of the trials at Nuremberg together with a large amount of documentary material.

Norsk Biografisk Leksikon. Particularly Volume XI (Oslo, 1952).

Det tyske overfall på Norge. Redegjørelse fra den norske regjering (Lillehammer, 1940). The first Norwegian official account of the attack on Norway.

Handlingar rörande Sveriges politik under andra världskriget. Frågor i samband med norska regjeringens vistelse utanför Norge (Stockholm, 1948). The Swedish account of governmental relations with Norway in the Second World War.

Riksrådsforhandlingene (Oslo, 1947). Edited by S. Steen. An official account of negotiations between April and September 1940.

3   *Newspapers*
Some newspapers have been of very great use, others have been referred to only occasionally. Of particular importance are the following:
Norwegian
Aftenposten
Arbeiderbladet
Fritt Folk. The NS party organ
Morgenbladet
Nationen
Norsk Lovtidend
Norsk Tidend. Published by the government-in-exile during the war
Tidens Tegn
Vår Hær
German
Die Deutsche Zeitung in Norwegen

Of lesser importance are the following:
Norwegian
  Adresseavisen
  Arbeideren
  Arbeiderenes Enhetsfront
  Dagbladet
  Fri Fagbevelse
  Norsk Arbeidsliv
German
  Berliner Lokalanzeiger
  Bremer Zeitung
  Diplomatisches Bulletin
  Hamburger Fremdenblatt
  Hamburger Tageblatt
  Monatshefte für Auswärtige Politik
Swedish
  Nya Dagligt Allehanda
  Stockholm Tidningen
French
  Le Temps
British
  The Times
American
  State Department Bulletin
Anglo-American
  The Norseman

4 *Diaries and other autobiographical material*
Norwegian
  Russland og vi, by Vidkun Quisling (Oslo, 1941).
  Fra de urolige Tredveårene, by Asbjørn Lindboe (Oslo, 1965).
German
  Jodl's Diary. Reprinted in *Die Welt als Geschichte* (Stuttgart, 1952 and 1953).
  Halder's Diary. Reprinted in *Kriegstagebuch*. Volume I (Stuttgart, 1962).
  Das politische Tagebuch Alfred Rosenberg. Edited by H. G. Seraphim (Munich, 1964).
  Inside Hitler's Headquarters, by Walter Warlimont (Bristol, 1964).

All the above memoirs are of great importance to an understanding of Quisling's activities. Listed below are some others of lesser importance:
Russia and Peace, by F. Nansen (London, 1923).
Armenia and the Near East, by F. Nansen (London, 1928).
Through the Caucasus to the Volga, by F. Nansen (London, 1931).

Biografiske Opplysninger til 25-aarsjubileet for Studentene i 1905. Quisling's
   autobiographical record (Oslo, 1930).
Fra mine unge år, by J. L. Quisling (Christiania, 1912).

5   *Pamphlets and published speeches of Quisling*
   Most of these were published or reissued by the NS press during the war.
Redegjørelse for Nordisk Folkereisnings Retningslinjer (Oslo, 1931).
Oppfordring til Nasjonal Samling (Oslo, 1933).
Quislings foredrag den 26 Oktober 1933 (Oslo, 1933).
Quislings foredrag i Lillehammer (Oslo, 1933).
Hvad vi vil (Oslo, 1934).
Nasjonal Samlings Program (Oslo, 1934).
Quislings Nyttårstale, 1935 (Oslo, 1935).
Norkse Arbeidere (Oslo, 1936).
Fra partipolitikk til fagstyre (Oslo, 1937).
Demokratiet går til grunne – en ny tid bryter fram (Oslo, 1939).
Det som skjedde 9 April (Oslo, 1940).
Et nytt Norge kaller (Oslo, 1940).
8 April 1941 og 9 April 1940 (Oslo, 1941).
Kampen mellom Arier og Jødemakt (Oslo, 1941).
Nasjonalt forfall og nasjonal gjenreising (Oslo, 1941).
Quislings appell til Hirden (Oslo, 1941).
Quislings nyttårstale, 1941 (Oslo, 1941).
Quislings oppfordring om regimentet Nordland (Oslo, 1941).
Quislings tale til Norges håndverkere (Oslo, 1941).
For Norges frihet og selvstendighet (Oslo, 1942), (Collected articles).
Fornyelsestanker i det norske folk (Oslo, 1942).
Quislings tale på Førertinget (Oslo, 1942).
Fenrisulven og Midgardsormen er sluppet løs (Oslo, 1943).
Norsk ungdom – Tysk ungdom (Oslo, 1943).
Opprop fra Ministerpresidenten til alle Nordmenn (Oslo, 1943).
Quislings tale den 1 Februar 1943 (Oslo, 1943).
Quislings tale den 17 Mai 1943 (Oslo, 1943).
Quislings tale den 14 Mai 1944 (Oslo, 1944).
Ved Terskelen til det avgjørende år (Oslo, 1945).

   In addition there are a number of collections of speeches and policy
statements, including the following:
Quislings skrivelse til Kongen i anledning hevdelsen av uniformsforbudet
   (Stavanger, 1934).
Quisling har sagt. Volumes I and II (Oslo, 1940, 1941).
Quislings tale i Stortinget 1932 (Oslo, 1941).
Quisling ruft Norwegen (Munich, 1942).
Quisling i kamp for Norge (Oslo, 1943).

Die nationale Revolution in Norwegen. Edited by Quisling and Lunde
(Oslo, 1944).
Quisling und Entwurf Europa-pakt (Oslo, 1944).

Finally there are two articles, not mentioned in the text, and the two
party publications which appeared so irregularly that they cannot be
considered as newspapers.
*Om at bebodde verdener finnes utenom jorden og betydningen derav for vår
livsanskuelse* (Oslo, 1929).
Fra det daglige liv i Russland (Oslo, 1930).
Samband. This appeared only briefly in the early 1930s.
Nasjonal Samling. This appeared a few times in 1933 and 1934.

6 Articles in journals and magazines relating to Quisling
Some of these articles contain references to valuable original material,
which is unavailable elsewhere. These include:
J. S. Worm-Müller in *Norsk Tidend* for 24 September and 4 October 1941.
N. C. Brögger in *Kirke og Kultur* (1945).
B. Vogt in *Samtiden* (1947).
S. Hartmann in *Militær Orientering* (1952).
A reprint of parts of Noack's diary in *Welt ohne Krieg* (1952).
S. Hartmann in *Samtiden* (1956).
M. Skodvin in *Det Kongelige Norske Videnskabers Selskabs* (1961).

Several articles previously published by myself elaborate upon some
points which have been mentioned only occasionally and briefly in the
text. These include:
P. M. Hayes in *History Today* (1966).
P. M. Hayes in *The Journal of Contemporary History* (1966).
P. M. Hayes in *Revue d'histoire de la deuxième guerre mondiale* (1967).
P. M. Hayes in *History Studies* (1968).

7 Secondary sources – books
This section has been subdivided into those books of which regular use
has been made, and those to which occasional reference has been made.

(i) Regular use
Derry, T. K. *The Campaign in Norway* (HMSO, 1952). The official history of the campaign, though, having been published in 1952, it does
not contain the more recently available material.
Hartmann, S. *Fører uten Folk* (Oslo, 1959). A collection of essays about
Quisling's life which lacks continuity but contains a good deal of
original material.
Hewins, R. *Quisling: Prophet without Honour* (London, 1965). A defence
of Quisling written by a journalist. Much of the original material is
neglected.

Hubatsch, W. *Weserübung: Die deutsche Besetzung von Dänemark und Norwegen* (Göttingen, 1960). An informative and scholarly account of German preparations for the invasion of Denmark and Norway.

Knudsen, H. F. *I was Quisling's secretary* (London, 1967). A passionate defence of Quisling by his companion for many years.

Østbye, H. N. *Ein Buch über Vidkun Quisling* (Oslo, 1941). A hagiography, written by one of Quisling's closest collaborators.

Riste, O., ed. *Norway and the Second World War* (Oslo, 1966). A brief account by three Norwegian scholars of some of the interesting aspects of the part played by Norway between 1939 and 1945.

Skodvin, M. *Striden om okkupasjonsstyret i Norge, fram til 25 September 1940* (Oslo, 1956). A detailed and scholarly account of governmental intrigues in the six months following the invasion of Norway.

Unstad, L. L. *Vidkun Quisling: The Norwegian enigma* (Susquehanna UP, 1964). A sympathetic account of Quisling's character and actions.

Vogt, B. *Mennesket Vidkun og Forræderen Quisling* (Oslo, 1965). An attempt to set Quisling's actions in their historical context.

Wyller, T. C. *Nyordning og Motstand* (Oslo, 1958). A scholarly account of the resistance of the organisations to pressure by Quisling and NS.

(ii) *Occasional reference*

Aall, H. H. *Social Individualism* (Oslo, 1939).

Ash, B. *Norway 1940* (London, 1964).

Baumann, M. *Nansen of the North* (London, 1937).

Beloff, M. *The Foreign Policy of Soviet Russia* (Oxford, 1963).

Berggrav, E. *Da Kampen kom* (Oslo, 1946).

Bonnevie, T. *Høyesterett og Riksrådsforhandlingene* (Oslo, 1947).

Castberg, F. *Juridiske stridsspørsmål i Norges politiske historie* (Oslo, 1961).

Christie, H. C. *Den norske kirke i kamp* (Oslo, 1945).

Churchill, W. S. *War Speeches.* Volume I (London, 1951).

Deutscher, I. *The Prophet Outcast* (London, 1963).

Gemzell, C.-A. *Raeder, Hitler und Skandinavien* (Lund, 1965).

Görlitz, W. *Der deutsche Generalstab* (Frankfurt, 1953).

Hagen, W. *Die geheime Front* (Vienna, 1950).

Hambro, C. J. *De første måneder* (Oslo, 1945).

Hemming-Sjöberg, A. *Domen över Quisling* (Stockholm, 1946).

Hibbert, C. *Benito Mussolini* (London, 1962).

Hilberg, R. *The destruction of the European Jews* (London, 1961).

Holmsen, A. and Jensen, M. *Norges Historie* (Oslo, 1949).

Hoprekstad, O. *Frå laerarstriden* (Bergen, 1946).

Høyer, L. N. *Nansen. A family portrait* (London, 1957).

Jessen, F. de. *Manuel historique de la question de Slesvig, 1906–1938* (Copenhagen, 1939).

Jong, L. de. *The German fifth column in the Second World War* (London, 1956).

Keilhau, W. *Det Norske folks liv og historie. Vår egen tid* (Oslo, 1951).

Kenney, R. *The Northern tangle* (London, 1946).

Kjeldstadli, S. *Hjemmestyrkene* (Oslo, 1959).

Koht, H. *For fred og fridom i krigstid* (Oslo, 1957).

Koht, H. *Frå skanse til skanse* (Oslo, 1947).

Koht, H. *Norsk utanrikspolitikk fram til 9 April 1940* (Oslo, 1947).

Koht, H. *Norway, neutral and invaded* (London, 1941).

Kordt, E. *Wahn und Wirklichkeit* (Stuttgart, 1947).

Lange, T. de. *Quisling-saken, Samlet rettsreferat med forord* (Hamar, 1945).

Mogens, V. *Tyskerne. Quisling og vi andre* (Oslo, 1945).

Moulton, J. L. *The Norwegian campaign of 1940* (London, 1966).

Myklebost, T. *They came as friends* (London, 1943).

Noack, U. *Norwegen zwischen Friedensvermittlung und Fremdherrschaft* (Krefeld, 1952).

Ørvik, N. *Sikkerhetspolitikken 1920–1939* (Oslo, 1960 and 1961).

Rauschning, H. *Hitler Speaks* (London, 1940).

Reynaud, P. *Au cœur de la mêlée* (Paris, 1951).

Reynolds, E. E. *Nansen* (London, 1932).

Rickman, A. R. *Swedish Iron Ore* (London, 1939).

Rosenberg, A. *Der Mythus des 20 Jahrhunderts* (Munich, 1934).

Scharffenberg, J. *Norske aktstykker til okkupasjonens forhistorie* (Oslo, 1950).

Scheen, R. *Norges sjøkrig* (Bergen, 1947).

Seip, D. A. *Hjemme og i fiendeland* (Oslo, 1946).

Shirer, W. *Berlin Diary* (London, 1941).

Singer, K. *Duel for the Northland* (London, 1945).

Skar, A. *Fagorganisasjonen under okkupasjonen* (Oslo, 1949).

Skeie, J. *Norges Forsvars historie* (Oslo, 1953).

Stagg, F. N. *South Norway* (London, 1958).

Starritt, S. S. *The life of Nansen* (London, 1930).

Sundell, O. *9 April* (Stockholm, 1948).

Trotsky, L. *The revolution betrayed* (London, 1937).

Turley, C. *Nansen of Norway* (London, 1933).

Webster Smith, B. *Fridtjof Nansen* (London, 1939).

Wheeler-Bennett, Sir John. *The Nemesis of Power* (London, 1961).

Whitehouse, J. H. *Nansen. A book of homage* (London, 1931).

Woodward, Sir Llewellyn. *British Foreign Policy in the Second World War* (HMSO, 1962).

Ziemke, E. F. *The German northern theatre of operations 1940–1945* (Washington, D.C. 1960).

Numerous other works peripheral to the subject have also been used, but these are not mentioned, as they are not essential for a full understanding of the topics discussed in the text.

Acknowledgements

I WOULD first like to thank the many Norwegians who have been very helpful in different ways – making documents available, discussing ideas and offering criticism. Dr Olav Riste, of the War History Department in Oslo, not only gave me invaluable advice but was also responsible for obtaining permission for me to work at the State Papers. Riksadvokat Andreas Aulie and Inspector of Police Lars L'Abée Lund were extremely helpful in making important documents available. Professor Magne Skodvin, of the University of Oslo, and Lt-Colonel Nils Borchgrevink, of the War History Department, did not spare their assistance. The staff of the Criminal Police HQ and the University Library in Oslo were unfailingly patient and courteous. The staff and students of Studenterhjemmet gave linguistic aid on numerous occasions.

I would like too to thank especially warmly Professor J. B. Joll and Dr A. L. C. Bullock, Master of St Catherine's College, Oxford, who acted as my supervisors during the years 1963–69 when I was writing my DPhil thesis. The help and encouragement of R. M. Hartwell and P. M. Williams, Fellows of Nuffield College, Oxford, sustained me in the task of converting the thesis into a book.

I have also been helped by the staffs of the Wiener Library, Nuffield College Library and the Institut für Zeitgeschichte. Nuffield College enabled me to begin research and liberally financed two trips to Norway. The late Warden and the Fellows of Keble College, Oxford, have been a constant source of encouragement since 1965. The Board of the Social Studies Faculty generously provided a grant for a third visit to Norway in the summer of 1967 and, together with Keble College, gave me a sabbatical term in the summer of 1968.

Finally, I would like to thank Mrs Joanna Gardner for typing the manuscript so efficiently, Mr Herbert Rees for invaluable literary assistance, and my wife for tolerating my long absences from home.

PAUL M. HAYES

Keble College, Oxford
January 1971

INDEX

DATE DUE

GAYLORD			PRINTED IN U.S.A.